What They're Saying about "They Say / I Say"

"Demystifies academic argumentation."
—**Patricia Bizzell,** *College of the Holy Cross*

"This book demystifies rhetorical moves, tricks of the trade that many students are unsure about. It's reasonable, helpful, nicely written . . . and hey, it's true. I would have found it immensely helpful myself in high school and college."
—**Mike Rose,** *University of California, Los Angeles*

"The best tribute to 'They Say / I Say' I've heard is this, from a student: 'This is one book I'm not selling back to the bookstore.' Nods all around the room. The students love this book."
—**Christine Ross,** *Quinnipiac University*

"The best guide ever for helping students to join the conversation!" —**Jami Hemmenway,** *Eureka College*

"The argument of this book is important—that there are 'moves' to academic writing . . . and that knowledge of them can be generative. The template format is a good way to teach and demystify the moves that matter. I like this book a lot."
– **David Bartholomae,** *University of Pittsburgh*

"It demonstrates the exact moves we want our students to make and helps them understand those moves conceptually."
—**Matt Mullins,** *University of North Carolina at Greensboro*

"Good readings, good tone, useful templates."
–**Jenny Mueller,** *McKendree University*

"The chapter on reading gives readers a roadmap for following the moves that authors make as they situate their discussions in larger conversations—and gets past the agree/disagree pattern of response. The idea that any text is part of a larger conversation is as helpful for reading as it is for writing."
—**Eileen Seifert,** *DePaul University*

"Students need to walk a fine line between their work and that of others, and this book helps them walk that line, providing specific methods and techniques for introducing, explaining, and integrating other voices with their own ideas."
—**Libby Miles,** *University of Rhode Island*

" '*They Say / I Say*' reveals the language of academic writing in a way that students seem to understand and incorporate more easily than they do with other writing books. Instead of a list of don'ts, the book provides a catalog of do's, which is always more effective." —**Amy Lea Clemons,** *Francis Marion University*

"Hands down it's the best composition book I've ever come across." —**Michael Jauchen,** *Colby-Sawyer College*

"Explains not just what good writing is but why it matters and why 'academic writing' even exists. Goes beyond the theoretical to the very practical, giving specific examples and illustrations of why it's important to make certain moves in writing."
—**Heather McPherson,** *University of Minnesota*

" '*They Say / I Say*' teaches students to use their own voices—to move from depending on the texts they read to conversing with those texts, from agreeing with the author to questioning what he or she says."
—**Pat Sherbert,** *National Math and Science Initiative*

"A well-organized, readable book that walks students through tricky concepts easily."
—**Eric Hudak,** *University of Texas at Arlington*

"Clear, fun to read, and students like it. The readings are interesting." —**Morani Kornberg-Weiss,** *University at Buffalo*

"Demystifies the process of argumentation, draws back the curtain on what writers do."
—**Jaclyn Lutke,** *Indiana University-Purdue University Indianapolis*

"THEY SAY / I SAY"

*The Moves That Matter
in Academic Writing*

WITH READINGS

Second Edition

"THEY SAY / I SAY"

The Moves That Matter
in Academic Writing

WITH READINGS

Second Edition

GERALD GRAFF
University of Illinois at Chicago

CATHY BIRKENSTEIN
University of Illinois at Chicago

RUSSEL DURST
University of Cincinnati

W · W · NORTON & COMPANY
NEW YORK   LONDON

W. W. Norton & Company has been independent since its founding in 1923, when William Warder Norton and Mary D. Herter Norton first published lectures delivered at the People's Institute, the adult education division of New York City's Cooper Union. The firm soon expanded its program beyond the Institute, publishing books by celebrated academics from America and abroad. By mid-century, the two major pillars of Norton's publishing program—trade books and college texts—were firmly established. In the 1950s, the Norton family transferred control of the company to its employees, and today—with a staff of four hundred and a comparable number of trade, college, and professional titles published each year—W. W. Norton & Company stands as the largest and oldest publishing house owned wholly by its employees.

Book design by Maggie Warner
Director of College Production: Jane Searle
Composition by Matrix Publishing Services, Inc.
Manufactured by RR Donnelley, Crawfordsville

Library of Congress Cataloging-in-Publication Data

Graff, Gerald.
    "They say/I say" : the moves that matter in academic writing : with readings /
    Gerald Graff, Cathy Birkenstein, Russel Durst. — 2nd ed.
        p. cm.
Includes bibliographical references and index.
ISBN 978-0-393-91275-3 (pbk.)
1. English language—Rhetoric—Handbooks, manuals, etc.   2. Persuasion
(Rhetoric)—Handbooks, manuals, etc.   3. Report writing—Handbooks, manuals,
etc.   4. Academic writing—Handbooks, manuals, etc.   5. College readers.
I. Birkenstein, Cathy.   II. Durst, Russel K., 1954-   III. Title.
    PE1431.G73 2011
    808'.042—dc23
    2011039045

W. W. Norton & Company, Inc., 500 Fifth Avenue, New York, N.Y. 10110-0017
www.wwnorton.com

W. W. Norton & Company Ltd., Castle House, 75/76 Wells Street, London W1T 3QT

1 2 3 4 5 6 7 8 9 0

To the great rhetorician Wayne Booth,
who cared deeply
about the democratic art
of listening closely to what others say.

CONTENTS

Contents

Contents

Contents

PREFACE

—⊡—

WHEN WE FIRST SET OUT to write this book, our goal was simple: to offer a version of *"They Say / I Say": The Moves That Matter in Academic Writing* with an anthology of readings that would demonstrate the rhetorical moves "that matter." And because *"They Say"* teaches students that academic writing is a means of entering a conversation, we looked for readings on topics that would engage students and inspire them to respond—and to enter the conversations.

The book has been more successful than we ever imagined possible, which we believe reflects the growing importance of academic writing as a focus of first-year writing courses, and the fact that students find practical strategies like the ones offered in this book to be particularly helpful.

The goal in writing *"They Say"* has always been to offer students a user-friendly model of writing that will help them put into practice the important principle that writing is a social activity. Proceeding from the premise that effective writers enter conversations of other writers and speakers, this book encourages students to engage with those around them—including those who disagree with them—instead of just expressing their ideas "logically." Our own experience teaching first-year writing students has led us to believe that to be persuasive, arguments need not only supporting evidence but also motivation and exigency, and that the surest way to achieve this motivation and exigency is to generate one's own arguments as a response to those of others—to something "they say." To help students write their way into the often daunting conversations of academia and the wider public sphere, the book provides templates to help them make sophisticated rhetorical moves that they might otherwise not think of attempting. Learning to make these rhetorical moves in writing also helps students become better readers of argument.

That the two versions of *"They Say / I Say"* are now being taught at more than 1,500 schools suggests that there is a widespread desire for explicit instruction that is understandable but not oversimplified, to help writers negotiate the basic moves necessary to "enter the conversation." Instructors have told us how much this book helps their students learn how to write academic discourse, and some students have written to us saying that it's helped them to "crack the code," as one student put it.

This second edition of *"They Say / I Say" with Readings* includes forty-four readings on five compelling and controversial issues. The readings provide a glimpse into some important conversations of our day—and will, we hope, provoke students to respond and thus to join in those conversations.

HIGHLIGHTS

Forty-four readings that will provoke students to think—and write. Taken from a wide variety of sources, including the *New York Times*, *Salon*, *Townhall.com*, the *Chronicle of Higher Education*, the *New Yorker*, *Sports Illustrated*, best-selling trade books, celebrated speeches, and more, the readings represent a range of perspectives on five important issues:

- Is Higher Education Worth the Price?
- Is Pop Culture Actually Good for You?
- Is Fast Food the New Tobacco?
- Why Does It Matter Who Wins the Big Game?
- What's Up with the American Dream?

The readings can function as sources for students' own writing, and the study questions that follow each reading focus students' attention on how each author uses the key rhetorical moves—and include one question that invites them to respond with their own views.

A chapter on reading (Chapter 12) encourages students to think of reading as an act of entering conversations. Instead of teaching students merely to identify the author's argument, this chapter shows them how to read with an eye for what arguments the author is responding to—in other words, to think carefully about why the writer is making the argument in the first place, and thus to recognize (and ultimately become a part of) the larger conversation that gives meaning to reading the text.

Two books in one, with a rhetoric up front and readings in the back. The two parts are linked by cross-references in the margins, leading from the rhetoric to specific examples in the readings and from the readings to the corresponding writing instruction. Teachers can therefore begin with either the rhetoric or the readings, and the links will facilitate movement between one section and the other.

What's New

Two new chapters in the anthology: Is Higher Education Worth the Price? and Why Does It Matter Who Wins the Big Game?

Thirty-two readings, including one scholarly piece and one essay written by a student in each chapter, added in response to requests from many teachers who wanted more complex and documented writing.

They Say / I Blog. Updated monthly, this blog provides up-to-the-minute readings on the issues covered in the book, along with questions that prompt students to literally join the conversation. Check it out at theysayiblog.com.

A chapter on writing in the social sciences. Chapter 13, "Analyze This," shows students that writing in the social sciences is fundamentally argumentative and provides templates to help them make the basic rhetorical moves that writers in those fields make.

A complete instructor's guide, with teaching tips for all the chapters, syllabi, summaries of the readings, and suggested answers to the study questions. Go to the Instructor Resources page, wwnorton.com/instructors, to access these materials.

We hope that this new edition of *"They Say / I Say" with Readings* will spark students' interest in some of the most pressing conversations of our day and provide them with some of the tools they need to engage in those conversations with dexterity and confidence.

Gerald Graff
Cathy Birkenstein
Russel Durst

Preface to *"They Say / I Say"*

—⌐◻⌐—

EXPERIENCED WRITING INSTRUCTORS have long recognized that writing well means entering into conversation with others. Academic writing in particular calls upon writers not simply to express their own ideas, but to do so as a response to what others have said. The first-year writing program at our own university, according to its mission statement, asks "students to participate in ongoing conversations about vitally important academic and public issues." A similar statement by another program holds that "intellectual writing is almost always composed in response to others' texts." These statements echo the ideas of rhetorical theorists like Kenneth Burke, Mikhail Bakhtin, and Wayne Booth as well as recent composition scholars like David Bartholomae, John Bean, Patricia Bizzell, Irene Clark, Greg Colomb, Lisa Ede, Peter Elbow, Joseph Harris, Andrea Lunsford, Elaine Maimon, Gary Olson, Mike Rose, John Swales and Christine Feak, Tilly Warnock, and others who argue that writing well means engaging the voices of others and letting them in turn engage us.

Yet despite this growing consensus that writing is a social, conversational act, helping student writers actually participate in these conversations remains a formidable challenge. This book aims to meet that challenge. Its goal is to demystify academic writing by isolating its basic moves, explaining them clearly, and representing them in the form of templates. In this way, we hope to help students become active participants in the important conversations of the academic world and the wider public sphere.

HIGHLIGHTS

- *Shows students that writing well means entering a conversation*, summarizing others ("they say") to set up one's own argument ("I say").
- *Demystifies academic writing*, showing students "the moves that matter" in language they can readily apply.
- *Provides user-friendly templates* to help writers make those moves in their own writing.

HOW THIS BOOK CAME TO BE

The original idea for this book grew out of our shared interest in democratizing academic culture. First, it grew out of arguments that Gerald Graff has been making throughout his career that schools and colleges need to invite students into the conversations and debates that surround them. More specifically, it is a practical, hands-on companion to his recent book, *Clueless in Academe: How Schooling Obscures the Life of the Mind*, in which he looks at academic conversations from the perspective of those who find them mysterious and proposes ways in which such mystification can be overcome. Second, this book grew out of writing templates that Cathy Birkenstein developed in the 1990s, for use in writing and literature courses she was teaching. Many students, she found, could readily grasp what it meant to support a thesis with evidence, to entertain a counterargument, to identify a textual contradiction, and ultimately to summarize and respond to challenging arguments, but they often had trouble putting these concepts into practice in their own writing. When Cathy sketched out templates on the board, however, giving her students some of the language and patterns that these sophisticated moves require, their writing—and even their quality of thought—significantly improved.

This book began, then, when we put our ideas together and realized that these templates might have the potential to open up and clarify academic conversation. We proceeded from the premise that all writers rely on certain stock formulas that they themselves didn't invent—and that many of these formulas are so commonly used that they can be represented in model templates that students can use to structure and even generate what they want to say.

As we developed a working draft of this book, we began using it in first-year writing courses that we teach at UIC. In classroom exercises and writing assignments, we found that students who otherwise struggled to organize their thoughts, or even to think of something to say, did much better when we provided them with templates like the following.

▸ In discussions of _____, a controversial issue is whether _____. While some argue that _____, others contend that _____.

▸ This is not to say that _____.

One virtue of such templates, we found, is that they focus writers' attention not just on what is being said, but on the *forms* that structure what is being said. In other words, they make students more conscious of the rhetorical patterns that are key to academic success but often pass under the classroom radar.

THE CENTRALITY OF "THEY SAY / I SAY"

The central rhetorical move that we focus on in this book is the "they say / I say" template that gives our book its title. In our view, this template represents the deep, underlying structure, the internal DNA as it were, of all effective argument. Effective persuasive writers do more than make well-supported claims ("I say"); they also map those claims relative to the claims of others ("they say").

Here, for example, the "they say / I say" pattern structures a passage from an essay by the media and technology critic Steven Johnson.

> For decades, we've worked under the assumption that mass culture follows a path declining steadily toward lowest-common-denominator standards, presumably because the "masses" want dumb, simple pleasures and big media companies try to give the masses what they want. But . . . the exact opposite is happening: the culture is getting more cognitively demanding, not less.
>
> STEVEN JOHNSON, *"Watching TV Makes You Smarter"*

In generating his own argument from something "they say," Johnson suggests *why* he needs to say what he is saying: to correct a popular misconception.

Even when writers do not explicitly identify the views they are responding to, as Johnson does, an implicit "they say" can often be discerned, as in the following passage by Zora Neale Hurston.

> I remember the day I became colored.
>
> ZORA NEALE HURSTON, *"How It Feels to Be Colored Me"*

In order to grasp Hurston's point here, we need to be able to reconstruct the implicit view she is responding to and questioning: that racial identity is an innate quality we are simply born with. On the contrary, Hurston suggests, our race is imposed on us by society—something we "become" by virtue of how we are treated.

As these examples suggest, the "they say / I say" model can improve not just student writing, but student reading comprehension as well. Since reading and writing are deeply reciprocal activities, students who learn to make the rhetorical moves represented by the templates in this book figure to become more adept at identifying these same moves in the texts they read. And if we are right that effective arguments are always in dialogue with other arguments, then it follows that in order to understand the types of challenging texts assigned in college, students need to identify the views to which those texts are responding.

Working with the "they say / I say" model can also help with invention, finding something to say. In our experience, students best discover what they want to say not by thinking about a subject in an isolation booth, but by reading texts, listening closely to what other writers say, and looking for an opening through which they can enter the conversation. In other words, listening closely to others and summarizing what they have to say can help writers generate their own ideas.

THE USEFULNESS OF TEMPLATES

Our templates also have a generative quality, prompting students to make moves in their writing that they might not otherwise make or even know they should make. The templates in this book can be particularly helpful for students who are unsure about what to say, or who have trouble finding enough to say, often because they consider their own beliefs so self-evident that they need not be argued for. Students like this are often helped, we've found, when we give them a simple template like the following one for entertaining a counterargument (or planting a naysayer, as we call it in Chapter 6).

► Of course some might object that _____. Although I concede that _____, I still maintain that _____.

What this particular template helps students do is make the seemingly counterintuitive move of questioning their own beliefs, of looking at them from the perspective of those who disagree. In so doing, templates can bring out aspects of students' thoughts that, as they themselves sometimes remark, they didn't even realize were there.

Other templates in this book help students make a host of sophisticated moves that they might not otherwise make: summarizing what someone else says, framing a quotation in one's own words, indicating the view that the writer is responding to, marking the shift from a source's view to the writer's own view, offering evidence for that view, entertaining and answering counterarguments, and explaining what is at stake in the first place. In showing students how to make such moves, templates do more than organize students' ideas; they help bring those ideas into existence.

OKAY, BUT TEMPLATES?

We are aware, of course, that some instructors may have reservations about templates. Some, for instance, may object that such formulaic devices represent a return to prescriptive forms of instruction that encourage passive learning or lead students to put their writing on automatic pilot.

This is an understandable reaction, we think, to kinds of rote instruction that have indeed encouraged passivity and drained writing of its creativity and dynamic relation to the social world. The trouble is that many students will never learn on their own to make the key intellectual moves that our templates represent. While seasoned writers pick up these moves unconsciously through their reading, many students do not. Consequently, we believe, students need to see these moves represented in the explicit ways that the templates provide.

The aim of the templates, then, is not to stifle critical thinking but to be direct with students about the key rhetorical moves that it comprises. Since we encourage students to modify and adapt the templates to the particularities of the arguments they are making, using such prefabricated formulas as learning tools need not result in writing and thinking that are themselves formulaic. Admittedly, no teaching tool can guarantee that students will engage in hard, rigorous thought. Our templates do, however, provide concrete prompts that can stimulate and shape such thought: What do "they say" about my topic? What would a naysayer say about my argument? What is my evidence? Do I need to qualify my point? Who cares?

In fact, templates have a long and rich history. Public orators from ancient Greece and Rome through the European Renaissance studied rhetorical *topoi* or "commonplaces," model passages and formulas that represented the different strategies available to public speakers. In many respects, our templates echo this classical rhetorical tradition of imitating established models.

The journal *Nature* requires aspiring contributors to follow a guideline that is like a template on the opening page of their manuscript: "Two or three sentences explaining what the main result [of their study] reveals in direct comparison with what was thought to be the case previously, or how the main result adds to previous knowledge." In the field of education, a form designed by the education theorist Howard Gardner asks post-doctoral fellowship applicants to complete the following template: "Most scholars in the field believe _____. As a result of my study, _____." That these two examples are geared toward postdoctoral fellows and veteran researchers shows that it is not only struggling undergraduates who can use help making these key rhetorical moves, but experienced academics as well.

Templates have even been used in the teaching of personal narrative. The literary and educational theorist Jane Tompkins devised the following template to help student writers make the often difficult move from telling a story to explaining what it means: "X tells a story about _____ to make the point that _____. My own experience with _____ yields a point that is similar/different/both similar and different. What I take away from my own experience with _____ is _____. As a result, I conclude _____." We especially like this template because it suggests that "they say / I say" argument need not be mechanical, impersonal, or dry, and that telling a story and making an argument are more compatible activities than many think.

WHY IT'S OKAY TO USE "I"

But wait—doesn't the "I" part of *"they say / I say"* flagrantly encourage the use of the first-person pronoun? Aren't we aware that some teachers prohibit students from using "I" or "we," on the grounds that these pronouns encourage ill-considered, subjective opinions rather than objective and reasoned arguments? Yes, we are aware of this first-person prohibition, but we think it has serious flaws. First, expressing ill-considered, subjective opinions is not necessarily the worst sin beginning writers can commit; it might be a starting point from which they can move on to more reasoned, less self-indulgent perspectives. Second, prohibiting students from using "I" is simply not an effective way of curbing students' subjectivity, since one can offer poorly argued, ill-supported opinions just as easily without it. Third and most important, prohibiting the first person tends to hamper students' ability not only to take strong positions but to differentiate their own positions from those of others, as we point out in Chapter 5. To be sure, writers can resort to various circumlocutions—"it will here be argued," "the evidence suggests," "the truth is"—and these may be useful for avoiding a monotonous series of "I believe" sentences. But except for avoiding such monotony, we see no good reason why "I" should be set aside in persuasive writing. Rather than prohibit "I," then, we think a better tactic is to give students practice at using it well and learning its use, both by supporting their claims with evidence and by attending closely to alternative perspectives—to what "they" are saying.

HOW THIS BOOK IS ORGANIZED

Because of its centrality, we have allowed the "they say / I say" format to dictate the structure of this book. So while Part 1 addresses the art of listening to others, Part 2 addresses how to offer one's own response. Part 1 opens with a chapter on "Starting with What Others Are Saying" that explains why it is generally advisable to begin a text by citing others rather than plunging directly into one's own views. Subsequent chapters take up the arts of summarizing and quoting what these others have to say. Part 2 begins with a chapter on different ways of responding, followed by chapters on marking the shift between what "they say" and what "I say," on introducing and answering objections, and on answering the all-important questions "so what?" and "who cares?" Part 3 offers strategies for "Tying It All Together," beginning with a chapter on connection and coherence; followed by a chapter on formal and informal language, arguing that academic discourse is often perfectly compatible with the informal language that students use outside school; and concluding with a chapter on the art of metacommentary, showing students how to guide the way readers understand a text. Part 4 offers guidance for entering the conversation, with chapters on class discussions, reading, and writing in the social sciences.

WHAT THIS BOOK DOESN'T DO

There are some things that this book does not try to do. We do not, for instance, cover logical principles of argument such as syllogisms, warrants, logical fallacies, or the differences between inductive and deductive reasoning. Although such concepts can be useful, we believe most of us learn the ins and outs of argumentative writing not by studying logical principles in the abstract, but by plunging into actual discussions and debates, trying out different patterns of response, and in this way getting a sense of what works to persuade different audiences and what doesn't. In our view, people learn more about arguing from hearing someone say, "You miss my point. What I'm saying is not _____, but _____," or "I agree with you that _____, and would even add that _____," than they do from studying the differences between inductive and deductive reasoning. Such formulas give students an immediate sense of what it feels like to enter a public conversation in a way that studying abstract warrants and logical fallacies does not.

ENGAGING WITH THE IDEAS OF OTHERS

One central goal of this book is to demystify academic writing by returning it to its social and conversational roots. Although writing may require some degree of quiet and solitude, the "they say / I say" model shows students that they can best develop their arguments not just by looking inward but by doing what they often do in a good conversation with friends and family— by listening carefully to what others are saying and engaging with other views.

This approach to writing therefore has an ethical dimension, since it asks writers not simply to keep proving and reasserting what they already believe but to stretch what they believe by putting it up against beliefs that differ, sometimes radically, from their own. In an increasingly diverse, global society, this ability to engage with the ideas of others is especially crucial to democratic citizenship.

Gerald Graff
Cathy Birkenstein

"THEY SAY / I SAY"

The Moves That Matter

in Academic Writing

WITH READINGS

Second Edition

"THEY SAY / I SAY"

*The Moves That Matter
in Academic Writing*

WITH READINGS

Second Edition

INTRODUCTION

Entering the Conversation

—▫—

THINK ABOUT AN ACTIVITY that you do particularly well: cooking, playing the piano, shooting a basketball, even something as basic as driving a car. If you reflect on this activity, you'll realize that once you mastered it you no longer had to give much conscious thought to the various moves that go into doing it. Performing this activity, in other words, depends on your having learned a series of complicated moves—moves that may seem mysterious or difficult to those who haven't yet learned them.

The same applies to writing. Often without consciously realizing it, accomplished writers routinely rely on a stock of established moves that are crucial for communicating sophisticated ideas. What makes writers masters of their trade is not only their ability to express interesting thoughts but their mastery of an inventory of basic moves that they probably picked up by reading a wide range of other accomplished writers. Less experienced writers, by contrast, are often unfamiliar with these basic moves and unsure how to make them in their own writing. This book is intended as a short, user-friendly guide to the basic moves of academic writing.

One of our key premises is that these basic moves are so common that they can be represented in *templates* that you can use right away to structure and even generate your own writing. Perhaps the most distinctive feature of this book is its presentation of many such templates, designed to help you successfully enter not only the world of academic thinking and writing, but also the wider worlds of civic discourse and work.

Instead of focusing solely on abstract principles of writing, then, this book offers model templates that help you put those principles directly into practice. Working with these templates can give you an immediate sense of how to engage in the kinds of critical thinking you are required to do at the college level and in the vocational and public spheres beyond.

Some of these templates represent simple but crucial moves like those used to summarize some widely held belief.

▸ Many Americans assume that _____.

Others are more complicated.

▸ On the one hand, _____. On the other hand, _____.

▸ Author X contradicts herself. At the same time that she argues _____, she also implies _____.

▸ I agree that _____.

▸ This is not to say that _____.

It is true, of course, that critical thinking and writing go deeper than any set of linguistic formulas, requiring that you question assumptions, develop strong claims, offer supporting reasons and evidence, consider opposing arguments, and so on. But these deeper habits of thought cannot be put into practice unless you have a language for expressing them in clear, organized ways.

STATE YOUR OWN IDEAS AS A RESPONSE TO OTHERS

The single most important template that we focus on in this book is the "they say _____ ; I say _____ " formula that gives our book its title. If there is any one point that we hope you will take away from this book, it is the importance not only of expressing your ideas ("I say") but of presenting those ideas as a *response to some other person or group* ("they say"). For us, the underlying structure of effective academic writing—and of responsible public discourse—resides not just in stating our own ideas but in listening closely to others around us, summarizing their views in a way that they will recognize, and responding with our own ideas in kind. Broadly speaking, academic writing is argumentative writing, and we believe that to argue well you need to do more than assert your own position. You need to enter a conversation, using what others say (or might say) as a launching pad or sounding board for your own views. For this reason, one of the main pieces of advice in this book is to write the voices of others into your text.

In our view, then, the best academic writing has one underlying feature: it is deeply engaged in some way with other people's views. Too often, however, academic writing is taught as a process of saying "true" or "smart" things in a vacuum, as if it were possible to argue effectively without being in conversation *with* someone else. If you have been taught to write a traditional five-paragraph essay, for example, you have learned how to develop a thesis and support it with evidence. This is good advice as far as it goes, but it leaves out the important fact that in the real world we don't make arguments without being provoked. Instead, we make arguments because someone has said or done something (or perhaps *not* said or done something) and we need to respond: "I

3

can't see why you like the Lakers so much"; "I agree: it was a great film"; "That argument is contradictory." If it weren't for other people and our need to challenge, agree with, or otherwise respond to them, there would be no reason to argue at all.

To make an impact as a writer, you need to do more than make statements that are logical, well supported, and consistent. You must also find a way of entering a conversation with others' views—with something "they say." If your own argument doesn't identify the "they say" that you're responding to, it probably won't make sense. As Figure 1 suggests, *what* you are saying may be clear to your audience, but *why* you are saying it won't be. For it is what others are saying and thinking that motivates our writing and gives it a reason for being. It follows, then, as Figure 2 suggests, that your own argument—the thesis or "I say" moment of your text—should always be a response to the arguments of others.

Many writers make explicit "they say / I say" moves in their writing. One famous example is Martin Luther King Jr.'s "Let-

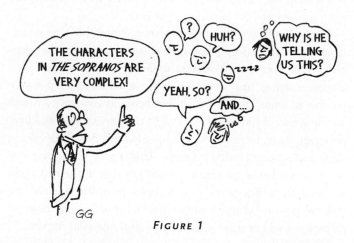

FIGURE 1

FIGURE 2

ter from Birmingham Jail," which consists almost entirely of King's eloquent responses to a public statement by eight clergymen deploring the civil rights protests he was leading. The letter—which was written in 1963, while King was in prison for leading a demonstration against racial injustice in Birmingham—is structured almost entirely around a framework of summary and response, in which King summarizes and then answers their criticisms. In one typical passage, King writes as follows.

> You deplore the demonstrations taking place in Birmingham. But your statement, I am sorry to say, fails to express a similar concern for the conditions that brought about the demonstrations.
> MARTIN LUTHER KING JR., "Letter from Birmingham Jail"

King goes on to agree with his critics that "It is unfortunate that demonstrations are taking place in Birmingham," yet he hastens to add that "it is even more unfortunate that the city's white power structure left the Negro community with no alternative." King's letter is so thoroughly conversational, in fact, that it could be rewritten in the form of a dialogue or play.

> King's critics:
> King's response:
> Critics:
> Response:

Clearly, King would not have written his famous letter were it not for his critics, whose views he treats not as objections to his already-formed arguments but as the motivating source of those arguments, their central reason for being. He quotes not only what his critics have said ("Some have asked: 'Why didn't you give the new city administration time to act?'"), but also things they *might* have said ("One may well ask: 'How can you advocate breaking some laws and obeying others?'")—all to set the stage for what he himself wants to say.

A similar "they say / I say" exchange opens an essay about American patriotism by the social critic Katha Pollitt, who uses her own daughter's comment to represent the national fervor of post-9/11 patriotism.

> My daughter, who goes to Stuyvesant High School only blocks from the former World Trade Center, thinks we should fly the American flag out our window. Definitely not, I say: The flag stands for jingoism and vengeance and war. She tells me I'm wrong—the flag means standing together and honoring the dead and saying no to terrorism. In a way we're both right. . . .
>
> KATHA POLLITT, "Put Out No Flags"

As Pollitt's example shows, the "they" you respond to in crafting an argument need not be a famous author or someone known to your audience. It can be a family member like Pollitt's daughter, or a friend or classmate who has made a provocative claim. It can even be something an individual or a group might say—or a side of yourself, something you once believed but no longer do, or something you partly believe but also doubt. The important thing is that the "they" (or "you" or "she") represent some wider group with which readers might identify—in Pollitt's case, those who patriotically believe in flying the flag. Pollitt's example also shows that responding to the views of others need not always involve unqualified opposition. By agreeing and disagreeing with her daughter, Pollitt enacts what we call the "yes and no" response, reconciling apparently incompatible views.

See Chapter 4 for more on agreeing, but with a difference.

While King and Pollitt both identify the views they are responding to, some authors do not explicitly state their views but instead allow the reader to infer them. See, for instance, if you can identify the implied or unnamed "they say" that the following claim is responding to.

> I like to think I have a certain advantage as a teacher of literature because when I was growing up I disliked and feared books.
>
> GERALD GRAFF, "Disliking Books at an Early Age"

In case you haven't figured it out already, the phantom "they say" here is the common belief that in order to be a good teacher of literature, one must have grown up liking and enjoying books.

As you can see from these examples, many writers use the "they say / I say" format to agree or disagree with others, to challenge standard ways of thinking, and thus to stir up controversy. This point may come as a shock to you if you have always had the impression that in order to succeed academically you need to play it safe and avoid controversy in your writing, making statements that nobody can possibly disagree with. Though this view of writing may appear logical, it is actually a recipe for flat, lifeless writing and for writing that fails to answer what we call the "so what?" and "who cares?" questions. "William Shakespeare wrote many famous plays and sonnets" may be a perfectly true statement, but precisely because nobody is likely to disagree with it, it goes without saying and thus would seem pointless if said.

WAYS OF RESPONDING

Just because much argumentative writing is driven by disagreement, it does not follow that *agreement* is ruled out. Although argumentation is often associated with conflict and opposition, the type of conversational "they say / I say" argument that we focus on in this book can be just as useful when you agree as when you disagree.

▸ She argues _____, and I agree because _____ .

▸ Her argument that _____ is supported by new research showing that _____ .

Nor do you always have to choose between either simply agreeing *or* disagreeing, since the "they say / I say" format also works to both agree and disagree at the same time, as Pollitt illustrates above.

▸ He claims that _____, and I have mixed feelings about it. On the one hand, I agree that _____. On the other hand, I still insist that _____.

This last option—agreeing and disagreeing simultaneously—is one we especially recommend, since it allows you to avoid a simple yes or no response and present a more complicated argument, while containing that complication within a clear "on the one hand / on the other hand" framework.

While the templates we offer in this book can be used to structure your writing at the sentence level, they can also be expanded as needed to almost any length, as the following elaborated "they say / I say" template demonstrates.

In recent discussions of _____, a controversial issue has been whether _____. On the one hand, some argue that _____. From this perspective, _____. On the other hand, however, others argue that _____. In the words of _____, one of this view's main proponents, "_____." According to this view, _____. In sum, then, the issue is whether _____ or _____.

My own view is that _____. Though I concede that _____, I still maintain that _____. For example, _____. Although some might object that _____, I would reply that _____. The issue is important because _____.

If you go back over this template, you will see that it helps you make a host of challenging moves (each of which is taken up in forthcoming chapters in this book). First, the template helps you open your text by identifying an issue in some ongoing conversation or debate ("In recent discussions of _____, a controversial issue has been _____ "), and then to map some of the voices in this controversy (by using the "on the one hand / on the other hand" structure). The template also helps you introduce a quotation ("In the words of"), to explain the quotation in your own words ("According to this view"), and—in a new paragraph—to state your own argument ("My own view is that"), to qualify your argument ("Though I concede that"), and then to support your argument with evidence ("For example"). In addition, the template helps you make one of the most crucial moves in argumentative writing, what we call "planting a naysayer in your text," in which you summarize and then answer a likely objection to your own central claim ("Although it might be objected that _____, I reply _____"). Finally, this template helps you shift between general, over-arching claims ("In sum, then") and smaller-scale, supporting claims ("For example").

Again, none of us is born knowing these moves, especially when it comes to academic writing. Hence the need for this book.

DO TEMPLATES STIFLE CREATIVITY?

If you are like some of our students, your initial response to templates may be skepticism. At first, many of our students complain that using templates will take away their originality and creativity and make them all sound the same. "They'll turn us into writing robots," one of our students insisted. Another agreed, adding, "Hey, I'm a jazz musician. And we don't play by set forms. We create our own." "I'm in college now," another student asserted; "this is third-grade-level stuff."

In our view, however, the templates in this book, far from being "third-grade-level stuff," represent the stock in trade of sophisticated thinking and writing, and they often require a great deal of practice and instruction to use successfully. As for the belief that pre-established forms undermine creativity, we think it rests on a very limited vision of what creativity is all about. In our view, the above template and the others in this book will actually help your writing become *more* original and creative, not less. After all, even the most creative forms of expression depend on established patterns and structures. Most songwriters, for instance, rely on a time-honored verse-chorus-verse pattern, and few people would call Shakespeare uncreative because he didn't invent the sonnet or the dramatic forms that he used to such dazzling effect. Even the most avant-garde, cutting-edge artists (like improvisational jazz musicians) need to master the basic forms that their work improvises on, departs from, and goes beyond, or else their work will come across as uneducated child's play. Ultimately, then, creativity and originality lie not in the avoidance of established forms but in the imaginative use of them.

Furthermore, these templates do not dictate the *content* of what you say, which can be as original as you can make it, but only suggest a way of formatting *how* you say it. In addition, once you begin to feel comfortable with the templates in this book, you will be able to improvise creatively on them to fit new situations and purposes and find others in your reading. In other words, the templates offered here are learning tools to get you started, not structures set in stone. Once you get used to using them, you can even dispense with them altogether, for the rhetorical moves they model will be at your fingertips in an unconscious, instinctive way.

But if you still need proof that writing templates do not stifle creativity, consider the following opening to an essay on the fast-food industry that we've included in this book.

If ever there were a newspaper headline custom-made for Jay Leno's monologue, this was it. Kids taking on McDonald's this week, suing the company for making them fat. Isn't that like middle-aged men suing Porsche for making them get speeding tickets? Whatever happened to personal responsibility?

I tend to sympathize with these portly fast-food patrons, though. Maybe that's because I used to be one of them.

DAVID ZINCZENKO, "Don't Blame the Eater"

Although Zinczenko relies on a version of the "they say / I say" formula, his writing is anything but dry, robotic, or uncreative. While Zinczenko does not explicitly use the words "they say" and "I say," the template still gives the passage its underlying structure: "*They say* that kids suing fast-food companies for making them fat is a joke; but *I say* such lawsuits are justified."

BUT ISN'T THIS PLAGIARISM?

"But isn't this plagiarism?" at least one student each year will usually ask. "Well, is it?" we respond, turning the question around into one the entire class can profit from. "We are, after all, asking you to use language in your writing that isn't your own—language that you 'borrow' or, to put it less delicately, steal from other writers."

Often, a lively discussion ensues that raises important questions about authorial ownership and helps everyone better understand the frequently confusing line between plagiarism and the legitimate use of what others say and how they say it. Students are quick to see that no one person owns a conventional formula like "on the one hand . . . on the other hand . . . " Phrases like "a controversial issue" are so commonly used and recycled that they are generic—community property that can be freely used without fear of committing plagiarism. It *is* plagiarism, however, if the words used to fill in the blanks of such formulas are borrowed from others without proper acknowledgment. In sum, then, while it is not plagiarism to recycle conventionally used formulas, it is a serious academic offense to take the substantive content from others' texts without citing the author and giving him or her proper credit.

PUTTING IN YOUR OAR

Though the immediate goal of this book is to help you become a better writer, at a deeper level it invites you to become a certain type of person: a critical, intellectual thinker who, instead of sitting passively on the sidelines, can participate in the debates and conversations of your world in an active and empowered way. Ultimately, this book invites you to become a critical thinker who can enter the types of conversations described eloquently by the philosopher Kenneth Burke in the following widely cited passage. Likening the world of intellectual exchange to a never-ending conversation at a party, Burke writes:

> You come late. When you arrive, others have long preceded you, and they are engaged in a heated discussion, a discussion too heated for them to pause and tell you exactly what it is about. . . . You listen for a while, until you decide that you have caught the tenor of the argument; then you put in your oar. Someone answers; you answer him; another comes to your defense; another aligns himself against you. . . . The hour grows late, you must depart. And you do depart, with the discussion still vigorously in progress.
>
> KENNETH BURKE, *The Philosophy of Literary Form*

What we like about this passage is its suggestion that stating an argument and "putting in your oar" can only be done in conversation with others; that we all enter the dynamic world of ideas not as isolated individuals but as social beings deeply connected to others who have a stake in what we say.

This ability to enter complex, many-sided conversations has taken on a special urgency in today's diverse, post-9/11 world, where the future for all of us may depend on our ability to put ourselves in the shoes of those who think very differently from us. The central piece of advice in this book—that we listen carefully to others, including those who disagree with us, and then engage with them thoughtfully and respectfully—can help us see beyond our own pet beliefs, which may not be shared by everyone. The mere act of crafting a sentence that begins "Of course, someone might object that _____ " may not seem like a way to change the world; but it does have the potential to jog us out of our comfort zones, to get us thinking critically about our own beliefs, and perhaps even to change our minds.

Exercises

1. Read the following paragraph from an essay by Emily Poe, a student at Furman University. Disregarding for the moment what Poe says, focus your attention on the phrases Poe uses to structure what she says (italicized here). Then write a new paragraph using Poe's as a model but replacing her topic, vegetarianism, with one of your own.

   The term "vegetarian" tends to be synonymous with "tree-hugger" in many people's minds. *They see* vegetarianism as a cult that brainwashes its followers into eliminating an essential part of their daily diets for an abstract goal of "animal welfare." *However,* few vegetarians choose their lifestyle just to follow the crowd. *On the contrary,* many of these supposedly brainwashed people are actually independent thinkers, concerned citizens, and compassionate human beings. *For the truth is* that there are many very good reasons for giving up meat. Perhaps the best reasons are to improve the environment, to encourage humane treatment of livestock, or to enhance one's own health. *In this essay, then,* closely examining a vegetarian diet as compared to a meat-eater's diet will show that vegetarianism is clearly the better option for sustaining the Earth and all its inhabitants.

2. Write a short essay in which you first summarize our rationale for the templates in this book and then articulate your own position in response. If you want, you can use the template below to organize your paragraphs, expanding and modifying it as necessary to fit what you want to say.

> ▸ In the Introduction to *"They Say / I Say": The Moves That Matter in Academic Writing,* Gerald Graff and Cathy Birkenstein provide templates designed to _____. Specifically, Graff and Birkenstein argue that the types of writing templates they offer _____. As the authors themselves put it, "_____." Although some people believe _____, Graff and Birkenstein insist that _____. In sum, then, their view is that _____.
>
> I [agree/disagree/have mixed feelings]. In my view, the types of templates that the authors recommend _____. For instance, _____. In addition, _____. Some might object, of course, on the grounds that _____. Yet I would argue that _____. Overall, then, I believe _____—an important point to make given _____.

1
"THEY SAY"

ONE

"They Say"

Starting with What Others Are Saying

——————

Not long ago we attended a talk at an academic conference where the speaker's central claim seemed to be that a certain sociologist—call him Dr. X—had done very good work in a number of areas of the discipline. The speaker proceeded to illustrate his thesis by referring extensively and in great detail to various books and articles by Dr. X and by quoting long passages from them. The speaker was obviously both learned and impassioned, but as we listened to his talk we found ourselves somewhat puzzled: the argument—that Dr. X's work was very important—was clear enough, but why did the speaker need to make it in the first place? Did anyone dispute it? Were there commentators in the field who had argued against X's work or challenged its value? Was the speaker's interpretation of what X had done somehow novel or revolutionary? Since the speaker gave no hint of an answer to any of these questions, we could only wonder why he was going on and on about X. It was only after the speaker finished and took questions from the audience that we got a clue: in response to one questioner, he referred to several critics who had vigorously See an example in Figure 1 on p. 4.

questioned Dr. X's ideas and convinced many sociologists that Dr. X's work was unsound.

This story illustrates an important lesson: that to give writing the most important thing of all—namely, a point—a writer needs to indicate clearly not only what his or her thesis is, but also what larger conversation that thesis is responding to. Because our speaker failed to mention what others had said about Dr. X's work, he left his audience unsure about why he felt the need to say what he was saying. Perhaps the point was clear to other sociologists in the audience who were more familiar with the debates over Dr. X's work than we were. But even they, we bet, would have understood the speaker's point better if he'd sketched in some of the larger conversation his own claims were a part of and reminded the audience about what "they say."

This story also illustrates an important lesson about the *order* in which things are said: to keep an audience engaged, a writer needs to explain what he or she is responding to—either before offering that response or, at least, very early in the discussion. Delaying this explanation for more than one or two paragraphs in a very short essay, three or four pages in a longer one, or more than ten or so pages in a book-length text reverses the natural order in which readers process material—and in which writers think and develop ideas. After all, it seems very unlikely that

See how an essay about Wal-Mart opens by quoting its critics, p. 620, ¶1.

our conference speaker first developed his defense of Dr. X and only later came across Dr. X's critics. As someone knowledgeable in his field, the speaker surely encountered the criticisms first and only then was compelled to respond and, as he saw it, set the record straight.

Therefore, when it comes to constructing an argument (whether orally or in writing), we offer you the following advice: remember that you are entering a conversation and therefore need to start with "what others are saying," as the title of this chapter recommends, and then introduce your own ideas as a response. Specifically, we suggest that you summarize what "they say" as soon as you can in your text, and remind readers of it at strategic points as your text unfolds. Though it's true that not all texts follow this practice, we think it's important for all writers to master it before they depart from it.

This is not to say that you must start with a detailed list of everyone who has written on your subject before you offer your own ideas. Had our conference speaker gone to the opposite extreme and spent most of his talk summarizing Dr. X's critics with no hint of what he himself had to say, the audience probably would have had the same frustrated "why-is-he-going-on-like-this?" reaction. What we suggest, then, is that as soon as possible you state your own position and the one it's responding to *together*, and that you think of the two as a unit. It is generally best to summarize the ideas you're responding to briefly, at the start of your text, and to delay detailed elaboration until later. The point is to give your readers a quick preview of what is motivating your argument, not to drown them in details right away.

Starting with a summary of others' views may seem to contradict the common advice that writers should lead with their own thesis or claim. Although we agree that you shouldn't keep readers in suspense too long about your central argument, we also believe that you need to present that argument as part of some larger conversation, indicating something about the arguments of others that you are supporting, opposing, amending, complicating, or qualifying. One added benefit of summarizing others' views as soon as you can: you let those others do some of the work of framing and clarifying the issue you're writing about.

Consider, for example, how George Orwell starts his famous essay "Politics and the English Language" with what others are saying.

Most people who bother with the matter at all would admit that the English language is in a bad way, but it is generally assumed that we cannot by conscious action do anything about it. Our civilization is decadent and our language—so the argument runs—must inevitably share in the general collapse. . . .

[But] the process is reversible. Modern English . . . is full of bad habits . . . which can be avoided if one is willing to take the necessary trouble.

GEORGE ORWELL, "Politics and the English Language"

Orwell is basically saying, "Most people assume that we cannot do anything about the bad state of the English language. But I say we can."

Of course, there are many other powerful ways to begin. Instead of opening with someone else's views, you could start with an illustrative quotation, a revealing fact or statistic, or—as we do in this chapter—a relevant anecdote. If you choose one of these formats, however, be sure that it in some way illustrates the view you're addressing or leads you to that view directly, with a minimum of steps.

In opening this chapter, for example, we devote the first paragraph to an anecdote about the conference speaker and then move quickly at the start of the second paragraph to the misconception about writing exemplified by the speaker. In the following opening, from a 2004 opinion piece in the *New York Times Book Review*, Christina Nehring also moves quickly from an anecdote illustrating something she dislikes to her own claim—that book lovers think too highly of themselves.

"I'm a reader!" announced the yellow button. "How about you?" I looked at its bearer, a strapping young guy stalking my town's Festival of Books. "I'll bet you're a reader," he volunteered, as though we were two geniuses well met. "No," I replied. "Absolutely not," I wanted to yell, and fling my Barnes & Noble bag at his feet. Instead, I mumbled something apologetic and melted into the crowd.

There's a new piety in the air: the self congratulation of book lovers.

CHRISTINA NEHRING, "Books Make You a Boring Person"

Nehring's anecdote is really a kind of "they say": book lovers keep telling themselves how great they are.

TEMPLATES FOR INTRODUCING WHAT "THEY SAY"

There are lots of conventional ways to introduce what others are saying. Here are some standard templates that we would have recommended to our conference speaker.

▸ A number of sociologists have recently suggested that X's work has several fundamental problems.

▸ It has become common today to dismiss _____.

▸ In their recent work, Y and Z have offered harsh critiques of _____ for _____.

TEMPLATES FOR INTRODUCING "STANDARD VIEWS"

The following templates can help you make what we call the "standard view" move, in which you introduce a view that has become so widely accepted that by now it is essentially the conventional way of thinking about a topic.

▸ Americans have always believed that <u>individual effort can triumph over circumstances</u>.

▸ Conventional wisdom has it that _____.

▸ Common sense seems to dictate that _____.

▸ The standard way of thinking about topic X has it that _____.

▸ It is often said that _____.

▸ My whole life I have heard it said that _____.

▸ You would think that _____.

▸ Many people assume that _____.

These templates are popular because they provide a quick and efficient way to perform one of the most common moves that writers make: challenging widely accepted beliefs, placing them on the examining table and analyzing their strengths and weaknesses.

TEMPLATES FOR MAKING WHAT "THEY SAY" SOMETHING *YOU* SAY

Another way to introduce the views you're responding to is to present them as your own. That is, the "they say" that you respond to need not be a view held by others; it can be one that you yourself once held or one that you are ambivalent about.

▸ I've always believed that <u>museums are boring</u>.

▸ When I was a child, I used to think that _____.

▸ Although I should know better by now, I cannot help thinking that
_____ .

▸ At the same time that I believe _____ , I also believe
_____ .

TEMPLATES FOR INTRODUCING
SOMETHING IMPLIED OR ASSUMED

Another sophisticated move a writer can make is to summarize
a point that is not directly stated in what "they say" but is
implied or assumed.

▸ Although none of them have ever said so directly, my teachers have
often given me the impression that <u>education will open doors</u>.

▸ One implication of X's treatment of _____ is that
_____ .

▸ X apparently assumes that _____ .

▸ While they rarely admit as much, _____ often take for granted
that _____ .

These are templates that can help you think analytically—
to look beyond what others say explicitly and to consider
their unstated assumptions, as well as the implications of their
views.

TEMPLATES FOR INTRODUCING
AN ONGOING DEBATE

Sometimes you'll want to open by summarizing a debate
that presents two or more views. This kind of opening

demonstrates your awareness that there are conflicting ways to look at your subject, the clear mark of someone who knows the subject and therefore is likely to be a reliable, trustworthy guide. Furthermore, opening with a summary of a debate can help you explore the issue you are writing about before declaring your own view. In this way, you can use the writing process itself to help you discover where you stand instead of having to commit to a position before you are ready to do so.

Here is a basic template for opening with a debate.

> ▸ In discussions of X, one controversial issue has been _____.
> On the one hand, _____ argues _____.
> On the other hand, _____ contends _____. Others
> even maintain _____. My own view is _____.

The cognitive scientist Mark Aronoff uses this kind of template in an essay on the workings of the human brain.

> Theories of how the mind/brain works have been dominated for centuries by two opposing views. One, rationalism, sees the human mind as coming into this world more or less fully formed— preprogrammed, in modern terms. The other, empiricism, sees the mind of the newborn as largely unstructured, a blank slate.
>
> MARK ARONOFF, "Washington Slept Here"

Another way to open with a debate involves starting with a proposition many people agree with in order to highlight the point(s) on which they ultimately disagree.

> ▸ When it comes to the topic of _____, most of us will readily
> agree that _____. Where this agreement usually

ends, however, is on the question of _____. Whereas some are convinced that _____, others maintain that _____ .

The political writer Thomas Frank uses a variation on this move.

> That we are a nation divided is an almost universal lament of this bitter election year. However, the exact property that divides us— elemental though it is said to be—remains a matter of some controversy.
>
> THOMAS FRANK, "American Psyche"

KEEP WHAT "THEY SAY" IN VIEW

We can't urge you too strongly to keep in mind what "they say" as you move through the rest of your text. After summarizing the ideas you are responding to at the outset, it's very important to continue to keep those ideas in view. Readers won't be able to follow your unfolding response, much less any complications you may offer, unless you keep reminding them what claims you are responding to.

In other words, even when presenting your own claims, you should keep returning to the motivating "they say." The longer and more complicated your text, the greater the chance that readers will forget what ideas originally motivated it—no matter how clearly you lay them out at the beginning. At strategic moments throughout your text, we recommend that you include what we call "return sentences." Here is an example.

▸ In conclusion, then, as I suggested earlier, defenders of
_____ can't have it both ways. Their assertion that _____
is contradicted by their claim that _____.

We ourselves use such return sentences at every opportunity in this book to remind you of the view of writing that our book questions—that good writing means making true or smart or logical statements about a given subject with little or no reference to what others say about it.

By reminding readers of the ideas you're responding to, return sentences ensure that your text maintains a sense of mission and urgency from start to finish. In short, they help ensure that your argument is a genuine response to others' views rather than just a set of observations about a given subject. The difference is huge. To be responsive to others and the conversation you're entering, you need to start with what others are saying and continue keeping it in the reader's view.

Exercises

1. The following is a list of arguments that lack a "they say"—any sense of who needs to hear these claims, who might think otherwise. Like the speaker in the cartoon on page 4 who declares that *The Sopranos* presents complex characters, these one-sided arguments fail to explain what view they are responding to—what view, in effect, they are trying to correct, add to, qualify, complicate, and so forth. Your job in this exercise is to provide each argument with such a counterview. Feel free to use any of the templates in this chapter that you find helpful.

a. Our experiments suggest that there are dangerous levels of chemical X in the Ohio groundwater.

b. Material forces drive history.

c. Proponents of Freudian psychology question standard notions of "rationality."

d. Male students often dominate class discussions.

e. The film is about the problems of romantic relationships.

f. I'm afraid that templates like the ones in this book will stifle my creativity.

2. Below is a template that we derived from the opening of David Zinczenko's "Don't Blame the Eater" (p. 391). Use the template to structure a passage on a topic of your own choosing. Your first step here should be to find an idea that you support that others not only disagree with but actually find laughable (or, as Zinczenko puts it, worthy of a Jay Leno monologue). You might write about one of the topics listed in the previous exercise (the environment, sports, gender relations, the meaning of a book or movie) or any other topic that interests you.

▸ If ever there was an idea custom-made for a Jay Leno monologue, this was it: _____. Isn't that like _____? Whatever happened to _____?

    I happen to sympathize with _____, though, perhaps because _____.

TWO

"Her Point Is"

The Art of Summarizing

—◻—

IF IT IS TRUE, as we claim in this book, that to argue persuasively you need to be in dialogue with others, then summarizing others' arguments is central to your arsenal of basic moves. Because writers who make strong claims need to map their claims relative to those of other people, it is important to know how to summarize effectively what those other people say. (We're using the word "summarizing" here to refer to any information from others that you present in your own words, including that which you paraphrase.)

Many writers shy away from summarizing—perhaps because they don't want to take the trouble to go back to the text in question and wrestle with what it says, or because they fear that devoting too much time to other people's ideas will take away from their own. When assigned to write a response to an article, such writers might offer their own views on the article's *topic* while hardly mentioning what the article itself argues or says. At the opposite extreme are those who do nothing *but* summarize. Lacking confidence, perhaps, in their own ideas, these writers so overload their texts with summaries of others' ideas that their own voice gets lost. And since these summaries are not animated by the writers' own interests, they often read like mere lists of things that X thinks or Y says—with no clear focus.

As a general rule, a good summary requires balancing what the original author is saying with the writer's own focus. Generally speaking, a summary must at once be true to what the original author says while also emphasizing those aspects of what the author says that interest you, the writer. Striking this delicate balance can be tricky, since it means facing two ways at once: both outward (toward the author being summarized) and inward (toward yourself). Ultimately, it means being respectful of others but simultaneously structuring how you summarize them in light of your own text's central claim.

See how Barack Obama summarizes part of the U.S. Constitution in a speech about race, p. 647, ¶4.

ON THE ONE HAND, PUT YOURSELF IN *THEIR* SHOES

To write a really good summary, you must be able to suspend your own beliefs for a time and put yourself in the shoes of someone else. This means playing what the writing theorist Peter Elbow calls the "believing game," in which you try to inhabit the worldview of those whose conversation you are joining—and whom you are perhaps even disagreeing with—and try to see their argument from their perspective. This ability to temporarily suspend one's own convictions is a hallmark of good actors, who must convincingly "become" characters whom in real life they may detest. As a writer, when you play the believing game well, readers should not be able to tell whether you agree or disagree with the ideas you are summarizing.

If, as a writer, you cannot or will not suspend your own beliefs in this way, you are likely to produce summaries that are so obviously biased that they undermine your credibility with readers. Consider the following summary.

> David Zinczenko's article, "Don't Blame the Eater," is nothing more than an angry rant in which he accuses the fast-food companies of an evil conspiracy to make people fat. I disagree because these companies have to make money. . . .

If you review what Zinczenko actually says (pp. 391–93), you should immediately see that this summary amounts to an unfair distortion. While Zinczenko does argue that the practices of the fast-food industry have the *effect* of making people fat, his tone is never "angry," and he never goes so far as to suggest that the fast-food industry conspires to make people fat with deliberately evil intent.

Another tell-tale sign of this writer's failure to give Zinczenko a fair hearing is the hasty way he abandons the summary after only one sentence and rushes on to his own response. So eager is this writer to disagree that he not only caricatures what Zinczenko says but also gives the article a hasty, superficial reading. Granted, there are many writing situations in which, because of matters of proportion, a one- or two-sentence summary is precisely what you want. Indeed, as writing professor Karen Lunsford (whose own research focuses on argument theory) points out, it is standard in the natural and social sciences to summarize the work of others quickly, in one pithy sentence or phrase, as in the following example.

> Several studies (Crackle, 1992; Pop, 2001; Snap, 1987) suggest that these policies are harmless; moreover, other studies (Dick, 2002; Harry, 2003; Tom, 1987) argue that they even have benefits.

But if your assignment is to respond in writing to a single author like Zinczenko, you will need to tell your readers enough about his or her argument so they can assess its merits on their own, independent of you.

When a writer fails to provide enough summary or to engage in a rigorous or serious enough summary, he or she often falls prey to what we call "the closest cliché syndrome," in which what gets summarized is not the view the author in question has actually expressed but a familiar cliché that the writer *mistakes* for the author's view (sometimes because the writer believes it and mistakenly assumes the author must too). So, for example, Martin Luther King Jr.'s passionate defense of civil disobedience in "Letter from Birmingham Jail" might be summarized not as the defense of political protest that it actually is but as a plea for everyone to "just get along." Similarly, Zinczenko's critique of the fast-food industry might be summarized as a call for over-weight people to take responsibility for their weight.

Whenever you enter into a conversation with others in your writing, then, it is extremely important that you go back to what those others have said, that you study it very closely, and that you not confuse it with something you already believe. A writer who fails to do this ends up essentially conversing with imaginary others who are really only the products of his or her own biases and preconceptions.

ON THE OTHER HAND, KNOW WHERE *YOU* ARE GOING

Even as writing an effective summary requires you to temporarily adopt the worldview of another, it does not mean ignoring your own view altogether. Paradoxically, at the same time that summarizing another text requires you to represent fairly what it says, it also requires that your own response exert a quiet influence. A good summary, in other words, has a focus or spin that allows the summary to fit with your own agenda while still being true to the text you are summarizing.

Thus if you are writing in response to the essay by Zinczenko, you should be able to see that an essay on the fast-food industry in general will call for a very different summary than will an essay on parenting, corporate regulation, or warning labels. If you want your essay to encompass all three topics, you'll need to subordinate these three issues to one of Zinczenko's general claims and then make sure this general claim directly sets up your own argument.

For example, suppose you want to argue that it is parents, not fast-food companies, who are to blame for children's obesity. To set up this argument, you will probably want to compose a summary that highlights what Zinczenko says about the fast-food industry *and parents*. Consider this sample.

In his article "Don't Blame the Eater," David Zinczenko blames the fast-food industry for fueling today's so-called obesity epidemic, not only by failing to provide adequate warning labels on its high-calorie foods but also by filling the nutritional void in children's lives left by their overtaxed working parents. With many parents working long hours and unable to supervise what their children eat, Zinczenko claims, children today are easily victimized by the low-cost, calorie-laden foods that the fast-food chains are all too eager to supply. When he was a young boy, for instance, and his single mother was away at work, he ate at Taco Bell, McDonald's, and other chains on a regular basis, and ended up overweight. Zinczenko's hope is that with the new spate of lawsuits against the food industry, other children with working parents will have healthier choices available to them, and that they will not, like him, become obese.

In my view, however, it is the parents, and not the food chains, who are responsible for their children's obesity. While it is true that many of today's parents work long hours, there are still several things that parents can do to guarantee that their children eat healthy foods. . . .

The summary in the first paragraph succeeds because it points in two directions at once—both toward Zinczenko's own text *and* toward the second paragraph, where the writer begins to establish her own argument. The opening sentence gives a sense of Zinczenko's general argument (that the fast-food chains are to blame for obesity), including his two main supporting claims (about warning labels and parents), but it ends with an emphasis on the writer's main concern: parental responsibility. In this way, the summary does justice to Zinczenko's arguments while also setting up the ensuing critique.

This advice—to summarize authors in light of your own arguments—may seem painfully obvious. But writers often summarize a given author on one issue even though their text actually focuses on another. To avoid this problem, you need to make sure that your "they say" and "I say" are well matched. In fact, aligning what they say with what you say is a good thing to work on when revising what you've written.

Often writers who summarize without regard to their own interests fall prey to what might be called "list summaries," summaries that simply inventory the original author's various points but fail to focus those points around any larger overall claim. If you've ever heard a talk in which the points were connected only by words like "and then," "also," and "in addition," you

THE EFFECT OF A TYPICAL LIST SUMMARY

FIGURE 3

know how such lists can put listeners to sleep—as shown in Figure 3. A typical list summary sounds like this.

> The author says many different things about his subject. *First* he says. . . . *Then* he makes the point that. . . . *In addition* he says. . . . *And then* he writes. . . . *Also* he shows that. . . . *And then* he says. . . .

It may be boring list summaries like this that give summaries in general a bad name and even prompt some instructors to discourage their students from summarizing at all.

In conclusion, writing a good summary means not just representing an author's view accurately, but doing so in a way that fits your own composition's larger agenda. On the one hand, it means playing Peter Elbow's believing game and doing justice to the source; if the summary ignores or misrepresents the source, its bias and unfairness will show. On the other hand, even as it does justice to the source, a summary has to have a slant or spin that prepares the way for your own claims. Once a summary enters your text, you should think of it as joint property—reflecting both the source you are summarizing and your own views.

SUMMARIZING SATIRICALLY

Thus far in this chapter we have argued that, as a general rule, good summaries require a balance between what someone else has said and your own interests as a writer. Now, however, we want to address one exception to this rule: the satiric summary, in which a writer deliberately gives his or her own spin to someone else's argument in order to reveal a glaring shortcoming in it. Despite our previous comments that well-crafted summaries generally strike a balance between heeding what someone else has said and your own independent interests, the satiric mode can at times be a very effective form of critique because it lets the summarized argument condemn itself without overt editorializing by you, the writer. If you've ever watched *The Daily Show*, you'll recall that it often merely summarizes silly things political leaders have said or done, letting their words or actions undermine themselves.

Consider another example. In late September 2001, former President George W. Bush in a speech to Congress urged the nation's "continued participation and confidence in the American economy" as a means of recovering from the terrorist attacks of 9/11. The journalist Allan Sloan criticized this proposal simply by summarizing it, observing that the president had equated "patriotism with shopping. Maxing out your credit cards at the mall wasn't self indulgence, it was a way to get back at Osama bin Laden." Sloan's summary leaves no doubt where he stands—he considers Bush's proposal ridiculous, or at least too simple.

USE SIGNAL VERBS THAT FIT THE ACTION

In introducing summaries, try to avoid bland formulas like "she says," or "they believe." Though language like this is sometimes serviceable enough, it often fails to reflect accurately what's been said. In some cases, "he says" may even drain the passion out of the ideas you're summarizing.

We suspect that the habit of ignoring the action in what we summarize stems from the mistaken belief we mentioned earlier that writing is about playing it safe and not making waves, a matter of piling up truths and bits of knowledge rather than a dynamic process of doing things to and with other people. People who wouldn't hesitate to *say* "X totally misrepresented," "attacked," or "loved" something when chatting with friends will in their writing often opt for far tamer and even less accurate phrases like "X said."

But the authors you summarize at the college level seldom simply "say" or "discuss" things; they "urge," "emphasize," and "complain about" them. David Zinczenko, for example, doesn't just *say* that fast-food companies contribute to obesity; he *complains* or *protests* that they do; he *challenges, chastises,* and *indicts* those companies. The Declaration of Independence doesn't just *talk about* the treatment of the colonies by the British; it *protests against* it. To do justice to the authors you cite, we recommend that when summarizing—or when introducing a quotation—you use vivid and precise signal verbs as often as possible. Though "he says" or "she believes" will sometimes be the most appropriate language for the occasion, your text will often be more accurate and lively if you tailor your verbs to suit the precise actions you're describing.

TEMPLATES FOR INTRODUCING SUMMARIES AND QUOTATIONS

- ► She advocates a radical revision of the juvenile justice system.

- ► They celebrate the fact that _____.

- ► _____, he admits.

VERBS FOR INTRODUCING SUMMARIES AND QUOTATIONS

VERBS FOR MAKING A CLAIM

argue	insist
assert	observe
believe	remind us
claim	report
emphasize	suggest

VERBS FOR EXPRESSING AGREEMENT

acknowledge	endorse
admire	extol
agree	praise

VERBS FOR EXPRESSING AGREEMENT

celebrate the fact that	reaffirm
corroborate	support
do not deny	verify

VERBS FOR QUESTIONING OR DISAGREEING

complain	qualify
complicate	question
contend	refute
contradict	reject
deny	renounce
deplore the tendency to	repudiate

VERBS FOR MAKING RECOMMENDATIONS

advocate	implore
call for	plead
demand	recommend
encourage	urge
exhort	warn

Exercises

1. To get a feel for Peter Elbow's "believing game," write a summary of some belief that you strongly disagree with. Then write a summary of the position that you actually hold on this topic. Give both summaries to a classmate or two, and see if they can tell which position you endorse. If you've succeeded, they won't be able to tell.

2. Write two different summaries of David Zinczenko's "Don't Blame the Eater" (pp. 391–93). Write the first one for an essay arguing that, contrary to what Zinczenko claims, there *are* inexpensive and convenient alternatives to fast-food restaurants. Write the second for an essay that questions whether being overweight is a genuine medical problem rather than a problem of cultural stereotypes. Compare your two summaries: though they are about the same article, they should look very different.

THREE

"As He Himself Puts It"

The Art of Quoting

—◻—

A KEY PREMISE of this book is that to launch an effective argument you need to write the arguments of others into your text. One of the best ways to do so is by not only summarizing what "they say," as suggested in Chapter 2, but by quoting their exact words. Quoting someone else's words gives a tremendous amount of credibility to your summary and helps ensure that it is fair and accurate. In a sense, then, quotations function as a kind of proof of evidence, saying to readers: "Look, I'm not just making this up. She makes this claim and here it is in her exact words."

Yet many writers make a host of mistakes when it comes to quoting, not the least of which is the failure to quote enough in the first place, if at all. Some writers quote too little— perhaps because they don't want to bother going back to the original text and looking up the author's exact words, or because they think they can reconstruct the author's ideas from memory. At the opposite extreme are writers who so overquote that they end up with texts that are short on commentary of their own—maybe because they lack confidence in their ability to comment on the quotations, or because they don't fully understand what they've quoted and therefore have trouble explaining what the quotations mean.

But the main problem with quoting arises when writers assume that quotations speak for themselves. Because the meaning of a quotation is obvious to *them*, many writers assume that this meaning will also be obvious to their readers, when often it is not. Writers who make this mistake think that their job is done when they've chosen a quotation and inserted it into their text. They draft an essay, slap in a few quotations, and whammo, they're done.

Such writers fail to see that quoting means more than simply enclosing what "they say" in quotation marks. In a way, quotations are orphans: words that have been taken from their original contexts and that need to be integrated into their new textual surroundings. This chapter offers two key ways to produce this sort of integration: (1) by choosing quotations wisely, with an eye to how well they support a particular part of your text, and (2) by surrounding every major quotation with a frame explaining whose words they are, what the quotation means, and how the quotation relates to your own text. The point we want to emphasize is that quoting what "they say" must always be connected with what *you* say.

See how one author connects what "they say" to what he wants to say, p. 314, ¶7–8.

Quote Relevant Passages

Before you can select appropriate quotations, you need to have a sense of what you want to do with them—that is, how they will support your text at the particular point where you insert them. Be careful not to select quotations just for the sake of demonstrating that you've read the author's work; you need to make sure they support your own argument.

However, finding relevant quotations is not always easy. In fact, sometimes quotations that were initially relevant to your argument, or to a key point in it, become less so as your text changes during the process of writing and revising. Given the evolving and messy nature of writing, you may sometimes think that you've found the perfect quotation to support your argument, only to discover later on, as your text develops, that your focus has changed and the quotation no longer works. It can be somewhat misleading, then, to speak of finding your thesis and finding relevant quotations as two separate steps, one coming after the other. When you're deeply engaged in the writing and revising process, there is usually a great deal of back-and-forth between your argument and any quotations you select.

FRAME EVERY QUOTATION

Finding relevant quotations is only part of your job; you also need to present them in a way that makes their relevance and meaning clear to your readers. Since quotations do not speak for themselves, you need to build a frame around them in which you do that speaking for them.

Quotations that are inserted into a text without such a frame are sometimes called "dangling" quotations for the way they're left dangling without any explanation. One former graduate teaching assistant we worked with, Steve Benton, calls these "hit-and-run" quotations, likening them to car accidents in which the driver speeds away and avoids taking responsibility for the dent in your fender or the smashed taillights, as in Figure 4.

On the following page is a typical hit-and-run quotation by a writer responding to an essay by the feminist philoso-

DON'T BE A HIT-AND-RUN QUOTER.

FIGURE 4

pher Susan Bordo, who laments that media pressures on young women to diet are spreading to previously isolated regions of the world like the Fiji islands.

> Susan Bordo writes about women and dieting. "Fiji is just one example. Until television was introduced in 1995, the islands had no reported cases of eating disorders. In 1998, three years after programs from the United States and Britain began broadcasting there, 62 percent of the girls surveyed reported dieting."
> I think Bordo is right. Another point Bordo makes is that. . . .

Since this writer fails to introduce the quotation adequately or explain why he finds it worth quoting, readers will have a hard time reconstructing what Bordo argued. Besides neglecting to say who Bordo is or even that the quoted words are hers, the writer does not explain how her words connect with anything he is saying or even what she says that he thinks is so "right." He simply abandons the quotation in his haste to zoom on to another point.

See how Michael Kimmelman introduces a quote on p. 515, ¶7.

To adequately frame a quotation, you need to insert it into what we like to call a "quotation sandwich," with the statement introducing it serving as the top slice of bread and the explanation following it serving as the bottom slice. The introductory or lead-in claims should explain who is speaking and set up what the quotation says; the follow-up statements should explain why you consider the quotation to be important and what you take it to say.

TEMPLATES FOR INTRODUCING QUOTATIONS

▸ X states, "not all steroids should be banned from sports."

▸ As the prominent philosopher X puts it, "_____."

▸ According to X, "_____."

▸ X himself writes, "_____."

▸ In her book, _____, X maintains that "_____."

▸ Writing in the journal *Commentary*, X complains that "_____."

▸ In X's view, "_____."

▸ X agrees when she writes, "_____."

▸ X disagrees when he writes, "_____."

▸ X complicates matters further when she writes, "_____."

TEMPLATES FOR EXPLAINING QUOTATIONS

The one piece of advice about quoting that our students say they find most helpful is to get in the habit of following every major quotation by explaining what it means, using a template like one of the ones below.

▸ Basically, X is warning that the proposed solution will only make the problem worse.

▸ In other words, X believes _____ .

▸ In making this comment, X urges us to _____ .

▸ X is corroborating the age-old adage that _____ .

▸ X's point is that _____ .

▸ The essence of X's argument is that _____ .

When offering such explanations, it is important to use language that accurately reflects the spirit of the quoted passage. It is quite serviceable to write "Bordo states" or "asserts" in introducing the quotation about Fiji. But given the fact that Bordo is clearly alarmed by the extension of the media's reach to Fiji, it is far more accurate to use language that reflects her alarm: "Bordo is alarmed that" or "is disturbed by" or "complains."

See pp. 39–40 for a list of action verbs for summarizing what others say.

Consider, for example, how the earlier passage on Bordo might be revised using some of these moves.

The feminist philosopher Susan Bordo deplores Western media's obsession with female thinness and dieting. Her basic complaint is that increasing numbers of women across the globe are being led to see themselves as fat and in need of a diet. Citing the islands of Fiji as a case in point, Bordo notes that "until television was introduced in 1995, the islands had no reported cases of eating disorders. In 1998, three years after programs from the United States

and Britain began broadcasting there, 62 percent of the girls sur-
veyed reported dieting" (149–50). Bordo's point is that the Western cult of dieting is spreading even to remote places across the
globe. Ultimately, Bordo complains, the culture of dieting will find
you, regardless of where you live.

Bordo's observations ring true to me because, now that I think
about it, most women I know, regardless of where they are from,
are seriously unhappy with their weight. . . .

This framing of the quotation not only better integrates Bordo's
words into the writer's text, but also serves to demonstrate the
writer's interpretation of what Bordo is saying. While "the feminist philosopher" and "Bordo notes" provide information that
readers need to know, the sentences that follow the quotation
build a bridge between Bordo's words and those of the writer.
The reference to 62 percent of Fijian girls dieting is no longer
an inert statistic (as it was in the flawed passage presented
earlier) but a quantitative example of how "the Western cult
of dieting is spreading . . . across the globe." Just as important, these sentences explain what Bordo is saying in the
writer's own words—and thereby make clear that the quotation is being used purposefully to set up the writer's own argument and has not been stuck in just for padding the essay or
the works-cited list.

BLEND THE AUTHOR'S WORDS
WITH YOUR OWN

The above framing material also works well because it accurately represents Bordo's words while giving those words the
writer's own spin. Notice how the passage refers several times

to the key concept of dieting, and how it echoes Bordo's references to "television" and to U.S. and British "broadcasting" by referring to "culture," which is further specified as "Western." Instead of simply repeating Bordo word for word, the follow-up sentences echo just enough of her language while still moving the discussion in the writer's own direction. In effect, the framing creates a kind of hybrid mix of Bordo's words and those of the writer.

CAN YOU OVERANALYZE A QUOTATION?

But is it possible to overexplain a quotation? And how do you know when you've explained a quotation thoroughly enough? After all, not all quotations require the same amount of explanatory framing, and there are no hard-and-fast rules for knowing how much explanation any quotation needs. As a general rule, the most explanatory framing is needed for quotations that may be hard for readers to process: quotations that are long and complex, that are filled with details or jargon, or that contain hidden complexities.

And yet, though the particular situation usually dictates when and how much to explain a quotation, we will still offer one piece of advice: when in doubt, go for it. It is better to risk being overly explicit about what you take a quotation to mean than to leave the quotation dangling and your readers in doubt. Indeed, we encourage you to provide such explanatory framing even when writing to an audience that you know to be familiar with the author being quoted and able to interpret your quotations on their own. Even in such cases, readers need to see how *you* interpret the quotation, since words—especially those of controversial figures—can be interpreted in various ways and used to support different, sometimes opposing, agendas. Your readers need to see what you make of the material you've quoted, if only to be sure that your reading of the material and theirs is on the same page.

How *Not* to Introduce Quotations

We want to conclude this chapter by surveying some ways *not* to introduce quotations. Although some writers do so, you should not introduce quotations by saying something like "Orwell asserts an idea that" or "A quote by Shakespeare says." Introductory phrases like these are both redundant and misleading. In the first example, you could write either "Orwell asserts that" or "Orwell's assertion is that," rather than redundantly combining the two. The second example misleads readers, since it is the writer who is doing the quoting, not Shakespeare (as "a quote by Shakespeare" implies).

The templates in this book will help you avoid such mistakes. Once you have mastered templates like "as X puts it," or "in X's own words," you probably won't even have to think about them—and will be free to focus on the challenging ideas that templates help you frame.

Exercises

1. Find a published piece of writing that quotes something that "they say." How has the writer integrated the quotation into his or her own text? How has he or she introduced the quotation, and what, if anything, has the writer said to explain it and tie it to his or her own text? Based on what you've read in this chapter, are there any changes you would suggest?

2. Look at something you have written for one of your classes. Have you quoted any sources? If so, how have you integrated the quotation into your own text? How have you introduced it? Explained what it means? Indicated how it relates to *your* text? If you haven't done all these things, revise your text to do so, perhaps using the Templates for Introducing Quotations (p. 46) and Explaining Quotations (pp. 46–47). If you've not written anything with quotations, try revising some academic text you've written to do so.

2
"I SAY"

FOUR

"Yes / No / Okay, But"

Three Ways to Respond

—◈—

THE FIRST THREE chapters of this book discuss the "they say" stage of writing, in which you devote your attention to the views of some other person or group. In this chapter we move to the "I say" stage, in which you offer your own argument as a response to what "they" have said.

Moving to the "I say" stage can be daunting in academia, where it often may seem that you need to be an expert in a field to have an argument at all. Many students have told us that they have trouble entering some of the high-powered conversations that take place in college or graduate school because they do not know enough about the topic at hand, or because, they say, they simply are not "smart enough." Yet often these same students, when given a chance to study in depth the contribution that some scholar has made in a given field, will turn around and say things like "I can see where she is coming from, how she makes her case by building on what other scholars have said. Perhaps had I studied the situation longer I could have come up with a similar argument." What these students came to realize is that good arguments are based not on knowledge that only a special class of experts has access to, but on everyday habits of mind that can be isolated, identified, and used by almost anyone. Though there's certainly no substitute for expertise and for knowing as much as possible about one's topic, the arguments that finally win the day are built, as the title of this chapter suggests, on some very basic rhetorical patterns that most of us use on a daily basis.

There are a great many ways to respond to others' ideas, but this chapter concentrates on the three most common and recognizable ways: agreeing, disagreeing, or some combination of both. Although each way of responding is open to endless variation, we focus on these three because readers come to any text needing to learn fairly quickly where the writer stands, and they do this by placing the writer on a mental map consisting of a few familiar options: the writer agrees with those he or she is responding to, disagrees with them, or presents some combination of both agreeing and disagreeing.

When writers take too long to declare their position relative to views they've summarized or quoted, readers get frustrated, wondering, "Is this guy agreeing or disagreeing? Is he *for* what this other person has said, *against* it, or what?" For this reason, this chapter's advice applies to reading as well as to writing. Especially with difficult texts, you need not only to find the position the writer is responding to—the "they say"—but also to determine whether the writer is agreeing with it, challenging it, or some mixture of the two.

ONLY *THREE* WAYS TO RESPOND?

Perhaps you'll worry that fitting your own response into one of these three categories will force you to oversimplify your argument or lessen its complexity, subtlety, or originality. This is certainly a serious concern for academics who are rightly skeptical of writing that is simplistic and reductive. We would argue, however, that the more complex and subtle your argument is, and the more it departs from the conventional ways people think, the more your readers will need to be able to place it on their mental map in order to process the complex details you present. That is, the complexity, subtlety, and originality of your response are more likely to stand out and be noticed if readers have a baseline sense of where you stand relative to any ideas you've cited. As you move through this chapter, we hope you'll agree that the forms of agreeing, disagreeing, and both agreeing and disagreeing that we discuss, far from being simplistic or one-dimensional, are able to accommodate a high degree of creative, complex thought.

It is always a good tactic to begin your response not by launching directly into a mass of details but by stating clearly whether you agree, disagree, or both, using a direct, no-nonsense formula such as: "I agree," "I disagree," or "I am of two minds. I agree that _____, but I cannot agree that _____." Once you have offered one of these straightforward statements (or one of the many varia-**See p. 21 for suggestions on previewing where you stand.** tions discussed below), readers will have a strong grasp of your position and then be able to appreciate the complications you go on to offer as your response unfolds.

Still, you may object that these three basic ways of responding don't cover all the options—that they ignore interpretive or analytical responses, for example. In other words, you might think that when you interpret a literary work you don't necessarily agree or disagree with anything but simply explain the work's meaning, style, or structure. Many essays about literature and the arts, it might be said, take this form—they interpret a work's meaning, thus rendering matters of agreeing or disagreeing irrelevant.

We would argue, however, that the most interesting interpretations in fact tend to be those that agree, disagree, or both—that instead of being offered solo, the best interpretations take strong stands relative to other interpretations. In fact, there would be no reason to offer an interpretation of a work of literature or art unless you were responding to the interpretations or possible interpretations of others. Even when you point out features or qualities of an artistic work that others have not noticed, you are implicitly disagreeing with what those interpreters have said by pointing out that they missed or overlooked something that, in your view, is important. In any effective interpretation, then, you need not only to state what you yourself take the work of art to mean but to do so relative to the interpretations of other readers—be they professional scholars, teachers, classmates, or even hypothetical readers (as in, "Although some readers might think that this poem is about _____, it is in fact about _____ ").

DISAGREE—AND EXPLAIN WHY

Disagreeing may seem like one of the simpler moves a writer can make, and it is often the first thing people associate with critical thinking. Disagreeing can also be the easiest way to generate an essay: find something you can disagree with in what has been said or might be said about your topic, summarize it, and argue with it. But disagreement in fact poses hidden challenges. You need to do more than simply assert that you disagree with a particular view; you also have to offer persuasive reasons *why* you disagree. After all, disagreeing means more than adding "not" to what someone else has said, more than just saying, "Although they say women's rights are improving,

I say women's rights are *not* improving." Such a response merely contradicts the view it responds to and fails to add anything interesting or new. To turn it into an argument, you need to give reasons to support what you say: because another's argument fails to take relevant factors into account; because it is based on faulty or incomplete evidence; because it rests on questionable assumptions; or because it uses flawed logic, is contradictory, or overlooks what you take to be the real issue. To move the conversation forward (and, indeed, to justify your very act of writing), you need to demonstrate that you have something to contribute.

See p. 257 for reasons why student loan debt is not a national crisis.

You can even disagree by making what we call the "duh" move, in which you disagree not with the position itself but with the assumption that it is a new or stunning revelation. Here is an example of such a move, used to open a 2003 essay on the state of American schools.

> According to a recent report by some researchers at Stanford University, high school students with college aspirations "often lack crucial information on applying to college and on succeeding academically once they get there."
>
> Well, duh. . . . It shouldn't take a Stanford research team to tell us that when it comes to "succeeding academically," many students don't have a clue.
>
> GERALD GRAFF, "Trickle-Down Obfuscation"

Like all of the other moves discussed in this book, the "duh" move can be tailored to meet the needs of almost any writing situation. If you find the expression "duh" too brash to use with your intended audience, you can always dispense with the term itself and write something like "It is true that _____; but we already knew that."

TEMPLATES FOR DISAGREEING, WITH REASONS

▸ X is mistaken because she overlooks <u>recent fossil discoveries in the South</u>.

▸ X's claim that _____ rests upon the questionable assumption that _____ .

▸ I disagree with X's view that _____ because, as recent research has shown, _____ .

▸ X contradicts herself/can't have it both ways. On the one hand, she argues _____ . On the other hand, she also says _____ .

▸ By focusing on _____ , X overlooks the deeper problem of _____ .

You can also disagree by making what we call the "twist it" move, in which you agree with the evidence that someone else has presented but show through a twist of logic that this evidence actually supports your own, contrary position. For example:

> X argues for stricter gun control legislation, saying that the crime rate is on the rise and that we need to restrict the circulation of guns. I agree that the crime rate is on the rise, but that's precisely why I oppose stricter gun control legislation. We need to own guns to protect ourselves against criminals.

In this example of the "twist it" move, the writer agrees with X's claim that the crime rate is on the rise but then argues that this increasing crime rate is in fact a valid reason for *opposing* gun control legislation.

At times you might be reluctant to express disagreement, for any number of reasons—not wanting to be unpleasant, to hurt someone's feelings, or to make yourself vulnerable to being disagreed with in return. One of these reasons may in fact explain why the conference speaker we described at the start of Chapter 1 avoided mentioning the disagreement he had with other scholars until he was provoked to do so in the discussion that followed his talk.

As much as we understand such fears of conflict and have experienced them ourselves, we nevertheless believe it is better to state our disagreements in frank yet considerate ways than to deny them. After all, suppressing disagreements doesn't make them go away; it only pushes them underground, where they can fester in private unchecked. Nevertheless, disagreements do not need to take the form of personal put-downs. Furthermore, there is usually no reason to take issue with *every* aspect of someone else's views. You can single out for criticism only those aspects of what someone else has said that are troubling, and then agree with the rest—although such an approach, as we will see later in this chapter, leads to the somewhat more complicated terrain of both agreeing and disagreeing at the same time.

AGREE—BUT WITH A DIFFERENCE

Like disagreeing, agreeing is less simple than it may appear. Just as you need to avoid simply contradicting views you disagree with, you also need to do more than simply echo views you agree with. Even as you're agreeing, it's important to bring something new and fresh to the table, adding something that makes you a valuable participant in the conversation.

There are many moves that enable you to contribute something of your own to a conversation even as you agree with what someone else has said. You may point out some unnoticed evidence or line of reasoning that supports X's claims that X herself hadn't mentioned. You may cite some corroborating personal experience, or a situation not mentioned by X that her views help readers understand. If X's views are particularly challenging or esoteric, what you bring to the table could be an accessible translation—an explanation for readers not already in the know. In other words, your text can usefully contribute to the conversation simply by pointing out unnoticed implications or explaining something that needs to be better understood.

Whatever mode of agreement you choose, the important thing is to open up some difference or contrast between your position and the one you're agreeing with rather than simply parroting what it says.

TEMPLATES FOR AGREEING

▸ I agree that <u>diversity in the student body is educationally valuable</u> because my experience at <u>Central University</u> confirms it.

▸ X is surely right about _____ because, as she may not be aware, recent studies have shown that _____ .

▸ X's theory of _____ is extremely useful because it sheds light on the difficult problem of _____ .

▸ Those unfamiliar with this school of thought may be interested to know that it basically boils down to _____ .

Some writers avoid the practice of agreeing almost as much as others avoid disagreeing. In a culture like America's that prizes originality, independence, and competitive individualism, writers sometimes don't like to admit that anyone else has made the same point, seemingly beating them to the punch. In our view, however, as long as you can support a view taken by someone else without merely restating what he or she has said, there is no reason to worry about being "unoriginal." Indeed, there is good reason to rejoice when you agree with others since those others can lend credibility to your argument. While you don't want to present yourself as a mere copycat of someone else's views, you also need to avoid sounding like a lone voice in the wilderness.

But do be aware that whenever you agree with one person's view, you are likely disagreeing with someone else's. It is hard to align yourself with one position without at least implicitly positioning yourself against others. The psychologist Carol Gilligan does just that in an essay in which she agrees with scientists who argue that the human brain is "hard-wired" for cooperation, but in so doing aligns herself against anyone who believes that the brain is wired for selfishness and competition.

> These findings join a growing convergence of evidence across the human sciences leading to a revolutionary shift in consciousness. . . . If cooperation, typically associated with altruism and self-sacrifice, sets off the same signals of delight as pleasures commonly associated with hedonism and self-indulgence; if the opposition between selfish and selfless, self vs. relationship biologically makes no sense, then a new paradigm is necessary to reframe the very terms of the conversation.
>
> CAROL GILLIGAN, "Sisterhood Is Pleasurable:
> A Quiet Revolution in Psychology"

In agreeing with some scientists that "the opposition between selfish and selfless . . . makes no sense," Gilligan implicitly disagrees with anyone who thinks the opposition *does* make sense. Basically, what Gilligan says could be boiled down to a template.

▸ I agree that ＿＿＿＿＿, a point that needs emphasizing since so many people still believe ＿＿＿＿＿.

▸ If group X is right that ＿＿＿＿＿, as I think they are, then we need to reassess the popular assumption that ＿＿＿＿＿.

What such templates allow you to do, then, is to agree with one view while challenging another—a move that leads into the domain of agreeing and disagreeing simultaneously.

Agree and Disagree Simultaneously

This last option is often our favorite way of responding. One thing we particularly like about agreeing and disagreeing simultaneously is that it helps us get beyond the kind of "is too" / "is not" exchanges that often characterize the disputes of young children and the more polarized shouting matches of talk radio and TV.

Templates for Agreeing and Disagreeing Simultaneously

"Yes and no." "Yes, but . . . " "Although I agree up to a point, I still insist . . . " These are just some of the ways you can make your argument complicated and nuanced while maintaining a clear, reader-friendly framework. The parallel structure—"yes

and no"; "on the one hand I agree, on the other I disagree"—enables readers to place your argument on that
map of positions we spoke of earlier in this chapter
while still keeping your argument sufficiently complex.

Another aspect we like about this option is that it
can be tipped subtly toward agreement or disagreement,
depending on where you lay your stress. If you want to
stress the disagreement end of the spectrum, you would use a template like the one below.

Dana Stevens says "yes, but" to an argument that TV makes us smarter, pp. 295–98.

▸ Although I agree with X up to a point, I cannot accept his overrid-
ing assumption that <u>religion is no longer a major force today</u>.

Conversely, if you want to stress your agreement more than
your disagreement, you would use a template like this one.

▸ Although I disagree with much that X says, I fully endorse his final
conclusion that _____ .

The first template above might be called a "yes, but . . . " move,
the second a "no, but . . . " move. Other versions include the
following.

▸ Though I concede that _____ , I still insist that _____ .

▸ X is right that _____ , but she seems on more dubious ground
when she claims that _____ .

▸ While X is probably wrong when she claims that _____ ,
she is right that _____ .

▸ Whereas X provides ample evidence that _____ , Y and Z's
research on _____ and _____ convinces me
that _____ instead.

Another classic way to agree and disagree at the same time is to make what we call an "I'm of two minds" or a "mixed feelings" move.

▶ I'm of two minds about X's claim that _____. On the one hand, I agree that _____. On the other hand, I'm not sure if _____.

▶ My feelings on the issue are mixed. I do support X's position that _____, but I find Y's argument about _____ and Z's research on _____ to be equally persuasive.

This move can be especially useful if you are responding to new or particularly challenging work and are as yet unsure where you stand. It also lends itself well to the kind of speculative investigation in which you weigh a position's pros and cons rather than come out decisively either for or against. But again, as we suggest earlier, whether you are agreeing, disagreeing, or both agreeing and disagreeing, you need to be as clear as possible, and making a frank statement that you are ambivalent is one way to be clear.

IS BEING UNDECIDED OKAY?

Nevertheless, writers often have as many concerns about expressing ambivalence as they do about expressing disagreement or agreement. Some worry that by expressing ambivalence they will come across as evasive, wishy-washy, or unsure of themselves. Others worry that their ambivalence will end up confusing readers who require decisive clear-cut conclusions.

The truth is that in some cases these worries are legitimate. At times ambivalence can frustrate readers, leaving them with the feeling that you failed in your obligation to offer the guidance they expect from writers. At other times, however, acknowledging that a clear-cut resolution of an issue is impossible can demonstrate your sophistication as a writer. In an academic culture that values complex thought, forthrightly declaring that you have mixed feelings can be impressive, especially after having ruled out the one-dimensional positions on your issue taken by others in the conversation. Ultimately, then, how ambivalent you end up being comes down to a judgment call based on different readers' responses to your drafts, on your knowledge of your audience, and on the challenges of your particular argument and situation.

Exercises

1. Read one of the essays in the readings section of this book, identifying those places where the author agrees with others, disagrees, or both.

2. Write an essay responding in some way to the essay that you worked with in the preceding exercise. You'll want to summarize and/or quote some of the author's ideas and make clear whether you're agreeing, disagreeing, or both agreeing and disagreeing with what he or she says. Remember that there are templates in this book that can help you get started; see Chapters 1–3 for templates that will help you represent other people's ideas, and Chapter 4 for templates that will get you started with your response.

FIVE

"AND YET"

Distinguishing What You Say
from What They Say

※

IF GOOD ACADEMIC WRITING involves putting yourself into dialogue with others, it is extremely important that readers be able to tell at every point when you are expressing your own view and when you are stating someone else's. This chapter takes up the problem of moving from what *they* say to what *you* say without confusing readers about who is saying what.

DETERMINE WHO IS SAYING WHAT
IN THE TEXTS YOU READ

Before examining how to signal who is saying what in your own writing, let's look at how to recognize such signals when they appear in the texts you read—an especially important skill when it comes to the challenging works assigned in school. Frequently, when students have trouble understanding difficult texts, it is not just because the texts contain unfamiliar ideas or words, but because the texts rely on subtle clues to let readers know when a particular view should be attributed to the writer or to someone else. Especially with texts that present a true dialogue of perspectives, readers need to be alert to the often subtle markers that indicate whose voice the writer is speaking in.

Consider how the social critic and educator Gregory Mantsios uses these "voice markers," as they might be called, to distinguish the different perspectives in his essay on America's class inequalities.

> "We are all middle-class," or so it would seem. Our national consciousness, as shaped in large part by the media and our political leadership, provides us with a picture of ourselves as a nation of prosperity and opportunity with an ever expanding middle-class life-style. As a result, our class differences are muted and our collective character is homogenized.
>
> Yet class divisions are real and arguably the most significant factor in determining both our very being in the world and the nature of the society we live in.
>
> GREGORY MANTSIOS, "Rewards and Opportunities:
> The Politics and Economics of Class in the U.S."

Although Mantsios makes it look easy, he is actually making several sophisticated rhetorical moves here that help him distinguish the common view he opposes from his own position.

In the opening sentence, for instance, the phrase "or so it would seem" shows that Mantsios does not necessarily agree with the view he is describing, since writers normally don't present views they themselves hold as ones that only "seem" to be true. Mantsios also places this opening view in quotation marks to signal that it is not his own. He then further distances himself from the belief being summarized in the opening paragraph by attributing it to "our national consciousness, as shaped in large part by the media and our political leadership," and then further attributing to this "consciousness" a negative, undesirable "result": one in which "our class differences" get "muted" and "our collective character" gets "homogenized," stripped of its diversity and distinctness. Hence, even before Mantsios has declared his own position in the second paragraph, readers can get a pretty solid sense of where he probably stands.

Furthermore, the second paragraph opens with the word "yet," indicating that Mantsios is now shifting to his own view (as opposed to the common view he has thus far been describing). Even the parallelism he sets up between the first and second paragraphs—between the first paragraph's claim that class differences do not exist and the second paragraph's claim that they do—helps throw into sharp relief the differences between the two voices. Finally, Mantsios's use of a direct, authoritative, declarative tone in the second paragraph also suggests a switch in voice. Although he does not use the words "I say" or "I argue," he clearly identifies the view he holds by presenting it not as one that merely *seems* to be true or that *others tell us* is true, but as a view that *is* true or, as Mantsios puts it, "real."

Paying attention to these voice markers is an important aspect of reading comprehension. Readers who fail to notice these markers often take an author's summaries of what someone else believes to be an expression of what the author himself or herself believes. Thus when we teach Mantsios's essay, some students invariably come away thinking that the statement "we are all middle-class" is Mantsios's own position rather than the perspective he is opposing, failing to see that in writing these words Mantsios acts as a kind of ventriloquist, mimicking what others say rather than directly expressing what he himself is thinking.

To see how important such voice markers are, consider what the Mantsios passage looks like if we remove them

> We are all middle-class. . . . We are a nation of prosperity and opportunity with an ever expanding middle-class life-style. . . .
>
> Class divisions are real and arguably the most significant factor in determining both our very being in the world and the nature of the society we live in.

In contrast to the careful delineation between voices in Mantsios's original text, this unmarked version leaves it hard to tell where his voice begins and the voices of others end. With the markers removed, readers cannot tell that "We are all middle-class" represents a view the author opposes, and that "Class divisions are real" represents what the author himself believes. Indeed, without the markers, especially the "Yet," readers might well miss the fact that the second paragraph's claim that "Class divisions are real" contradicts the first paragraph's claim that "We are all middle-class."

See how Cal Thomas begins with a view he then tries to refute on p. 568, ¶2–3.

TEMPLATES FOR SIGNALING WHO IS SAYING WHAT IN YOUR OWN WRITING

To avoid confusion in your own writing, make sure that at every point your readers can clearly tell who is saying what. To do so, you can use as voice-identifying devices many of the templates presented in previous chapters.

▸ Although X makes the best possible case for <u>universal, government-funded health care</u>, <u>I am not persuaded</u>.

▸ My view, however, contrary to what X has argued, is that _____.

▸ Adding to X's argument, I would point out that _____.

▸ According to both X and Y, _____.

▸ Politicians, X argues, should _____.

▸ Most athletes will tell you that _____.

BUT I'VE BEEN TOLD NOT TO USE "I"

Notice that the first three templates above use the first-person "I" or "we," as do many of the templates in this book, thereby contradicting the common advice about avoiding the first person in academic writing. Although you may have been told that the "I" word encourages subjective, self-indulgent opinions rather than well-grounded arguments, we believe that texts using "I" can be just as well supported—or just as self-indulgent—as those that don't. For us, well-supported arguments are grounded in persuasive reasons and evidence, not in the use or nonuse of any particular pronouns.

Furthermore, if you consistently avoid the first person in your writing, you will probably have trouble making the key move addressed in this chapter: differentiating your views from those of others, or even offering your own views in the first place. But don't just take our word for it. See for yourself how freely the first person is used by the writers quoted in this book, and by the writers assigned in your courses.

Nevertheless, certain occasions may warrant avoiding the first person and writing, for example, that "she is correct" instead of "I think that she is correct." Since it can be monotonous to read an unvarying series of "I" statements ("I believe . . . I think . . . I argue"), it is a good idea to mix first-person assertions with ones like the following.

- ▸ X is right that <u>certain common patterns can be found in the communities</u>.

- ▸ The evidence shows that _____ .

- ▸ X's assertion that _____ does not fit the facts.

- ▸ Anyone familiar with _____ should agree that _____ .

One might even follow Mantsios's lead, as in the following template.

- ▸ But _____ are real, and are arguably the most significant factor in _____ .

One the whole, however, academic writing today, even in the sciences and social sciences, makes use of the first person fairly liberally.

ANOTHER TRICK FOR IDENTIFYING WHO IS SPEAKING

To alert readers about whose perspective you are describing at any given moment, you don't always have to use overt voice markers like "X argues" followed by a summary of the argument. Instead, you can alert readers about whose voice you're speaking in by *embedding* a reference to X's argument in your own sentences. Hence, instead of writing:

Liberals believe that cultural differences need to be respected. I have a problem with this view, however.

you might write:

I have a problem with *what liberals call cultural differences*.

There is a major problem with the liberal doctrine of *so-called cultural differences*.

You can also embed references to something you yourself have previously said. So instead of writing two cumbersome sentences like:

Earlier in this chapter we coined the term "voice markers." We would argue that such markers are extremely important for reading comprehension.

you might write:

We would argue that "voice markers," as we identified them earlier, are extremely important for reading comprehension.

Embedded references like these allow you to economize your train of thought and refer to other perspectives without any major interruption.

TEMPLATES FOR EMBEDDING VOICE MARKERS

▶ X overlooks what I consider an important point about <u>cultural differences</u>.

▶ My own view is that what X insists is a _____ is in fact a
  _____ .

▶ I wholeheartedly endorse what X calls _____ .

▶ These conclusions, which X discusses in _____ , add weight
  to the argument that _____ .

When writers fail to use voice-marking devices like the ones discussed in this chapter, their summaries of others' views tend to become confused with their own ideas—and vice versa. When readers cannot tell if you are summarizing your own views or endorsing a certain phrase or label, they have to stop and think: "Wait. I thought the author disagreed with this claim. Has she actually been asserting this view all along?" or "Hmmm, I thought she would have objected to this kind of phrase. Is she actually endorsing it?" Getting in the habit of using voice markers will keep you from confusing your readers and help alert you to similar markers in the challenging texts you read.

Exercises

1. To see how one writer signals when she is asserting her own views and when she is summarizing those of someone else, read the following passage by the social historian Julie Charlip. As you do so, identify those spots where Charlip refers to the views of others and the signal phrases she uses to distinguish her views from theirs.

   Marx and Engels wrote: "Society as a whole is more and more splitting up into two great hostile camps, into two great classes directly facing each other—the bourgeoisie and the proletariat" (10). If only that were true, things might be more simple. But in late twentieth-century America, it seems that society is splitting more and more into a plethora of class factions—the working class, the working poor, lower-middle class, upper-middle class, lower uppers, and upper uppers. I find myself not knowing what class I'm from.

In my days as a newspaper reporter, I once asked a sociology professor what he thought about the reported shrinking of the middle class. Oh, it's not the middle class that's disappearing, he said, but the working class. His definition: if you earn thirty thousand dollars a year working in an assembly plant, come home from work, open a beer and watch the game, you are working class; if you earn twenty thousand dollars a year as a school teacher, come home from work to a glass of white wine and PBS, you are middle class.

How do we define class? Is it an issue of values, lifestyle, taste? Is it the kind of work you do, your relationship to the means of production? Is it a matter of how much money you earn? Are we allowed to choose? In this land of supposed classlessness, where we don't have the tradition of English society to keep us in our places, how do we know where we really belong? The average American will tell you he or she is "middle class." I'm sure that's what my father would tell you. But I always felt that we were in some no man's land, suspended between classes, sharing similarities with some and recognizing sharp, exclusionary differences from others. What class do I come from? What class am I in now? As an historian, I seek the answers to these questions in the specificity of my past.

> JULIE CHARLIP, "A Real Class Act: Searching
> for Identity in the Classless Society"

2. Study a piece of your own writing to see how many perspectives you account for and how well you distinguish your

own voice from those you are summarizing. Consider the following questions:

a. How many perspectives do you engage?
b. What other perspectives might you include?
c. How do you distinguish your views from the other views you summarize?
d. Do you use clear voice-signaling phrases?
e. What options are available to you for clarifying who is saying what?
f. Which of these options are best suited for this particular text?

If you find that you do *not* include multiple views or clearly distinguish between your views and others', revise your text to do so.

SIX

"SKEPTICS MAY OBJECT"

Planting a Naysayer in Your Text

———

THE WRITER Jane Tompkins describes a pattern that repeats itself whenever she writes a book or an article. For the first couple of weeks when she sits down to write, things go relatively well. But then in the middle of the night, several weeks into the writing process, she'll wake up in a cold sweat, suddenly realizing that she has overlooked some major criticism that readers will surely make against her ideas. Her first thought, invariably, is that she will have to give up on the project, or that she will have to throw out what she's written thus far and start over. Then she realizes that "this moment of doubt and panic is where my text really begins." She then revises what she's written in a way that incorporates the criticisms she's anticipated, and her text becomes stronger and more interesting as a result.

This little story contains an important lesson for all writers, experienced and inexperienced alike. It suggests that even though most of us are upset at the idea of someone criticizing our work, such criticisms can actually work to our advantage. Although it's naturally tempting to ignore criticism of our ideas, doing so may in fact be a big mistake, since our writing improves when we not only listen to these objections but give them an explicit hearing in our writing. Indeed, no single device more quickly improves a piece of writing than planting a naysayer in the text—saying, for example, that "although some readers may object" to something in your argument, you "would reply that _____."

ANTICIPATE OBJECTIONS

But wait, you say. Isn't the advice to incorporate critical views a recipe for destroying your credibility and undermining your argument? Here you are, trying to say something that will hold up, and we want you to tell readers all the negative things someone might say against you?

Exactly. We *are* urging you to tell readers what others might say against you, but our point is that doing so will actually *enhance* your credibility, not undermine it. As we argue throughout this book, writing well does not mean piling up uncontroversial truths in a vacuum; it means engaging others in a dialogue or debate—not only by opening your text with a summary of what others *have* said, as we suggest in Chapter 1, but also by imagining what others *might* say against your argument as it unfolds. Once you see writing as an act of entering a conversation, you should also see how opposing arguments can work for you rather than against you.

Paradoxically, the more you give voice to your critics' objections, the more you tend to disarm those critics, especially if you go on to answer their objections in convincing ways. When you entertain a counterargument, you make a kind of preemptive strike, identifying problems with your argument before others can point them out for you. Furthermore, by entertaining counterarguments, you show respect for your readers, treating them not as gullible dupes who will believe anything you say but as independent, critical thinkers who are aware that your view is not the only one in town. In addition, by imagining what others might say against your claims, you come across as a generous, broad-minded person who is confident enough to open himself or herself to debate—like the writer in Figure 5.

Conversely, if you don't entertain counterarguments, you may very likely come across as closed-minded, as if you think your beliefs are beyond dispute. You might also leave important questions hanging and concerns about your arguments unaddressed. Finally, if you fail to plant a naysayer in your text, you may find that you have very little to say. Our own students often say that entertaining counterarguments makes it easier to generate enough text to meet their assignment's page-length requirements.

Planting a naysayer in your text is a relatively simple move, as you can see by looking at the following passage from a book by the writer Kim Chernin. Having spent some thirty pages complaining about the pressure on American women to lose weight and be thin, Chernin inserts a whole chapter entitled "The Skeptic," opening it as follows.

> At this point I would like to raise certain objections that have been inspired by the skeptic in me. She feels that I have been ignoring some of the most common assumptions we all make about our bodies and these she wishes to see addressed. For example: "You know perfectly well," she says to me, "that you feel better when you lose weight. You buy new clothes. You look at yourself more eagerly in the mirror. When someone invites you to a party you don't stop and ask yourself whether you want to go. You feel sexier. Admit it. You like yourself better."
>
> KIM CHERNIN, *The Obsession:*
> *Reflections on the Tyranny of Slenderness*

FIGURE 5

The remainder of Chernin's chapter consists of her answers to this inner skeptic. In the face of the skeptic's challenge to her book's central premise (that the pressure to diet seriously harms women's lives), Chernin responds neither by repressing the skeptic's critical voice nor by giving in to it and relinquishing her own position. Instead, she embraces that voice and writes it into her text. Note too that instead of dispatching this naysaying voice quickly, as many of us would be tempted to do, Chernin stays with it and devotes a full paragraph to it. By borrowing some of Chernin's language, we can come up with templates for entertaining virtually any objection.

TEMPLATES FOR ENTERTAINING OBJECTIONS

▸ At this point I would like to raise some objections that have been inspired by the skeptic in me. She feels that I have been ignoring the complexities of the situation.

▸ Yet some readers may challenge my view by insisting that _____ .

▸ Of course, many will probably disagree on the grounds that _____ .

Note that the objections in the above templates are attributed not to any specific person or group, but to "skeptics," "readers," or "many." This kind of nameless, faceless naysayer is perfectly appropriate in many cases. But the ideas that motivate arguments and objections often can—and, where possible, should—be ascribed to a specific ideology or school of thought (for example, liberals, Christian fundamentalists, neopragmatists) rather than to anonymous anybodies. In other words, naysayers can be labeled, and you can add precision and impact to your writing by identifying what those labels are.

TEMPLATES FOR NAMING YOUR NAYSAYERS

▸ Here many *feminists* would probably object that gender does influence language.

▸ But *social Darwinists* would certainly take issue with the argument that _____ .

▸ *Biologists*, of course, may want to question whether _____ .

▸ Nevertheless, both *followers and critics of Malcolm X* will probably suggest otherwise and argue that _____ .

To be sure, some people dislike such labels and may even resent having labels applied to themselves. Some feel that labels put individuals in boxes, stereotyping them and glossing over what makes each of us unique. And it's true that labels can be used inappropriately, in ways that ignore individuality and promote stereotypes. But since the life of ideas, including many of our most private thoughts, is conducted through groups and types rather than solitary individuals, intellectual exchange requires labels to give definition and serve as a convenient shorthand. If you categorically reject all labels, you give up an important resource and even mislead readers by presenting yourself and others as having no connection to anyone else. You also miss an opportunity to generalize the importance and relevance of your work to some larger conversation. When you attribute a position you are summarizing to liberalism, say, or historical materialism, your argument is no longer just about your own solitary views but about the intersection of broad ideas and habits of mind that many readers may already have a stake in.

The way to minimize the problem of stereotyping, then, is not to categorically reject labels but to refine and qualify their use, as the following templates demonstrate.

▸ Although not all *Christians* think alike, some of them will probably dispute my claim that _____ .

▸ *Non-native English speakers* are so diverse in their views that it's hard to generalize about them, but some are likely to object on the grounds that _____ .

Another way to avoid needless stereotyping is to qualify labels carefully, substituting "pro bono lawyers" for "lawyers" in general, for example, or "quantitative sociologists" for all "social scientists," and so on.

TEMPLATES FOR INTRODUCING OBJECTIONS INFORMALLY

Objections can also be introduced in more informal ways. For instance, you can frame objections in the form of questions.

▸ But is my proposal realistic? What are the chances of its actually being adopted?

▸ Yet is it necessarily true that _____ ? Is it always the case, as I have been suggesting, that _____ ?

▸ However, does the evidence I've cited prove conclusively that _____ ?

You can also let your naysayer speak directly.

▸ "Impossible," some will say. "You must be reading the research selectively."

Moves like this allow you to cut directly to the skeptical voice itself, as the singer-songwriter Joe Jackson does in the following excerpt from a 2003 *New York Times* article complaining about the restrictions on public smoking in New York City bars and restaurants.

> I like a couple of cigarettes or a cigar with a drink, and like many other people, I only smoke in bars or nightclubs. Now I can't go to any of my old haunts. Bartenders who were friends have turned into cops, forcing me outside to shiver in the cold and curse under my breath. . . . It's no fun. Smokers are being demonized and victimized all out of proportion.
>
> "Get over it," say the anti-smokers. "You're the minority." I thought a great city was a place where all kinds of minorities could thrive. . . . "Smoking kills," they say. As an occasional smoker with otherwise healthy habits, I'll take my chances. Health consciousness is important, but so are pleasure and freedom of choice.
>
> JOE JACKSON, "Want to Smoke? Go to Hamburg"

Jackson could have begun his second paragraph, in which he shifts from his own voice to that of his imagined naysayer, more formally, as follows: "Of course anti-smokers will object that since we smokers are in the minority, we should simply stop complaining and quietly make the sacrifices we are being called on to make for the larger social good." Or "Anti-smokers might insist, however, that the smoking minority should submit to

See the essay on *Family Guy* (p. 299) that addresses naysayers throughout.

the non-smoking majority." We think, though, that Jackson gets the job done in a far more lively way with the more colloquial form he chooses. Borrowing a standard move of playwrights and novelists, Jackson cuts directly to the objectors' view and then to his own retort, then back to the objectors'

See Chapter 5 for more advice on using voice markers.

view and then to his own retort again, thereby creating a kind of dialogue or miniature play within his own text. This move works well for Jackson, but only because he uses quotation marks and other voice markers to make clear at every point whose voice he is in.

REPRESENT OBJECTIONS FAIRLY

Once you've decided to introduce a differing or opposing view into your writing, your work has only just begun, since you still need to represent and explain that view with fairness and generosity. Although it is tempting to give opposing views short shrift, to hurry past them, or even to mock them, doing so is usually counterproductive. When writers make the best case

See pp. 31–32 for more on the believing game.

they can for their critics (playing Peter Elbow's "believing game"), they actually bolster their credibility with readers rather than undermine it. They make readers think, "This is a writer I can trust."

We recommend, then, that whenever you entertain objections in your writing, you stay with them for several sentences or even paragraphs and take them as seriously as possible. We also recommend that you read your summary of opposing views with an outsider's eye: put yourself in the shoes of someone who disagrees with you and ask if such a reader would recognize himself in your summary. Would that reader think you have taken his views seriously, as beliefs that reasonable people might hold?

Or would he detect a mocking tone or an oversimplification of his views?

There will always be certain objections, to be sure, that you believe do not deserve to be represented, just as there will be objections that seem so unworthy of respect that they inspire ridicule. Remember, however, that if you do choose to mock a view that you oppose, you are likely to alienate those readers who don't already agree with you—likely the very readers you want to reach. Also be aware that in mocking another's view you may contribute to a hostile argument culture in which someone may ridicule you in return.

ANSWER OBJECTIONS

Do be aware that when you represent objections successfully, you still need to be able to answer those objections persuasively. After all, when you write objections into a text, you take the risk that readers will find those objections more convincing than the argument you yourself are advancing. In the editorial quoted above, for example, Joe Jackson takes the risk that readers will identify more with the anti-smoking view he summarizes than with the pro-smoking position he endorses.

This is precisely what Benjamin Franklin describes happening to himself in *The Autobiography of Benjamin Franklin* (1793), when he recalls being converted to Deism (a religion that exalts reason over spirituality) by reading *anti*-Deist books. When he encountered the views of Deists being negatively summarized by authors who opposed them, Franklin explains, he ended up finding the Deist position more persuasive. To avoid having this kind if unintentional reverse effect on

readers, you need to do your best to make sure that any counterarguments you address are not more convincing than your
own claims. It is good to address objections in your writing,
but only if you are able to overcome them.

One surefire way to *fail* to overcome an objection is to dismiss it out of hand—saying, for example, "That's just wrong."
The difference between such a response (which offers no supporting reasons whatsoever) and the types of nuanced responses
we're promoting in this book is the difference between bullying your readers and genuinely persuading them.

Often the best way to overcome an objection is not to try
to refute it completely but to agree with part of it while challenging only the part you dispute. In other words, in answering counterarguments, it is often best to say "yes, but" or "yes
and no," treating the counterview as an opportunity to revise
and refine your own position. Rather than build your argument into an impenetrable fortress, it is often best to
make concessions while still standing your ground, as
Kim Chernin does in the following response to the
counter-argument quoted above. While in the voice
of the "skeptic," Chernin writes: "Admit it. You like yourself
better when you've lost weight." In response, Chernin replies
as follows.

See pp. 61–66
for more on
agreeing, with
a difference.

> Can I deny these things? No woman who has managed to lose
> weight would wish to argue with this. Most people feel better about
> themselves when they become slender. And yet, upon reflection,
> it seems to me that there is something precarious about this well-
> being. After all, 98 percent of people who lose weight gain it back.
> Indeed, 90 percent of those who have dieted "successfully" gain
> back more than they ever lost. Then, of course, we can no longer
> bear to look at ourselves in the mirror.

In this way, Chernin shows how you can use a counterview to improve and refine your overall argument by making a concession. Even as she concedes that losing weight feels good in the short run, she argues that in the long run the weight always returns, making the dieter far more miserable.

TEMPLATES FOR MAKING CONCESSIONS WHILE STILL STANDING YOUR GROUND

▸ Although I grant that the book is poorly organized, I still maintain that it raises an important issue.

▸ Proponents of X are right to argue that _____. But they exaggerate when they claim that _____.

▸ While it is true that _____, it does not necessarily follow that _____.

▸ On the one hand, I agree with X that _____. But on the other hand, I still insist that _____.

Templates like these show that answering naysayers' objections does not have to be an all-or-nothing affair in which you either definitively refute your critics or they definitively refute you. Often the most productive engagements among differing views end with a combined vision that incorporates elements of each one.

But what if you've tried out all the possible answers you can think of to an objection you've anticipated and you *still* have a nagging feeling that the objection is more convincing than your argument itself? In that case, the best remedy is to go back and make some fundamental revisions to your argument, even reversing your position completely if need be. Although finding out late in the game that you aren't fully convinced by your own argument can be painful, it can actually make your final text more intellectually honest, challenging, and serious. After all, the goal of writing is not to keep proving that whatever you initially said is right, but to stretch the limits of your thinking. So if planting a strong naysayer in your text forces you to change your mind, that's not a bad thing. Some would argue that that is what the academic world is all about.

Exercises

1. Read the following passage by the cultural critic Eric Schlosser. As you'll see, he hasn't planted any naysayers in this text. Do it for him. Insert a brief paragraph stating an objection to his argument and then responding to the objection as he might.

The United States must declare an end to the war on drugs. This war has filled the nation's prisons with poor drug addicts and small-time drug dealers. It has created a multibillion-dollar black market, enriched organized crime groups and promoted the corruption of government officials throughout the world. And it has not stemmed the widespread use of illegal drugs. By any rational measure, this war has been a total failure.

We must develop public policies on substance abuse that are guided not by moral righteousness or political expediency but by common sense. The United States should immediately decriminalize the cultivation and possession of small amounts of marijuana for personal use. Marijuana should no longer be classified as a Schedule I narcotic, and those who seek to use marijuana as medicine should no longer face criminal sanctions. We must shift our entire approach to drug abuse from the criminal justice system to the public health system. Congress should appoint an independent commission to study the harm-reduction policies that have been adopted in Switzerland, Spain, Portugal, and the Netherlands. The commission should recommend policies for the United States based on one important criterion: what works.

In a nation where pharmaceutical companies advertise powerful antidepressants on billboards and where alcohol companies run amusing beer ads during the Super Bowl, the idea of a "drug-free society" is absurd. Like the rest of American society, our drug policy would greatly benefit from less punishment and more compassion.

ERIC SCHLOSSER, "A People's Democratic Platform"

2. Look over something you've written that makes an argument. Check to see if you've anticipated and responded to any objections. If not, revise your text to do so. If so, have you anticipated all the likely objections? Who if anyone have you attributed the objections to? Have you represented the objections fairly? Have you answered them well enough, or do you think you now need to qualify your own argument? Could you use any of the language suggested in this chapter? Does the introduction of a naysayer strengthen your argument? Why or why not?

SEVEN

"So What? Who Cares?"

Saying Why It Matters

———⌐□⌐———

BASEBALL IS the national pastime. Bernini was the best sculptor of the baroque period. All writing is conversational. So what? Who cares? Why does any of this matter?

How many times have you had reason to ask these questions? Regardless of how interesting a topic may be to you as a writer, readers always need to know what is at stake in a text and why they should care. All too often, however, these questions are left unanswered—mainly because writers and speakers assume that audiences will know the answers already or will figure them out on their own. As a result, students come away from lectures feeling like outsiders to what they've just heard, just as many of us feel left hanging after talks we've attended. The problem is not necessarily that the speakers lack a clear, well-focused thesis or that the thesis is inadequately supported with evidence. Instead, the problem is that the speakers don't address the crucial question of why their arguments matter.

That this question is so often left unaddressed is unfortunate since the speakers generally *could* offer interesting, engaging answers. When pressed, for instance, most academics will tell you that their lectures and articles matter because they address some belief that needs to be corrected or updated—and because their arguments have important, real-world consequences. Yet many academics fail to identify these reasons and consequences explicitly in what they say and write. Rather than assume that audiences will know why their claims matter, all writers need to answer the "so what?" and "who cares?" questions up front. Not everyone can claim to have a cure for cancer or a solution to end poverty. But writers who fail to show that others *should* care or already *do* care about their claims will ultimately lose their audiences' interest.

This chapter focuses on various moves that you can make to answer the "who cares?" and "so what?" questions in your own writing. In one sense, the two questions get at the same thing: the relevance or importance of what you are saying. Yet they get at this significance in different ways. Whereas "who cares?" literally asks you to identify a person or group who cares about your claims, "so what?" asks about the real-world applications and consequences of those claims—what difference it would make if they were accepted. We'll look first at ways of making clear who cares.

"WHO CARES?"

To see how one writer answers the "who cares?" question, consider the following passage from the science writer Denise Grady. Writing in the *New York Times*, she explains some of the latest research into fat cells.

> Scientists used to think body fat and the cells it was made of were pretty much inert, just an oily storage compartment. But within the past decade research has shown that fat cells act like chemical factories and that body fat is potent stuff: a highly active

tissue that secretes hormones and other substances with profound and sometimes harmful effects. . . .

In recent years, biologists have begun calling fat an "endocrine organ," comparing it to glands like the thyroid and pituitary, which also release hormones straight into the bloodstream.

DENISE GRADY, "The Secret Life of a Potent Cell"

Notice how Grady's writing reflects the central advice we give in this book, offering a clear claim and also framing that claim as a response to what someone else has said. In so doing, Grady immediately identifies at least one group with a stake in the new research that sees fat as "active," "potent stuff": namely, the scientific community, which formerly believed that body fat is inert. By referring to these scientists, Grady implicitly acknowledges that her text is part of a larger conversation and shows who besides herself has an interest in what she says.

Consider, however, how the passage would read had Grady left out what "scientists used to think" and simply explained the new findings in isolation.

Within the past few decades research has shown that fat cells act like chemical factories and that body fat is potent stuff: a highly active tissue that secretes hormones and other substances. In recent years, biologists have begun calling fat an "endocrine organ," comparing it to glands like the thyroid and pituitary, which also release hormones straight into the bloodstream.

Though this statement is clear and easy to follow, it lacks any indication that anyone needs to hear it. Okay, one nods while reading this passage, fat is an active, potent thing. Sounds plausible enough; no reason to think it's not true. But does anyone really care? Who, if anyone, is interested?

TEMPLATES FOR INDICATING WHO CARES

To address "who cares?" questions in your own writing, we suggest using templates like the following, which echo Grady in refuting earlier thinking.

▸ Parents used to think spanking was necessary. But recently [or within the past few decades] experts suggest that it can be counterproductive.

▸ This interpretation challenges the work of those critics who have long assumed that _____.

▸ These findings challenge the work of earlier researchers, who tended to assume that _____.

▸ Recent studies like these shed new light on _____, which previous studies had not addressed.

Grady might have been more explicit by writing the "who cares?" question directly into her text, as in the following template.

▸ But who really cares? Who besides me and a handful of recent researchers has a stake in these claims? At the very least, the researchers who formerly believed _____ should care.

To gain greater authority as a writer, it can help to name specific people or groups who have a stake in your claims and to go into some detail about their views.

▸ Researchers have long assumed that _____. For instance, one eminent scholar of cell biology, _____, assumed in _____, her seminal work on cell structures and functions, that fat cells _____. As _____ herself put it, " _____ " (2007). Another leading scientist, _____, argued that fat cells

"_____" (2006). Ultimately, when it came to the nature of fat, the basic assumption was that _____.

    But a new body of research shows that fat cells are far more complex and that _____.

In other cases, you might refer to certain people or groups who *should* care about your claims.

▸ If sports enthusiasts stopped to think about it, many of them might simply assume that the most successful athletes _____. However, new research shows _____.

▸ These findings challenge neoliberals' common assumption that _____.

▸ At first glance, teenagers might say _____. But on closer inspection _____.

As these templates suggest, answering the "who cares?" question involves establishing the type of contrast between what others say and what you say that is central to this book. Ultimately, such templates help you create a dramatic tension or clash of views in your writing that readers will feel invested in and want to see resolved.

"So What?"

Although answering the "who cares?" question is crucial, in many cases it is not enough, especially if you are writing for general readers who don't necessarily have a strong investment in the particular clash of views you are setting up. In the case of Grady's argument about fat cells, such readers may still wonder why it matters that some researchers think fat cells are active, while others think they're inert. Or, to move to a different field of study, American literature, *so what* if some scholars disagree about Huck Finn's relationship with the runaway slave Jim in Mark Twain's *Adventures of Huckleberry Finn?* Why should anyone besides a few specialists in the field care about such disputes? What, if anything, hinges on them?

The best way to answer such questions about the larger consequences of your claims is to appeal to something that your audience already figures to care about. Whereas the "who cares?" question asks you to identify an interested person or group, the "so what?" question asks you to link your argument to some larger matter that readers already deem important. Thus in analyzing *Huckleberry Finn,* a writer could argue that seemingly narrow disputes about the hero's relationship with Jim actually shed light on whether Twain's canonical, widely read novel is a critique of racism in America or is itself marred by it.

Let's see how Grady invokes such broad, general concerns in her article on fat cells. Her first move is to link researchers' interest in fat cells to a general concern with obesity and health.

> Researchers trying to decipher the biology of fat cells hope to find new ways to help people get rid of excess fat or, at least, prevent obesity from destroying their health. In an increasingly obese world, their efforts have taken on added importance.

Further showing why readers should care, Grady's next move is to demonstrate the even broader relevance and urgency of her subject matter.

> Internationally, more than a billion people are overweight. Obesity and two illnesses linked to it, heart disease and high blood pressure, are on the World Health Organization's list of the top 10 global health risks. In the United States, 65 percent of adults weigh too much,

compared with about 56 percent a decade ago, and government researchers blame obesity for at least 300,000 deaths a year.

What Grady implicitly says here is "Look, dear reader, you may think that these questions about the nature of fat cells I've been pursuing have little to do with everyday life. In fact, however, these questions are extremely important—particularly in our 'increasingly obese world' in which we need to prevent obesity from destroying our health."

See Jason Zinser's "so what" statements on p. 363, ¶2.
Notice that Grady's phrase "in an increasingly _____ world" can be adapted as a strategic move to address the "so what?" question in other fields as well. For example, a sociologist analyzing back-to-nature movements of the past thirty years might make the following statement.

> In a world increasingly dominated by cellphones and sophisticated computer technologies, these attempts to return to nature appear futile.

This type of move can be readily applied to other disciplines because no matter how much disciplines may differ from one another, the need to justify the importance of one's concerns is common to them all.

TEMPLATES FOR ESTABLISHING WHY YOUR CLAIMS MATTER

▸ *Huckleberry Finn* matters/is important because it is one of the most widely taught novels in the American school system.

▸ Although X may seem trivial, it is in fact crucial in terms of today's concern over _____.

▸ Ultimately, what is at stake here is _____.

▸ These findings have important implications for the broader domain of _____.

▸ If we are right about _____, then major consequences follow for _____.

▸ These conclusions/This discovery will have significant applications in _____ as well as in _____.

Finally, you can also treat the "so what?" question as a related aspect of the "who cares?" question.

▸ Although X may seem of concern to only a small group of _____, it should in fact concern anyone who cares about _____.

All these templates help you hook your readers. By suggesting the real-world applications of your claims, the templates not only demonstrate that others care about your claims but also tell your readers why *they* should care. Again, it bears repeating that simply stating and proving your thesis isn't enough. You also need to frame it in a way that helps readers care about it.

WHAT ABOUT READERS WHO ALREADY KNOW WHY IT MATTERS?

At this point, you might wonder if you need to answer the "who cares?" and "so what?" questions in *everything* you write. Is it really necessary to address these questions if you're proposing something so obviously consequential as, say, a treatment for autism or a program to eliminate illiteracy? Isn't it obvious that everyone cares about such problems? Does it really need to be spelled out? And what about when you're writing for audiences who you know are already interested in your claims and who understand perfectly well why they're important? In other words, do you always need to address the "so what?" and "who cares?" questions?

See how two authors explain why fast food advertisements matter on pp. 472–73, ¶53–54.
As a rule, yes—although it's true that you can't keep answering them forever and at a certain point must say enough is enough. Although a determined skeptic can infinitely ask why something matters—"Why should I care about earning a salary? And why should I care about supporting a family?"—you have to stop answering at some point in your text. Nevertheless, we urge you to go as far as possible in answering such questions. If you take it for granted that readers will somehow intuit the answers to "so what?" and "who cares?" on their own, you may make your work seem less interesting than it actually is, and you run the risk that readers will dismiss your text as irrelevant and unimportant. By conrast, when you are careful to explain who cares and why, it's a little like bringing a cheerleading squad into your text. And though some expert readers might already know why your claims matter, even they need to be reminded. Thus the safest move is to be as explicit as possible in answering the "so what?" question, even for those already in the know. When you step back from the text and explain why it matters, you are urging your audience to keep reading, pay attention, and care.

Exercises

1. Find several texts (scholarly pieces, newspaper articles, emails, memos, etc.) and see whether they answer the "so

what?" and "who cares?" questions. Probably some do, some don't. What difference does it make whether they do or do not? How do the authors who answer these questions do so? Do they use any strategies or techniques that you could borrow for your own writing? Are there any strategies or techniques recommended in this chapter, or that you've found or developed on your own, that you'd recommend to these authors?

2. Look over something you've written yourself. Do you indicate "so what?" and "who cares"? If not, revise your text to do so. You might use the following template to get started.

My point here (that _____) should interest those who _____. Beyond this limited audience, however, my point should speak to anyone who cares about the larger issue of _____.

3

TYING IT ALL TOGETHER

EIGHT

"AS A RESULT"

Connecting the Parts

—◻—

WE ONCE HAD a student named Bill, whose characteristic sentence pattern went something like this.

> Spot is a good dog. He has fleas.

"Connect your sentences," we urged in the margins of Bill's papers. "What does Spot being good have to do with his fleas?" "These two statements seem unrelated. Can you connect them in some logical way?" When comments like these yielded no results, we tried inking in suggested connections for him.

> Spot is a good dog, *but* he has fleas.
> Spot is a good dog, *even though* he has fleas.

But our message failed to get across, and Bill's disconnected sentence pattern persisted to the end of the semester.

And yet Bill did focus well on his subjects. When he mentioned Spot the dog (or Plato, or any other topic) in one sentence, we could count on Spot (or Plato) being the topic of the following sentence as well. This was not the case with some of Bill's classmates, who sometimes changed topic from sentence to sentence or even from clause to clause within a single sentence. But because Bill neglected to mark his connections, his writing was as frustrating to read as theirs. In all these cases, we had to struggle to figure out on our own how the sentences and paragraphs connected or failed to connect with one another.

What makes such writers so hard to read, in other words, is that they never gesture back to what they have just said or forward to what they plan to say. "Never look back" might be their motto, almost as if they see writing as a process of thinking of something to say about a topic and writing it down, then thinking of something else to say about the topic and writing that down too, and on and on until they've filled the assigned number of pages and can hand the paper in. Each sentence basically starts a new thought, rather than growing out of or extending the thought of the previous sentence.

When Bill talked about his writing habits, he acknowledged that he never went back and read what he had written. Indeed, he told us that, other than using his computer software to check for spelling errors and make sure that his tenses were all aligned, he never actually reread what he wrote before turning it in. As Bill seemed to picture it, writing was something one did while sitting at a computer, whereas reading was a separate activity generally reserved for an easy chair, book in hand. It had never occurred to Bill that to write a good sentence he had to think about how it connected to those that came before and after; that he had to think hard about how that sentence fit into the sentences that surrounded it. Each sentence for Bill existed in a sort of tunnel isolated from every other sentence on the page. He never bothered to fit all the parts of his essay together because he apparently thought of writing as a matter of piling up information or observations rather than building a sustained argument. What we suggest in this chapter, then, is that you converse not only with others in your writing but with yourself: that you establish clear relations between one statement and the next by connecting those statements.

This chapter addresses the issue of how to connect all the parts of your writing. The best compositions establish a sense of momentum and direction by making explicit connections among their different parts, so that what is said in one sentence (or paragraph) both sets up what is to come and is clearly informed by what has already been said. When you write a sentence, you create an expectation in the reader's mind that the next sentence will in some way echo and extend it, even if—*especially if*—that next sentence takes your argument in a new direction.

It may help to think of each sentence you write as having arms that reach backward and forward, as Figure 6 suggests. When your sentences reach outward like this, they establish connections that help your writing flow smoothly in a way readers appreciate. Conversely, when writing lacks such connections and moves in fits and starts, readers repeatedly have to go back over the sentences and guess at the connections on their own. To prevent such disconnection and make your writing flow, we advise

YOUR
LAST
SENTENCE

YOUR
NEXT
SENTENCE

FIGURE 6

following a "do it yourself" principle, which means that it is your job as a writer to do the hard work of making the connections rather than, as Bill did, leaving this work to your readers.

This chapter offers several strategies you can use to put this principle into action: (1) using transition terms (like "therefore" and "as a result"); (2) adding pointing words (like "this" or "such"); (3) developing a set of key terms and phrases for each text you write; and (4) repeating yourself, but with a difference—a move that involves repeating what you've said, but with enough variation to avoid being redundant. All these moves require that you always look back and, in crafting any one sentence, think hard about those that precede it.

Notice how we ourselves have used such connecting devices thus far in this chapter. The second paragraph of this chapter, for example, opens with the transitional "And yet," signaling a change in direction, while the opening sentence of the third includes the phrase "in other words," telling you to expect a restatement of a point we've just made. If you look through this book, you should be able to find many sentences that contain some word or phrase that explicitly hooks them back to something said earlier, to something about to be said, or both. And many sentences in *this* chapter repeat key terms related to the idea of connection: "connect," "disconnect," "link," "relate," "forward," and "backward."

USE TRANSITIONS

For readers to follow your train of thought, you need not only to connect your sentences and paragraphs to each other, but also to mark the kind of connection you are making. One of the easiest ways to make this move is to use *transitions* (from the Latin root *trans*, "across"), which help you cross from one point to another in your text. Transitions are usually placed at or near the start of sentences so they can signal to readers where your text is going: in the same direction it has been moving, or in a new direction. More specifically, transitions tell readers whether your text is echoing a previous sentence or paragraph ("in other words"), adding something to it ("in addition"), offering an example of it ("for example"), generalizing from it ("as a result"), or modifying it ("and yet").

The following is a list of commonly used transitions, categorized according to their different functions.

ADDITION

also	indeed
and	in fact
besides	moreover
furthermore	so too
in addition	

EXAMPLE

after all	specifically
as an illustration	to take a case in point
for example	consider
for instance	

ELABORATION

actually	to put it another way
by extension	to put it bluntly
in short	to put it succinctly
that is	ultimately
in other words	

COMPARISON

along the same lines	likewise
in the same way	similarly

CONTRAST

although	nevertheless
but	nonetheless
by contrast	on the contrary
conversely	on the other hand
despite	regardless
even though	whereas
however	while yet
in contrast	

CAUSE AND EFFECT

accordingly	so
as a result	then
consequently	therefore
hence	thus
since	

CONCESSION

admittedly	naturally
although it is true	of course
granted	to be sure

CONCLUSION

as a result	in sum
consequently	therefore
hence	thus
in conclusion	to sum up
in short	to summarize

Ideally, transitions should operate so unobtrusively in a piece of writing that they recede into the background and readers do not even notice that they are there. It's a bit like what happens when drivers use their turn signals before turning right or left: just as other drivers recognize such signals almost uncon‑sciously, readers should process transition terms with a mini‑mum of thought. But even though such terms should function unobtrusively in your writing, they can be among the most pow‑erful tools in your vocabulary. Think how your heart sinks when someone, immediately after praising you, begins a sentence with "but" or "however." No matter what follows, you know it won't be good.

Notice that some transitions can help you not only to move from one sentence to another, but to combine two or more sen‑tences into one. Combining sentences in this way helps prevent the choppy, staccato effect that arises when too many short sen‑tences are strung together, one after the other. For instance, to combine Bill's two choppy sentences ("Spot is a good dog. He has fleas.") into one, better-flowing sentence, we suggested that he rewrite them as "Spot is a good dog, *even though* he has fleas."

Transitions like these not only guide readers through the twists and turns of your argument but also help ensure that you *have* an argument in the first place. In fact, we think of words like "but," "yet," "nevertheless," "besides," and others as argu‑ment words, since it's hard to use them without making some kind of argument. The word "therefore," for instance, commits you to making sure that the claims preceding it lead logically to the conclusion that it introduces. "For example" also assumes an argument, since it requires the material you are introducing to stand as an instance or proof of some preceding generaliza‑tion. As a result, the more you use transitions, the more you'll be able not only to connect the parts of your text but also to construct a strong argument in the first place. And if you draw on them frequently enough, using them should eventually become second nature.

To be sure, it is possible to overuse transitions, so take time See how Robert Frank uses transitions on p. 580, ¶3–4. to read over your drafts carefully and eliminate any transitions that are unnecessary. But following the maxim that you need to learn the basic moves of argument before you can deliberately depart from them, we advise you not to forgo explicit transition terms until you've first mastered their use. In all our years of teaching, we've read countless essays that suffered from having few or no transitions, but cannot recall one in which the transitions were overused. Seasoned writers sometimes omit explicit transitions, but only because they rely heavily on the other types of connecting devices that we turn to in the rest of this chapter.

Before doing so, however, let us warn you about inserting transitions without really thinking through their meanings—using "therefore," say, when your text's logic actually requires "nevertheless" or "however." So beware. Choosing transition terms should involve a bit of mental sweat, since the whole point of using them is to make your writing *more* reader-friendly, not less. The only thing more frustrating than reading Bill-style passages like "Spot is a good dog. He has fleas" is reading mis-connected sentences like "Spot is a good dog. For example, he has fleas."

Use Pointing Words

Another way to connect the parts of your argument is by using pointing words—which, as their name implies, point or refer backward to some concept in the previous sentence. The most common of these pointing words include "this," "these," "that," "those," "their," and "such" (as in "these pointing words" near the start of this sentence) and simple pronouns like "his," "he," "her," "she," "it," and "their." Such terms help you create the flow we spoke of earlier that enables readers to move effortlessly through your text. In a sense, these terms are like an invisible hand reaching out of your sentence, grabbing what's needed in the previous sentences and pulling it along.

Like transitions, however, pointing words need to be used carefully. It's dangerously easy to insert pointing words into your text that don't refer to a clearly defined object, assuming that because the object you have in mind is clear to you it will also be clear to your readers. For example, consider the use of "this" in the following passage.

> Alexis de Tocqueville was highly critical of democratic societies, which he saw as tending toward mob rule. At the same time, he accorded democratic societies grudging respect. *This* is seen in Tocqueville's statement that . . .

When "this" is used in such a way it becomes an ambiguous or free-floating pointer, since readers can't tell if it refers to Tocqueville's critical attitude toward democratic societies, his grudging respect for them, or some combination of both. "This what?" readers mutter as they go back over such passages and try to figure them out. It's also tempting to try to cheat with pointing words, hoping that they will conceal or make up for conceptual confusions that may lurk in your argument. By referring to a fuzzy idea as "this" or "that," you might hope the fuzziness will somehow come across as clearer than it is.

You can fix problems caused by a free-floating pointer by making sure there is one and only one possible object in the vicinity that the pointer could be referring to. It also often helps to name the object the pointer is referring to at the same time that you point to it, replacing the bald "this" in the example above with a more precise phrase like "this ambivalence toward democratic societies" or "this grudging respect."

REPEAT KEY TERMS AND PHRASES

A third strategy for connecting the parts of your argument is to develop a constellation of key terms and phrases, including their synonyms and antonyms, that you repeat throughout your text. When used effectively, your key terms should be items that readers could extract from your text in order to get a solid sense of your topic. Playing with key terms also can be a good way to come up with a title and appropriate section headings for your text.

Notice how often Martin Luther King Jr. uses the key words "criticism," "statement," "answer," and "correspondence" in the opening paragraph of his famous "Letter from Birmingham Jail."

> Dear Fellow Clergymen:
>
>   While confined here in the Birmingham city jail, I came across your recent *statement* calling my present activities "unwise and untimely." Seldom do I pause to *answer criticism* of my work and ideas. If I sought to *answer* all the *criticisms* that cross my desk, my secretaries would have little time for anything other than *such correspondence* in the course of the day, and I would have no time for constructive work. But since I feel that you are men of genuine good will and that your *criticisms* are sincerely set forth, I want to try to *answer* your *statement* in what I hope will be patient and reasonable terms.
>
>   MARTIN LUTHER KING JR., *"Letter from Birmingham Jail"*

Even though King uses the terms "criticism" and "answer" three times each and "statement" twice, the effect is not overly repetitive. In fact, these key terms help build a sense of momentum in the paragraph and bind it together.

For another example of the effective use of key terms, consider the following passage, in which the historian Susan Douglas develops a constellation of sharply contrasting key terms around the concept of "cultural schizophrenics": women like herself who, Douglas claims, have mixed feelings about the images of ideal femininity with which they are constantly bombarded by the media.

> In a variety of ways, the mass media helped make us the cultural schizophrenics we are today, women who rebel against yet submit to prevailing images about what a desirable, worthwhile woman should be. . . . [T]he mass media has engendered in many women a kind of cultural identity crisis. We are ambivalent toward femininity on the one hand and feminism on the other. Pulled in opposite directions—told we were equal, yet told we were subordinate; told we could change history but told we were trapped by history—we got the bends at an early age, and we've never gotten rid of them.
>
> When I open *Vogue*, for example, I am simultaneously infuriated and seduced. . . . I adore the materialism; I despise the materialism. . . . I want to look beautiful; I think wanting to look beautiful is about the most dumb-ass goal you could have. The magazine stokes my desire; the magazine triggers my bile. And this doesn't only happen when I'm reading *Vogue*; it happens all the time. . . . On the one hand, on the other hand—that's not just me—that's what it means to be a woman in America.
>
> To explain this schizophrenia . . .
>
> SUSAN DOUGLAS, *Where the Girls Are:*
> *Growing Up Female with the Mass Media*

In this passage, Douglas establishes "schizophrenia" as a key concept and then echoes it through synonyms like "identity crisis," "ambivalent," "the bends"—and even demonstrates it through a series of contrasting words and phrases:

> rebel against / submit
> told we were equal / told we were subordinate
> told we could change history / told we were trapped by history
> infuriated / seduced
> I adore / I despise
> I want / I think wanting . . . is about the most dumb-ass goal
> stokes my desire / triggers my bile
> on the one hand / on the other hand

These contrasting phrases help flesh out Douglas's claim that women are being pulled in two directions at once. In so doing, they bind the passage together into a unified whole that, despite its complexity and sophistication, stays focused over its entire length.

Repeat Yourself—but with a Difference

The last technique we offer for connecting the parts of your text involves repeating yourself, but with a difference—which basically means saying the same thing you've just said, but in a slightly different way that avoids sounding monotonous. To effectively connect the parts of your argument and keep it moving forward, be careful not to leap from one idea to a different idea or introduce new ideas cold. Instead, try to build bridges between your ideas by echoing what you've just said while simultaneously moving your text into new territory.

Several of the connecting devices discussed in this chapter are ways of repeating yourself in this special way. Key terms, pointing terms, and even many transitions can be used in a way that not only brings something forward from the previous sentence but in some way alters it. When Douglas, for instance, uses the key term "ambivalent" to echo her earlier reference to schizophrenics, she is repeating herself with a difference—repeating the same concept, but with a different word that adds new associations.

In addition, when you use transition phrases like "in other words" and "to put it another way," you repeat yourself with a difference, since these phrases help you restate earlier claims but in a different register. When you open a sentence with "in other words," you are basically telling your readers that in case they didn't fully understand what you meant in the last sentence, you are now coming at it again from a slightly different angle, or that since you're presenting a very important idea, you're not going to skip over it quickly but will explore it further to make sure your readers grasp all its aspects.

We would even go so far as to suggest that after your first sentence, almost every sentence you write should refer back to previous statements in some way. Whether you are writing a "furthermore" comment that adds to what you have just said or a "for example" statement that illustrates it, each sentence should echo at least one element of the previous sentence in some discernible way. Even when your text changes direction and requires transitions like "in contrast," "however," or "but," you still need to mark that shift by linking the sentence to the one just before it, as in the following example.

Cheyenne loved basketball. Nevertheless, she feared her height would put her at a disadvantage.

These sentences work because even though the second sentence changes course and qualifies the first, it still echoes key concepts from the first. Not only does "she" echo "Cheyenne," since both refer to the same person, but "feared" echoes "loved" by establishing the contrast mandated by the term "nevertheless." "Nevertheless," then, is not an excuse for changing subjects radically. It too requires repetition to help readers shift gears with you and follow your train of thought.

Repetition, in short, is the central means by which you can move from point A to point B in a text. To introduce one last analogy, think of the way experienced rock climbers move up a steep slope. Instead of jumping or lurching from one handhold to the next, good climbers get a secure handhold on the position they have established before reaching for the next ledge. The same thing applies to writing. To move smoothly from point to point in your argument, you need to firmly ground what you say in what you've already said. In this way, your writing remains focused while simultaneously moving forward.

"But hold on," you may be thinking. "Isn't repetition precisely what sophisticated writers should avoid, on the grounds that it will make their writing sound simplistic—as if they are belaboring the obvious?" Yes and no. On the one hand, writers certainly can run into trouble if they merely repeat themselves and nothing more. On the other hand, repetition is key to creating continuity in writing. It is impossible to stay on track in a piece of writing if you don't repeat your points throughout the length of the text. Furthermore, writers would never make an impact on readers if they didn't repeat their main points often enough to reinforce those points and make them stand out above subordinate points. The trick therefore is not to avoid repeating yourself but to repeat yourself in varied and interesting enough ways that you advance your argument without sounding tedious.

Exercises

1. Read the following opening to Chapter 2 of *The Road to Wigan Pier*, by George Orwell. Annotate the connecting devices by underlining the transitions, circling the key terms, and putting boxes around the pointing terms.

Our civilisation . . . is founded on coal, more completely than one realises until one stops to think about it. The machines that keep us alive, and the machines that make the machines, are all directly or indirectly dependent upon coal. In the metabolism of the Western world the coal-miner is second in importance only to the man who ploughs the soil. He is a sort of grimy cary-atid upon whose shoulders nearly everything that is not grimy is supported. For this reason the actual process by which coal is extracted is well worth watching, if you get the chance and are willing to take the trouble.

When you go down a coal-mine it is important to try and get to the coal face when the "fillers" are at work. This is not easy, because when the mine is working visitors are a nuisance and are not encouraged, but if you go at any other time, it is possi-ble to come away with a totally wrong impression. On a Sun-day, for instance, a mine seems almost peaceful. The time to go there is when the machines are roaring and the air is black with coal dust, and when you can actually see what the miners have to do. At those times the place is like hell, or at any rate like my own mental picture of hell. Most of the things one imagines in hell are there—heat, noise, confusion, darkness, foul air, and, above all, unbearably cramped space. Everything except the fire, for there is no fire down there except the feeble beams of Davy lamps and electric torches which scarcely penetrate the clouds of coal dust.

When you have finally got there—and getting there is a job in itself: I will explain that in a moment—you crawl through the last line of pit props and see opposite you a shiny black wall three or four feet high. This is the coal face. Overhead is the smooth ceiling made by the rock from which the coal has been cut; underneath is the rock again, so that the gallery you are in is only as high as the ledge of coal itself, probably not much more than a yard. The first impression of all, overmastering everything else for a while, is the frightful, deafening din from the conveyor belt which carries the coal away. You cannot see very far, because the fog of coal dust throws back the beam of your lamp, but you can see on either side of you the line of half-naked kneeling men, one to every four or five yards, driving their shovels under the fallen coal and flinging it swiftly over their left shoulders . . . .

GEORGE ORWELL, *The Road to Wigan Pier*

2. Read over something you've written with an eye for the devices you've used to connect the parts. Underline all the transitions, pointing terms, key terms, and repetition. Do you see any patterns? Do you rely on certain devices more than others? Are there any passages that are hard to follow—and if so, can you make them easier to read by trying any of the other devices discussed in this chapter?

NINE

"Ain't So / Is Not"

Academic Writing Doesn't Always Mean Setting Aside Your Own Voice

———□———

HAVE YOU EVER gotten the impression that writing well in college means setting aside the kind of language you use in everyday conversation? That to impress your instructors you need to use big words, long sentences, and complex sentence structures? If so, then we're here to tell you that it ain't necessarily so. On the contrary, academic writing can—and in our view *should*—be relaxed, easy to follow, and even a little bit fun. Although we don't want to suggest that you avoid using sophisticated, academic terms in your writing, we encourage you to draw upon the kinds of expressions and turns of phrase that you use every day when conversing with family and friends. In this chapter, we want to show you how you can write effective academic arguments while holding on to some of your own voice.

This point is important, since you may well become turned off from writing if you think your everyday language practices have to be checked at the classroom door. You may end up feeling like a student we know who, when asked how she felt about the writing she does in college, answered, "I do it because I have to, but it's just not me!"

This is not to suggest that *any* language you use among friends has a place in academic writing. Nor is it to suggest that you may fall back on colloquial usage as an excuse for not learning more rigorous forms of expression. After all, learning these more rigorous forms of expression and developing a more intellectual self is a major reason for getting an education. We do, however, wish to suggest that relaxed, colloquial language can often enliven academic writing and even enhance its rigor and precision. Such informal language also helps you connect with readers in a personal as well as an intellectual way. In our view, then, it is a mistake to assume that the academic and the everyday are completely separate languages that can never be used together.

Mix Academic and Colloquial Styles

Many successful writers blend academic, professional language with popular expressions and sayings. Consider, for instance, the following passage from a scholarly article about the way teachers respond to errors in student writing.

> Marking and judging formal and mechanical errors in student papers is one area in which composition studies seems to have a multiple-personality disorder. On the one hand, our mellow, student-centered, process-based selves tend to condemn marking formal errors at all. Doing it represents the Bad Old Days. Ms. Fidditch and Mr. Flutesnoot with sharpened red pencils, spilling innocent blood across the page. Useless detail work. Inhumane, perfectionist standards, making our students feel stupid, wrong,

trivial, misunderstood. Joseph Williams has pointed out how arbitrary and context-bound our judgments of formal error are. And certainly our noting of errors on student papers gives no one any great joy; as Peter Elbow says, English is most often associated *either* with grammar or with high literature—"two things designed to make folks feel most out of it."

ROBERT CONNORS AND ANDREA LUNSFORD,
"Frequency of Formal Errors in Current College Writing,
or Ma and Pa Kettle Do Research"

This passage blends writing styles in several ways. First, it places informal, relaxed expressions like "mellow," "the Bad Old Days," and "folks" alongside more formal, academic phrases like "multiple-personality disorder," "student-centered," "process-based," and "arbitrary and context-bound." Even the title of the piece, "Frequency of Formal Errors in Current College Writing, or Ma and Pa Kettle Do Research," blends formal, academic usage on the left side of the comma with a popular-culture reference to the fictional movie characters Ma and Pa Kettle on the right. Second, to give vivid, concrete form to their discussion of grading disciplinarians, Connors and Lunsford conjure up such archetypal, imaginary figures as the stuffy, old-fashioned taskmasters Ms. Fidditch and Mr. Flutesnoot. Through such imaginative uses of language, Connors and Lunsford inject greater force into what might otherwise have been dry, scholarly prose.

Formal/informal mixings like this can be found in countless other texts, though more frequently in the humanities than the sciences, and more frequently still in journalism. Notice how the food industry critic Eric Schlosser describes some changes in the city of Colorado Springs in his best-selling book on fast foods in the United States.

> The loopiness once associated with Los Angeles has come full
> blown to Colorado Springs—the strange, creative energy that crops
> up where the future's consciously being made, where people walk
> the fine line separating a visionary from a total nutcase.
>
> ERIC SCHLOSSER, *Fast Food Nation*

Schlosser could have played it safe and referred not to the "loop-
iness" but to the "eccentricity" associated with Los Angeles, or
to "the fine line separating a visionary from a lunatic" instead
of " . . . a total nutcase." His decision, however, to go with the
more adventuresome, colorful terms gives a liveliness to his
writing that would have been lacking with the more conventional terms.

Another example of writing that blends the informal with
the formal comes from an essay on the American novelist Willa
Cather by the literary critic Judith Fetterley. Discussing "how
very successful Cather has been in controlling how we think
about her," Fetterley, building on the work of another scholar,
writes as follows.

> As Merrill Skaggs has put it, "She is neurotically controlling and
> self-conscious about her work, but she knows at all points what she
> is doing. Above all else, she is self-conscious."
>   Without question, Cather was a control freak.
>
> JUDITH FETTERLEY, "Willa Cather and the
> Question of Sympathy: The Unofficial Story"

This passage demonstrates not only that specialized phrases
from psychology like "self-conscious" and "neurotically controlling" are compatible with everyday, popular expressions like
"control freak," but also that translating the one type of language into the other, the specialized into the everyday, can help

drive home a point. By translating Skaggs's polysyllabic description of Cather as "neurotically controlling and self-conscious" into the succinct, if blunt, claim that "Without question, Cather was a control freak," Fetterley suggests that one need not choose between rarified, See p. 380 for an essay that mixes colloquial and academic styles. academic ways of talking and the everyday language of casual conversation. Indeed, her passage offers a simple recipe for blending the high and the low: first make your point in the language of a professional field, and then make it again in everyday language—a great trick, we think, for underscoring a point.

While one effect of blending languages like this is to give your writing more punch, another is to make a political statement—about the way, for example, society unfairly overvalues some dialects and devalues others. For instance, in the titles of two of her books, *Talkin and Testifyin: The Language of Black America* and *Black Talk: Words and Phrases from the Hood to the Amen Corner*, the language scholar Geneva Smitherman mixes African American vernacular phrases with more scholarly language in order to suggest, as she explicitly argues in these books, that black English vernacular is as legitimate a variety of language as "standard" English. Here are three typical passages.

In Black America, the oral tradition has served as a fundamental vehicle for gittin ovuh. That tradition preserves the Afro-American heritage and reflects the collective spirit of the race.

Blacks are quick to ridicule "educated fools," people who done gone to school and read all dem books and still don't know nothin!

. . . it is a socially approved verbal strategy for black rappers to talk about how bad they is.

—Geneva Smitherman, *Talkin and Testifyin:*
The Language of Black America

In these examples, Smitherman blends the standard written English of phrases like "oral tradition" and "fundamental vehicle" with black oral vernacular like "gittin ovuh," "dem books," and "how bad they is." Indeed, she even blends standard English spelling with that of black English variants like "dem" and "ovuh," thus mimicking what some black English vernacular actually sounds like. Although some scholars might object to these unconventional practices, this is precisely Smitherman's point: that our habitual language practices need to be opened up, and that the number of participants in the academic conversation needs to be expanded.

Along similar lines, the writer and activist Gloria Anzaldúa mixes standard English with Tex-Mex, a hybrid blend of English, Castilian Spanish, a North Mexican dialect, and the Indian language Nahuatl, to make a political point about the suppression of the Spanish language in the United States.

> From this racial, ideological, cultural, and biological cross-pollination, an "alien" consciousness is presently in the making—a new *mestiza* consciousness, *una conciencia de mujer.*
>
> —Gloria Anzaldúa,
> *Borderlands / La Frontera: The New Mestiza*

Like Smitherman, Anzaldúa gets her point across not only through what she says but through the way she says it, literally showing that the new hybrid, or *mestiza*, consciousness that she describes is, as she puts it, "presently in the making." Ultimately, these passages suggest that blending languages— what Vershawn Ashanti Young calls "code meshing"—can call into question the very idea that the languages are distinct and separate.

WHEN TO MIX STYLES?
CONSIDER YOUR AUDIENCE AND PURPOSE

Because there are so many options in writing, you should never feel limited in your choice of words, as if such choices are set in stone. You can always experiment with your language and improve it. You can always dress it up, dress it down, or some combination of both. In dressing down your language, for example, you can make the claim that somebody "failed to notice" something by saying instead that it "flew under the radar." Or you can state that the person was "unaware" of something by saying that he was "out to lunch." You could even recast the title of this book, *"They Say / I Say,"* as a teenager might say it: "I'm Like / She Goes."

But how do you know when it is better to play things straight and stick to standard English, and when to be more adventuresome and mix things up? When, in other words, should you write "failed to notice" and when is it okay (or more effective) to write "flew under the radar"? Is it *always* appropriate to mix styles? And when you do so, how do you know when enough is enough?

In all situations, think carefully about your audience and purpose. When you write a letter applying for a job, for instance, or submit a grant proposal, where your words will be weighed by an official screening body, using language that's too colloquial or slangy may well jeopardize your chances of success. On such occasions, it is usually best to err on the safe side, conforming as closely as possible to the conventions of standard written English. In other situations for other audiences, however, there is room to be more creative—in this book, for example. Ultimately, your judgments about the appropriate language for the situation should always take into account your likely audience and your purpose in writing.

Although it may have been in the past, academic writing in most disciplines today is no longer the linguistic equivalent of a black-tie affair. To succeed as a writer in college, then, you need not always limit your language to the strictly formal. Although academic writing does rely on complex sentence patterns and on specialized, disciplinary vocabularies, it is surprising how often such writing draws on the languages of the street, popular culture, our ethnic communities, and home. It is by blending these languages that what counts as "standard" English changes over time and the range of possibilities open to academic writers continues to grow.

Exercises

1. Take a paragraph from this book and dress it down, rewriting it in informal colloquial language. Then rewrite the same paragraph again by dressing it up, making it much more formal. Then rewrite the paragraph one more time in a way that blends the two styles. Share your paragraphs with a classmate, and discuss which versions are most effective and why.

2. Find something you've written for a course, and study it to see whether you've used any of your own everyday expressions, any words or structures that are not "academic." If by chance you don't find any, see if there's a place or two where shifting into more casual or unexpected language would help you make a point, get your reader's attention, or just add liveliness to your text. Be sure to keep your audience and purpose in mind, and use language that will be appropriate to both.

TEN

"BUT DON'T GET ME WRONG"

The Art of Metacommentary

—⊡—

WHEN WE TELL PEOPLE that we are writing a chapter on the art of metacommentary, they often give us a puzzled look and tell us that they have no idea what "metacommentary" is. "We know what commentary is," they'll sometimes say, "but what does it mean when it's *meta*?" Our answer is that whether or not they know the term, they practice the art of metacommentary on a daily basis whenever they make a point of explaining something they've said or written: "What I meant to say was _____," "My point was not _____, but _____," or "You're probably not going to like what I'm about to say, but _____." In such cases, they are not offering new points but telling an audience how to interpret what they have already said or are about to say. In short, then, metacommentary is a way of commenting on your claims and telling others how—and how *not*—to think about them.

It may help to think of metacommentary as being like the chorus in a Greek play that stands to the side of the drama unfolding on the stage and explains its meaning to the audience—or like a voice-over narrator who comments on and explains the action in a television show or movie. Think of metacommentary as a sort of second text that stands alongside your main text and explains what it means. In the main text you say something; in the metatext you guide your readers in interpreting and processing what you've said.

What we are suggesting, then, is that you think of your text as two texts joined at the hip: a main text in which you make your argument and another in which you "work" your ideas, distinguishing your views from others they may be confused with, anticipating and answering objections, connecting one point to another, explaining why your claim might be controversial, and so forth. Figure 7 demonstrates what we mean.

THE MAIN TEXT SAYS SOMETHING, THE METATEXT TELLS READERS HOW—AND HOW NOT—TO THINK ABOUT IT.
FIGURE 7

USE METACOMMENTARY TO CLARIFY AND ELABORATE

But why do you need metacommentary to tell readers what you mean and guide them through your text? Can't you just clearly say what you mean up front? The answer is that, no matter how clear and precise your writing is, readers can still fail to understand it in any number of ways. Even the best writers can provoke reactions in readers that they didn't intend, and even good readers can get lost in a complicated argument or fail to see how one point connects with another. Readers may also fail to see what follows from your argument, or they may follow your reasoning and examples yet fail to see the larger conclusion you draw from them. They may fail to see your argument's overall significance, or mistake what you are saying for a related argument that they have heard before but that you want to distance yourself from. As a result, no matter how straightforward a writer you are, readers still need you to help them grasp what you really mean. Because the written word is prone to so much mischief and can be interpreted in so many different ways, we need metacommentary to keep misinterpretations and other communication misfires at bay.

David Foster Wallace uses a lot of metacommentary; see, e.g., p. 199, ¶3.

Another reason to master the art of metacommentary is that it will help you develop your ideas and generate more text. If you have ever had trouble producing the required number of pages for a writing project, metacommentary can help you add both length and depth to your writing. We've seen many students who try to produce a five-page paper sputter to a halt at two or three pages, complaining they've said everything they can think of about their topic. "I've stated my thesis and presented my reasons and evidence," students have told us. "What else is there to do?" It's almost as if such writers have generated a thesis and don't know what to do with it. When these students learn to use metacommentary, however, they get more out of their ideas and write longer, more substantial texts. In sum, metacommentary can help you extract the full potential from your ideas, drawing out important implications, explaining ideas from different perspectives, and so forth.

So even when you may think you've said everything possible in an argument, try inserting the following types of metacommentary.

▸ In other words, <u>she doesn't realize how right she is</u>.

▸ What _____ really means is _____.

▸ My point is not _____ but _____.

▸ Ultimately, then, my goal is to demonstrate that _____.

Ideally, such metacommentary should help you recognize some implications of your ideas that you didn't initially realize were there.

Let's look at how the cultural critic Neil Postman uses metacommentary in the following passage describing the shift he sees in American culture as it moves away from print and reading to television and movies.

> *It is my intention in this book to show* that a great . . . shift has taken place in America, with the result that the content of much of our public discourse has become dangerous nonsense. *With this in view, my task in the chapters ahead is* straightforward. *I must, first, demonstrate* how, under the governance of the printing press, discourse in America was different from what it is now— generally coherent, serious and rational; *and then* how, under the

governance of television, it has become shriveled and absurd. *But to avoid the possibility that my analysis will be interpreted as* standard-brand academic whimpering, a kind of elitist complaint against "junk" on television, *I must first explain that* . . . I appreciate junk as much as the next fellow, *and I know full well that* the printing press has generated enough of it to fill the Grand Canyon to overflowing. Television is not old enough to have matched printing's output of junk.

NEIL POSTMAN, *Amusing Ourselves to Death:*
Public Discourse in the Age of Show Business

To see what we mean by metacommentary, look at the phrases above that we have italicized. With these moves, Postman essentially stands apart from his main ideas to help readers follow and understand what he is arguing.

He previews what he will argue: *It is my intention in this book to show* . . .

He spells out how he will make his argument: *With this in view, my task in these chapters* . . . *is.* . . . *I must, first, demonstrate* . . . *and then* . . .

He distinguishes his argument from other arguments it may easily be confused with: *But to avoid the possibility that my analysis will be interpreted as* . . . *I must first explain that* . . .

TITLES AS METACOMMENTARY

Even the title of Postman's book, *Amusing Ourselves to Death: Public Discourse in the Age of Show Business*, functions as a form of metacommentary since, like all titles, it stands apart from the text itself and tells readers the book's main point: that the very pleasure provided by contemporary show business is destructive.

Titles, in fact, are one of the most important forms of metacommentary, functioning rather like carnival barkers telling passersby what they can expect if they go inside. Subtitles, too, function as metacommentary, further explaining or elaborating on the main title. The subtitle of this book, for example, not only explains that it is about "the moves that matter in academic writing," but indicates that "they say / I say" is one of these moves. Thinking of a title as metacommentary can actually help you develop sharper titles, ones that, like Postman's, give readers a hint of what your argument will be. Contrast such titles with unhelpfully open-ended ones like "Shakespeare" or "Steroids" or "English Essay," or essays with no titles at all. Essays with vague titles (or no titles) send the message that the writer has simply not bothered to reflect on what he or she is saying and is uninterested in guiding or orienting readers.

Use Other Moves as Metacommentary

Many of the other moves covered in this book function as metacommentary: entertaining objections, adding transitions, framing quotations, answering "so what?" and "who cares?" When you entertain objections, you stand outside of your text and imagine what a critic might say; when you add transitions, you essentially explain the relationship between various claims. And when you answer the "so what?" and "who cares?" questions, you look beyond your central argument and explain who should be interested in it and why.

TEMPLATES FOR INTRODUCING METACOMMENTARY

TO WARD OFF POTENTIAL MISUNDERSTANDINGS

The following moves help you differentiate certain views from ones they might be mistaken for.

▸ Essentially, I am arguing not that <u>we should give up the policy</u>, but that we should monitor effects far more closely.

▸ This is not to say _____, but rather _____.

▸ X is concerned less with _____ than with _____.

TO ALERT READERS TO AN ELABORATION OF A PREVIOUS IDEA

The following moves elaborate on a previous point, saying to readers: "In case you didn't get it the first time, I'll try saying the same thing in a different way."

▸ In other words, _____.

▸ To put it another way, _____.

▸ What X is saying here is that _____.

TO PROVIDE READERS WITH A ROADMAP TO YOUR TEXT

This move orients readers, clarifying where you have been and where you are going—and making it easier for them to process and follow your text.

▸ Chapter 2 explores _____, while chapter 3 examines _____.

▸ Having just argued that _____, I want now to complicate the point by _____.

TO MOVE FROM A GENERAL CLAIM TO A SPECIFIC EXAMPLE

These moves help you explain a general point by providing a concrete example that illustrates what you're saying.

- For example, _____ .

- _____ , for instance, demonstrates _____ .

- Consider _____ , for example.

- To take a case in point, _____ .

TO INDICATE THAT A CLAIM IS MORE, LESS, OR EQUALLY IMPORTANT

The following templates help you give relative emphasis to the claim that you are introducing, showing whether that claim is of more or less weight than the previous one, or equal to it.

- Even more important, _____ .

- But above all, _____ .

- Incidentally, we will briefly note, _____ .

- Just as important, _____ .

- Equally, _____ .

- Finally, _____ .

TO EXPLAIN A CLAIM WHEN YOU ANTICIPATE OBJECTIONS

Here's a template to help you anticipate and respond to possible objections.

- Although some readers may object that _____ , I would answer that _____ .

TO GUIDE READERS TO YOUR MOST GENERAL POINT

These moves show that you are wrapping things up and tying up various subpoints previously made.

Chapter 6 has more templates for anticipating objections.

▶ In sum, then, _____.

▶ My conclusion, then, is that _____.

▶ In short, _____.

In this chapter we have tried to show that the most persuasive writing often doubles back and comments on its own claims in ways that help readers negotiate and process them. Instead of simply piling claim upon claim, effective writers are constantly "stage managing" how their claims will be recieved. It's true of course that to be persuasive a text has to have strong claims to argue in the first place. But even the strongest arguments will flounder unless writers use metacommentary to prevent potential misreadings and make their arguments shine.

Exercises

1. Read an essay or article and annotate it to indicate the different ways the author uses metacommentary. Use the templates on pp. 135–37 as your guide. For example, you may want to circle transitional phrases and write "trans" in the margins, to put brackets around sentences that elaborate on earlier sentences and mark them "elab," or underline sentences in which the author sums up what he or she has been saying, writing "sum" in the margins.

   How does the author use metacommentary? Does the author follow any of the templates provided in this book word for word? Did you find any forms of metacommentary not discussed in this chapter? If so, can you identify them, name them, and perhaps devise templates based on them for use in your own writing? And finally, how do you think the author's use of metacommentary enhances (or harms) his or her writing?

2. Complete each of the following metacommentary templates in any way that makes sense.

▸ In making a case for the medical use of marijuana, I am not saying that _____ .

▸ But my argument will do more than prove that one particular industrial chemical has certain toxic properties. In this article, I will also

_____ .

▸ My point about the national obsessions with sports reinforces the belief held by many _____ that _____ .

▸ I believe, therefore, that the war is completely unjustified. But let me back up and explain how I arrived at this conclusion: _____ . In this way, I came to believe that this war is a big mistake.

4

ENTERING THE CONVERSATION

ELEVEN

"I TAKE YOUR POINT"

Entering Class Discussions

Have you ever been in a class discussion that feels less like a genuine meeting of the minds than like a series of discrete, disconnected monologues? You make a comment, say, that seems provocative to you, but the classmate who speaks after you makes no reference to what you said, instead going off in an entirely different direction. Then, the classmate who speaks next makes no reference either to you or to any one else, making it seem as if everyone in the conversation is more interested in their own ideas than in actually conversing with anyone else.

We like to think that the principles this book advances can help improve class discussions, which increasingly include various forms of online communication. Particularly important for class discussion is the point that our own ideas become more cogent and powerful the more responsive we are to others, and the more we frame our claims not in isolation but as responses to what others before us have said. Ultimately, then, a good face-to-face classroom discussion (or online communication) doesn't just happen spontaneously. It requires the same sorts of disciplined moves and practices used in many writing situations, particularly that of identifying to what and to whom you are responding.

FRAME YOUR COMMENTS AS A RESPONSE
TO SOMETHING THAT HAS ALREADY BEEN SAID

The single most important thing you need to do when joining a class discussion is to link what you are about to say to something that has already been said.

▸ I really liked Aaron's point about the two sides being closer than they seem. I'd add that both seem rather moderate.

▸ I take your point, Nadia, that _____. Still . . .

▸ Though Sheila and Ryan seem to be at odds about _____, they may actually not be all that far apart.

In framing your comments this way, it is usually best to name both the person and the idea you're responding to. If you name the person alone ("I agree with Aaron because _____"), it may not be clear to listeners what part of what Aaron said you are referring to. Conversely, if you only summarize what Aaron said without naming him, you'll probably leave your classmates wondering whose comments you're referring to.

But won't you sound stilted and deeply redundant in class if you try to restate the point your classmate just made? After all, in the case of the first template above, the entire class will have just heard Aaron's point about the two sides being closer than they seem. Why then would you need to restate it?

We agree that in oral situations, it does often sound artificial to restate what others just said precisely because they just said it. It would be awkward if, on being asked to pass the salt at lunch, one were to reply: "If I understand you correctly, you have asked me to pass the salt. Yes, I can, and here it is." But in oral discussions about complicated issues that are open to multiple interpretations, we usually do need to resummarize what others have said to make sure that everyone is on the same page. Since Aaron may have made several points when he spoke and may have been followed by other commentators, the class will probably need you to summarize which point of his you are referring to. And even if Aaron made only one point, restating that point is helpful, not only to remind the group what his point was (since some may have missed or forgotten it) but also to make sure that he, you, and others have interpreted his point in the same way.

TO CHANGE THE SUBJECT,
INDICATE EXPLICITLY THAT YOU ARE DOING SO

It is fine to try to change the conversation's direction. There's just one catch: you need to make clear to listeners that this is what you are doing. For example:

▸ So far we have been talking about <u>the characters in the film</u>. But isn't the real issue here <u>the cinematography</u>?

▸ I'd like to change the subject to one that hasn't yet been addressed.

You can try to change the subject without indicating that you are doing so. But you risk that your comment will come across as irrelevant rather than as a thoughtful contribution that moves the conversation forward.

BE EVEN MORE EXPLICIT
THAN YOU WOULD BE IN WRITING

Because listeners in an oral discussion can't go back and reread what you just said, they are more easily overloaded than are readers of a print text. For this reason, in a class discussion you will do well to take some extra steps to help listeners follow your train of thought. (1) When you make a comment, limit yourself to one point only though you can elaborate on this point, fleshing it out with examples and evidence. If you feel you must make two points, either unite them under one larger umbrella point, or make one point first and save the other for later. Trying to bundle two or more claims into one comment can result in neither getting the attention it deserves. (2) Use metacommentary to highlight your key point so that listeners can readily grasp it.

▸ In other words, what I'm trying to get at here is _____.

▸ My point is this: _____.

▸ My point, though, is not _____, but _____.

▸ This distinction is important because _____.

TWELVE

"WHAT'S MOTIVATING THIS WRITER?"

Reading for the Conversation

—◻—

"WHAT IS THE AUTHOR'S ARGUMENT? What is he or she trying to say?" For many years, these were the first questions we would ask our classes in a discussion of an assigned reading. The discussion that resulted was often halting, as our students struggled to get a handle on the argument, but eventually, after some awkward silences, the class would come up with something we could all agree was an accurate summary of the author's main thesis. Even after we'd gotten over that hurdle, however, the discussion would often still seem forced, and would limp along as we all struggled with the question that naturally arose next: Now that we had determined what the author was saying, what did we ourselves have to say?

For a long time we didn't worry much about these halting discussions, justifying them to ourselves as the predictable result of assigning difficult, challenging readings. Several years ago, however, as we started writing this book and began thinking about writing as the art of entering conversations, we latched onto the idea of leading with some different questions: "What other argument(s) is the writer responding to?" "Is the writer disagreeing or agreeing with something, and if so what?" "What is motivating the writer's argument?" "Are there other ideas that you have encountered in this class or elsewhere that might be pertinent?" The results were often striking. The discussions that followed tended to be far livelier and to draw in a greater number of students. We were still asking students to look for the main argument, but we were now asking them to see that argument as a response to some other argument that provoked it, gave it a reason for being, and helped all of us see why we should care about it.

What had happened, we realized, was that by changing the opening question, we changed the way our students approached reading, and perhaps the way they thought about academic work in general. Instead of thinking of the argument of a text as an isolated entity, they now thought of that argument as one that responded to and provoked other arguments. Since they were now dealing not with *one* argument but at least *two* (the author's argument and the one[s] he or she was responding to), they now had alternative ways of seeing the topic at hand. This meant that, instead of just trying to understand the view presented by the author, they were more able to question that view intelligently and engage in the type of discussion and debate that is the hallmark of a college education. In our discussions, animated debates often arose between students who found the author's argument convincing and others who were more convinced by the view it was challenging. In the best of these debates, the binary positions would be questioned by other students, who suggested each was too simple, that both might be right or that a third alternative was possible. Still other students might object that the discussion thus far had missed the author's real point and suggest that we all go back to the text and pay closer attention to what it actually said.

We eventually realized that the move from reading for the author's argument in isolation to reading for how the author's argument is in conversation with the arguments of others helps readers become active, critical readers rather than passive recipients of knowledge. On some level, reading for the conversation is more rigorous and demanding than reading for what one author says. It asks that you determine not only what the author thinks, but how what the author thinks fits with what others think, and ultimately with what you yourself think. Yet on another level, reading this way is a lot simpler and more familiar than reading for the thesis alone, since it returns writing to the familiar, everyday act of communicating with other people about real issues.

DECIPHERING THE CONVERSATION

We suggest, then, that when assigned a reading, you imagine the author not as sitting alone in an empty room hunched over a desk or staring at a screen, but as sitting in a crowded coffee shop talking to others who are making claims that he or she is engaging with. In other words, imagine the author as participating in an ongoing, multisided, conversation in which everyone is trying to persuade others to agree or at least to take his or her position seriously.

The trick in reading for the conversation is to figure out *what views the author is responding to* and *what the author's own argument is*—or, to put it in the terms used in this book, to determine the "they say" and how the author responds to it. One of the challenges in reading for the "they say" and "I say" can be figuring out which is which, since it may not be obvious when writers are summarizing others and when they are speaking for themselves. Readers need to be alert for any changes in voice that a writer might make, since instead of using explicit road-mapping phrases like "although many believe," authors may simply summarize the view that they want to engage with and indicate only subtly that it is not their own.

Consider again the opening to the selection by David Zinczenko on p. 391.

> If ever there were a newspaper headline custom made for Jay Leno's monologue, this was it. Kids taking on McDonald's this week, suing the company for making them fat. Isn't that like middle-aged men suing Porsche for making them get speeding tickets? Whatever happened to personal responsibility?
>
> I tend to sympathize with these portly fast-food patrons, though. Maybe that's because I used to be one of them.
>
> —DAVID ZINCZENKO, "Don't Blame the Eater"

Whenever we teach this passage, some students inevitably assume that Zinczenko must be espousing the view expressed in his first paragraph: that suing McDonald's is ridiculous. When their reading is challenged by their classmates, these students point to the page and reply, "Look. It's right here on the page. This is what Zinczenko wrote. These are his exact words." The assumption these students are making is that if something appears on the page, the author must endorse it. In fact, however, we ventriloquize views that we don't believe in, and may in fact passionately disagree with, all the time. The central clues that Zinczenko disagrees with the view expressed in his opening

See Chapter 6 for more discussion of naysayers.

paragraph come in the second paragraph, when he finally offers a first-person declaration and uses a constrastive transition, "though," thereby resolving any questions about where he stands.

When the "They Say" Is Unstated

Another challenge can be identifying the "they say" when it is not explicitly identified. Whereas Zinczenko offers an up-front summary of the view he is responding to, other writers assume that their readers are so familiar with these views that they need not name or summarize them. In such cases, you the reader have to reconstruct the unstated "they say" that is motivating the text through a process of inference.

See, for instance, if you can reconstruct the position that Tamara Draut is challenging in the opening paragraph of her essay "The Growing College Gap."

> "The first in her family to graduate from college." How many times have we heard that phrase, or one like it, used to describe a successful American with a modest background? In today's United States, a four-year degree has become the all-but-official ticket to middle-class security. But if your parents don't have much money or higher education in their own right, the road to college—and beyond—looks increasingly treacherous. Despite a sharp increase in the proportion of high school graduates going on to some form of postsecondary education, socio-economic status continues to exert a powerful influence on college admission and completion; in fact, gaps in enrollment by class and race, after declining in the 1960s and 1970s, are once again as wide as they were thirty years ago, and getting wider, even as college has become far more crucial to lifetime fortunes.
>
> —Tamara Draut, "The Growing College Gap"

You might think that the "they say" here is embedded in the third sentence: They say (or we all think) that a four-year degree is "the all-but-official ticket to middle-class security," and you might assume that Draut will go on to disagree.

If you read the passage this way, however, you would be mistaken. Draut is not questioning whether a college degree has become "the ticket to middle-class security," but whether most Americans can obtain that ticket, whether college is within the financial reach of most American families. You may have been thrown off by the "but" following the statement that college has become a prerequisite for middle-class security. However, unlike the "though" in Zinczenko's opening, this "but" does not signal that Draut will be disagreeing with the view she has just summarized, a view that in fact she takes as a given. What Draut disagrees with is that this ticket to middle-class security is still readily available to the middle and working classes.

Were one to imagine Draut in a room talking with others with strong views on this topic, one would need to picture her challenging not those who think college is a ticket to financial security (something she agrees with and takes for granted), but those who think the doors of college are open to anyone willing to put forth the effort to walk through them. The view that Draut is challenging, then, is not summarized in her opening. Instead, she assumes that readers are already so familiar with this view that it need not be stated.

Draut's example suggests that in texts where the central "they say" is not immediately identified, you have to construct it yourself based on the clues the text provides. You have to start by locating the writer's thesis and then imagine some of the arguments that might be made against it. What would it look like to disagree with this view? In Draut's case, it is relatively easy to construct a counterargument: it is the familiar faith in the American Dream of equal opportunity when it comes to access to college. Figuring out the counterargument not only reveals what motivated Draut as a writer but helps you respond to her essay as an active, critical reader. Constructing this counterargument can also help you recognize how Draut challenges your own views, questioning opinions that you previously took for granted.

WHEN THE "THEY SAY" IS ABOUT SOMETHING "NOBODY HAS TALKED ABOUT"

Another challenge in reading for the conversation is that writers sometimes build their arguments by responding to a *lack* of discussion. These writers build their case not by playing off views that can be identified (like faith in the American Dream or the idea that we are responsible for our body weight), but by pointing to something others have overlooked. As the writing theorists John M. Swales and Christine B. Feak point out, one effective way to "create a research space" and "establish a niche" in the academic world is "by indicating a gap in . . . previous research." Much research in the sciences and humanities takes this "Nobody has noticed X" form.

In such cases, the writer may be responding to scientists, for example, who have overlooked an obscure plant that offers insights into global warming, or to literary critics who have been so busy focusing on the lead character in a play that they have overlooked something important about the minor characters.

READING PARTICULARLY CHALLENGING TEXTS

Sometimes it is difficult to figure out the views that writers are responding to not because these writers do not identify those views but because their language and the concepts they are dealing with are particularly challenging. Consider, for instance, the first two sentences of *Gender Trouble: Feminism and the Subversion of Identity*, a book by the feminist philosopher and literary theorist Judith Butler, thought by many to be a particularly difficult academic writer.

> Contemporary feminist debates over the meaning of gender lead time and again to a certain sense of trouble, as if the indeterminacy of gender might eventually culminate in the failure of feminism. Perhaps trouble need not carry such a negative valence.
>
> —JUDITH BUTLER, *Gender Trouble: Feminism and the Subversion of Identity*

There are many reasons readers may stumble over this relatively short passage, not the least of which is that Butler does not explicitly indicate where her own view begins and the view she is responding to ends. Unlike Zinczenko, Butler does not use the first-person "I" or a phrase such as "in my own view" to show that the position in the second sentence is her own. Nor does Butler offer a clear transition such as "but" or "however" at the start of the second sentence to indicate, as Zinczenko does with "though," that in the second sentence she is questioning the argument she has summarized in the first. And finally, like many academic writers, Butler uses abstract, unfamiliar words that many readers may need to look up, like "gender" (sexual identity, male or female), "indeterminacy" (the quality of being impossible to define or pin down), "culminate" (finally result in), and "negative valence" (a term borrowed from chemistry, roughly denoting "negative significance" or "meaning"). For all these reasons, we can imagine many readers feeling intimidated before they reach the third sentence of Butler's book.

But readers who break down this passage into its essential parts will find that it is actually a lucid piece of writing that conforms to the classic "they say / I say" pattern. Though it can be difficult to spot the clashing arguments in the two sentences, close analysis reveals that the first sentence offers a way of looking at a certain type of "trouble" in the realm of feminist politics that is being challenged in the second.

To understand difficult passages of this kind, you need to translate them into your own words—to build a bridge, in effect, between the passage's unfamiliar terms and ones more familiar to you. Building such a bridge should help you connect what you already know to what the author is saying—and will then help you move from reading to writing, providing you with some of the language you will need to summarize the text. One major challenge in translating the author's words into your own, however, is to stay true to what the author is actually saying, avoiding what we call "the closest cliché syndrome," in which one mistakes a commonplace idea for an author's more complex one (mistaking Butler's critique of the concept of "woman," for instance, for the common idea that women must have equal rights). The work of complex writers like Butler, who frequently challenge conventional thinking, cannot always be collapsed into the types of ideas most of us are already familiar with. Therefore, when you translate, do not try to fit the ideas of such writers into your preexisting beliefs, but instead allow your own views to be challenged. In building a bridge to the writers you read, it is often necessary to meet those writers more than halfway.

For more on the closest cliché syndrome, see Chapter 2.

So what, then, does Butler's opening say? Translating Butler's words into terms that are easier to understand, we can see that the first sentence says that for many feminists today, "the indeterminacy of gender"—the inability to define the essence of sexual identity—spells the end of feminism; that for many feminists the inability to define "gender," presumably the building block of the feminist movement, means serious "trouble" for feminist politics. In contrast, the second sentence suggests that this same "trouble" need not be thought of in such "negative" terms, that the inability to define femininity, or "gender trouble" as Butler calls it in her book's title, may not be such a bad thing—and, as she goes on to argue in the pages that follow, may even be something that feminist activists can profit from. In other words, Butler suggests, highlighting uncertainties about masculinity and femininity can be a powerful feminist tool.

Pulling all these inferences together, then, the opening sentences can be translated as follows: "While many contemporary feminists believe that uncertainty about what it means to be a woman will undermine feminist politics, I, Judith Butler, believe that this uncertainty can actually help strengthen feminist politics." Translating Butler's point into our own book's basic move: "They say that if we cannot define 'woman,' feminism is in big trouble. But I say that this type of trouble is precisely what feminism needs." Despite its difficulty, then, we hope you agree that this initially intimidating passage does make sense if you stay with it.

We hope it is clear that critical reading is a two-way street. It is just as much about being open to the way that writers can challenge you, maybe even transform you, as it is about questioning those writers. And if you translate a writer's argument into your own words as you read, you should allow the text to take you outside the ideas that you already hold and to introduce you to new terms and concepts. Even if you end up disagreeing with an author, you first have to show that you have really listened to what he or she is saying, have fully grasped his or her arguments, and can accurately summarize those arguments. Without such deep, attentive listening, any critique you make will be superficial and decidedly *uncritical*. It will be a critique that says more about you than about the writer or idea you're supposedly responding to.

In this chapter we have tried to show that reading for the conversation means looking not just for the thesis of a text in isolation but for the view or views that motivate that thesis— the "they say." We have also tried to show that reading for the conversation means being alert for the different strategies writers use to engage the view(s) that are motivating them, since not all writers engage other perspectives in the same way. Some writers explicitly identify and summarize a view they are responding to at the outset of their text and then return to it frequently as their text unfolds. Some refer only obliquely to a view that is motivating them, assuming that readers will be able to reconstruct that view on their own. Other writers may not explicitly distinguish their own view from the views they are questioning in ways that all of us find clear, leaving some readers to wonder whether a given view is the writer's own or one that he or she is challenging. And some writers push off against the "they say" that is motivating them in a challenging academic language that requires readers to translate what they are saying into more accessible, everyday terms. In sum, then, though most persuasive writers do follow a conversational "they say / I say" pattern, they do so in a great variety of ways. What this means for readers is that they need to be armed with various strategies for detecting the conversations in what they read, even when those conversations are not self-evident.

THIRTEEN

"ANALYZE THIS"

Writing in the Social Sciences

ERIN ACKERMAN

———□———

SOCIAL SCIENCE is the study of people—how they behave and relate to one another, and the organizations and institutions that facilitate these interactions. People are complicated, so any study of human behavior is at best partial, taking into account some elements of what people do and why, but not always explaining those actions definitively. As a result, it is the subject of constant conversation and argument.

Consider some of the topics studied in the social sciences: minimum wage laws, violence against women, tobacco regulation, the 2000 election, employment discrimination. Got an opinion on any of these topics? You aren't alone. But in the writing you do as a student of the social sciences, you need to

ERIN ACKERMAN is a professor of political science at John Jay College, City University of New York. Her research and teaching interests include American and comparative constitutional law, women and law, the law and politics of reproductive health, biomedical policy, and American political development.

write about more than just your opinions. Good writing in the social sciences, as in other academic disciplines, requires that you demonstrate that you have thought about what it is you think. The best way to do that is to bring your views into conversation with those expressed by others and to test what you and others think against a review of data. In other words, you'll need to start with what others say and then present what you say as a response.

Consider the following example from a book about contemporary American political culture:

> Claims of deep national division were standard fare after the 2000 elections, and to our knowledge few commentators have publicly challenged them. . . . In sum, contemporary observers of American politics have apparently reached a new consensus around the proposition that old disagreements about economics now pale in comparison to new divisions based on sexuality, morality, and religion, divisions so deep as to justify fears of violence and talk of war in describing them.
>
>   This short book advocates a contrary thesis: the sentiments expressed in the previously quoted pronouncements of scholars, journalists, and politicos range from simple exaggeration to sheer nonsense. . . . Many of the activists in the political parties and various cause groups do, in fact, hate each other and regard themselves as combatants in a war. But their hatreds and battles are not shared by the great mass of the American people. . . .
>
> MORRIS P. FIORINA, *Culture War?*
> *The Myth of a Polarized America*, 2004

In other words, "they" (journalists, pundits, other political scientists) say that the American public is deeply divided, whereas Fiorina replies that they have misinterpreted the evidence—

specifically, that they have generalized from a few exceptional cases (activists). Even the title of the book calls into question an idea held by others, one Fiorina labels a "myth."

This chapter explores some of the basic moves social science writers make. In addition, writing in the social sciences generally includes several core components: a strong introduction and thesis, a literature review, and the writer's own analysis, including presentation of data and consideration of implications. Much of your own writing will include one or more of these components as well. The introduction sets out the thesis, or point, of the paper, briefly explaining what you will say in your text and how it fits into the preexisting conversation. The literature review summarizes what has already been said on your topic. Your analysis allows you to present data—the information about human behavior you are measuring or testing against what other people have said—and to explain the conclusions you have drawn based on your investigation. Do you agree, disagree, or some combination of both, with what has been said by others? What reasons can you give for why you feel that way? And so what? Who should be interested in what you have to say, and why?

THE INTRODUCTION AND THESIS: "THIS PAPER CHALLENGES ..."

Your introduction sets forth what you plan to say in your essay. You might evaluate the work of earlier scholars or certain widely held assumptions and find them incorrect when measured against new data. Alternatively, you might point out that an author's work is largely correct, but that it could use some qualifications or be extended in some way. Or you might identify a gap in our knowledge—we know a great deal about topic

X but almost nothing about some other closely related topic. In each of these instances, your introduction needs to cover both "they say" and "I say" perspectives. If you stop after the "they say," your readers won't know what you are bringing to the conversation. Similarly, if you were to jump right to the "I say" portion of your argument, readers might wonder why you need to say anything at all.

Sometimes you join the conversation at a point where the discussion seems settled. One or more views about a topic have become so widely accepted among a group of scholars or society at large that these views are essentially the conventional way of thinking about the topic. You may wish to offer new reasons to support this interpretation, or you may wish to call these standard views into question. To do so, you must first introduce and identify these widely held beliefs and then present your own view. In fact, much of the writing in the social sciences takes the form of calling into question that which we think we already know. Consider the following example from a 2001 article from *The Journal of Economics Perspectives*:

> Fifteen years ago, Milton Friedman's 1957 treatise *A Theory of the Consumption Function* seemed badly dated. Dynamic optimization theory had not been employed much in economics when Friedman wrote, and utility theory was still comparatively primitive, so his statement of the "permanent income hypothesis" never actually specified a formal mathematical model of behavior derived explicitly from utility maximization . . . [W]hen other economists subsequently found multiperiod maximizing models that could be solved explicitly, the implications of those models differed sharply from Friedman's intuitive description of his "model." Furthermore, empirical tests in the 1970s and 1980s often rejected these rigorous versions of the permanent income hypothesis in favor of an

alternative hypothesis that many households simply spent all of their current income.

Today, with the benefit of a further round of mathematical (and computational) advances, Friedman's (1957) original analysis looks more prescient than primitive . . .

CHRISTOPHER D. CARROLL, "A Theory of Consumption
Function, With and Without Liquidity Constraints,"
The Journal of Economic Perspectives, 2001

This introduction makes clear that Carroll will defend Milton Friedman against some major criticisms of his work. Carroll mentions what has been said about Friedman's work and then goes on to say that the critiques turn out to be wrong and to suggest that Friedman's work reemerges as persuasive. A template of Carroll's introduction might look something like this: Economics research in the last fifteen years suggested Friedman's 1957 treatise was _____ because _____. In other words, they say that Friedman's work is not accurate because of _____, _____, and _____. Recent research convinces me, however, that Friedman's work makes sense.

In some cases, however, there may not be a strong consensus among experts on a topic. You might enter the ongoing debate by casting your vote with one side or another or by offering an alternative view. In the following example, Shari Berman identifies two competing accounts of how to explain world events in the twentieth century and then puts forth a third view.

Conventional wisdom about twentieth-century ideologies rests on two simple narratives. One focuses on the struggle for dominance between democracy and its alternatives. . . . The other narrative focuses on the competition between free-market capitalism and its rivals. . . . Both of these narratives obviously contain some truth.

. . . Yet both only tell part of the story, which is why their common conclusion—neoliberalism as the "end of History"—is unsatisfying and misleading.

What the two conventional narratives fail to mention is that a third struggle was also going on: between those ideologies that believed in the primacy of economics and those that believed in the primacy of politics.

SHARI BERMAN, "The Primacy of Economics versus the Primacy of Politics: Understanding the Ideological Dynamics of the Twentieth Century," *Perspectives on Politics*, 2009

After identifying the two competing narratives, Berman suggests a third view—and later goes on to argue that this third view explains current debates over globalization. A template for this type of introduction might look something like this: In recent discussions of _____, a controversial aspect has been _____. On the one hand, some argue that _____. On the other hand, others argue that _____. Neither of these arguments, however, considers the alternative view that _____.

Given the complexity of many of the issues studied in the social sciences, however, you may sometimes agree *and* disagree with existing views—pointing out things that you believe are correct or have merit, while disagreeing with or refining other points. In the example below, anthropologist Sally Engle Merry agrees with another scholar about something that is a key trait of modern society but argues that this trait has a different origin than the other author identifies.

For more on different ways of responding, see Chapter 4.

Although I agree with Rose that an increasing emphasis on governing the soul is characteristic of modern society, I see the transformation not as evolutionary but as the product of social mobilization and political struggle.

SALLY ENGLE MERRY, "Rights, Religion, and Community:
Approaches to Violence against Women in the
Context of Globalization," *Law and Society Review*, 2001

Here are some templates for agreeing and disagreeing:

▶ Although I agree with X up to a point, I cannot accept his overall conclusion that _____.

▶ Although I disagree with X on _____ and _____, I agree with her conclusion that _____.

▶ Political scientists studying _____ have argued that it is caused by _____. While _____ contributes to the problem, _____ is also an important factor.

In the process of examining people from different angles, social scientists sometimes identify gaps—areas that have not been explored in previous research. In a 1998 article on African American neighborhoods, sociologist Mary Pattillo identifies such a gap.

The research on African Americans is dominated by inquiries into the lives of the black poor. Contemporary ethnographies and journalistic descriptions have thoroughly described deviance, gangs, drugs, intergender relations and sexuality, stymied aspiration, and family patterns in poor neighborhoods (Dash 1989; Hagedorn 1988; Kotlowitz 1991; Lemann 1991; MacLeoad 1995; Sullivan 1989; Williams 1989). Yet, the majority of African Americans are not poor (Billingsley 1992). A significant part of the black experience, namely that of working and middle-class blacks, remains unexplored. We have little information about what black middle-class neighborhoods look like and how social life is organized within them. . . . this article begins to fill this empirical and theoretical gap using ethnographic data collected in Groveland, a middle-class black neighborhood in Chicago.

> Mary E. Pattillo, "Sweet Mothers and Gangbangers:
> Managing Crime in a Black Middle-Class
> Neighborhood," *Social Forces*, 1998

Pattillo explains that much has been said about poor African American neighborhoods. But, she says, we have little information about the experience of working-class and middle-class black neighborhoods—a gap that her article will address.

Here are some templates for introducing gaps in the existing research:

▶ Studies of X have indicated _____. It is not clear, however, that this conclusion applies to _____.

▶ _____ often take for granted that _____. Few have investigated this assumption, however.

▶ X's work tells us a great deal about _____. Can this work be generalized to _____?

Again, a good introduction indicates what you have to say in the larger context of what others have said. Throughout the rest of your paper, you will move back and forth between the "they say" and the "I say," adding more details.

THE LITERATURE REVIEW:
"PRIOR RESEARCH INDICATES . . ."

In the literature review, you explain what "they say" in more detail, summarizing, paraphrasing, or quoting the viewpoints to which you are responding. But you need to balance what they are saying with your own focus. You need to characterize someone else's work fairly and accurately but set up the points you yourself want to make by selecting the details that are relevant to your own perspective and observations.

It is common in the social sciences to summarize several arguments at once, identifying their major arguments or findings in a single paragraph.

> How do employers in a low-wage labor market respond to an increase in the minimum wage? The prediction from conventional economic theory is unambiguous: a rise in the minimum wage leads perfectly competitive employers to cut employment (George J. Stigler, 1946). Although studies in the 1970's based on aggregate teenage employment rates usually confirmed this prediction, earlier studies based on comparisons of employment at affected and unaffected establishments often did not (e.g., Richard A. Lester, 1960, 1964). Several recent studies that rely on a similar comparative methodology have failed to detect a negative employment effect of higher minimum wages. Analyses of the 1990–1991 increases in the federal minimum wage (Lawrence F. Katz and Krueger, 1992; Card, 1992a) and of an earlier increase in the minimum wage in California (Card, 1992b) find no adverse employment impact.
>
> DAVID CARD AND ALAN KRUEGER,
> "Minimum Wages and Employment: A Case Study of the
> Fast-Food Industry in New Jersey and Pennsylvania,"
> *The American Economic Review*, 1994;

Card and Krueger cite the key findings and conclusions of works that are relevant to the question they are investigating and the point they plan to address, asking "How do employers in a low-wage labor market respond to an increase in the minimum wage?" They go on, as good writers should, to answer the question they ask. And they do so by reviewing others who have answered that question, noting that this question has been answered in different, sometimes contradictory, ways.

Such summaries are brief, bringing together relevant arguments by several scholars to provide an overview of scholarly work on a particular topic. In writing such a summary, you need to ask yourself how the authors themselves might describe their positions and also consider what in their work is relevant for the point you wish to make. This kind of summary is especially appropriate when you have a large amount of research material on a topic and want to identify the major strands of a debate or to show how the work of one author builds on that of another. Here are some templates for overview summaries:

▸ In addressing the question of _____, political scientists have considered several explanations for _____. X argues that _____. According to Y and Z, another plausible explanation is _____.

▸ What is the effect of _____ on _____? Previous work on _____ by X and by Y and Z supports _____.

Sometimes you may need to say more about the works you cite. On a midterm or final exam, for example, you may need to demonstrate that you have a deep familiarity with a particular work. And in some disciplines of the social sciences, longer, more detailed literature reviews are the standard. Your instructor and the articles he or she has assigned are your best guides for the length and level of detail of your literature review. Other times, the work of certain authors is especially important for your argument, and therefore you need to provide more details to explain what these authors have said. See how Martha Derthick summarizes an argument that is central to her 2001 book about the politics of tobacco regulation.

> The idea that governments could sue to reclaim health care costs from cigarette manufacturers might be traced to "Cigarettes and Welfare Reform," an article published in the *Emory Law Journal* in 1977 by Donald Gasner, a law professor at the University of Southern Illinois. Garner suggested that state governments could get a cigarette manufacturer to pay the direct medical costs "of looking after patients with smoking diseases." He drew an analogy to the Coal Mine Health and Safety Act of 1969, under which coal mine operators are required to pay certain disability benefits for coal miners suffering from pneumoconiosis, or black lung disease.
>
> MARTHA DERTHICK, *Up In Smoke: From Legislation to Litigation in Tobacco Politics*, 2005

Note that Derthick identifies the argument she is summarizing, quoting its author directly and then adding details about a precedent for the argument.

You may want to include direct quotations of what others have said, as Derthick does. Using an author's exact words helps you demonstrate that you are representing him or her fairly. But you cannot simply insert a quotation; you need to explain to your readers what it means for your point. Consider the following example drawn from a 2004 political science book on the debate over tort reform.

> The essence of *agenda setting* was well enunciated by E. E. Schattschneider: "In politics as in everything else, it makes a great

difference whose game we play" (1960, 47). In short, the ability to define or control the rules, terms, or perceived options in a contest over policy greatly affects the prospects for winning."

WILLIAM HALTOM AND MICHAEL McCANN, *Distorting the Law: Politics, Media, and the Litigation Crisis*, 2004

Notice how Haltom and McCann first quote Schattschneider and then explain in their own words how political agenda setting can be thought of as a game, with winners and losers.

Remember that whenever you summarize, quote, or paraphrase the work of others, credit must be given in the form of a citation to the original work. The words may be your own, but if the idea comes from someone else you must give credit to the original work. There are several formats for documenting sources. Consult your instructor for help choosing which citation style to use.

THE ANALYSIS

The literature review covers what others have said on your topic. The analysis allows you to present and support your own response. In the introduction you indicate whether you agree, disagree, or some combination of both with what others have said. You will want to expand on how you have formed your opinion and why others should care about your topic.

"The Data Indicate . . ."

The social sciences use data to develop and test explanations. Data can be quantitative or qualitative and can come from a number of sources. You might use statistics related to GDP growth, unemployment, voting rates, or demographics. Or you could use surveys, interviews, or other first-person accounts.

Regardless of the type of data used, it is important to do three things: define your data, indicate where you got the data, and then say what you have done with your data. In a 2005 journal article, political scientist Joshua C. Wilson examines a court case about protests at an abortion clinic and asks whether each side of the conflict acts in a way consistent with their general views on freedom of speech.

[T]his paper relies on close readings of in-person, semi-structured interviews with the participants involved in the real controversy that was the *Williams* case.

Thirteen interviews ranging in length from 40 minutes to 1 hour and 50 minutes were conducted for this paper. Of those interviewed, all would be considered "elites" in terms of political psychology/political attitude research—six were active members of Solano Citizens for Life . . . ; two were members of Planned Parenthood Shasta-Diablo management; one was the lawyer who obtained the restraining order, temporary injunction, and permanent injunction for Planned parenthood; one was the lawyer for the duration of the case for Solano Citizens for life; two were lawyers for Planned Parenthood on appeal; and one was the Superior Court judge who heard arguments for, and finally crafted, the restraining order and injunctions against Solano Citizens for Life. During the course of the interviews, participants were asked a range of questions about their experiences and thoughts in relation to the Williams case, as well as their beliefs about the interpretation and limits of the First Amendment right to free speech—both in general, and in relation to the Williams case.

JOSHUA C. WILSON. "When Rights Collide:
Anti-Abortion Protests and the Ideological Dilemma
in *Planned Parenthood Shasta-Diablo, Inc. v. Williams*,"
Studies in Law, Politics, and Society, 2005

Wilson identifies and describes his qualitative data—interviews conducted with key parties in the conflict—and explains the nature of the questions he asked.

If your data are quantitative, you will need to explain them similarly. See how political scientist Brian Arbour explains the quantitative data he used to study for a 2009 article in *The Forum* how a change of rules might have affected the outcome of the 2008 Democratic primary contest between Hillary Clinton and Barack Obama.

> I evaluate these five concerns about the Democratic system of delegate allocation by "rerunning" the Obama-Clinton contest with a different set of allocation rules, those in effect for the 2008 Republican presidential contest. . . . Republicans allow each state to make their own rules, leading to "a plethora of selection plans" (Shapiro & Bello 2008, 5) . . . To "rerun" the Democratic primary under Republican rules, I need data on the results of the Democratic primary for each state and congressional district and on the Republican delegate allocation rules for each state. The Green Papers (www.thegreenpapers.com), a website that serves as an almanac of election procedures, rules, and results, provides each of these data sources. By "rerunning" the Democratic primaries and caucuses, I use the exact results of each contest.
>
> BRIAN ARBOUR, "Even Closer, Even Longer: What If the 2008 Democratic Primary Used Republican Rules?" *The Forum*, 2009

Note that Arbour identifies his data as primary voting results and the rules for Republican primaries. In the rest of the paper, Arbour shows how his use of these data suggests that political commentators who thought Republican rules would have clarified the close race between Clinton and Obama were wrong and the race would have been "even closer, even longer."

Here are some templates for discussing data:

▸ In order to test the hypothesis that _____, we assessed _____. Our calculations suggest _____.

▸ I used _____ to investigate _____. The results of this investigation indicate _____.

"But Others May Object . . ."

No matter how strongly your data support your argument, there are almost surely other perspectives (and thus other data) that you need to acknowledge. By considering possible objections to your argument and taking them seriously, you demonstrate that you've done your work and that you're aware of other perspectives—and most important, you present your own argument as part of an ongoing conversation.

See how economist Christopher Carroll acknowledges that there may be objections to his argument about how people allocate their income between consumption and savings.

> I have argued here that the modern version of the dynamically optimizing consumption model is able to match many of the important features of the empirical data on consumption and saving behavior. There are, however, several remaining reasons for discomfort with the model.
>
> CHRISTOPHER D. CARROLL, "A Theory of Consumption
> Function, With and Without Liquidity Constraints,"
> *The Journal of Economic Perspectives,* 2001

Carroll then goes on to identify the possible limitations of his mathematical analysis.

Someone may object because there are related phenomena that your analysis does not explain or because you do not have the right data to investigate a particular question. Or perhaps someone may object to assumptions underlying your argument or how you handled your data. Here are some templates for considering naysayers:

▸ _____ might object that _____ .

▸ Is my claim realistic? I have argued _____ , but readers may question _____ .

▸ My explanation accounts for _____ but does not explain _____ . This is because _____ .

"Why Should We Care?"

Who should care about your research, and why? Since the social sciences attempt to explain human behavior, it is important to consider how your research affects the assumptions we make about human behavior. In addition, you might offer recommendations for how other social scientists might continue to explore an issue, or what actions policymakers should take.

In the following example, sociologist Devah Pager identifies the implications of her study of the way having a criminal record affects a person applying for jobs.

> [I]n terms of policy implications, this research has troubling conclusions. In our frenzy of locking people up, our "crime control" policies may in fact exacerbate the very conditions that lead to crime in the first place. Research consistently shows that finding quality steady employment is one of the strongest predictors of

desistance from crime (Shover 1996; Sampson and Laub 1993; Uggen 2000). The fact that a criminal record severely limits employment opportunities—particularly among blacks—suggests that these individuals are left with few viable alternatives.

> DEVAH PAGER, "The Mark of a Criminal Record,"
> *The American Journal of Sociology*, 2003

Pager's conclusion that a criminal record negatively affects employment chances creates a vicious circle, she says: steady employment discourages recidivism, but a criminal record makes it harder to get a job.

In answering the "so what?" question, you need to explain why your readers should care. Although sometimes the implications of your work may be so broad that they would be of interest to almost anyone, it's never a bad idea to identify explicitly any groups of people who will find your work important.

Templates for establishing why your claims matter:

▶ X is important because _____.

▶ Ultimately, what is at stake here is _____.

▶ The finding that _____ should be of interest to _____ because _____.

As noted at the beginning of this chapter, the complexity of people allows us to look at their behavior from many different viewpoints. Much has been, and will be, said about how and why people do the things they do. As a result, we can look at writing in the social sciences as an ongoing conversation. When you join this conversation, the "they say / I say" framework will help you figure out what has already been said (they say) and what you can add (I say). The components of social science writing presented in this chapter are tools to help you join that conversation.

READINGS

FOURTEEN

IS HIGHER EDUCATION WORTH THE PRICE?

—◻—

WHAT IS THE VALUE of college? What do students learn there to justify the experience and the cost? Why do the vast majority of families want their children to attend college? Why do more and more jobs require a college education? Will the growing costs of higher education eventually reverse these trends by straining people's ability to afford it?

Some people cite the practical benefits of college as providing professional education, enabling graduates to embark on high-paying careers. Others believe that college is not only about learning how to earn a living, important as that goal may be, but also about learning how to live: how to be an informed and involved citizen, how to communicate effectively, how to understand other cultures and peoples, how to think and reflect. For many students, college is a time of personal growth and social development—a chance to make friends, get to know people from different backgrounds, and explore new ideas and activities.

The readings in this chapter focus on the future of higher education in the United States, adopting various notions of what college can and should entail. The chapter begins with an article by Andrew Hacker and Claudia Dreifus examining shortfalls in the higher education system and proposing improvements.

Other authors in the chapter argue, in different ways, that the experience of higher education is already very valuable indeed. Sanford Ungar writes about the benefits of a liberal-arts education, as opposed to the pre-professional training that more and more of today's students choose. David Foster Wallace, in a commencement address, speaks to the importance of college as an opportunity to learn self-understanding and critical awareness. Liz Addison, drawing on her own experiences, articulates the often underappreciated value of a community college education. In a similar vein, Kevin Carey discusses the benefits of for-profit education, including that which takes place online.

Not everyone shares the perspective that college is universally beneficial, however. Charles Murray advances the view that many students who currently go to college would be better off attending a vocational program or going right to work after high school. Mike Rose makes the case for a broader definition of intelligence, one that encompasses the types of skills that people who do physical labor develop through their work.

In the final reading in the chapter, Robin Wilson takes on the issue of the cost of higher education, specifically student loan debt.

Are Colleges Worth
the Price of Admission?

ANDREW HACKER AND CLAUDIA DREIFUS

—◻—

TUITION CHARGES at both public and private colleges have more than doubled—in real dollars—compared with a generation ago.

For most Americans, educating their offspring will be the largest financial outlay, after their home mortgage, they'll ever make. And if parents can't or won't pay, young people often find themselves burdened with staggering loans. Graduating with six figures' worth of debt is becoming increasingly common.

So are colleges giving good value for those investments? What are families buying? What are individuals—and our society as a whole—gaining from higher education?

ANDREW HACKER AND CLAUDIA DREIFUS are the authors of *Higher Education? How Colleges Are Wasting Our Money and Failing Our Kids—and What We Can Do About It* (2010). This article, adapted from that book, originally appeared on July 11, 2010, in the *Chronicle of Higher Education*. Hacker is professor emeritus of political science at Queens College of the City of New York. Dreifus, who teaches international affairs and media at Columbia University, writes the "Conversation with . . ." column for the Science section of the *New York Times*.

Several years ago, we set out to answer those questions and began studying institutions and interviewing higher-education leaders, policy makers, and students across the country. Our conclusion: Colleges are taking on too many roles and doing none of them well. They are staffed by casts of thousands and dedicated to everything from esoteric research to vocational training—and have lost track of their basic mission to challenge the minds of young people. Higher education has become a colossus—a \$420-billion industry—immune from scrutiny and in need of reform.

Here are some proposals that might begin to set things right: ⁵

Engage all students. We believe all Americans can do college work, so universal enrollment should be our nation's goal. But for that to happen, professors must make an effort to reach their students—and not, as former Secretary of Education William Bennett once said, "teach their dissertation or next article." Colleges should demand good teaching. They must become conscientious, caring, and attentive to every corner of their classrooms.

Make students use their minds. What should happen to students at college? They should become more thoughtful and interesting people. But some 64 percent of undergraduate students are enrolled in vocational majors, instead of choosing fields like philosophy, literature, or the physical sciences. We'd like to persuade them that supposedly impractical studies are a wiser use of college and ultimately a better investment. The undergraduate years are an interlude that will never come again, a time to liberate the imagination and stretch one's intellect without worrying about a possible payoff. We want that opportunity for everyone, not just the offspring of professional parents.

Replace tenure with multiyear contracts. Despite fears concerning academic freedom, higher education will lose nothing by ending tenure but will reap major gains. We conclude this reluctantly. But tenure takes a huge toll at every academic level. Professors who possess it have no reason to improve their teaching, take on introductory courses, or, in fact, accept any tasks not to their liking. Meanwhile, junior faculty members pay a brutal price by succumbing to intellectual caution. If we could achieve only one reform, that would be it.

Allow fewer sabbaticals. We hear often that academics need every seventh year to recharge their mental batteries, yet we've found no evidence that this happens during a sojourn in Tuscany. We next hear that faculty members require relief from teaching to better conduct their research. Nearly 500,000 assistant, associate, and full professors could now be eligible for sabbaticals. Do we really need that many new books or articles?

End exploitation of adjuncts. It is immoral and unseemly to 10 have a person teaching the same course as an ensconced faculty member but for one-sixth of the pay of his or her tenured colleague down the hall. Adjuncts should receive the same per-course compensation as an assistant professor, including health insurance and other benefits. Most adjuncts are committed teachers who were overproduced by Ph.D. factories, more politely called graduate schools. Finding money to eradicate that outcast group should have highest priority—higher, certainly, than building a mega-athletic complex or a new campus in Abu Dhabi.

Make presidents be public servants. They should say "thanks, but no" if their trustees offer them salaries of $1-million, or anything near it. Colleges contend that they must pump up what they pay to get the best administrators. We're not opposed to talent, but higher education needs something more. The head of the Food and Drug Administration puts in a full day for under $200,000, as do four-star generals. Presidents needn't take vows of poverty, but do they really need quasicorporate stipends to take the job?

Spin off medical schools, research centers, and institutes. Postgraduate training has a place, as long as it doesn't divert faculties from working with undergraduates or preoccupy presidents, who should be focusing on education—not angling for another center on antiterrorist technologies. For people who want to do research, plenty of other places exist—the Brookings Institution, the Rand Corporation, the Howard Hughes Medical Institute—all of which do excellent work without university ties. Princeton University has succeeded quite nicely without a medical school—which often becomes the most costly complex on a campus, commandeering resources, attention, and even mission. In fact, the "school" often becomes a minute part of a medical complex: Johns Hopkins has fewer than 500 medical students, but atop them sits an empire with more than 30,000 employees.

Give techno-teaching a fair hearing. Nothing outshines a superb teacher, whether in small seminars or large lecture halls. Yet a gripping performance on a screen may be preferable to a live teacher of doubtful competence. Unlike a textbook, software can pose interactive questions, review answers, and tell students to try again, offering hints on where they may have gone wrong. Other computer programs can meld clips from movies, plays, or ballet. Techno-teaching can't rival a seminar pondering Fermat's last theorem or *King Lear*, but until we improve classroom instruction, new methods shouldn't be dismissed out of hand.

Spread donations around. Too many benefactors donate to institutions that are already well provided for. Even in economic downturns, gifts to the wealthiest colleges keep coming in. So here's a suggestion for their donors: Pick another college—there's a long, deserving list—and send your check where it will truly do some good.

As we traveled around the country researching our book, we, 15 in fact, found some colleges that we thought were doing their job well:

The University of Mississippi. In 1962 the Supreme Court ordered Ole Miss to admit James Meredith, a black Air Force veteran. In the riots that greeted his admission, two died and dozens were injured. President John F. Kennedy had to send in federal troops.

Today Ole Miss is a university where reconciliation and civility are at the heart of the educational mission. Much of the transformation has been the work of Robert Khayat, who retired from the chancellorship in 2009. In his 14 years there, he raised academic standards, tripled African American enrollment, and banned Confederate flags from athletic events. Under his leadership the university reached into its past for different pieces of the state's history. Think Eudora Welty, William Faulkner, and Tennessee Williams. Ole Miss has a Center for the Study of Southern Culture that focuses on the art, literature, music, and food of the region, black and white. Indeed, of all the flagship colleges we have visited, we have found Ole Miss the most appealing. The campus has the feel of a liberal-arts college. Its Sally McDonnell Barksdale Honors College offers as fine an education as one might find at Carleton or Kenyon Colleges.

Raritan Valley Community College. A two-year college in New Jersey where all students commute and 40 percent study part time, Raritan provides a better introduction to college work than many four-year institutions. It has no megalectures. Its classes don't exceed 40 students, and many are seminar size. Team teaching is encouraged, with both professors present throughout the term. Like most two-year colleges, Raritan's classes are taught mainly by adjuncts. Many have been with Raritan for a while, are good in their fields, and can work closely with students because classes are small. The signal fact about Raritan and colleges like it is that you can get a start with the liberal arts at a tenth of the cost of many private tuitions, and a third of what flagship colleges charge. More than that, you can learn with professors who know your name and have an interest in your future.

University of Notre Dame. Perhaps because of its religious base, the university has successfully avoided the faddish academic trends and compulsive consumerism that has overwhelmed many other colleges. The campus looks relatively spartan. Teaching appears to have genuine import; Notre Dame has a 13-to-one student-faculty ratio, and only 10 percent of the classes are taught by graduate assistants. The president, the Rev. John Jenkins, has himself taught undergraduates—and he personally counsels them if they are suffering a spiritual crisis. Interestingly, for a university famous for football, sports don't seem to overwhelm. On Notre Dame's Web site, it is academics and student life that are trumpeted. It's as if the administrators are saying, "Listen, we have our priorities."

The Cooper Union for the Advancement of Science and Art. 20 While many Ivies describe themselves as meritocracies, Cooper Union, a no-tuition college for engineering, fine arts, and architecture, actually is one. Art and architecture applicants are considered not only by their standardized-test scores, but through a "home test" of six or 10 open-ended questions. When one sits around a table with Cooper seniors and they speak of their futures, their tone is different from students we've met elsewhere. Without the miseries of debt, they contemplate limitless possibilities. Cooper can do that because it dedicates its endowment to a tuition-free education; other well-endowed universities might do well to follow suit.

Berea College. Berea, a liberal-arts college rated by *U.S. News & World Report* as one of "the best comprehensive" colleges in the South, also does not charge tuition. Instead, students are asked to contribute 10 hours a week of labor. Most of them come from the top 20 percent of their high schools and from families where the annual income is under $50,000 a year. For those fortunate enough to win admission, a first-rate education is proffered. The student-faculty ratio is 10-to-one with no graduate teaching assistants substituting for professors.

Arizona State University. At a distance, Arizona State seems like just another oversized state university: a giant credential factory with a football team. But look closer and one quickly sees that it may well be the most experimental institution in the country, a university where the old rules are up for grabs and anyone with an interesting idea can get a hearing. Many academic departments have been dissolved and re-formed within new interdisciplinary institutes, breaking the stranglehold of the disciplines that is so deadly at most colleges. Like Ole Miss, Arizona State has a first rate Honor's College. Good, bad, smart, stupid, it's possible to get new things started at this university. Even some old-time professors, tenured long before the reformer Michael Crow assumed the presidency, told us that they found it exciting to be working at an institution with so much buzz.

University of Maryland-Baltimore County. The Meyerhoff Scholars Program has greatly increased the number of African-Americans in the biological sciences and engineering. In addition, although the university is a research institution focused on science and engineering, undergraduate instruction in the liberal arts is not an afterthought. President Freeman A. Hrabowski sets a tone at the top that says teaching undergraduates is important, and the faculty knows he means it. Of all the research universities we've visited, it is the place that has most capably connected research with undergraduate education.

University of Colorado at Boulder. Despite one of the longest-running football scandals in college sports and the debacle of Ward Churchill (an ethnic-studies professor who compared the victims of the World Trade Center bombing to a Nazi war criminal, and who was later charged with research misconduct), the University of Colorado is capable of doing some things right. For example, in the undergraduate course, "Physics for Everyday Life," founded by the Nobel Prize winner Carl Wieman, the lessons are broken down into modules. A feedback system employing computers and clickers means that the lecturer never moves faster than the students. Trained and supervised graduate teaching assistants keep track of the students, and the lead professor gets weekly reports on their progress. Above all, the course is taught in a way that is interesting to students.

Massachusetts Institute of Technology. It's good to be a contingent at MIT. One part-time writing professor we know teaches two and a half courses a year and coordinates internships. For that, she earns half the compensation of a senior professor, plus benefits for five contract years. Depending on the discipline, part-timers who teach a half-time load are eligible for health insurance, making MIT the contingents' Valhalla. So far as we've heard, decency, fair pay, and health insurance have yet to bankrupt it—and they probably wouldn't other institutions, either.

Western Oregon University. A former teachers' college, Western Oregon does its job without any frills or pretense and with utter seriousness and dedication. Most of its students are either rural or working class; a majority are the first in their families to attend college. Costs are kept at a minimum. The university even offers a "tuition promise" to entering freshmen: Their fees will remain constant throughout their four years. Although the campus is attractive and modern, it has few of the bells and whistles that are routine at other institutions. While salaries are modest, faculty members are enthusiastic. There are no star professors, little research, and the administrative pool is bare bones. All energy is focused on one thing: educating undergraduates.

Evergreen State College. Evergreen is very much a product of the 1960s, when the State of Washington created a new type of public college—one rooted in the ideas of the progressive-education movement. There are no grades or set curriculum. At the end of each quarter, professors present students with long written evaluations of their work; the students, in turn, do the same for their teachers. Courses are cross-disciplinary and team taught, and they are invented or redesigned annually. Despite the university's reputation as a countercultural bastion, 82 percent of its graduates found full-time employment within a year, and 93 percent of those who applied got into graduate schools. For students who want to spend four years in an atmosphere of pure learning, this is the place.

The institutions that we've cited are exceptions to our premise that higher education has lost track of its original and enduring purpose. They reinforce our view that college should be a cultural journey, an intellectual expedition, a voyage confronting new ideas and information. Many colleges with national names and universities with imperial plans could learn a lot from them.

Joining the Conversation

1. Andrew Hacker and Claudia Dreifus, reporting the results of a large-scale study, quickly give their conclusion: "Colleges are taking on too many roles and doing none of them well." They then list a number of proposals to improve higher education. Describe in a sentence or two the type of educational transformation they seem to be advocating.

2. Hacker and Dreifus also list some colleges that they believe are doing a better job than most. What are some common threads linking these institutions?

3. These authors say forcefully what they think, but do they tell us what anyone else thinks? What objections can you think of to their views on higher education?

4. How do you think Hacker and Dreifus might respond to what David Foster Wallace (pp. 198–209) says about the "real value of a real education, which has almost nothing to do with knowledge, and everything to do with simple awareness"?

5. How would Hacker and Dreifus evaluate your school? Reread what they say about the colleges they think are "doing their job well," and then write a paragraph evaluating your school.

The New Liberal Arts

SANFORD J. UNGAR

—◻—

HARD ECONOMIC TIMES inevitably bring scrutiny of all accepted ideals and institutions, and this time around liberal-arts education has been especially hard hit. Something that has long been held up as a uniquely sensible and effective approach to learning has come under the critical gaze of policy makers and the news media, not to mention budget-conscious families.

But the critique, unfortunately, seems to be fueled by reliance on common misperceptions. Here are a few of those misperceptions, from my vantage point as a liberal-arts college president, and my reactions to them:

SANFORD J. UNGAR is the president of Goucher College in Baltimore, Maryland. He is the author of *Fresh Blood: The New American Immigrants* (1998) and *Africa: The People and Politics of an Emerging Continent* (1986). Ungar has also worked in broadcast journalism both at National Public Radio and at the Voice of America, the U.S. government-funded broadcast network for a global audience. His extensive print journalism work includes articles in *Newsweek*, the *Economist*, and the *Washington Post*. This article first appeared in the *Chronicle of Higher Education* on March 5, 2010.

Misperception No. 1: A liberal-arts degree is a luxury that most families can no longer afford. "Career education" is what we now must focus on. Many families are indeed struggling, in the depths of the recession, to pay for their children's college education. Yet one could argue that the traditional, well-rounded preparation that the liberal arts offer is a better investment than ever—that the future demands of citizenship will require not narrow technical or job-focused training, but rather a subtle understanding of the complex influences that shape the world we live in.

No one could be against equipping oneself for a career. But the "career education" bandwagon seems to suggest that short-cuts are available to students that lead directly to high-paying jobs—leaving out "frills" like learning how to write and speak well, how to understand the nuances of literary texts and scientific concepts, how to collaborate with others on research.

Many states and localities have officials or task forces in charge of "work-force development," implying that business and industry will communicate their needs and educational institutions will dutifully turn out students who can head straight to the factory floor or the office cubicle to fulfill them. But history is filled with examples of failed social experiments that treated people as work units rather than individuals capable of inspiration and ingenuity. It is far wiser for students to prepare for change—and the multiple careers they are likely to have—than to search for a single job track that might one day become a dead end.

I recently heard Geoffrey Garin, president of Hart Research Associates, suggest that the responsibility of higher education today is to prepare people "for jobs that do not yet exist." It may be that studying the liberal arts is actually the best form of career education.

Misperception No. 2: College graduates are finding it harder to get good jobs with liberal-arts degrees. Who wants to hire

See Chapter 4 for tips on explaining why you disagree.

somebody with an irrelevant major like philosophy or French? Yes, recent graduates have had difficulty in the job market, but the recession has not differentiated among major fields of study in its impact. A 2009 survey for the Association of American Colleges and Universities actually found that more than three-quarters of our nation's employers recommend that collegebound students pursue a "liberal education." An astounding 89 percent said they were looking for more emphasis on "the ability to effectively communicate orally and in writing," and almost as many urged the development of better "critical thinking and analytical reasoning skills." Seventy percent said they were on the lookout for "the ability to innovate and be creative."

It is no surprise, then, that a growing number of corporations, including some in highly technical fields, are headed by people with liberal-arts degrees. Plenty of philosophy and physics majors work on Wall Street, and the ability to analyze and compare literature across cultures is a skill linked to many other fields, including law and medicine. Knowledge of foreign languages is an advantage in all lines of work. What seemed a radical idea in business education 10 years or so ago—that critical and creative thinking is as "relevant" as finance or accounting—is now commonplace.

Misperception No. 3: The liberal arts are particularly irrelevant for low-income and first-generation college students. They, more than their more-affluent peers, must focus on something more practical and marketable. It is condescending to imply that those who have less cannot understand and appreciate the finer elements of knowledge—another way of saying, really, that the rich folks will do the important thinking, and the lower classes will simply carry out their ideas. That is just a form of prejudice and cannot be supported intellectually.

Perhaps students who come with prior acquaintance with 10 certain fields and a reservoir of experience have an advantage at the start of college. But in my experience, it is often the people who are newest to certain ideas and approaches who are the most original and inventive in the discussion and application of those ideas. They catch up quickly.

We should respect what everyone brings to the table and train the broadest possible cross section of American society to participate in, and help shape, civil discourse. We cannot assign different socioeconomic groups to different levels or types of education. This is a country where a mixed-race child raised overseas by a stuggling single mother who confronts impossible odds can grow up to be president. It is precisely a liberal education that allowed him to catch up and move ahead.

Misperception No. 4: One should not, in this day and age, study only the arts. The STEM fields—science, technology, engineering, and mathematics—are where the action is. The liberal arts encompass the broadest possible range of disciplines in the natural sciences, the humanities, and the social sciences. In fact, the historical basis of a liberal education is in the classical artes liberales, comprising the trivium (grammar, logic, and rhetoric) and the quadrivium (arithmetic, geometry, astronomy, and music). Another term sometimes substituted for liberal arts, for the sake of clarity, is "the arts and sciences." Thus, many universities have colleges, divisions, or schools of arts and sciences among their academic units.

To be sure, there is much concern about whether America is keeping up with China and other rising economies in the STEM disciplines. No evidence suggests, however, that success in scientific and technical fields will be greater if it comes at the expense of a broad background in other areas of the liberal arts.

Misperception No. 5: It's the liberal Democrats who got this country into trouble in recent years, so it's ridiculous to continue indoctrinating our young people with a liberal education. A liberal education, as properly defined above, has nothing whatsoever to do with politics—except insofar as politics is one of the fields that students often pursue under its rubric. On the contrary, because of its inclusiveness and its respect for classical traditions, the liberal arts could properly be described as a conservative approach to preparation for life. It promotes the idea of listening to all points of view and not relying on a single ideology, and examining all approaches to solving a problem rather than assuming that one technique or perspective has all the answers. That calm and balanced sort of dialogue may be out of fashion in the American public arena today, when shouting matches are in vogue and many people seek information only from sources they know in advance they agree with. But it may be only liberal education that can help lead the way back to comity and respectful conversation about issues before us.

Misperception No. 6: America is the only country in the world that clings to such an old-fashioned form of postsecondary education as the liberal arts. Other countries, with more practical orientations, are running way ahead of us. It is often difficult to explain the advantages of a liberal-arts education to people from other cultures, where it is common to specialize early. In many places, including Europe, the study of law or medicine 15 often begins directly after high school, without any requirement to complete an undergraduate degree first. We should recognize, however, that a secondary education in some systems—say, those that follow the model of the German Gymnasium—often includes much that is left out of the typical high-school curriculum in America. One need only look in on a student preparing for the baccalaureat examination in France to understand the distinction: Mastery of philosophical and scientific concepts is mandatory.

Further, in recent years delegations from China have been visiting the United States and asking pointed questions about the liberal arts, seemingly because they feel there may be good reason to try that approach to education. The Chinese may be coming around to the view that a primary focus on technical training is not serving them adequately—that if they aspire to world leadership, they will have to provide young people with a broader perspective. Thus, it is hardly a propitious moment to toss out, or downgrade, one element of higher education that has served us so well.

Misconception No. 7: The cost of American higher education is spiraling out of control, and liberal-arts colleges are becoming irrelevant because they are unable to register gains in productivity or to find innovative ways of doing things. There is plenty wrong with American higher education, including the runaway costs. But the problem of costs goes beyond individual institutions. Government at all levels has come nowhere close to supporting colleges in ways that allow them to provide the kind of access and affordability that's needed. The best way to understand genuine national priorities is to follow the money, and by that standard, education is really not all that important to this country.

Many means exist to obtain a liberal education, including at some large universities, public and private. The method I happen to advocate, for obvious reasons, is the small, residential liberal-arts college, usually independent, where there is close interaction between faculty members and students and, at its best, a sense of community emerges that prepares young people to develop high standards for themselves and others.

Efficiency is hardly the leading quality of liberal-arts colleges, and indeed, their financial model is increasingly coming into question. But because of their commitment to expand need-based financial aid, the net cost of attending a small liberal-arts college can be lower than that of a large public university. One can only hope that each institution will find ways to cut costs and develop distinguishing characteristics that help it survive through the tough times ahead.

The debate over liberal education will surely continue 20 through the recession and beyond, but it would be helpful to put these misperceptions aside. Financial issues cannot be ignored, but neither can certain eternal verities: Through immersion in liberal arts, students learn not just to make a living, but also to live a life rich in values and character. They come to terms with complexity and diversity, and otherwise devise means to solve problems—rather than just complaining about them. They develop patterns that help them understand how to keep learning for the rest of their days.

Joining the Conversation

1. Summarize in a few sentences the seven misperceptions that Sanford Ungar discusses. These of course are all things that "they say"—and that he uses to launch what he wants to

say. How does calling them "misperceptions" affect the way you read his argument? Would you read it any differently if he instead called them "common assumptions"?

2. See paragraph 6, where Geoffrey Garin suggests that "the responsibility of higher education today is to prepare people 'for jobs that do not yet exist.'" Thus, according to Ungar, "It may be that studying the liberal arts is actually the best form of career education." How would you respond to this claim?

3. Misperception 5 relates liberal education to political affiliation. What does Ungar have to say on this issue, and what do you think about his response?

4. On what specific points do you think Ungar would agree with Andrew Hacker and Claudia Dreifus (pp. 179–88)? On what points would he be likely to disagree?

5. Write your own essay listing and explaining five assumptions about college education. Follow Ungar's essay as a model, and use the "they say / I say" pattern to organize your essay, with each assumption as a "they say" that sets up what you want to say.

Kenyon Commencement Speech

DAVID FOSTER WALLACE

—◻—

GREETINGS AND CONGRATULATIONS to Kenyon's graduating class of 2005. There are these two young fish swimming along and they happen to meet an older fish swimming the other way, who nods at them and says "Morning, boys. How's the water?" And the two young fish swim on for a bit, and then eventually one of them looks over at the other and goes "What the hell is water?"

This is a standard requirement of U.S. commencement speeches, the deployment of didactic little parable-ish stories. The story turns out to be one of the better, less bullshitty conventions of the genre, but if you're worried that I plan to present myself here as the wise, older fish explaining what water is

DAVID FOSTER WALLACE (1962–2008) was a novelist and essayist. His books include the novel *Infinite Jest* (1996), the short story collection *Brief Interviews with Hideous Men* (1999), and the essay collections *A Supposedly Fun Thing I'll Never Do Again* (1997) and *Consider the Lobster* (2005). This talk was delivered as the commencement speech at Kenyon College on May 21, 2005, and has been reprinted as *This Is Water: Some Thoughts, Delivered on a Significant Occasion, about Living a Compassionate Life* (2009).

to you younger fish, please don't be. I am not the wise old fish. The point of the fish story is merely that the most obvious, important realities are often the ones that are hardest to see and talk about. Stated as an English sentence, of course, this is just a banal platitude, but the fact is that in the day-to-day trenches of adult existence, banal platitudes can have life-or-death importance, or so I wish to suggest to you on this dry and lovely morning.

Of course the main requirement of speeches like this is that I'm supposed to talk about your liberal arts education's meaning, to try to explain why the degree you are about to receive has actual human value instead of just a material payoff. So let's talk about the single most pervasive cliché in the commencement speech genre, which is that a liberal arts education is not so much about filling you up with knowledge as it is about "teaching you how to think." If you're like me as a student, you've never liked hearing this, and you tend to feel a bit insulted by the claim that you needed anybody to teach you how to think, since the fact that you even got admitted to a college this good seems like proof that you already know how to think. But I'm going to posit to you that the liberal arts cliché turns out not to be insulting at all, because the really significant education in thinking that we're supposed to get in a place like this isn't really about the capacity to think, but rather about the choice of what to think about. If your total freedom of choice regarding what to think about seems too obvious to waste time discussing, I'd ask you to think about fish and water, and to bracket for just a few minutes your scepticism about the value of the totally obvious.

Here's another didactic little story. There are these two guys sitting together in a bar in the remote Alaskan wilderness. One of the guys is religious, the other is an atheist, and the two are

arguing about the existence of God with that special intensity
that comes after about the fourth beer. And the atheist says:
"Look, it's not like I don't have actual reasons for not believing in God. It's not like I haven't ever experimented with the
whole God and prayer thing. Just last month I got caught away
from the camp in that terrible blizzard, and I was totally lost
and I couldn't see a thing, and it was fifty below, and so I tried
it: I fell to my knees in the snow and cried out 'Oh, God, if
there is a God, I'm lost in this blizzard, and I'm gonna die if
you don't help me.'" And now, in the bar, the religious guy
looks at the atheist all puzzled. "Well then you must believe
now," he says, "After all, here you are, alive." The atheist just
rolls his eyes. "No, man, all that was was a couple Eskimos happened to come wandering by and showed me the way back to
camp."

It's easy to run this story through kind of a standard liberal 5
arts analysis: the exact same experience can mean two totally
different things to two different people, given those people's
two different belief templates and two different ways of constructing meaning from experience. Because we prize tolerance and diversity of belief, nowhere in our liberal arts analysis
do we want to claim that one guy's interpretation is true and
the other guy's is false or bad. Which is fine, except we also
never end up talking about just where these individual templates and beliefs come from. Meaning, where they come from
inside the two guys. As if a person's most basic orientation
toward the world, and the meaning of his experience were
somehow just hard-wired, like height or shoe size; or automatically absorbed from the culture, like language. As if how
we construct meaning were not actually a matter of personal,
intentional choice. Plus, there's the whole matter of arro-
gance. The nonreligious guy is so totally certain in his dis-

missal of the possibility that the passing Eskimos had anything to do with his prayer for help. True, there are plenty of religious people who seem arrogant and certain of their own interpretations, too. They're probably even more repulsive than atheists, at least to most of us. But religious dogmatists' problem is exactly the same as the story's unbeliever: blind certainty, a close-mindedness that amounts to an imprisonment so total that the prisoner doesn't even know he's locked up.

The point here is that I think this is one part of what teaching me how to think is really supposed to mean. To be just a little less arrogant. To have just a little critical awareness about myself and my certainties. Because a huge percentage of the stuff that I tend to be automatically certain of is, it turns out, totally wrong and deluded. I have learned this the hard way, as I predict you graduates will, too.

Here is just one example of the total wrongness of something I tend to be automatically sure of: everything in my own immediate experience supports my deep belief that I am the absolute center of the universe; the realest, most vivid and important person in existence. We rarely think about this sort of natural, basic self-centredness because it's so socially repulsive. But it's pretty much the same for all of us. It is our default setting, hard-wired into our boards at birth. Think about it: there is no experience you have had that you are not the absolute center of. The world as you experience it is there in front of you or behind you, to the left or right of you, on your TV or your monitor. And so on. Other people's thoughts and feelings have to be communicated to you somehow, but your own are so immediate, urgent, real.

Please don't worry that I'm getting ready to lecture you about compassion or other-directedness or all the so-called virtues. This is not a matter of virtue. It's a matter of my choosing to do the work of somehow altering or getting free of my natural, hard-wired default setting which is to be deeply and literally self-centered and to see and interpret everything through this lens of self. People who can adjust their natural default setting this way are often described as being "well-adjusted," which I suggest to you is not an accidental term.

Given the triumphant academic setting here, an obvious question is how much of this work of adjusting our default setting involves actual knowledge or intellect. This question gets very tricky. Probably the most dangerous thing about an academic education—at least in my own case—is that it enables my tendency to over-intellectualize stuff, to get lost in abstract argument inside my head, and instead of simply paying attention to what is going on right in front of me, paying attention to what is going on inside me.

As I'm sure you guys know by now, it is extremely difficult 10 to stay alert and attentive, instead of getting hypnotized by the constant monologue inside your own head (which may be happening right now). Twenty years after my own graduation, I have come gradually to understand that the liberal arts cliché about teaching you how to think is actually shorthand for a much deeper, more serious idea: learning how to think really means learning how to exercise some control over how and what you think. It means being conscious and aware enough to choose what you pay attention to and to choose how you construct meaning from experience. Because if you cannot exercise this kind of choice in adult life, you will be totally hosed. Think of the old cliché about "the mind being an excellent servant but a terrible master."

This, like many clichés, so lame and unexciting on the surface, actually expresses a great and terrible truth. It is not the least bit coincidental that adults who commit suicide with firearms almost always shoot themselves in the head. They shoot the terrible master. And the truth is that most of these suicides are actually dead long before they pull the trigger.

And I submit that this is what the real, no bullshit value of your liberal arts education is supposed to be about: how to keep from going through your comfortable, prosperous, respectable adult life dead, unconscious, a slave to your head and to your natural default setting of being uniquely, completely, imperially alone day in and day out. That may sound like hyperbole, or abstract nonsense. Let's get concrete. The plain fact is that you graduating seniors do not yet have any clue what "day in day out" really means. There happen to be whole, large parts of adult American life that nobody talks about in commencement speeches. One such part involves boredom, routine and petty frustration. The parents and older folks here will know all too well what I'm talking about.

By way of example, let's say it's an average adult day, and you get up in the morning, go to your challenging, white-collar, college-graduate job, and you work hard for eight or ten hours, and at the end of the day you're tired and somewhat stressed and all you want is to go home and have a good supper and maybe unwind for an hour, and then hit the sack early because, of course, you have to get up the next day and do it all again. But then you remember there's no food at home. You haven't had time to shop this week because of your challenging job, and so now after work you have to get in your car and drive to the supermarket. It's the end of the work day and the traffic is apt to be very bad. So getting to the store takes way longer than it should, and when you finally get there, the supermarket is very crowded, because of course it's the time of day when all the other people with jobs also try to squeeze in some grocery shopping. And the store is hideously lit and infused with soul-killing muzak or corporate pop and it's pretty much the last place you want to be but you can't just get in and quickly out; you have to wander all over the huge, over-lit store's confusing aisles to find the stuff you want and you have to manoevre your junky cart through all these other tired, hurried people with carts (et cetera, et cetera, cutting stuff out because this is a long ceremony) and eventually you get all your supper supplies, except now it turns out there aren't enough checkout lanes open even though it's the end-of-the-day rush. So the checkout line is incredibly long, which is stupid and infuriating. But you can't take your frustration out on the frantic lady working the register, who is overworked at a job whose daily tedium and meaninglessness surpasses the imagination of any of us here at a prestigious college.

But anyway, you finally get to the checkout line's front, and you pay for your food, and you get told to "Have a nice day" in a voice that is the absolute voice of death. Then you have to take your creepy, flimsy, plastic bags of groceries in your cart with the one crazy wheel that pulls maddeningly to the left, all the way out through the crowded, bumpy, littery parking lot, and then you have to drive all the way home through slow, heavy, SUV-intensive, rush-hour traffic, et cetera et cetera.

Everyone here has done this, of course. But it hasn't yet been part of you graduates' actual life routine, day after week after month after year.

But it will be. And many more dreary, annoying, seemingly meaningless routines besides. But that is not the point. The point is that petty, frustrating crap like this is exactly where the work of choosing is gonna come in. Because the traffic jams and crowded aisles and long checkout lines give me time to think, and if I don't make a conscious decision about how to think and what to pay attention to, I'm gonna be pissed and miserable every time I have to shop. Because my natural default setting is the certainty that situations like this are really all about me. About *my* hungriness and *my* fatigue and *my* desire to just get home, and it's going to seem for all the world like everybody else is just in my way. And who are all these people in my way? And look at how repulsive most of them are, and how stupid and cow-like and dead-eyed and nonhuman they seem in the checkout line, or at how annoying and rude it is that people are talking loudly on cell phones in the middle of the line. And look at how deeply and personally unfair this is. Or, of course, if I'm in a more socially conscious liberal arts form of my default setting, I can spend time in the end-of-the-day traffic being disgusted about all the huge, stupid, lane-blocking SUVs and Hummers and V-12 pickup trucks, burning their wasteful, selfish, 40-gallon tanks of gas, and I can dwell on the fact that the patriotic or religious bumper-stickers always seem to be on the biggest, must disgustingly selfish vehicles, driven by the ugliest (this is an example of how *not* to think, though) most disgustingly selfish vehicles, driven by the ugliest, most inconsiderate and aggressive drivers. And I can think about how our children's children will despise us for wasting all the future's fuel, and probably screwing up the climate, and how spoiled and stupid and selfish and disgusting we all are, and how modern consumer society just sucks, and so forth and so on.

You get the idea.

If I choose to think this way in a store and on the freeway, fine. Lots of us do. Except thinking this way tends to be so easy and automatic that it doesn't have to be a choice. It is my natural default setting. It's the automatic way that I experience the boring, frustrating, crowded parts of adult life when I'm operating on the automatic, unconscious belief that I am the center of the world, and that my immediate needs and feelings are what should determine the world's priorities.

The thing is that, of course, there are totally different ways to think about these kinds of situations. In this traffic, all these vehicles stopped and idling in my way, it's not impossible that some of these people in SUVs have been in horrible auto accidents in the past, and now find driving so terrifying that their therapist has all but ordered them to get a huge, heavy SUV so they can feel safe enough to drive. Or that the Hummer that just cut me off is maybe being driven by a father whose little child is hurt or sick in the seat next to him, and he's trying to get this kid to the hospital, and he's in a bigger, more legitimate hurry than I am: it is actually I who am in *his* way.

Or I can choose to force myself to consider the likelihood 20 that everyone else in the supermarket's checkout line is just as bored and frustrated as I am, and that some of these people probably have harder, more tedious and painful lives than I do.

Again, please don't think that I'm giving you moral advice, or that I'm saying you are supposed to think this way, or that anyone expects you to just automatically do it. Because it's hard. It takes will and effort, and if you are like me, some days you won't be able to do it, or you just flat out won't want to.

But most days, if you're aware enough to give yourself a choice, you can choose to look differently at this fat, dead-eyed, over-made-up lady who just screamed at her kid in the checkout line. Maybe she's not usually like this. Maybe she's been up three straight nights holding the hand of a husband who is dying of bone cancer. Or maybe this very lady is the low-wage clerk at the motor vehicle department, who just yesterday helped your spouse resolve a horrific, infuriating, red-tape problem through some small act of bureaucratic kindness. Of course, none of this is likely, but it's also not impossible.

It just depends what you want to consider. If you're automatically sure that you know what reality is, and you are operating on your default setting, then you, like me, probably won't consider possibilities that aren't annoying and miserable. But if you really learn how to pay attention, then you will know there are other options. It will actually be within your power to experience a crowded, hot, slow, consumer-hell type situation as not only meaningful, but sacred, on fire with the same force that made the stars: love, fellowship, the mystical oneness of all things deep down.

Not that that mystical stuff is necessarily true. The only thing that's capital-T True is that you get to decide how you're gonna try to see it.

This, I submit, is the freedom of a real education, of learning how to be well-adjusted. You get to consciously decide what has meaning and what doesn't. You get to decide what to worship.

Because here's something else that's weird but true: in the day-to-day trenches of adult life, there is actually no such thing as atheism. There is no such thing as not worshipping. Everybody worships. The only choice we get is what to worship. And the compelling reason for maybe choosing some sort of god or spiritual-type thing to worship—be it JC or Allah, be it YHWH or the Wiccan Mother Goddess, or the Four Noble Truths, or some inviolable set of ethical principles—is that pretty much anything else you worship will eat you alive. If you worship money and things, if they are where you tap real meaning in life, then you will never have enough, never feel you have enough. It's the truth. Worship your body and beauty and sexual allure and you will always feel ugly. And when time and age start showing, you will die a million deaths before they finally grieve you. On one level, we all know this stuff already.

It's been codified as myths, proverbs, clichés, epigrams, parables; the skeleton of every great story. The whole trick is keeping the truth up front in daily consciousness.

Worship power, you will end up feeling weak and afraid, and you will need ever more power over others to numb you to your own fear. Worship your intellect, being seen as smart, you will end up feeling stupid, a fraud, always on the verge of being found out. But the insidious thing about these forms of worship is not that they're evil or sinful, it's that they're unconscious. They are default settings.

They're the kind of worship you just gradually slip into, day after day, getting more and more selective about what you see and how you measure value without ever being fully aware that that's what you're doing.

And the so-called real world will not discourage you from operating on your default settings, because the so-called real world of men and money and power hums merrily along in a pool of fear and anger and frustration and craving and worship of self. Our own present culture has harnessed these forces in ways that have yielded extraordinary wealth and comfort and personal freedom. The freedom all to be lords of our tiny skull-sized kingdoms, alone at the center of all creation. This kind of freedom has much to recommend it. But of course there are all different kinds of freedom, and the kind that is most precious you will not hear much talk about much in the great outside world of wanting and achieving. . . . The really important kind of freedom involves attention and awareness and discipline, and being able truly to care about other people and to sacrifice for them over and over in myriad petty, unsexy ways every day.

That is real freedom. That is being educated, and understanding how to think. The alternative is unconsciousness, the default setting, the rat race, the constant gnawing sense of having had, and lost, some infinite thing.

I know that this stuff probably doesn't sound fun and breezy or grandly inspirational the way a commencement speech is supposed to sound. What it is, as far as I can see, is the capital-T Truth, with a whole lot of rhetorical niceties stripped away. You are, of course, free to think of it whatever you wish. But please don't just dismiss it as just some finger-wagging Dr. Laura sermon. None of this stuff is really about morality or religion or dogma or big fancy questions of life after death.

The capital-T Truth is about life *before* death.

It is about the real value of a real education, which has almost nothing to do with knowledge, and everything to do with simple awareness; awareness of what is so real and essential, so hidden in plain sight all around us, all the time, that we have to keep reminding ourselves over and over: "This is water, this is water."

It is unimaginably hard to do this, to stay conscious and alive in the adult world day in and day out. Which means yet another grand cliché turns out to be true: your education really *is* the job of a lifetime. And it commences: now.

I wish you way more than luck.

Joining the Conversation

1. According to David Foster Wallace, there are "whole parts of adult American life that nobody talks about in commencement speeches," including "boredom, routine, and petty frustration." Looking at the speech as a whole, why do you think he raises this point, instead of focusing on more

positive and inspiring topics that are more typical of commencement speeches?

2. This speech contains several examples of metacommentary, in which Wallace essentially tells the audience how to interpret what he is saying. In paragraph 2, for example, he explains "the point of the fish story." Find two or three other examples of metacommentary and consider Wallace's purpose in including them.

3. How does Wallace's argument about the value of the knowledge acquired in college compare with Mike Rose's discussion (pp. 243–54) of the knowledge acquired on the job in blue-collar occupations?

4. In paragraph 28, Wallace argues against focusing on "extraordinary wealth and comfort and personal freedom" and in favor of a different kind of freedom, which he characterizes as "being educated, and understanding how to think." Has he convinced you? Why or why not?

5. Some say that this is one of the best commencement speeches given in recent years. What do you think? Write an essay responding to what Wallace says here. Start by summarizing or quoting from his speech.

Two Years Are Better Than Four

LIZ ADDISON

—◻︎—

OH, THE HAND WRINGING. "College as America used to understand it is coming to an end," bemoans Rick Perlstein and his beatnik friend of fallen face. Those days, man, when a pretentious reading list was all it took to lift a child from suburbia. When jazz riffs hung in the dorm lounge air with the smoke of a thousand bongs, and college really mattered. Really mattered?

Rick Perlstein thinks so. It mattered so much to him that he never got over his four years at the University of Privilege. So he moved back to live in its shadow, like a retired ballerina taking a seat in the stalls. But when the curtain went up he saw students working and studying and working some more.

LIZ ADDISON majored in biology at Southern Maine Community College and graduated in 2008. She now studies veterinary medicine at the Royal Veterinary College in London and plans to practice in Virginia once she graduates. This essay, published on September 26, 2007, was a runner-up in a *New York Times Magazine* college essay contest. The essay responds to Rick Perlstein's opinion piece "What's the Matter with College?" in which he argues that universities no longer matter as much as they once did.

Adults before their time. Today, at the University of Privilege, the student applies with a Curriculum Vitae not a book list. Shudder.

Thus, Mr. Perlstein concludes, the college experience—a rite of passage as it was meant it to be—must have come to an end. But he is wrong. For Mr. Perlstein, so rooted in his own nostalgia, is looking for himself—and he would never think to look for himself in the one place left where the college experience of self-discovery does still matter to those who get there. My guess, reading between the lines, is that Mr. Perlstein has never set foot in an American community college.

The philosophy of the community college, and I have been to two of them, is one that unconditionally allows its students to begin. Just begin. Implicit in this belief is the understanding that anything and everything is possible. Just follow any one of the 1,655 road signs, and pop your head inside—yes, they let anyone in—and there you will find discoveries of a first independent film, a first independent thought, a first independent study. This college experience remains as it should. This college brochure is not marketing for the parents—because the parents, nor grandparents, probably never went to college themselves.

Upon entry to my first community college I had but one 5 O'level to my name. These now disbanded qualifications once marked the transition from lower to upper high school in the Great British education system. It was customary for the average student to proceed forward with a clutch of O'levels, say eight or nine. On a score of one, I left school hurriedly at sixteen. Thomas Jefferson once wrote, "Everybody should have an education proportional to their life." In my case, my life became proportional to my education. But, in doing so, it had the good fortune to land me in an American community college and now, from that priceless springboard, I too seek admission to the University of Privilege. Enter on empty and leave with a head full of dreams? How can Mr. Perlstein say college does not matter anymore?

The community college system is America's hidden public service gem. If I were a candidate for office I would campaign from every campus. Not to score political points, but simply to make sure that anyone who is looking to go to college in this country knows where to find one. Just recently, I read an article in the *New York Times* describing a "college application essay" workshop for low-income students. I was strangely disturbed that those interviewed made no mention of community college. Mr. Perlstein might have been equally disturbed, for the thrust of the workshop was no different to that of an essay coach to the affluent. "Make Life Stories Shine," beams the headline. Or, in other words, prove yourself worldly, insightful, cultured, mature, before you get to college.

Yet, down at X.Y.C.C. it is still possible to enter the college experience as a rookie. That is the understanding—that you will grow up a little bit with your first English class, a bit more with your first psychology class, a whole lot more with your first biology, physics, chemistry. That you may shoot through the roof with calculus, philosophy, or genetics. "College is the key," a young African American student writes for the umpteenth torturous revision of his college essay, "as well as hope." Oh, I wanted desperately to say, please tell him about community college. Please tell him that hope can begin with just one placement test.

When Mr. Perlstein and friends say college no longer holds importance, they mourn for both the individual and society. Yet, arguably, the community college experience is more critical to the nation than that of former beatnik types who, lest we forget, did not change the world. The community colleges of America cover this country college by college and community by community. They offer a network of affordable future, of accessible hope, and an option to dream. In the cold light of day, is it perhaps not more important to foster students with dreams rather than a building take-over?

I believe so. I believe the community college system to be one of America's uniquely great institutions. I believe it should be celebrated as such. "For those who find it necessary to go to a two-year college," begins one University of Privilege admissions paragraph. None too subtle in its implication, but very true. For some students, from many backgrounds, would never breathe the college experience if it were not for the community college. Yes, it is here that Mr. Perlstein will find his college years of self-discovery, and it is here he will find that college does still matter.

Joining the Conversation

1. What view is Liz Addison responding to? Write out a sentence or two summarizing the "they say."
2. Addison discusses her own educational experience as part of her argument. What role does this use of autobiographical narrative play in her argument?
3. How does Addison make clear that her topic is really important—and that it should matter to readers?
4. In closing, Addison writes of community colleges: "It is here that Mr. Perlstein will find his college years of self-discovery, and it is here he will find that college does still matter." Do you think college still matters? Write an essay responding to this point from your own perspective as a college student.

Why Do You Think They're Called For-Profit Colleges?

KEVIN CAREY

—⊡—

MICHAEL CLIFFORD believes that education is the only path to world peace. He never went to college, but sometimes he calls himself "Doctor." Jerry Falwell is one of his heroes. Clifford has made millions of dollars from government programs but doesn't seem to see the windfall that way. Improbably, he has come to symbolize the contradictions at the heart of the growing national debate over for-profit higher education.

Until recently, for-profits were mostly mom-and-pop trade schools. Twenty years ago, a series of high-profile Congressional hearings, led by Senator Sam Nunn, revealed widespread fraud in the industry, and the resulting reforms almost wiped the schools

KEVIN CAREY researches higher education for Education Sector, a Washington, D.C., think tank, and has also written for publications including the *New Republic*, the *Washington Post*, the *Los Angeles Times*, and the *New York Daily News*. He was Indiana's assistant state budget director and adviser to both the governor and the Indiana Senate Democratic Caucus. Carey currently teaches education policy at Johns Hopkins University and contributes a monthly column to the *Chronicle of Higher Education*, where this article first appeared on July 25, 2010.

A billboard promoting the University of Phoenix, a large for-profit university system.

out. But they hung on and returned with a vengeance in the form of publicly traded giants like the University of Phoenix.

Entrepreneurs like Clifford, meanwhile, have been snapping up dying nonprofit colleges and quickly turning them into money-making machines.

Most of that money comes from the federal government, in the form of Pell Grants and subsidized student loans. Phoenix alone is on pace to reap $1-billion from Pell Grants this year, along with $4-billion from federal loans. A quarter of all federal aid goes to for-profits, while they enroll only 10 percent of students.

Unfortunately, a large and growing number of graduates of 5 for-profit colleges are having trouble paying those loans back.

Horror stories of aggressive recruiters' inducing students to take out huge loans for nearly worthless degrees are filling the news. The Obama administration, flush with victory after vanquishing the student-loan industry this year, has proposed cutting off federal aid to for-profits that saddle students with unmanageable debt. Congress has rolled out the TV cameras for a new round of hearings that are putting for-profits on the hot seat. One observer called the event "the Nunn hearings on steroids."

The new scrutiny of for-profits is welcome. Without oversight, the combination of government subsidies and financially unsophisticated consumers guarantees outright fraud or programs that, while technically legitimate, are so substandard that the distinction of legitimacy has no meaning. For-profit owners and advocates have a hard time admitting that.

I spoke with Michael Clifford recently as he was driving down the California coast to meet with a higher-education charity he runs. He's an interesting man—sincere, optimistic, a true believer in higher education and his role as a force for good. A musician and born-again Christian, he learned at the knee of the University of Phoenix's founder, John Sperling. In 2004, Clifford led the sale of a destitute Baptist institution called Grand Canyon University to investors. Six years later, enrollment has increased substantially, much of it online. The ownership company started selling shares to the public in 2008 and is worth nearly $1-billion today, making Clifford a wealthy man. He has since repeated the formula elsewhere, partnering with notables like General Electric's former chief executive, Jack Welch. Some of the colleges that Clifford has purchased have given him honorary degrees (thus "Doctor" Michael Clifford).

Clifford will concede, in the abstract, to abuses in the for-profit industry. But he rejects the Obama administration's proposal to cut off federal aid to for-profits at which student-debt payments after graduation exceed a certain percentage of the graduates' income. In fact, he denies that colleges have any responsibility whatsoever for how much students borrow and whether they can pay it back. He won't even acknowledge that student borrowing is related to how much colleges charge.

The refusal is the industry line, and it is crazy nonsense. As a rule, for-profits charge much more than public colleges and universities. Many of their students come from moderate- and low-income backgrounds. You don't need a college degree to know that large debt plus small income equals high risk of default. The for-profit Corinthian Colleges (as of mid-July, market cap: $923-million) estimated in official documents filed with the Securities and Exchange Commission that more than half the loans it makes to its own students will go bad. Corinthian still makes a profit, because it gets most of its money from loans guaranteed by Uncle Sam.

Other industry officials, like the for-profit lobbyist Harris 10 Miller, would have you believe that government money that technically passes through the hands of students on its way from the public treasury to the for-profit bottom line isn't a government subsidy at all. In that regard, for-profits lately have been trying to rebrand themselves as "market based" higher education. To understand how wrong this is, look no further than the "90/10 rule," a federal rule that bars for-profits from receiving more than 90 percent of their revenue from federal aid. The fact that the rule exists at all, and that Miller is working to water it down (it used to be the 85/15 rule), shows that for-profits operate in nothing like a subsidy-free market.

The federal government has every right to regulate the billions of taxpayer dollars it is pouring into the pockets of for-profit shareholders. The sooner abusive colleges are prevented from loading students with crushing debt in exchange for low-value degrees, the better.

But that doesn't mean for-profit higher education is inherently bad. The reputable parts of the industry are at the forefront of much technological and organizational innovation. For-profits exist in large part to fix educational market failures left by traditional institutions, and they profit by serving students that public and private nonprofit institutions too often ignore. While old-line research universities were gilding their walled-off academic city-states, the University of Phoenix was building no-frills campuses near freeway exits so working students could take classes in the evening. Who was more focused on the public interest? Some of the colleges Clifford bought have legacies that stretch back decades. Who else was willing to save them? Not the government, or the church, or the more fortunate colleges with their wealthy alumni and endowments that reach the sky.

The for-profit Kaplan University recently struck a deal with the California community-college system to provide courses that the bankrupt public colleges cannot. The president of the system's faculty senate objected: The deal was not "favorable to faculty," she said. Whose fault is that? Kaplan, or the feckless voters and incompetent politicians who have driven California to ruin?

Wal-Mart recently announced a deal with the for-profit American Public University to teach the giant retailer's employees. What ambitious president or provost is planning to make her reputation educating $9-an-hour cashiers?

Traditional institutions tend to respond to such ventures by 15 indicting the quality of for-profit degrees. The trouble is, they have very little evidence beyond the real issue of default rates to prove it. That's because traditional institutions have long resisted subjecting themselves to any objective measures of academic quality. They've pointed instead to regional accreditation, which conveniently allows colleges to decide for themselves whether they're doing a good job.

But many for-profit institutions have regional accreditation, too. That's what people like Clifford are buying when they invest in troubled colleges. Accreditation has become like a taxicab medallion, available for bidding on the open market. As a result, long-established public and private nonprofit colleges are left with no standards with which to make the case against their for-profit competitors. At one recent Congressional hearing, the Senate education committee's chairman, Tom Harkin, said of the for-profits, "We don't know how many students graduate, how many get jobs, how schools that are not publicly traded spend their [federal] dollars, and how many for-profit students default over the long term." All true—and just as true when the words "for-profit" are removed. There's no doubt that the worst for-profits are ruthlessly exploiting the commodified college degree. But they didn't commodify it in the first place.

For-profits fill a void left by traditional institutions that once believed their world was constant. Fast-developing methods of teaching students over the Internet have given the velocity of change a turbo boost. In such a volatile situation, all kinds of unexpected people make their way into the picture. And once they get there, they tend to stick around. Traditional institutions hoping that Congress will rid them of for-profit competition will very likely be disappointed.

Joining the Conversation

1. What, according to Kevin Carey, are the main problems with for-profit colleges? What does he list as some of their

positive qualities? Would you say that the article as a whole argues for a positive or negative view of for-profit colleges? How well does it succeed in supporting this position?

2. Much of this article discusses Michael Clifford, an entrepreneur in the business of for-profit colleges. Why do you think the author focuses on one individual in the article? How, if at all, does the portrait of Clifford enhance the discussion?

3. This essay was written for the *Chronicle of Higher Education*, a daily newspaper read by college and university professors and administrators. How would it be different if Carey had written it for an audience of college students? Or parents of college students?

4. Who is Carey responding to? How can you tell? Does he say?

5. We included this essay because it addresses the question this chapter asks: is a college education worth the price? Whatever kind of college you attend, do you think it's worth it? At this point in your college career, do you think it's going to help you achieve whatever goals you have? Are there any ways you think the school you attend could better serve your needs? Write a paragraph or two exploring these questions.

Are Too Many People Going to College?

CHARLES MURRAY

—◻—

To ASK WHETHER too many people are going to college requires us to think about the importance and nature of a liberal education. "Universities are not intended to teach the knowledge required to fit men for some special mode of gaining their livelihood," John Stuart Mill told students at the University of St. Andrews in 1867. "Their object is not to make skillful lawyers, or physicians, or engineers, but capable and cultivated human beings." If this is true (and I agree that it is), why say that too many people are going to college? Surely a mass democracy should encourage as many people as possible to become "capable and cultivated human beings" in Mill's sense. We should not restrict the availability of a liberal

CHARLES MURRAY works at the American Enterprise Institute, a conservative think tank in Washington, D.C. He is the coauthor, with Richard Herrnstein, of *The Bell Curve* (1994). Murray has also written articles for the *New Criterion*, the *Washington Post*, the *Wall Street Journal*, and the *New York Times*. This essay, adapted from his book, *Real Education: Four Simple Truths for Bringing America's Schools Back to Reality* (2008), first appeared on Sept. 8, 2008, in *The American*, the journal of the American Enterprise Institute.

education to a rarefied intellectual elite. More people should be going to college, not fewer.

Yes and no. More people should be getting the basics of a liberal education. But for most students, the places to provide those basics are elementary and middle school. E. D. Hirsch Jr. is the indispensable thinker on this topic, beginning with his 1987 book *Cultural Literacy: What Every American Needs to Know.* Part of his argument involves the importance of a body of core knowledge in fostering reading speed and comprehension. With regard to a liberal education, Hirsch makes three points that are germane here:

See Chapter 4 for ways to agree, but with a difference.

Full participation in any culture requires familiarity with a body of core knowledge. To live in the United States and not recognize Teddy Roosevelt, Prohibition, the Minutemen, Wall Street, smoke-filled rooms, or Gettysburg is like trying to read without knowing some of the ten thousand most commonly used words in the language. It signifies a degree of cultural illiteracy about America. But the core knowledge transcends one's own country. Not to recognize Falstaff, Apollo, the Sistine Chapel, the Inquisition, the twenty-third Psalm, or Mozart signifies cultural illiteracy about the West. Not to recognize the solar system, the Big Bang, natural selection, relativity, or the periodic table is to be scientifically illiterate. Not to recognize the Mediterranean, Vienna, the Yangtze River, Mount Everest, or Mecca is to be geographically illiterate.

This core knowledge is an important part of the glue that holds the culture together. All American children, of whatever ethnic heritage, and whether their families came here 300 years ago or three months ago, need to learn about the Pilgrims, Valley Forge, Duke Ellington, Apollo 11, Susan B. Anthony,

George C. Marshall, and the Freedom Riders. All students need to learn the iconic stories. For a society of immigrants such as ours, the core knowledge is our shared identity that makes us Americans together rather than hyphenated Americans.

K–8 are the right years to teach the core knowledge, and the **effort should get off to a running start in elementary school.** Starting early is partly a matter of necessity: There's a lot to learn, and it takes time. But another reason is that small children enjoy learning myths and fables, showing off names and dates they have memorized, and hearing about great historical figures and exciting deeds. The educational establishment sees this kind of curriculum as one that forces children to memorize boring facts. That conventional wisdom is wrong on every count. The facts can be fascinating (if taught right); a lot more than memorization is entailed; yet memorizing things is an indispensable part of education, too; and memorizing is something that children do much, much better than adults. The core knowledge is suited to ways that young children naturally learn and enjoy learning. Not all children will be able to do the reading with the same level of comprehension, but the fact-based nature of the core knowledge actually works to the benefit of low-ability students—remembering facts is much easier than making inferences and deductions. The core knowledge curriculum lends itself to adaptation for students across a wide range of academic ability.

In the 20 years since *Cultural Literacy* was published, Hirsch and his colleagues have developed and refined his original formulation into an inventory of more than 6,000 items that approximate the core knowledge broadly shared by literate Americans. Hirsch's Core Knowledge Foundation has also developed a detailed, grade-by-grade curriculum for K–8, complete with lists of books and other teaching materials.

The Core Knowledge approach need not stop with eighth grade. High school is a good place for survey courses in the humanities, social sciences, and sciences taught at a level below the demands of a college course and accessible to most students in the upper two-thirds of the distribution of academic ability. Some students will not want to take these courses, and it can be counterproductive to require them to do so, but high school can put considerable flesh on the liberal education skeleton for students who are still interested.

Liberal Education in College

Saying "too many people are going to college" is not the same as saying that the average student does not need to know about history, science, and great works of art, music, and literature. They do need to know—and to know more than they are currently learning. So let's teach it to them, but let's not wait for college to do it.

Liberal education in college means taking on the tough stuff. A high-school graduate who has acquired Hirsch's core knowledge will know, for example, that John Stuart Mill was an important 19th-century English philosopher who was associated with something called Utilitarianism and wrote a famous book called *On Liberty*. But learning philosophy in college, which is an essential component of a liberal education, means that the student has to be able to read and understand the actual text of *On Liberty*. That brings us to the limits set by the nature of college-level material. Here is the first sentence of *On Liberty*: "The subject of this essay is not the so-called liberty of the will, so unfortunately opposed to the misnamed doctrine of philosophical necessity; but civil, or social liberty: the nature and limits of the power which can be legitimately exercised by society over the individual." I will not burden you with *On Liberty*'s last sentence. It is 126 words long. And Mill is one of the more accessible philosophers, and *On Liberty* is one of Mill's more accessible works. It would be nice if everyone could acquire a fully formed liberal education, but they cannot.

Specifically: When College Board researchers defined "college readiness" as the SAT score that is associated with a 65 percent chance of getting at least a 2.7 grade point average in college during the freshman year, and then applied those criteria (hardly demanding in an era of soft courses and grade inflation) to the freshmen in a sample of 41 major colleges and universities, the threshold "college readiness" score was found to be 1180 on the combined SAT math and verbal tests. It is a score that only about 10 percent of American 18-year-olds would achieve if they all took the SAT, in an age when more than 30 percent of 18-year-olds go to college.

Should all of those who do have the academic ability to absorb a college-level liberal education get one? It depends. Suppose we have before us a young woman who is in the 98th percentile of academic ability and wants to become a lawyer and eventually run for political office. To me, it seems essential that she spend her undergraduate years getting a rigorous liberal education. Apart from a liberal education's value to her, the nation will benefit. Everything she does as an attorney or as an elected official should be informed by the kind of wisdom that a rigorous liberal education can encourage. It is appropriate to push her into that kind of undergraduate program.

But the only reason we can get away with pushing her is that the odds are high that she will enjoy it. The odds are high because she is good at this sort of thing—it's no problem for her to read *On Liberty* or *Paradise Lost*. It's no problem for her to come up with an interesting perspective on what she's read and weave it into a term paper. And because she's good at it, she is also likely to enjoy it. It is one of Aristotle's central themes in his discussion of human happiness, a theme that John Rawls later distilled into what he called the Aristotelian Principle: "Other things equal, human beings enjoy the exercise of the irrealized capacities (their innate or trained abilities), and this enjoyment increases the more the capacity is realized, or the greater its complexity." And so it comes to pass that those who take the hardest majors and who enroll in courses that look most like an old fashioned liberal education are concentrated among the students in the top percentiles of academic ability. Getting a liberal education consists of dealing with complex intellectual material day after day, and dealing with complex intellectual material is what students in the top few percentiles are really good at, in the same way that other people are really good at cooking or making pottery. For these students, doing it well is fun.

Every percentile down the ability ladder—and this applies to all abilities, not just academic—the probability that a person will enjoy the hardest aspects of an activity goes down as well. Students at the 80th percentile of academic ability are still smart kids, but the odds that they will respond to a course that assigns Mill or Milton are considerably lower than the odds that a student in the top few percentiles will respond. Virtue has nothing to do with it. Maturity has nothing to do with it. Appreciation of the value of a liberal education has nothing to do with it. The probability that a student will enjoy *Paradise Lost* goes down as his linguistic ability goes down, but so does the probability that he works on double acrostic puzzles in his spare time or regularly plays online Scrabble, and for the identical reason. The lower down the linguistic ladder he is, the less fun such activities are.

And so we return to the question: Should all of those who have the academic ability to absorb a college-level liberal education get one? If our young woman is at the 80th percentile of linguistic ability, should she be pushed to do so? She has enough intellectual capacity, if she puts her mind to it and works exceptionally hard.

The answer is no. If she wants to, fine. But she probably 15 won't, and there's no way to force her. Try to force her (for example, by setting up a demanding core curriculum), and she will transfer to another school, because she is in college for vocational training. She wants to write computer code. Start a business. Get a job in television. She uses college to take vocational courses that pertain to her career interests. A large proportion of people who are theoretically able to absorb a liberal education have no interest in doing so.

And reasonably so. Seen dispassionately, getting a traditional liberal education over four years is an odd way to enjoy spending one's time. Not many people enjoy reading for hour after hour, day after day, no matter what the material may be. To enjoy reading *On Liberty* and its ilk—and if you're going to absorb such material, you must in some sense enjoy the process—is downright peculiar. To be willing to spend many more hours writing papers and answers to exam questions about that material approaches masochism.

We should look at the kind of work that goes into acquiring a liberal education at the college level in the same way that we look at the grueling apprenticeship that goes into becoming a master chef: something that understandably attracts only a few people. Most students at today's colleges choose not to take the courses that go into a liberal education because the capabilities they want to develop lie elsewhere. These students are not lazy, any more than students who don't want to spend hours learning how to chop carrots into a perfect eighth-inch dice are lazy. A liberal education just doesn't make sense for them.

For Learning How to Make a Living, the Four-Year Brick-and-Mortar Residential College Is Increasingly Obsolete

We now go from one extreme to the other, from the ideal of liberal education to the utilitarian process of acquiring the knowledge that most students go to college to acquire—practical and vocational. The question here is not whether the traditional four-year residential college is fun or valuable as a place to grow up, but when it makes sense as a place to learn how to make a living. The answer is: in a sensible world, hardly ever.

Start with the time it takes—four years. Assuming a semester system with four courses per semester, four years of class work means 32 semester-long courses. The occupations for which "knowing enough" requires 32 courses are exceedingly rare. For some professions—medicine and law are the obvious examples—a rationale for four years of course work can be concocted (combining pre-med and pre-law undergraduate courses with three years of medical school and law school), but for every other occupation, the body of knowledge taught in classrooms can be learned more quickly. Even Ph.D.s don't require four years of course work. The Ph.D. is supposed to signify expertise, but that expertise comes from burrowing deep into a specialty, not from dozens of courses.

Those are the jobs with the most stringent academic require- 20
ments. For the student who wants to become a good hotel
manager, software designer, accountant, hospital administra-
tor, farmer, high-school teacher, social worker, journalist,
optometrist, interior designer, or football coach, four years of
class work is ridiculous. Actually becoming good in those occupations will take longer than four years, but most of the competence is acquired on the job. The two-year community
college and online courses offer more flexible options for tai-
loring course work to the real needs of the job.

A brick-and-mortar campus is increasingly obsolete. The
physical infrastructure of the college used to make sense for
three reasons. First, a good library was essential to higher learning, and only a college faculty and student body provided the
economies of scale that made good libraries affordable. Second,
scholarship flourishes through colleagueships, and the college
campus made it possible to put scholars in physical proximity
to each other. Third, the best teaching requires interaction
between teachers and students, and physical proximity was the
only way to get it. All three rationales for the brick-and-
mortar campus are fading fast.

The rationale for a physical library is within a few years of
extinction. Even now, the Internet provides access, for a price,
to all the world's significant technical journals. The books are
about to follow. Google is scanning the entire text of every
book in the libraries of Harvard, Princeton, Stanford, Oxford,
the New York Public Library, the Bavarian State Library,
Ghent University Library, Keio Library (Tokyo), the National
Library of Catalonia, University of Lausanne, and an expanding list of others. Collectively, this project will encompass close
to the sum total of human knowledge. It will be completely
searchable. Everything out of copyright will be free. Everything

still under copyright will be accessible for a fee. Libraries will still be a selling point for colleges, but as a place for students to study in pleasant surroundings—an amenity in the same way that an attractive student union is an amenity. Colleges and universities will not need to exist because they provide libraries.

The rationale for colleges based on colleagueships has eroded. Until a few decades ago, physical proximity was important because correspondence and phone calls just weren't as good. As email began to spread during the 1980s, physical proximity became less important. As the capacity of the Internet expanded in the 1990s, other mechanisms made those interactions richer. Now, regular emails from professional groups inform scholars of the latest publications in their field of interest. Specialized chat groups enable scholars to bounce new ideas off other people working on the same problems. Drafts are exchanged effortlessly and comments attached electronically. Whether physical proximity still has any advantages depends mostly on the personality of the scholar. Some people like being around other people during the workday and prefer face-to-face conversations to emails. For those who don't, the value of being on a college campus instead of on a mountaintop in Montana is nil. Their electronic access to other scholars is incomparably greater than any scholar enjoyed even within the world's premier universities before the advent of the Internet. Like the library, face-to-face colleagueships will be an amenity that colleges continue to provide. But colleges and universities will not need to exist because they provide a community of scholars.

The third rationale for the brick-and-mortar college is that it brings teachers together with students. Working against that rationale is the explosion in the breadth and realism of what is known as distance learning. The idea of distance learning is surprisingly old—Isaac Pitman was teaching his shorthand system to British students through the postal service in the 1840s, and the University of London began offering degrees for correspondence students in 1858—but the technology of distance learning changed little for the next century. The advent of inexpensive videocassettes in the 1980s opened up a way for students to hear and see lectures without being in the classroom. By the early 1990s, it was possible to buy college-level courses on audio or videotape, taught by first-rate teaching professors, on a wide range of topics, for a few hundred dollars. But without easy interaction between teacher and student, distance learning remained a poor second-best to a good college seminar.

Once again, the Internet is revolutionizing everything. As personal computers acquired the processing power to show high-definition video and the storage capacity to handle big video files, the possibilities for distance learning expanded by orders of magnitude. We are now watching the early expression of those possibilities: podcasts and streaming videos in real time of professors' lectures, online discussions among students scattered around the country, online interaction between students and professors, online exams, and tutorials augmented by computer-aided instruction software.

Even today, the quality of student-teacher interactions in a virtual classroom competes with the interactions in a brick-and-mortar classroom. But the technology is still in its early stages of development and the rate of improvement is breathtaking. Compare video games such as Myst and SimCity in the 1990s to their descendants today; the Walkman you used in the 1990s to the iPod you use today; the cell phone you used in the 1990s to the BlackBerry or iPhone you use today. Whatever technical limitations might lead you to say, "Yes, but it's still not the same as being there in the classroom," are probably within a few years of being outdated.

College Isn't All It's Cracked Up to Be

College looms so large in the thinking of both parents and students because it is seen as the open sesame to a good job. Reaping the economic payoff for college that shows up in econometric analyses is a long shot for large numbers of young people.

When high-school graduates think that obtaining a B.A. will help them get a higher-paying job, they are only narrowly correct. Economists have established beyond doubt that people with B.A.s earn more on average than people without them. But why does the B.A. produce that result? For whom does the B.A. produce that result? For some jobs, the economic premium for a degree is produced by the actual education that has gone into getting the degree. Lawyers, physicians, and engineers can earn their high incomes only by deploying knowledge and skills that take years to acquire, and degrees in law, medicine, and engineering still signify competence in those knowledges and skills. But for many other jobs, the economic premium for the B.A. is created by a brutal fact of life about the American job market: Employers do not even interview applicants who do not hold a B.A. Even more brutal, the advantage conferred by the B.A. often has nothing to do with the content of the education. Employers do not value what the student learned, just that the student has a degree.

Employers value the B.A. because it is a no-cost (for them) screening device for academic ability and perseverance. The more people who go to college, the more sense it makes for employers to require a B.A. When only a small percentage of people got college degrees, employers who required a B.A.

would have been shutting themselves off from access to most of the talent. With more than a third of 23-year-olds now getting a B.A., many employers can reasonably limit their hiring pool to college graduates because bright and ambitious high-school graduates who can go to college usually do go to college. An employer can believe that exceptions exist but rationally choose not to expend time and money to identify them. Knowing this, large numbers of students are in college to buy their admission ticket—the B.A.

But while it is true that the average person with a B.A. makes 30 more than the average person without a B.A., getting a B.A. is still going to be the wrong economic decision for many high-school graduates. Wages within occupations form a distribution. Young people with okay-but-not-great academic ability who are thinking about whether to go after a B.A. need to consider the competition they will face after they graduate. Let me put these calculations in terms of a specific example, a young man who has just graduated from high school and is trying to decide whether to become an electrician or go to college and major in business, hoping to become a white-collar manager. He is at the 70th percentile in linguistic ability and logical mathematical ability—someone who shouldn't go to college by my standards, but who can, in today's world, easily find a college that will give him a degree. He is exactly average in interpersonal and intrapersonal ability. He is at the 95th percentile in the small-motor skills and spatial abilities that are helpful in being a good electrician.

He begins by looking up the average income of electricians and managers on the Bureau of Labor Statistics website, and finds that the mean annual income for electricians in 2005 was $45,630, only about half of the $88,450 mean for management occupations. It looks as if getting a B.A. will buy him a huge wage premium. Should he try to get the B.A. on economic grounds?

To make his decision correctly, our young man must start by throwing out the averages. He has the ability to become an excellent electrician and can reasonably expect to be near the top of the electricians' income distribution. He does not have it in him to be an excellent manager, because he is only average in interpersonal and intrapersonal ability and only modestly above average in academic ability, all of which are important for becoming a good manager, while his competitors for those slots will include many who are high in all of those abilities. Realistically, he should be looking at the incomes toward the bottom of the distribution of managers. With that in mind, he goes back to the Bureau of Labor Statistics website and discovers that an electrician at the 90th percentile of electricians' incomes made $70,480 in 2005, almost twice the income of a manager at the 10th percentile of managers' incomes ($37,800). Even if our young man successfully completes college and gets a B.A. (which is far from certain), he is likely to make less money than if he becomes an electrician.

Then there is job security to consider. A good way to make sure you always can find work is to be among the best at what you do. It also helps to have a job that does not require you to compete with people around the globe. When corporations downsize, they lay off mediocre managers before they lay off top electricians. When the economy gets soft, top electricians can find work when mediocre managers cannot. Low-level management jobs can often be outsourced to India, whereas electricians' jobs cannot.

What I have said of electricians is true throughout the American job market. The income for the top people in a wide variety of occupations that do not require a college degree is higher than the average income for many occupations that require a B.A. Furthermore, the range and number of such jobs are expanding rapidly. The need for assembly-line workers in factories (one of the most boring jobs ever invented) is falling, but the demand for skilled technicians of every kind—in healthcare, information technology, transportation networks, and every other industry that relies on high-tech equipment—is expanding. The service sector includes many low-skill, low-paying jobs, but it also includes growing numbers of specialized jobs that pay well (for example, in healthcare and the entertainment and leisure industries). Construction offers an array of high-paying jobs for people who are good at what they do. It's not just skilled labor in the standard construction trades that is in high demand. The increase in wealth in American society has increased the demand for all sorts of craftsmanship. Today's high-end homes and office buildings may entail the work of specialized skills in stonework, masonry, glazing, painting, cabinetmaking, machining, landscaping, and a dozen other crafts. The increase in wealth is also driving an increased demand for the custom-made and the exquisitely wrought, meaning demand for artisans in everything from pottery to jewelry to metalworking. There has never been a time in history when people with skills not taught in college have been in so much demand at such high pay as today, nor a time when the range of such jobs has been so wide. In today's America, finding a first-rate lawyer or physician is easy. Finding first-rate skilled labor is hard.

Intrinsic Rewards

The topic is no longer money but job satisfaction—intrinsic 35 rewards. We return to our high-school graduate trying to decide between going to college and becoming an electrician. He knows that he enjoys working with his hands and likes the idea of not being stuck in the same place all day, but he also likes the idea of being a manager sitting behind a desk in a big office, telling people what to do and getting the status that goes with it.

However, he should face facts that he is unlikely to know on his own, but that a guidance counselor could help him face. His chances of getting the big office and the status are slim. He is more likely to remain in a cubicle, under the thumb of the boss in the big office. He is unlikely to have a job in which he produces something tangible during the course of the day.

If he becomes a top electrician instead, he will have an expertise that he exercises at a high level. At the end of a workday, he will often be able to see that his work made a difference in the lives of people whose problems he has solved. He will not be confined to a cubicle and, after his apprenticeship, will be his own supervisor in the field. Top electricians often become independent contractors who have no boss at all.

The intrinsic rewards of being a top manager can be just as great as those of a top electrician (though I would not claim they are greater), but the intrinsic rewards of being a mediocre manager are not. Even as people in white-collar jobs lament the soullessness of their work, the intrinsic rewards of exercising technical skills remain undiminished.

Finally, there is an overarching consideration so important it is hard to express adequately: the satisfaction of being good at what one does for a living (and knowing it), compared to the melancholy of being mediocre at what one does for a living (and knowing it). This is another truth about living a human life that a 17-year-old might not yet understand on his own, but that a guidance counselor can bring to his attention. Guidance counselors and parents who automatically encourage young people to go to college straight out of high school regardless of their skills and interests are being thoughtless about the best interests of young people in their charge.

The Dark Side of the B.A. as Norm

It is possible to accept all that I have presented as fact and still 40 disagree with the proposition that too many people are going to college. The argument goes something like this:

The meaning of a college education has evolved since the 19th century. The traditional liberal education is still available for students who want it, but the curriculum is appropriately broader now, and includes many courses for vocational preparation that today's students want. Furthermore, intellectual requirements vary across majors. It may be true that few students can complete a major in economics or biology, but larger proportions can handle the easier majors. A narrow focus on curriculum also misses the important nonacademic functions of college. The lifestyle on today's campuses may leave something to be desired, but four years of college still give youngsters in late adolescence a chance to encounter different kinds of people, to discover new interests, and to decide what they want to make of their lives. And if it is true that some students spend too much of their college years partying, that was also true of many Oxford students in the 18th century. Lighten up.

If the only people we had to worry about were those who are on college campuses and doing reasonably well, this position would have something to be said for it. It does not address the issues of whether four years makes sense or whether a residential facility makes sense; nevertheless, college as it exists is not an intrinsically evil place for the students who are there and are coping academically. But there is the broader American society to worry about as well. However unintentionally, we have made something that is still inaccessible to a majority of the population—the B.A.—into a symbol of first-class citizenship. We have done so at the same time that other class divisions are becoming more powerful. Today's college system is implicated in the emergence of class-riven America.

The problem begins with the message sent to young people that they should aspire to college no matter what. Some politicians are among the most visible offenders, treating every failure to go to college as an injustice that can be remedied by increasing government help. American educational administrators reinforce the message by instructing guidance counselors to steer as many students as possible toward a college-prep track (more than 90 percent of high-school students report that their guidance counselors encouraged them to go to college). But politicians and educators are only following the lead of the larger culture. As long as it remains taboo to acknowledge that college is intellectually too demanding for most young people, we will continue to create crazily unrealistic expectations among the next generation. If "crazily unrealistic" sounds too strong, consider that more than 90 percent of high school seniors expect to go to college, and more than 70 percent of them expect to work in professional jobs.

One aspect of this phenomenon has been labeled misaligned ambitions, meaning that adolescents have career ambitions that are inconsistent with their educational plans. Data from the Sloan Study of Youth and Social Development conducted during the 1990s indicate that misaligned ambitions characterized more than half of all adolescents. Almost always, the misalignment is in the optimistic direction, as adolescents aspire to be attorneys or physicians without understanding the educational hurdles they must surmount to achieve their goals.

They end up at a four-year institution not because that is where they can take the courses they need to meet their career goals, but because college is the place where B.A.s are handed out, and everyone knows that these days you've got to have a B.A. Many of them drop out. Of those who entered a four-year college in 1995, only 58 percent had gotten their B.A. five academic years later. Another 14 percent were still enrolled. If we assume that half of that 14 percent eventually get their B.A.s, about a third of all those who entered college hoping for a B.A. leave without one.

If these numbers had been produced in a culture where the 45 B.A. was a nice thing to have but not a big deal, they could be interpreted as the result of young adults deciding that they didn't really want a B.A. after all. Instead, these numbers were produced by a system in which having a B.A. is a very big deal indeed, and that brings us to the increasingly worrisome role of the B.A. as a source of class division. The United States has always had symbols of class, and the college degree has always been one of them. But through the first half of the 20th century, there were all sorts of respectable reasons a person might not go to college—not enough money to pay for college; needing to work right out of high school to support a wife, parents, or younger siblings; or the commonly held belief that going straight to work was better preparation for a business career than going to college. As long as the percentage of college graduates remained small, it also remained true, and everybody knew it, that the majority of America's intellectually most able people did not have B.A.s.

Over the course of the 20th century, three trends gathered strength. The first was the increasing proportion of jobs screened for high academic ability due to the advanced level of education they require—engineers, physicians, attorneys, college teachers, scientists, and the like. The second was the increasing market value of those jobs. The third was the open-ing up of college to more of those who had the academic abil-ity to go to college, partly because the increase in American wealth meant that more parents could afford college for their children, and partly because the proliferation of scholarships and loans made it possible for most students with enough aca-demic ability to go.

The combined effect of these trends has been to overturn the state of affairs that prevailed through World War II. Now the great majority of America's intellectually most able peo-ple do have a B.A. Along with that transformation has come a downside that few anticipated. The acceptable excuses for not going to college have dried up. The more people who go to college, the more stigmatizing the failure to complete col-lege becomes. Today, if you do not get a B.A., many people assume it is because you are too dumb or too lazy. And all this because of a degree that seldom has an interpretable substan-tive meaning.

Let's approach the situation from a different angle. Imagine that America had no system of postsecondary education and you were made a member of a task force assigned to create one from scratch. Ask yourself what you would think if one of your colleagues submitted this proposal:

First, we will set up a common goal for every young person that represents educational success. We will call it a B.A. We will then make it difficult or impossible for most people to achieve this goal. For those who can, achieving the goal will take four years no matter what is being taught. We will attach an economic reward for reaching the goal that often has little to do with the content of what has been learned. We will lure large numbers of people who do not possess adequate ability or motivation to try to achieve the goal and then fail. We will then stigmatize everyone who fails to achieve it.

What I have just described is the system that we have in 50 place. There must be a better way.

Joining the Conversation

1. The "I say" here is explicit: "too many people are going to college." We know what Charles Murray thinks. But why does he think this? In the rest of his essay, he tells us why. Summarize his argument, noting all the reasons and evidence he gives to support his claim.
2. Is Murray right—are too many people going to college? If you disagree, why? Whether or not you agree with him, do you find his argument persuasive?
3. In the middle of the essay is a lengthy narrative about someone who is trying to decide what to be when he grows up, an electrician or a manager. What does this narrative contribute to Murray's argument? Where would the argument be without the narrative?
4. Compare Murray's argument that college is a waste of time for many with Sanford Ungar's argument (pp. 190–96) that anyone can benefit from a college education. Which one do you find more convincing?
5. In one or two paragraphs, reflect on why you chose your current school. Did you consider, first and foremost, how your college would help you "learn how to make a living," as Murray would recommend? Did you consider other potential benefits of your college education? If you could have a well-paying job without a college education, would you go to college anyway?

Blue-Collar Brilliance

MIKE ROSE

—⧉—

MY MOTHER, Rose Meraglio Rose (Rosie), shaped her adult identity as a waitress in coffee shops and family restaurants. When I was growing up in Los Angeles during the 1950s, my father and I would occasionally hang out at the restaurant until her shift ended, and then we'd ride the bus home with her. Sometimes she worked the register and the counter, and we sat there; when she waited booths and tables, we found a booth in the back where the waitresses took their breaks.

There wasn't much for a child to do at the restaurants, and so as the hours stretched out, I watched the cooks and waitresses and listened to what they said. At mealtimes, the pace of the kitchen staff and the din from customers picked up. Weaving in and out around the room, waitresses warned behind

MIKE ROSE is a professor at the UCLA Graduate School of Education and Information Studies. He is well known for his writing on issues of literacy, including the books *Lives on the Boundary: The Struggles and Achievements of America's Underprepared* (1989) and *An Open Language: Selected Writing on Literacy, Learning, and Opportunity* (2006). This article originally appeared in 2009 in the *American Scholar*, a magazine published by the Phi Beta Kappa Society.

Rosie solved technical problems and human problems on the fly.

you in impassive but urgent voices. Standing at the service window facing the kitchen, they called out abbreviated orders. Fry four on two, my mother would say as she clipped a check onto the metal wheel. Her tables were deuces, four-tops, or six-tops according to their size; seating areas also were nicknamed. The racetrack, for instance, was the fast-turnover front section. Lingo conferred authority and signaled know-how.

Rosie took customers' orders, pencil poised over pad, while fielding questions about the food. She walked full tilt through the room with plates stretching up her left arm and two cups of coffee somehow cradled in her right hand. She stood at a table or booth and removed a plate for this person, another for that person, then another, remembering who had the hamburger, who had the fried shrimp, almost always getting it right. She would haggle with the cook about a returned order and rush by us, saying, He gave me lip, but I got him. She'd take a minute to flop down in the booth next to my father. I'm all in, she'd say, and whisper something about a customer. Gripping the outer edge of the table with one hand, she'd watch the room and note, in the flow of our conversation, who needed a refill, whose order was taking longer to prepare than it should, who was finishing up.

I couldn't have put it in words when I was growing up, but what I observed in my mother's restaurant defined the world of adults, a place where competence was synonymous with physical work. I've since studied the working habits of blue-collar workers and have come to understand how much my mother's kind of work demands of both body and brain. A waitress acquires knowledge and intuition about the ways and the rhythms of the restaurant business. Waiting on seven to nine tables, each with two to six customers, Rosie devised memory strategies so that she could remember who ordered what. And because she knew the average time it took to prepare different dishes, she could monitor an order that was taking too long at the service station.

Like anyone who is effective at physical work, my mother 5 learned to work smart, as she put it, to make every move count. She'd sequence and group tasks: What could she do first, then second, then third as she circled through her station? What tasks could be clustered? She did everything on the fly, and when problems arose—technical or human—she solved them within the flow of work, while taking into account the emotional state of her co-workers. Was the manager in a good mood? Did the cook wake up on the wrong side of the bed? If so, how could she make an extra request or effectively return an order?

And then, of course, there were the customers who entered the restaurant with all sorts of needs, from physiological ones, including the emotions that accompany hunger, to a sometimes complicated desire for human contact. Her tip depended on how well she responded to these needs, and so she became adept at reading social cues and managing feelings, both the customers' and her own. No wonder, then, that Rosie was intrigued by psychology. The restaurant became the place where she studied human behavior, puzzling over the problems of her regular customers and refining her ability to deal with people in a difficult world. She took pride in being among the public, she'd say. There isn't a day that goes by in the restaurant that you don't learn something.

My mother quit school in the seventh grade to help raise her brothers and sisters. Some of those siblings made it through high school, and some dropped out to find work in railroad yards, factories, or restaurants. My father finished a grade or two in primary school in Italy and never darkened the schoolhouse door again. I didn't do well in school either. By high school I had accumulated a spotty academic record and many hours of hazy disaffection. I spent a few years on the vocational track, but in my senior year I was inspired by my English teacher and managed to squeak into a small college on probation.

My freshman year was academically bumpy, but gradually I began to see formal education as a means of fulfillment and as a road toward making a living. I studied the humanities and later the social and psychological sciences and taught for ten years in a range of situations—elementary school, adult education courses, tutoring centers, a program for Vietnam veterans who wanted to go to college. Those students had socio-economic and educational backgrounds similar to mine. Then I went back to graduate school to study education and cognitive psychology and eventually became a faculty member in a school of education

Intelligence is closely associated with formal education—the type of schooling a person has, how much and how long—and most people seem to move comfortably from that notion to a belief that work requiring less schooling requires less intelligence. These assumptions run through our cultural history, from the post-Revolutionary War period, when mechanics were characterized by political rivals as illiterate and therefore incapable of participating in government, until today. More than once I've heard a manager label his workers as "a bunch of dummies." Generalizations about intelligence, work, and social class deeply affect our assumptions about ourselves and each other, guiding the ways we use our minds to learn, build knowledge, solve problems, and make our way through the world.

Although writers and scholars have often looked at the working class, they have generally focused on the values such workers exhibit rather than on the thought their work requires—a subtle but pervasive omission. Our cultural iconography promotes the muscled arm, sleeve rolled tight against biceps, but no brightness behind the eye, no image that links hand and brain.

One of my mother's brothers, Joe Meraglio, left school in the ninth grade to work for the Pennsylvania Railroad. From there he joined the Navy, returned to the railroad, which was already in decline, and eventually joined his older brother at General Motors where, over a 33-year career, he moved from working on the assembly line to supervising the paint-and-body department. When I was a young man, Joe took me on a tour of the factory. The floor was loud—in some places deafening—and when I turned a corner or opened a door, the smell of chemicals knocked my head back. The work was repetitive and taxing, and the pace was inhumane.

Still, for Joe the shop floor provided what school did not; it was like schooling, he said, a place where you're constantly learning. Joe learned the most efficient way to use his body by acquiring a set of routines that were quick and preserved energy. Otherwise he would never have survived on the line.

As a foreman, Joe constantly faced new problems and became a consummate multi-tasker, evaluating a flurry of demands quickly, parceling out physical and mental resources, keeping a number of ongoing events in his mind, returning to whatever task had been interrupted, and maintaining a cool head under the pressure of grueling production schedules. In the midst of all this, Joe learned more and more about the auto industry, the technological and social dynamics of the shop floor, the machinery and production processes, and the basics of paint chemistry and of plating and baking. With further promotions, he not only solved problems but also began to find problems to solve: Joe initiated the redesign of the nozzle on a paint sprayer, thereby eliminating costly and unhealthy overspray. And he found a way to reduce energy costs on the baking ovens without affecting the quality of the paint. He lacked formal knowledge of how the machines under his supervision worked, but he had direct experience with them, hands-on knowledge, and was savvy about their quirks and operational capabilities. He could experiment with them.

In addition, Joe learned about budgets and management. Coming off the line as he did, he had a perspective of workers' needs and management's demands, and this led him to think

With an eighth-grade education, Joe (hands together) advanced to supervisor of a G.M. paint-and-body department.

of ways to improve efficiency on the line while relieving some of the stress on the assemblers. He had each worker in a unit learn his or her co-workers' jobs so they could rotate across stations to relieve some of the monotony. He believed that rotation would allow assemblers to get longer and more frequent breaks. It was an easy sell to the people on the line. The union, however, had to approve any modification in job duties, and the managers were wary of the change. Joe had to argue his case on a number of fronts, providing him a kind of rhetorical education.

Eight years ago I began a study of the thought processes 15 involved in work like that of my mother and uncle. I catalogued the cognitive demands of a range of blue-collar and service jobs, from waitressing and hair styling to plumbing and welding. To gain a sense of how knowledge and skill develop, I observed experts as well as novices. From the details of this close examination, I tried to fashion what I called "cognitive biographies" of blue-collar workers. Biographical accounts of the lives of scientists, lawyers, entrepreneurs, and other professionals are rich with detail about the intellectual dimension of their work. But the life stories of working-class people are few and are typically accounts of hardship and courage or the achievements wrought by hard work.

Our culture—in Cartesian fashion—separates the body from the mind, so that, for example, we assume that the use of a tool does not involve abstraction. We reinforce this notion by defining intelligence solely on grades in school and numbers on IQ tests. And we employ social biases pertaining to a person's place on the occupational ladder. The distinctions among blue, pink, and white collars carry with them attributions of character, motivation, and intelligence. Although we rightly acknowledge and amply compensate the play of mind in white-collar and professional work, we diminish or erase it in considerations about other endeavors—physical and service work particularly. We also often ignore the experience of everyday work in administrative deliberations and policymaking.

But here's what we find when we get in close. The plumber seeking leverage in order to work in tight quarters and the hair stylist adroitly handling scissors and comb manage their bodies strategically. Though work-related actions become routine with experience, they were learned at some point through observation, trial and error, and, often, physical or verbal assistance from a co-worker or trainer. I've frequently observed novices talking to themselves as they take on a task, or shaking their head or hand as if to erase an attempt before trying again. In fact, our traditional notions of routine performance could keep us from appreciating the many instances within routine where quick decisions and adjustments are made. I'm struck by the thinking-in-motion that some work requires, by all the mental activity that can be involved in simply getting from one place to another: the waitress rushing back through her station to the kitchen or the foreman walking the line.

The use of tools requires the studied refinement of stance, grip, balance, and fine-motor skills. But manipulating tools is intimately tied to knowledge of what a particular instrument can do in a particular situation and do better than other similar tools. A worker must also know the characteristics of the material one is engaging—how it reacts to various cutting or compressing devices, to degrees of heat, or to lines of force. Some of these things demand judgment, the weighing of options, the consideration of multiple variables, and, occasionally, the creative use of a tool in an unexpected way.

In manipulating material, the worker becomes attuned to aspects of the environment, a training or disciplining of perception that both enhances knowledge and informs perception. Carpenters have an eye for length, line, and angle; mechanics troubleshoot by listening; hair stylists are attuned to shape, texture, and motion. Sensory data merge with concept, as when an auto mechanic relies on sound, vibration, and even smell to understand what cannot be observed.

Planning and problem solving have been studied since the 20 earliest days of modern cognitive psychology and are considered core elements in Western definitions of intelligence. To work is to solve problems. The big difference between the psychologist's laboratory and the workplace is that in the former the problems are isolated and in the latter they are embedded in the real-time flow of work with all its messiness and social complexity.

Much of physical work is social and interactive. Movers determining how to get an electric range down a flight of stairs require coordination, negotiation, planning, and the establishing of incremental goals. Words, gestures, and sometimes a quick pencil sketch are involved, if only to get the rhythm right. How important it is, then, to consider the social and communicative dimension of physical work, for it provides the medium for so much of work's intelligence.

Given the ridicule heaped on blue-collar speech, it might seem odd to value its cognitive content. Yet, the flow of talk at work provides the channel for organizing and distributing tasks, for troubleshooting and problem solving, for learning new information and revising old. A significant amount of teaching, often informal and indirect, takes place at work. Joe Meraglio saw that much of his job as a supervisor involved instruction. In some service occupations, language and communication are central: observing and interpreting behavior and expression, inferring mood and motive, taking on the perspective of others, responding appropriately to social cues, and knowing when you're understood. A good hair stylist, for instance, has the ability to convert vague requests (I want something light and summery) into an appropriate cut through questions, pictures, and hand gestures.

Verbal and mathematical skills drive measures of intelligence in the Western Hemisphere, and many of the kinds of work I studied are thought to require relatively little proficiency in either. Compared to certain kinds of white-collar occupations, that's true. But written symbols flow through physical work.

Numbers are rife in most workplaces: on tools and gauges, as measurements, as indicators of pressure or concentration or temperature, as guides to sequence, on ingredient labels, on lists and spreadsheets, as markers of quantity and price. Certain jobs require workers to make, check, and verify calculations, and to collect and interpret data. Basic math can be involved, and some workers develop a good sense of numbers and patterns. Consider, as well, what might be called material mathematics: mathematical functions embodied in materials and actions, as when a carpenter builds a cabinet or a flight of stairs. A simple mathematical act can extend quickly beyond itself. Measuring, for example, can involve more than recording the dimensions of an object. As I watched a cabinetmaker measure a long strip of wood, he read a number off the tape out loud, looked back over his shoulder to the kitchen wall, turned back to his task, took another measurement, and paused for a moment in thought. He was solving a problem involving the molding, and the measurement was important to his deliberation about structure and appearance.

In the blue-collar workplace, directions, plans, and reference books rely on illustrations, some representational and others, like blueprints, that require training to interpret. Esoteric symbols—visual jargon—depict switches and receptacles, pipe fittings, or types of welds. Workers themselves often make sketches on the job. I frequently observed them grab a pencil to sketch something on a scrap of paper or on a piece of the material they were installing.

Though many kinds of physical work don't require a high literacy level, more reading occurs in the blue-collar workplace than is generally thought, from manuals and catalogues to work orders and invoices, to lists, labels, and forms. With routine tasks, for example, reading is integral to understanding production quotas, learning how to use an instrument, or applying a product. Written notes can initiate action, as in restaurant orders or reports of machine malfunction, or they can serve as memory aids.

True, many uses of writing are abbreviated, routine, and repetitive, and they infrequently require interpretation or analysis. But analytic moments can be part of routine activities, and seemingly basic reading and writing can be cognitively rich. Because workplace language is used in the flow of other activities, we can overlook the remarkable coordination of words, numbers, and drawings required to initiate and direct action.

If we believe everyday work to be mindless, then that will affect the work we create in the future. When we devalue the full range of everyday cognition, we offer limited educational opportunities and fail to make fresh and meaningful instructional connections among disparate kinds of skill and knowledge. If we think that whole categories of people—identified by class or occupation—are not that bright, then we reinforce social separations and cripple our ability to talk across cultural divides.

Affirmation of diverse intelligence is not a retreat to a softhearted definition of the mind. To acknowledge a broader range of intellectual capacity is to take seriously the concept of cognitive variability, to appreciate in all the Rosies and Joes the thought that drives their accomplishments and defines who they are. This is a model of the mind that is worthy of a democratic society.

Joining the Conversation

1. This essay begins with a fairly detailed description of Mike Rose's mother at her work as a waitress in the 1950s, when

he was a child. How is this description related to his argument? Is it an effective opening? Why or why not?

2. How would you summarize Rose's overall argument? What evidence does he offer as support? How convincing is his argument?

3 Where does Rose mention differing views, and what is his reason for bringing them up? What are these other views, and who holds them?

4. How do you think Rose would respond to Charles Murray's argument (pp. 222–42) that many students lack the intellectual potential to succeed in college?

5. Write an essay in which you consider the intellectual demands of a kind of work that you have done or are interested in.

A Lifetime of Student Debt? Not Likely

ROBIN WILSON

—▣—

ONE COLLEGE GRADUATE had smashed a ceramic piggy bank, while another had adorned a life-size human statue with nothing but a silver ball and chain. A third drew a picture of a woman in a red coat stumbling down a seemingly endless pathway. The objects were all part of an art show last month in which graduates expressed fear and frustration over their student-loan debt.

The show joins a number of increasingly high-pitched campaigns aimed at exposing what some consider a national crisis: Student-loan borrowing that is threatening the financial future of today's college students. In January a lawyer with $100,000 in education debt started a Facebook campaign urging the federal government to "free us of our obligations to repay our out-of-control student loan debt." *Forbes* magazine published an article that same month called "The Great College Hoax," which said

ROBIN WILSON, a reporter for the *Chronicle of Higher Education*, is a graduate of the College of Wooster in Ohio and won a prize from the Education Writers Association in 2004 for her reporting on college faculty. This article was the cover story for the May 22, 2009, issue of the *Chronicle of Higher Education*.

that the decision to borrow to attend college often amounts to a "financial disaster." A month later, a book came out decrying college debt, with the title *The Student Loan Scam: The Most Oppressive Debt in U.S. History and How We Can Fight Back.*

But is it really all that bad?

"There are some really poignant, painful stories," says Michael S. McPherson, an economist and president of the Spencer Foundation, which supports educational research. "But they aren't the typical American experience."

In fact, despite stories of a large number of students who face ₅ gargantuan debt, about a third of graduates leave college with no debt at all for their education. Of the 65 percent who face debt, the average they owe is around $20,000. That's just below the starting price of a 2009 Ford Escape.

"Most people borrow a reasonable amount of money, they pay it back, and they are better for having gone to college," says Mr. McPherson.

But for a vocal minority of borrowers, problems with student-loan debt are very real. About 8 percent of undergraduates borrow at least double the national average.

Why do some students borrow more than $40,000 for a bachelor's degree when average borrowing is only half that? The answer is almost never that they are from very low-income families and need that much money to get a four-year degree. Public four-year colleges charged an average of just $6,585 for in-state tuition and fees in 2008–9. The total cost, including textbooks, room and board, and other living expenses, averages $18,326 a year and financial aid brings that figure down for many students.

More often, the problem among students who go heavily into debt is that they are determined to attend their dream college, no matter the cost.

"People don't pay attention to the debt," says Mark 10
Kantrowitz, publisher of FinAid, a Web site about student aid.
"They want to be able to pay for the school they have wanted
to go to for as long as they can remember, and they are willing to do whatever it takes."

"Life Sentence"?

Students whom financial-aid experts call "overborrowers"
capture most of the media's attention. "If you are a writer
vying for a story on Page 1, which story do you want to write?"
asks Mr. McPherson. "Is it going to be the careful story driven
by the data, or is it going to be the headline that can scare
people?"

He's talking about headlines like the one on a CNN report
in 2006 that called student loans "A Life Sentence" and said:
"Forget about getting married and buying a home. This generation is thinking about next month's payment."

But data on the average student-loan borrower tell a very
different story. Figures compiled by the U.S. Education Department show that while roughly two-thirds of students graduated
from four-year colleges in 2003–4 with some education debt,
on average they borrowed $19,202. Those who attended pub-
lic institutions graduated with an average debt of $17,277, and
those from private colleges $21,957.

The data have been updated by the Project on Student Debt,
a nonprofit research-and-policy organization, which found that
for the Class of 2007, graduates' average debt was $18,482 at
public colleges and $23,065 at private ones.

Jill McCusker graduated in 2007 from Stonehill College, a 15
Roman Catholic institution in Massachusetts. Her $30,000 in
education loans put her above the average, but she is manag-

ing her $300-a-month payments by living with her mother for now. She doesn't regret her decision to attend Stonehill or even to borrow $30,000—although it has caused her to delay her plans to live in an apartment in Boston with a friend. "I really love the school and I felt it would look good on a résumé," says Ms. McCusker, who earns $39,000 a year working in an entry-level position for buyers at the headquarters of Talbots, a chain of women's clothing stores.

Ms. McCusker is among the silent majority of borrowers who are repaying their student loans without much complaint (see related articles). Her story stands in stark contrast to thousands of others on a new Facebook page that calls on the U.S. government to forgive all student loans. Robert Applebaum, who started the page, has been amazed to attract 188,766 friends and counting. With nearly $100,000 in education debt, though, he has a story far different from Ms. McCusker's. Mr. Applebaum incurred his loans during law school, for which the average graduate borrowed $70,933 in 2003–4.

Part of the confusion over the student-loan issue is that undergraduate debt is frequently conflated with graduate and professional-school debt—which is typically much, much higher. In 2003–4, for example, medical-school graduates borrowed an average of $113,661. Student-aid experts say the higher debt makes sense for people who earn degrees in law, business, and medicine because they are much more capable of landing high-paying jobs and paying off larger loans. (Mr. Applebaum has struggled because he went to an expensive law school but then took a low-paying job with the district attorney's office in Brooklyn, N.Y.)

Still, many economists say borrowing for any kind of higher education is generally a smart idea. That's partly because student loans typically carry low interest rates. "College is a very good investment, and most students take out too few loans, not too many," says Caroline M. Hoxby, a professor of economics at Stanford University.

Anthony P. Carnevale, director of Georgetown University's Center on Education and the Workforce, agrees. "From an economist's point of view, debt is the very best way to pay for education because you're shifting the cost forward until you'll be earning more money," he says. "You borrow cheap money. It's really a very good bargain."

Patrick M. Callan, president of the National Center for Public Policy and Higher Education, is not as sanguine about the value of borrowing. Still, "the only thing worse than borrowing," he says, "is not borrowing and not going to college at all."

Data on salaries back him up. According to the Census Bureau, the average college graduate earned $57,181 in 2007, while the average high-school graduate earned just $31,286. That means college graduates earned about 80 percent more that year than high-school graduates did. Over a lifetime, those extra earnings stack up. According to a 2002 report by the Census Bureau, a college graduate can expect to earn nearly $1 million more in lifetime earnings than a high-school graduate can.

"Alarmists have tried to change the public story on student-loan debt" by questioning whether borrowing for college is worth it, says Sandy Baum, a senior analyst at the College Board. But a student who graduates with $20,000 in debt should be able to make at least that amount in extra earnings in one to two years' time, she calculates, simply by having earned a college diploma.

Even in this economy, college graduates are much better off than high-school graduates. Yes, white-collar employees are losing their jobs. But the unemployment rate for people over 25 years old who hold at least a bachelor's degree is 4.4 percent, compared with 9.3 percent for people that age who hold only a high-school diploma, according to the Bureau of Labor Statistics.

Borrowing Risk

People concerned about student-loan debt say the problem is not that college isn't worth borrowing for, or even that today's average loan amount is too much.

What bothers advocacy groups like the Project on Student Debt is how many more students are borrowing now compared with a decade ago, how much more they are borrowing, and what that says about the affordability of a college education. 25

In 1993, the project has found, fewer than half of graduating seniors had loans, compared with 65 percent in 2003–4. Among those with loans, the average debt has more than doubled, from $9,250 in 1993 to $19,200 in 2003–4.

"It used to be that, 10 to 20 years ago, if you went to a four-year public institution, had a low to moderate income, and worked a reasonable amount part time in school, there was enough aid. And public institutions were better financed, so you could come out with no debt," says Lauren J. Asher, acting president of the group. "That same student now would have to borrow to get their education. A college degree is still a good investment, but the financial risk for the student has increased."

Indeed, Ms. Asher points out that more college graduates are carrying unmanageably high student-loan debts of at least $40,000. A study by the project found that in 1993, only about

1.3 percent of graduating seniors had borrowed the current equivalent of at least $40,000. By 2004 the proportion had risen to 7.7 percent.

High student-loan debt, says Ms. Asher, "can ruin someone for life." Many borrowers who find themselves in trouble use options under the federal loan program that allow them to postpone repayments on their loans for years. The problem is that because interest keeps racking up during such a deferment and after a default, the amount a borrower owes can soar.

That's what happened to Alan M. Collinge, founder of StudentLoanJustice.org, an advocacy group. He took out $38,000 in loans, which included $1,500 for an undergraduate degree and $23,000 for a master's program in aerospace engineering. In 1999 he took a research position at the University of Southern California at $35,000 a year. By 2001, after he had spent $6,000 on an invention that didn't pan out and had a car accident that cost him $1,500, he realized that he could no longer pay his bills, including his $362-a-month education debt. He went to his boss, asked for a 30-percent pay raise, and quickly found himself out of a job and in default on his student loans. His student-loan debt now has reached $120,000.

In February, Mr. Collinge published *The Student Loan Scam*, which blames lenders for using harsh collection tactics and failing to work with distressed borrowers—some of whose stories he details in the book and on his Web site. He acknowledges that these borrowers fall at the margins of the student-loan experience, but argues, "The margins are important because those are real people."

It is not that difficult for borrowers to find themselves in trouble, Ms. Asher says. "People lose control of their finances, and sometimes they make choices you wish they hadn't made."

That could probably be said of Darla M. Horn, who organized the student-loan-debt art show last month in Long Island City, N.Y. Ms. Horn says she has taken responsibility for repaying her $80,000 in undergraduate student loans. Until recently she earned $100,000 a year and could afford her repayments of $650 a month. (She is between jobs now and recently put her loans in forbearance while she worked on the art show, which she said was meant "to boost awareness of the growing burden of student-loan debt in an ever-tightening, ever-globalizing economy.") But she says she is not sure anyone should lend college students so much money, even if they are willing to take it.

Ms. Horn didn't have to borrow all that she did to earn a four-year degree, but she wanted to get far away from the small Texas town on the Louisiana border where she grew up. So she enrolled at the State University of New York College at Purchase and borrowed about $25,000 a year for the final three years to pay her out-of-state tuition. "There really wasn't a whole lot of thinking behind it," says Ms. Horn, whose parents hadn't saved much for her higher education. "I could have gone to a public school in Texas for less, but I wanted to go to New York and start a new life."

When she graduated, she realized that she didn't even know 35 how much money she had borrowed. "I can humbly say that I was completely financially illiterate," she says. "I was just signing the documents and faxing them back."

Experiences like Ms. Horn's aren't uncommon, say higher-education experts. Indeed, heavy borrowers are not necessarily poor students who would have been forced to forgo higher education if they hadn't received extravagant sums. Rather, some students enroll in high-priced for-profit programs only to learn later that their certificates or degrees are not as useful on the job market as they had expected. Students who attend four-year programs at for-profit institutions borrow much more on average—about $28,138 each in 2003–4—than students at nonprofit institutions do. Others borrow large amounts to attend pricey traditional four-year colleges but have no idea what kind of jobs they might land upon graduation and so have no way to judge whether they will be able to repay their loans.

"Intimidated by the Complexity"

Meanwhile, it is no one's job to talk with students about whether the amounts they are borrowing line up with their professional aspirations or even their immediate job prospects.

"College academic advisers are intimidated by the complexity of financial aid," says Jacqueline E. King, assistant vice president for policy analysis at the American Council on Education. Financial-aid offices say to students, "You make the academic decisions, and we will try to get you the money to pay for it," she says. Sitting down with each student to judge the wisdom of the amount he or she has borrowed would be impossible, particularly at large universities, she says.

Donald A. Saleh, vice president for enrollment management at Syracuse University, says it does try to advise students. According to a recent analysis by *U.S. News & World Report*, 63 percent of students in Syracuse's class of 2007 took out education loans, borrowing an average of $27,152. That landed the university on the magazine's list of universities with the heaviest student borrowing. (*U.S. News* uses the mean when calculating average debt, while Syracuse uses the median, which is only $22,600 on average per student).

"We can advise students about what we think is right, and 40
we will caution students," says Mr. Saleh. "But if they have the
legal ability to borrow the money, we can't prevent that from
happening."

New York University—where student borrowers graduated
with an average of $33,637 in debt in 2007—has begun con-
tacting high-school seniors it has admitted to make sure they
understand the debt load they could incur if they enroll (*The
Chronicle*, May 1).

Deanne Loonin, director of the Student Loan Borrower
Assistance Project at the National Consumer Law Center, says
students shouldn't rely on their colleges to warn them about
overborrowing. "It's too great a conflict of interest for schools
that are essentially selling a product to be expected to be the
ones who are going to be conservative financial counselors,"
she says.

Besides, students are not always open to such advice. "Making the college choice is a very emotional decision," says
Allesandra Lanza, a spokeswoman for American Student Assistance, a loan-guarantee agency in Boston. "It is not just the
education you are receiving, but this whole idea of an experience that will change your life," she says. That makes it difficult for people to step back and ask, "Is this the most valuable
use of your dollars?"

Sometimes the hopes and dreams of an entire family can get
caught up in a decision about where to attend college. That's
particularly the case at religious institutions, says John Maguire,
who is chairman of Maguire Associates, a higher-education
consulting firm in Bedford, Mass. "For families who believe
deeply in the mission of a Christian college, this is a school
they'll spend any amount of money on," he says. "When people are saying, 'This will make a huge difference in my kid's

life,' they are not talking about income. They are talking about whether their kid is going to go to church on Sundays, whether they will raise their own kids in the church, or even whether they will get into heaven."

Robert A. Sevier, senior vice president at Stamats Inc., 45 a higher-education marketing firm in Cedar Rapids, Iowa, doesn't have a lot of sympathy for college graduates who find they cannot repay their education loans. Overborrowing for college isn't much different than overborrowing for a home, he says. "People live outside their means."

But that doesn't describe most college graduates, he adds. "In spite of all the hysterical extremes, there are a lot of people in the middle who are making things work. They are graduating from college with $20,000 in debt; they are going to graduate school, getting jobs, and buying homes within their means."

Living Just "Like Normal People" on a Schoolteacher's Salary

Robert Carter

Bunker Hill, W.Va.; graduated from Bryan College (Tenn.) 2006; student-loan debt at graduation: $30,000. Paying off his student loans on a schoolteacher's salary has forced Robert Carter to make some tough decisions. He still drives his 2001 Ford Escape, which has 150,000 miles, and he and his wife couldn't afford to buy a big enough home in the county where he teaches, so they had to look farther out.

But Mr. Carter says they still enjoy many aspects of the American dream. "We definitely have been able to live like normal people," he says. "We have satellite TV, we have Internet, we both keep cellphones. We function. It's not like you see us and you say, Man, that guy needs a handout."

In fact, Mr. Carter says he and his wife, Jing Chen, who is pregnant and is substitute teaching, are quite comfortable. "If some of my college friends were to come and hang out with us for the day they might be impressed," he says. "They get to sit on a nice couch, have a nice meal, and watch TV on a big screen. It's not all luxury for sure, but we're doing OK."

Mr. Carter earns $41,000 teaching science to sixth and sev- 50 enth graders at Johnson-Williams Middle School in Virginia, where he is chairman of his department. And he just completed a two-year master's degree at Shenandoah University—paid for in part by the university and by his school district—that will bring him an extra $6,250 a year. He also earns a few thousand dollars more each year working at a shoe store on Saturdays and during summers.

Mr. Carter is from Virginia, and he knows he could have attended a public university in the state for less than what he paid in tuition at Bryan, a Christian college in Tennessee. His parents didn't help him with his education bills, so he was on his own and had to borrow more than the average student does.

"It was definitely worth it," he says. "I've picked up some lessons at Bryan that are mostly a credit to the education professors that I don't feel I could have gotten everywhere else. The professors helped me shape my philosophy and with tests I've had to take to be a teacher. Every time I left one of those tests, I felt like I remembered learning that at Bryan."

While Mr. Carter was pursing his master's degree, his student loans were in deferral. The $200-a-month repayments start again in August. Mr. Carter is prepared. "We bought a house for probably at least $40,000 less than what we qualified for," he says.

Still, he is always looking for ways to spend less. Recently, when he called his satellite-television provider and asked if it could do anything for him, the company knocked $10 a month off the bill.

When it comes to entertainment, Mr. Carter and his wife 55 don't need much. On weekends, they rent movies for $1 a night and visit their families who live nearby.

But making his loan payments will cause Mr. Carter some pain. He has always considered himself a big saver, and with all of his bills now he just can't put money in the bank. "The hardest thing about the student loans is that your budget is right at the max, so there isn't a lot of room for saving," he says. "It becomes one of those things that you can't do, and I feel like on that I've lost a part of me."

"I Didn't Want to Borrow More Than I Could Reasonably Pay Back"

Sara M. Harrington

Iowa City, Iowa; graduated from U. of Iowa, 2004; student-loan debt at graduation: $23,000. Before 8 a.m. every weekday, Sara M. Harrington and her husband fit their 9-month-old daughter into her car seat and drive a mile to a babysitter's house before going on to the University of Iowa, where Sara's husband drops her at her office. He drives three more blocks to his own office, in the information-technology department of a local hospital. They do the whole thing in reverse at 4:30 p.m.

Limiting themselves to just one car, a Ford Freestyle, is a sacrifice the couple have made so they can pay off their student loans. Each of them graduated with around $23,000 in education debt, and their monthly repayments total $500—the third-highest item on their monthly budget, after the mortgage and the day-care bill.

Because of their education loans, Ms. Harrington says, they were also frugal when they bought a 1,700 square-foot home, in 2006. "We didn't buy the most expensive house we could afford, knowing that we have these student-loan expenses for 10 years," she says.

They also use cloth diapers and Ms. Harrington continues 60 to breast-feed their baby, in part to save money. And instead of expensive nights out, most of their weekend entertainment is getting together over potluck dinners with other couples.

But Ms. Harrington says borrowing for her education was worth it. She knew enough from her work-study job in the financial-aid office as an undergraduate not to overborrow. "My parents would have borrowed for me, but I felt because it was my education, it was my responsibility," she says. "I willingly took it on myself. But I didn't want to borrow more than I could reasonably pay back with a major in psychology."

Ms. Harrington earns $36,000 a year working as a full-time counselor in the university's Office of Financial Aid. Her portion of the loan repayments amounts to $245 a month. Despite the sacrifices, she says, she doesn't feel deprived: "I have a car, a house, and a baby, and I've been able to move forward with my life."

The Harringtons also have enough left in their monthly budget to stash money away for expensive purchases, like the big-screen television set and the patio furniture they recently bought. Now they are saving to do some landscaping and for new kitchen countertops.

Working in the financial-aid office has given Ms. Harrington a lot of insight into how students pay for college. She and her husband are already saving for their baby daughter's education.

"I don't want her to graduate with an enormous amount 65 of debt equal to a mortgage on a nice home," says Ms. Harrington. "We plan to teach her savvy money skills from a young age."

For a First-Generation Graduate, Debt Was the Best Decision

Jennifer M. Holl

Chadds Ford, Pa.; graduated from Denison U., 1999; student-loan debt at graduation: $20,000. Before Jennifer M. Holl graduated from Denison University with a bachelor's degree in American history 10 years ago, she sat down with a student-loan officer to go over her promissory notes and calculate her monthly student-loan repayments. When the loan officer tallied up the loans and told Ms. Holl she owed $20,000, the young graduate burst into tears.

"That's when reality hit me," says Ms. Holl, who hadn't thought about the debt in one lump sum.

Now, a decade after graduation, Ms. Holl says the $20,000 she borrowed was one of the best spending decisions she has ever made.

"Honestly I don't regret it at all, and I'd do it again in a heartbeat," she says. "Denison opened up a gateway of opportunities, socially and educationally."

Ms. Holl, whose parents never attended college and 70 couldn't help with her education bills, had qualified for a full ride at Ohio State University. But she wanted to attend Denison because of the personal attention she thought she would get from professors.

"I chose to go to what I thought was the best school that I could get into in the state of Ohio," she says. "I knew it was expensive."

Over the last 10 years, her loan repayments have totaled between $115 and $175 a month, except for the two years she postponed her repayments while she earned a master's degree in history with a certificate in museum studies from the University of Delaware. Ms. Holl believes her degree from Denison helped her land a full scholarship at Delaware.

Over the years, Ms. Holl has sort of forgotten about her monthly student-loan repayments. They come directly out of her paychecks. "I'm so used to thinking of that money as not being mine I don't even feel it," she says. Still, she probably would have bought a better car by now. She drives a 2001 Volkswagen Jetta with 80,000 miles that is paid off. "It's not a clunker," says Ms. Holl. "But for safety, I'd like to upgrade." That is partly because she has a 20-month-old daughter now.

Ms. Holl and her husband don't take big vacations. "We go to the New Jersey shore," she says. "It's two-and-a-half hours away, and my in-laws have a house so we can go for free."

Ms. Holl's husband works for QVC and had no education 75 loans. One of the first things the couple did when they got married six years ago was use $3,500 they got in wedding gifts to pay down one of her student loans.

Three years ago, they were able to afford a Cape Cod on a half-acre of land in southeastern Pennsylvania that Ms. Holl says "is nicer than a starter house but not a mansion." And after their daughter was born, Ms. Holl scaled back to working part time. She earns $31,000 for 28 hours a week as a registrar at the Delaware Art Museum and is responsible for making arrangements when the museum borrows or lends artwork.

Working as a night manager at McDonald's would probably pay more, she says, but Ms. Holl is pleased that despite her education loans, she could take a lower-paying job with a non-profit organization.

After graduate school, she initially worked in the for-profit sector as a historic-preservation specialist for an engineering consulting firm. "I knew in a relatively short span of time that my heart yearned for the nonprofit world," she says. "While I certainly appreciated the higher salary and benefits that my first job provided for me, I don't miss the frenzied pace, travel, and total emphasis on the bottom line."

Ms. Holl's part-time work schedule, plus her husband's ability to work flextime, allows them—along with Ms. Holl's mother-in-law—to take care of their daughter themselves and eliminate day-care bills.

Back when she was a high-school student in northeastern 80 Ohio, living at home with her parents and two siblings in a modest 1,000-square-foot home, Ms. Holl says, she didn't imagine ever earning a master's degree or working in a museum.

"In my head I'd always wanted that, but given my family background I didn't think it was a possibility," she says. "Without the loans there is no way I could have done it."

Joining the Conversation

1. Robin Wilson makes clear in her opening paragraphs what view she is arguing against. What is that view, and how does she characterize it?

2. This article seems to offer a factual account of the current state of student debt, but it makes an implicit argument

about how students should approach the issue of debt. What is her argument?

3. What are some strategies Wilson employs to emphasize that this is an important topic?

4. Wilson makes considerable use of numerical data and statistics to support her argument. Choose two examples of such data and use them to make an opposing argument.

5. Wilson says that in many cases "the problem among students who go heavily in debt is that they are determined to attend their dream college, no matter the cost." What is her stance on these extreme cases? Take the position of a student who is amassing a large amount of debt to attend his or her dream school, and respond to Wilson's critique.

From *The Influencing Machine: Brooke Gladstone on the Media*, by Brooke Gladstone and Jeff Neufield.

FIFTEEN

IS POP CULTURE ACTUALLY
GOOD FOR YOU?

—▢—

IS THERE ANYBODY UNDER FIFTY whose parents haven't worried that he or she was watching too much TV? It almost goes without saying that most people believe that excessive exposure to the popular media—not only to television shows like *American Idol*, but also to Hollywood films, tabloid magazines, Facebook, video games, and the Internet—both dumbs us down and makes us more likely to tolerate acts of violence if not to commit them ourselves. An article in the *New Yorker* even suggests that the abuse of prisoners by the American military in Iraq and at Guantánamo was directly influenced by the hit TV series *24*, whose hero often resorts to torture to extract information from villains.

Some of the writers in this chapter, however, argue that such alarmist views of the popular media are seriously overstated. Steven Johnson, for example, acknowledges that TV shows and video games do perhaps "dumb us down" but argues that the more sophisticated ones actually deepen our intelligence and sharpen our ability to follow multiple plot lines and narratives. Similarly, Jason Zinser argues that programs such as *The Daily*

Show may enlighten their audiences, while Antonia Peacocke suggests that *Family Guy* insightfully satirizes United States culture, even if it sometimes takes its jokes too far. Tom Bissell challenges the idea that video games are an intellectual wasteland, insisting that certain games are both cognitively challenging and aesthetically pleasing. David Crystal makes the case that text messaging is a creative form of communication that enriches the English language.

These views are countered by Roz Chast, who shows what instant messaging might have done to Shakespeare's lofty language. Malcolm Gladwell questions the potential of Twitter and other social media to play more than a superficial role in attracting people to participate in political movements, and Dennis Baron points out that just as a new technology can kindle uprisings, so too can it be used to suppress them. Dana Stevens, on the other hand, doesn't buy any of the above arguments, questioning those who think that TV and other forms of popular culture are "good" for us as well as those who think the opposite.

The final author in this unit, Gerald Graff, shifts the focus of the discussion slightly, suggesting that it matters less whether we read Marvel comics or *Macbeth*, as long as we approach what we read with a critical eye and question it in analytical, intellectual ways.

Watching TV Makes You Smarter

STEVEN JOHNSON

SCIENTIST A: *Has he asked for anything special?*
SCIENTIST B: *Yes, this morning for breakfast . . . he requested something
called "wheat germ, organic honey and tiger's milk."*
SCIENTIST A: *Oh, yes. Those were the charmed substances that some years
ago were felt to contain life-preserving properties.*
SCIENTIST B: *You mean there was no deep fat? No steak or cream pies or
. . . hot fudge?*
SCIENTIST A: *Those were thought to be unhealthy.*

—From Woody Allen's Sleeper

ON JANUARY 24, the Fox network showed an episode of its
hit drama *24*, the real-time thriller known for its cliffhanger
tension and often-gruesome violence. Over the preceding
weeks, a number of public controversies had erupted around

STEVEN JOHNSON is the author of seven books, among them *Everything Bad Is Good for You: How Today's Popular Culture Is Actually
Making Us Smarter* (2005) and *Where Good Ideas Come From: The Natural History of Innovation* (2010). Johnson is also a contributing editor for *Wired*, writes a monthly column for *Discover*, and teaches
journalism at New York University. The piece included here was first
published in the *New York Times Magazine* in 2005; it is an excerpt
from *Everything Bad Is Good for You*.

24, mostly focused on its portrait of Muslim terrorists and its penchant for torture scenes. The episode that was shown on the twenty-fourth only fanned the flames higher: in one scene, a terrorist enlists a hit man to kill his child for not fully supporting the jihadist cause; in another scene, the secretary of defense authorizes the torture of his son to uncover evidence of a terrorist plot.

But the explicit violence and the post-9/11 terrorist anxiety are not the only elements of *24* that would have been unthinkable on prime-time network television 20 years ago. Alongside the notable change in content lies an equally notable change in form. During its 44 minutes—a real-time hour, minus 16 minutes for commercials—the episode connects the lives of 21 distinct characters, each with a clearly defined "story arc," as the Hollywood jargon has it: a defined personality with motivations and obstacles and specific relationships with other characters. Nine primary narrative threads wind their way through those 44 minutes, each drawing extensively upon events and information revealed in earlier episodes. Draw a map of all those intersecting plots and personalities, and you get structure that—where formal complexity is concerned—more closely resembles *Middlemarch* than a hit TV drama of years past like *Bonanza*.

For decades, we've worked under the assumption that mass culture follows a path declining steadily toward lowest-common-denominator standards, presumably because the **For other ways of representing "standard views," see p. 23.** "masses" want dumb, simple pleasures and big media companies try to give the masses what they want. But as that *24* episode suggests, the exact opposite is happening: the culture is getting more cognitively demanding, not less. To make sense of an episode of *24*, you have to integrate far more information than you would have a few decades ago watching a comparable show. Beneath the violence and the ethnic stereotypes, another trend appears: to keep up with entertainment like *24*, you have to pay attention, make inferences, track shifting social relationships. This is what I call the Sleeper Curve: the most debased forms of mass diversion— video games and violent television dramas and juvenile sit-coms—turn out to be nutritional after all.

I believe that the Sleeper Curve is the single most important new force altering the mental development of young people today, and I believe it is largely a force for good: enhancing our cognitive faculties, not dumbing them down. And yet you almost never hear this story in popular accounts of today's media. Instead, you hear dire tales of addiction, violence, mindless escapism. It's assumed that shows that promote smoking or gratuitous violence are bad for us, while those that thunder against teen pregnancy or intolerance have a positive role in society. Judged by that morality-play standard, the story of popular culture over the past 50 years—if not 500—is a story of decline: the morals of the stories have grown darker and more ambiguous, and the antiheroes have multiplied.

The usual counterargument here is that what media have 5 lost in moral clarity, they have gained in realism. The real world doesn't come in nicely packaged public-service announcements, and we're better off with entertainment like *The Sopranos* that reflects our fallen state with all its ethical ambiguity. I happen to be sympathetic to that argument, but it's not the one I want to make here. I think there is another way to assess the social virtue of pop culture, one that looks at media as a kind of cognitive workout, not as a series of life lessons. There may indeed be more "negative messages" in the mediasphere today. But that's not the only way to evaluate whether our television shows or video games are having a positive impact. Just as important—if not more important—is the kind of thinking you have to do to make sense of a cultural experience. That is where the Sleeper Curve becomes visible.

Televised Intelligence

Consider the cognitive demands that televised narratives place on their viewers. With many shows that we associate with "quality" entertainment—*The Mary Tyler Moore Show*, *Murphy Brown*, *Frasier*—the intelligence arrives fully formed in the words and actions of the characters on-screen. They say witty things to one another and avoid lapsing into tired sitcom clichés, and we smile along in our living rooms, enjoying the company of these smart people. But assuming we're bright enough to understand the sentences they're saying, there's no intellectual labor involved in enjoying the show as a viewer. You no more challenge your mind by watching these intelligent shows than you challenge your body watching *Monday Night Football*. The intellectual work is happening on-screen, not off.

But another kind of televised intelligence is on the rise. Think of the cognitive benefits conventionally ascribed to reading: attention, patience, retention, the parsing of narrative threads. Over the last half-century, programming on TV has increased the demands it places on precisely these mental faculties. This growing complexity involves three primary elements: multiple threading, flashing arrows and social networks.

According to television lore, the age of multiple threads began with the arrival in 1981 of *Hill Street Blues*, the Steven Bochco police drama invariably praised for its "gritty realism." Watch an episode of *Hill Street Blues* side by side with any major drama from the preceding decades—*Starsky and Hutch*, for instance, or *Dragnet*—and the structural transformation will jump out at you. The earlier shows follow one or two lead characters, adhere to a single dominant plot and reach a decisive conclusion at the end of the episode. Draw an outline of the narrative threads in almost every *Dragnet* episode, and it will be a single line: from the initial crime scene, through the investigation, to the eventual cracking of the case. A typical *Starsky and Hutch* episode offers only the slightest variation on this linear formula: the introduction of a comic subplot that usually appears only at the tail ends of the episode, creating a structure that looks like the graph below. The vertical axis represents the number of individual threads, and the horizontal axis is time.

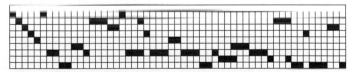

Starsky and Hutch (any episode)

A *Hill Street Blues* episode complicates the picture in a number of profound ways. The narrative weaves together a collection of distinct strands—sometimes as many as 10, though at least half of the threads involve only a few quick scenes scattered through the episode. The number of primary characters—and not just bit parts—swells significantly. And the episode has fuzzy borders: picking up one or two threads from previous episodes at the outset and leaving one or two threads open at the end. Charted graphically, an average episode looks like this graph:

Hill Street Blues (episode 85)

Critics generally cite *Hill Street Blues* as the beginning of "serious drama" narrative in the television medium—differentiating the series from the single-episode dramatic programs from the 1950s, which were Broadway plays performed in front of a camera. But the *Hill Street* innovations weren't all that original; they'd long played a defining role in popular television, just not during the evening hours. The structure of a *Hill Street* episode—and indeed of all the critically acclaimed dramas that followed, from *thirtysomething* to *Six Feet Under*—is the structure of a soap opera. *Hill Street Blues* might have sparked a new golden age of television drama during its seven-year run, but it did so by using a few crucial tricks that *Guiding Light* and *General Hospital* mastered long before.

Bochco's genius with *Hill Street* was to marry complex narrative structure with complex subject matter. *Dallas* had already shown that the extended, interwoven threads of the soap-opera genre could survive the weeklong interruptions of a prime-time show, but the actual content of *Dallas* was fluff. (The most probing issue it addressed was the question, now folkloric, of who shot J.R.) *All in the Family* and *Rhoda* showed that you could tackle complex social issues, but they did their tackling in the comfort of the sitcom living room. *Hill Street* had richly drawn characters confronting difficult social issues and a narrative structure to match.

Since *Hill Street* appeared, the multi-threaded drama has become the most widespread fictional genre on prime time: *St. Elsewhere, L.A. Law, thirtysomething, Twin Peaks, N.Y.P.D. Blue, E.R., The West Wing, Alias, Lost.* (The only prominent holdouts in drama are shows like *Law and Order* that have essentially updated the venerable *Dragnet* format and thus remained anchored to a single narrative line.) Since the early 1980s, however, there has been a noticeable increase in narrative complexity in these dramas. The most ambitious show on TV to date, *The Sopranos*, routinely follows up to a dozen distinct threads over the course of an episode, with more than 20 recurring characters. An episode from late in the first season looks like this:

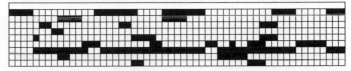

The Sopranos (episode 8)

The total number of active threads equals the multiple plots of *Hill Street*, but here each thread is more substantial. The show doesn't offer a clear distinction between dominant and minor plots; each story line carries its weight in the mix. The episode also displays a chordal mode of storytelling entirely absent from *Hill Street*: a single scene in *The Sopranos* will often connect to three different threads at the same time, layering one plot atop another. And every single thread in this *Sopranos* episode builds on events from previous episodes and continues on through the rest of the season and beyond.

Put those charts together, and you have a portrait of the Sleeper Curve rising over the past 30 years of popular television. In a sense, this is as much a map of cognitive changes in the popular mind as it is a map of on-screen developments, as if the media titans decided to condition our brains to follow ever-larger numbers of simultaneous threads. Before *Hill Street*, the conventional wisdom among television execs was that audiences wouldn't be comfortable following more than three plots in a single episode, and indeed, the *Hill Street* pilot, which was shown in January 1981, brought complaints from viewers that the show was too complicated. Fast-forward two decades, and shows like *The Sopranos* engage their audiences with narratives that make *Hill Street* look like *Three's Company*. Audiences happily embrace that complexity because they've been trained by two decades of multi-threaded dramas.

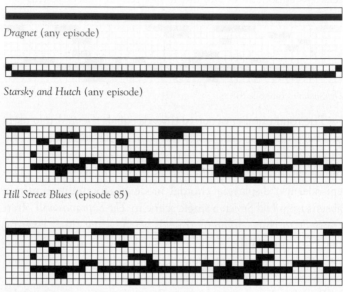

Dragnet (any episode)

Starsky and Hutch (any episode)

Hill Street Blues (episode 85)

The Sopranos (episode 8)

Multi-threading is the most celebrated structural feature of the modern television drama, and it certainly deserves some of the honor that has been doled out to it. And yet multi-threading is only part of the story.

The Case for Confusion

Shortly after the arrival of the first-generation slasher movies— *Halloween, Friday the 13th*—Paramount released a mock-slasher flick called *Student Bodies*, parodying the genre just as the

Scream series would do 15 years later. In one scene, the obligatory nubile teenage baby sitter hears a noise outside a suburban house; she opens the door to investigate, finds nothing and
then goes back inside. As the door shuts behind her, the camera swoops in on the doorknob, and we see that she has left
the door unlocked. The camera pulls back and then swoops
down again for emphasis. And then a flashing arrow appears
on the screen, with text that helpfully explains: "Unlocked!"

That flashing arrow is parody, of course, but it's merely an
exaggerated version of a device popular stories use all the time.
When a sci-fi script inserts into some advanced lab a non-
scientist who keeps asking the science geeks to explain what
they're doing with that particle accelerator, that's a flashing
arrow that gives the audience precisely the information it needs
in order to make sense of the ensuing plot. ("Whatever you do,
don't spill water on it, or you'll set off a massive explosion!")
These hints serve as a kind of narrative hand-holding. Implicitly, they say to the audience, "We realize you have no idea
what a particle accelerator is, but here's the deal: all you need
to know is that it's a big fancy thing that explodes when wet."
They focus the mind on relevant details: "Don't worry about
whether the baby sitter is going to break up with her boyfriend.
Worry about that guy lurking in the bushes." They reduce the
amount of analytic work you need to do to make sense of a
story. All you have to do is follow the arrows.

By this standard, popular television has never been harder
to follow. If narrative threads have experienced a population
explosion over the past 20 years, flashing arrows have grown
correspondingly scarce. Watching our pinnacle of early '80s TV
drama, *Hill Street Blues*, we find there's an informational whole-
ness to each scene that differs markedly from what you see on
shows like *The West Wing* or *The Sopranos* or *Alias* or *E.R.*

Hill Street has ambiguities about future events: will a con-
victed killer be executed? Will Furillo marry Joyce Davenport?
Will Renko find it in himself to bust a favorite singer for
cocaine possession? But the present tense of each scene explains
itself to the viewer with little ambiguity. There's an open question or a mystery driving each of these stories—how will it
all turn out?—but there's no mystery about the immediate
activity on the screen. A contemporary drama like *The West
Wing*, on the other hand, constantly embeds mysteries into the
present-tense events: you see characters performing actions or
discussing events about which crucial information has been
deliberately withheld. Anyone who has watched more than a
handful of *The West Wing* episodes closely will know the feeling: scene after scene refers to some clearly crucial but unex-
plained piece of information, and after the sixth reference,
you'll find yourself wishing you could rewind the tape to figure
out what they're talking about, assuming you've missed something. And then you realize that you're supposed to be confused. The open question posed by these sequences is not "How
will this turn out in the end?" The question is "What's happening right now?"

The deliberate lack of hand-holding extends down to the 20
microlevel of dialogue as well. Popular entertainment that
addresses technical issues—whether they are the intricacies
of passing legislation, or of performing a heart bypass, or of
operating a particle accelerator—conventionally switches
between two modes of information in dialogue: texture and
substance. Texture is all the arcane verbiage provided to
convince the viewer that they're watching Actual Doctors
at Work; substance is the material planted amid the background texture that the viewer needs to make sense of
the plot.

Conventionally, narratives demarcate the line between texture and substance by inserting cues that flag or translate the important data. There's an unintentionally comical moment in the 2004 blockbuster *The Day After Tomorrow* in which the beleaguered climatologist (played by Dennis Quaid) announces his theory about the imminent arrival of a new ice age to a gathering of government officials. In his speech, he warns that "we have hit a critical desalinization point!" At this moment, the writer-director Roland Emmerich—a master of brazen arrow-flashing—has an official follow with the obliging remark: "It would explain what's driving this extreme weather." They might as well have had a flashing "Unlocked!" arrow on the screen.

The dialogue on shows like *The West Wing* and *E.R.*, on the other hand, doesn't talk down to its audiences. It rushes by, the words accelerating in sync with the high-speed tracking shots that glide through the corridors and operating rooms. The characters talk faster in these shows, but the truly remarkable thing about the dialogue is not purely a matter of speed; it's the willingness to immerse the audience in information that most viewers won't understand. Here's a typical scene from *E.R.*:

[WEAVER AND WRIGHT push a gurney containing a 16-year-old girl. Her parents, JANNA AND FRANK MIKAMI, follow close behind. CARTER AND LUCY fall in.]

WEAVER: 16-year-old, unconscious, history of biliary atresia.

CARTER: Hepatic coma?

WEAVER: Looks like it.

MR. MIKAMI: She was doing fine until six months ago.

CARTER: What medication is she on?

MRS. MIKAMI: Ampicillin, tobramycin, vitamins a, d and k.

LUCY: Skin's jaundiced.

WEAVER: Same with the sclera. Breath smells sweet.

CARTER: Fetor hepaticus?

WEAVER: Yep.

LUCY: What's that?

WEAVER: Her liver's shut down. Let's dip a urine. [To CARTER] Guys, it's getting a little crowded in here, why don't you deal with the parents? Start lactulose, 30 cc's per NG.

CARTER: We're giving medicine to clean her blood.

WEAVER: Blood in the urine, two-plus.

CARTER: The liver failure is causing her blood not to clot.

MRS. MIKAMI: Oh, God. . . .

CARTER: Is she on the transplant list?

MR. MIKAMI: She's been Status 2a for six months, but they haven't been able to find her a match.

CARTER: Why? What's her blood type?

MR. MIKAMI: AB.

[This hits CARTER like a lightning bolt. LUCY gets it, too. They share a look.]

There are flashing arrows here, of course—"The liver failure is causing her blood not to clot"—but the ratio of medical jargon to layperson translation is remarkably high. From a purely narrative point of view, the decisive line arrives at the very end: "AB." The 16-year-old's blood type connects her to an earlier plot line, involving a cerebral-hemorrhage victim who—after being dramatically revived in one of the opening scenes—ends up brain-dead. Far earlier, before the liver-failure scene above, Carter briefly discusses harvesting the hemorrhage victim's organs for transplants, and another doctor makes a passing reference to his blood type being the rare AB (thus making him an unlikely donor). The twist here revolves around a statistically unlikely event happening at the E.R.—an otherwise perfect liver donor showing up just in time to donate his liver to a recipient with the same rare blood type. But the show reveals this twist with remarkable subtlety. To make sense of that last "AB" line—and the look of disbelief on Carter's and Lucy's faces—you have to recall a passing remark uttered earlier regarding a character who belongs to a completely different thread. Shows like *E.R.* may have more blood and guts than popular TV had a generation ago, but when it comes to story-telling, they possess a quality that can only be described as subtlety and discretion.

Even Bad TV Is Better

Skeptics might argue that I have stacked the deck here by focusing on relatively highbrow titles like *The Sopranos* or *The West Wing*, when in fact the most significant change in the last five years of narrative entertainment involves reality TV. Does the contemporary pop cultural landscape look quite as promising if the representative show is *Joe Millionaire* instead of *The West Wing*?

I think it does, but to answer that question properly, you have to avoid the tendency to sentimentalize the past. When people talk about the golden age of television in the early '70s—invoking shows like *The Mary Tyler Moore Show* and *All in the Family*—they forget to mention how awful most television programming was during much of that decade. If you're going to look at pop-culture trends, you have to compare apples to apples, or in this case, lemons to lemons. The relevant comparison is not between *Joe Millionaire* and *MASH*; it's between *Joe Millionaire* and *The Newlywed Game*, or between *Survivor* and *The Love Boat*.

What you see when you make these head-to-head compar- 25 isons is that a rising tide of complexity has been lifting programming at the bottom of the quality spectrum and at the top.

The Sopranos is several times more demanding of its audiences than *Hill Street* was, and *Joe Millionaire* has made comparable advances over *Battle of the Network Stars*. This is the ultimate test of the Sleeper Curve theory: even the junk has improved.

If early television took its cues from the stage, today's reality programming is reliably structured like a video game: a series of competitive tests, growing more challenging over time. Many reality shows borrow a subtler device from gaming culture as well: the rules aren't fully established at the outset. You learn as you play.

On a show like *Survivor* or *The Apprentice*, the participants— and the audience—know the general objective of the series, but each episode involves new challenges that haven't been ordained in advance. The final round of the first season of *The Apprentice*, for instance, threw a monkey wrench into the strategy that governed the play up to that point, when Trump announced that the two remaining apprentices would have to assemble and manage a team of subordinates who had already been fired in earlier episodes of the show. All of a sudden the overarching objective of the game—do anything to avoid being fired—presented a potential conflict to the remaining two contenders: the structure of the final round favored the survivor who had maintained the best relationships with his comrades. Suddenly, it wasn't enough just to have clawed your way to the top; you had to have made friends while clawing. The original *Joe Millionaire* went so far as to undermine the most fundamental convention of all—that the show's creators don't openly lie to the contestants about the prizes—by inducing a construction worker to pose as man of means while 20 women competed for his attention.

Reality programming borrowed another key ingredient from games: the intellectual labor of probing the system's rules for weak spots and opportunities. As each show discloses its conventions, and each participant reveals his or her personality traits and background, the intrigue in watching comes from figuring out how the participants should best navigate the environment that has been created for them. The pleasure in these shows comes not from watching other people being humiliated on national television; it comes from depositing other people in a complex, high-pressure environment where no established strategies exist and watching them find their bearings. That's why the water-cooler conversation about these shows invariably tracks in on the strategy displayed on the previous night's episode: why did Kwame pick Omarosa in that final round? What devious strategy is Richard Hatch concocting now?

When we watch these shows, the part of our brain that monitors the emotional lives of the people around us—the part that tracks subtle shifts in intonation and gesture and facial expression—scrutinizes the action on the screen, looking for clues. We trust certain characters implicitly and vote others off the island in a heartbeat. Traditional narrative shows also trigger emotional connections to the characters, but those connections don't have the same participatory effect, because traditional narratives aren't explicitly about strategy. The phrase "Monday-morning quarterbacking" describes the engaged feeling that spectators have in relation to games as opposed to stories. We absorb stories, but we second-guess games. Reality programming has brought that second-guessing to prime time, only the game in question revolves around social dexterity rather than the physical kind.

The Rewards of Smart Culture

The quickest way to appreciate the Sleeper Curve's cognition training is to sit down and watch a few hours of hit 30 programming from the late '70s on Nick at Nite or the SOAP-net channel or on DVD. The modern viewer who watches a show like *Dallas* today will be bored by the content—not just because the show is less salacious than today's soap operas (which it is by a small margin) but also because the show contains far less information in each scene, despite the fact that its soap-opera structure made it one of the most complicated narratives on television in its prime. With *Dallas*, the modern viewer doesn't have to think to make sense of what's going on, and not having to think is boring. Many recent hit shows—*24*, *Survivor*, *The Sopranos*, *Alias*, *Lost*, *The Simpsons*, *E.R.*—take the opposite approach, layering each scene with a thick network of affiliations. You have to focus to follow the plot, and in focusing you're exercising the parts of your brain that map social networks, that fill in missing information, that connect multiple narrative threads.

Of course, the entertainment industry isn't increasing the cognitive complexity of its products for charitable reasons. The Sleeper Curve exists because there's money to be made by making culture smarter. The economics of television syndication and DVD sales mean that there's a tremendous financial pressure to make programs that can be watched multiple times, revealing new nuances and shadings on the third viewing. Meanwhile, the Web has created a forum for annotation and commentary that allows more complicated shows to prosper, thanks to the fan sites where each episode of shows like *Lost* or *Alias* is dissected with an intensity usually reserved for Talmud scholars. Finally, interactive games have trained a new generation of media consumers to probe complex environments and to think on their feet, and that gamer audience has now come to expect the same challenges from their television shows. In the end, the Sleeper Curve tells us something about the human mind. It may be drawn toward the sensational where content is concerned—sex does sell, after all. But the mind also likes to be challenged; there's real pleasure to be found in solving puzzles, detecting patterns or unpacking a complex narrative system.

In pointing out some of the ways that popular culture has improved our minds, I am not arguing that parents should stop paying attention to the way their children amuse themselves. What I am arguing for is a change in the criteria we use to determine what really is cognitive junk food and what is genuinely nourishing. Instead of a show's violent or tawdry content, instead of wardrobe malfunctions or the F-word, the true test should be whether a given show engages or sedates the mind. Is it a single thread strung together with predictable punch lines every 30 seconds? Or does it map a complex social network? Is your on-screen character running around shooting everything in sight, or is she trying to solve problems and manage resources? If your kids want to watch reality TV, encourage them to watch *Survivor* over *Fear Factor*. If they want to watch a mystery show, encourage *24* over *Law and Order*. If they want to play a violent game, encourage *Grand Theft Auto* over *Quake*. Indeed, it might be just as helpful to have a rating system that used mental labor and not obscenity and violence as its classification scheme for the world of mass culture.

Kids and grown-ups each can learn from their increasingly shared obsessions. Too often we imagine the blurring of kid and grown-up cultures as a series of violations: the 9-year-olds who have to have nipple broaches explained to them thanks to Janet Jackson; the middle-aged guy who can't wait to get home to his Xbox. But this demographic blur has a commendable side that we don't acknowledge enough. The kids are forced to think like grown-ups: analyzing complex social networks, managing resources, tracking subtle narrative intertwinings, recognizing long-term patterns. The grown-ups, in turn, get to learn from the kids: decoding each new technological wave, parsing the interfaces and discovering the intellectual rewards of play. Parents should see this as an opportunity, not a crisis. Smart culture is no longer something you force your kids to ingest, like green vegetables. It's something you share.

Joining the Conversation

1. Steven Johnson makes clear in his opening paragraphs what view he is arguing against. What is that view (his "they say")? How does the dialogue from the Woody Allen movie *Sleeper* relate to that view?

2. Johnson's own argument relates to the intellectual effects of television viewing. Find his thesis statement, locate his supporting discussion, and write a concise summary of the whole argument.

3. Pick an example of popular entertainment that Johnson discusses or another one of comparable quality that you are familiar with, and imagine how someone could use it to make a case *against* Johnson's argument.

4. Compare Johnson's view with that of Dana Stevens, whose essay "Thinking Outside the Idiot Box" follows on p. 285. Which piece do you find more persuasive, and why?

5. Write a response to Johnson using your own experiences and observations as support for what you say. Consider the audience you wish to address, and craft your opening and choice of examples with that audience in mind.

Thinking Outside the Idiot Box

DANA STEVENS

———⌐———

Does watching TV make you smarter?
Duh . . . I dunno.

IF WATCHING TV really makes you smarter, as Steven Johnson argued in an article in yesterday's *New York Times Magazine* (an excerpt from his forthcoming book) then I guess I need
to watch a lot more of it, because try as I might, I could make
no sense of Johnson's piece. As far as I can tell, his thesis is
that television shows have slowly grown more and more complicated over the last two decades (this paradigm shift apparently having begun with *Hill Street Blues*, the Gutenberg Bible
of the smart-TV era), so that now, like rats in a behaviorist's
maze, trained viewers can differentiate among up to 12 distinct
plotlines in shows like *The Sopranos*. (The technical term for

DANA STEVENS is *Slate's* movie critic and has also written for the *New
York Times*, *Bookforum*, and the *Atlantic*. Stevens has a Ph.D. in comparative literature from the University of California at Berkeley.
"Thinking Outside the Idiot Box" was first published in *Slate* on March
25, 2005, as a direct response to "Watching TV Makes You Smarter,"
the article by Steven Johnson on pp. 277–94.

this great leap forward in human cognition: "multi-threading.") In other words, if I understand correctly, watching TV teaches you to watch more TV—a truth already grasped by the makers of children's programming like *Teletubbies*, which is essentially a tutorial instructing toddlers in the basics of vegging out.

As long as Johnson defines intelligence strictly in quantitative cog-sci terms ("attention, patience, retention, the parsing of narrative threads," etc.), his case may seem solid. Those of us who grew up in caveman days, fashioning crude stone tools while watching *Starsky and Hutch,* are indeed now better positioned than our forebears to follow such complex narrative fare as *The Sopranos* (though the analogy is faulty in that *The Sopranos* is clearly one of the high-end, sophisticated shows of its day, better compared to '70s offerings like *Soap* or *Mary Hartman, Mary Hartman*). But does that make us any smarter?

Not only does Johnson fail to account for the impact of the 16 minutes' worth of commercials that interrupt any given episode of, say, *24* (a show he singles out as particularly "nutritional"), but he breezily dismisses recent controversies about the program's representation of Muslim terrorists or its implicit endorsement of torture, preferring to concentrate on how the show's formal structure teaches us to "pay attention, make inferences, track shifting social relationships." Wait a minute—isn't a fictional program's connection to real-life political events like torture and racial profiling one of the "social relationships" we should be paying attention *to*? *24* is the perfect example of a TV show that challenges its audience's cognitive faculties with intricate plotlines and rapid-fire information while actively discouraging them from thinking too much about the vigilante ethic it portrays. It's really good at teaching you to think . . . about future episodes of *24*.

A mix of formal and informal styles is appropriate in *Slate*. See Chapter 9 on mixing styles in academic writing.

Johnson's claim for television as a tool for brain enhancement seems deeply, hilariously bogus—not unlike the graphically mesmerizing plot diagram he provides of "any episode" of *Starsky and Hutch* as a foil for the far fancier grid representing *The Sopranos*. (No matter how many times I return to that *Starsky and Hutch* diagram, it remains funny—in contrast to, say, the latest episode of *Joey*.) But I don't know that I have a lot more sympathy for the wet-blanket Puritanism of the anti-TV crowd.

Today being the first day of this year's TV Turnoff Week, there are a lot of articles out there about what Lisa Simpson would call the "endumbening" effect of television viewing. [An] interview with Kalle Lasn, a co-founder of TV Turnoff Week who also edits the "culture-jamming" journal *Adbusters*, focuses on the TV-B-Gone, a hand-held remote-control device that can switch off most television sets from between 20 and 50 feet away, restoring calm to public places like airports, bars, or banks. The device seems appealingly subversive, but ultimately, its function as a tool of social control can't help but invoke the very content-based censorship that the PBS crowd so deplores. There's an inescapably patronizing tone in the marketing of the TV-B-Gone, illustrated by Lasn's explanation of why he failed to zap one bank of public screens: "I was at the airport the other day, and there was a big TV set that a number of people were watching, and for some reason I didn't want to switch it off because it was some nature show." SO a football game in a bar is zapworthy, but spacing out to leopards in the Qantas terminal is A-OK! What if the nature show is violent, like the Discovery Channel's *Animal Face-Off*? What if the zapper is not an anti-television liberal, but a right-winger offended by *Will and Grace*'s living arrangement, or Janet Jackson's breast? Who decides?

From the vantage point of someone who watches a hell of a lot of TV (but still far less than the average American), the medium seems neither like a brain-liquefying poison nor a salutary tonic. Certainly for young children, who are fresh meat for the advertising industry, the idea of a week (or an entire childhood) without TV makes a lot of sense. But shouldn't grown men and women be trusted to judge their own dosages, just as they would decide on the number of drinks they can handle at the bar? And shouldn't we choose our favorite shows because we like them, not because they force our otherwise helpless cortexes to "manag[e] resources" and "recognize long-term patterns"? There couldn't be a better time to test Steven Johnson's theory than National TV Turnoff Week—just turn the set off till Sunday and see if you get any dumber. I'd participate in the experiment myself, but in my case, watching television is definitely a smart thing to do—I get paid for it.

Joining the Conversation

1. In her opening paragraph, Dana Stevens summarizes Steven Johnson's thesis statement from "Watching TV Makes You Smarter." How can you tell she is not speaking for herself here, but rather is describing a view that she disagrees with? What metacommentary signals her intent?
2. What specific criticisms does Stevens make of Johnson's essay? Which one is most persuasive to you, and why?
3. What exactly is Stevens's position?
4. How might Steven Johnson answer Stevens's objections?
5. Write an essay taking your own stand on the intellectual merits of television, considering the arguments of Dana Stevens and Steven Johnson and framing your essay as a response to one of them.

Family Guy *and Freud:*
Jokes and Their Relation
to the Unconscious

ANTONIA PEACOCKE

WHILE SLOUCHING IN FRONT of the television after a long day, you probably don't think a lot about famous psychologists of the twentieth century. Somehow, these figures don't come up often in prime-time—or even daytime—TV programming. Whether you're watching *Living Lohan* or the *NewsHour*, the likelihood is that you are not thinking of Sigmund Freud, even if you've heard of his book *Jokes and Their Relation to the Unconscious*. I say that you should be.

What made me think of Freud in the first place, actually, was *Family Guy*, the cartoon created by Seth MacFarlane.

ANTONIA PEACOCKE is a student at Harvard University, where she is majoring in philosophy. She was born in London and moved to New York at age 10, on exactly the same day that the fourth Harry Potter book came out. She's always loved writing and worked as a copy editor and columnist for her high school newspaper—and received the Catherine Fairfax MacRae Prize for Excellence in Both English and Mathematics. A National Merit Scholar, she wrote the essay here specifically for this book, using the MLA style of documentation.

(Seriously—stay with me here.) Any of my friends can tell you that this program holds endless fascination for me; as a matter of fact, my high school rag-sheet "perfect mate" was the baby Stewie Griffin, a character on the show. Embarrassingly enough, I have almost reached the point at which I can perform one-woman versions of several episodes. I know every website that streams the show for free, and I still refuse to return the five *Family Guy* DVDs a friend lent me in 2006. Before I was such a devotee, however, I was adamantly opposed to the program for its particular brand of humor.

It will come as no surprise that I was not alone in this view; many still denounce *Family Guy* as bigoted and crude. *New York Times* journalist Stuart Elliott claimed just this year that "the characters on the Fox television series *Family Guy* . . . purposely offen[d] just about every group of people you could name." Likewise Stephen Dubner, co-author of *Freakonomics*, called *Family Guy* "a cartoon comedy that packs more gags per minute about race, sex, incest, bestiality, etc. than any other show [he] can think of." Comparing its level of offense to that of Don Imus's infamous comments about the Rutgers women's basketball team in the same year, comments that threw the popular CBS radio talk-show host off the air, Dubner said he wondered why Imus couldn't get away with as much as *Family Guy* could.

Dubner did not know about all the trouble *Family Guy* has had. In fact, it must be one of the few television shows in history that has been canceled not just once, but twice. After its premiere in April 1999, the show ran until August 2000, but was besieged by so many complaints, some of them from MacFarlane's old high school headmaster, Rev. Richardson W. Schell, that Fox shelved it until July 2001 (Weinraub). Still afraid of causing a commotion, though, Fox had the car-

Peter and Stewie Griffin

toon censored and irregularly scheduled; as a result, its ratings fell so low that 2002 saw its second cancellation (Weinraub). But then it came back with a vengeance—I'll get into
that later.

Family Guy has found trouble more recently, too. In 2007 5
comedian Carol Burnett sued Fox for 6 million dollars, claiming that the show's parody of the Charwoman, a character
that she had created for *The Carol Burnett Show*, not only
violated copyright but also besmirched the character's name
in revenge for Burnett's refusal to grant permission to use her
theme song ("Carol Burnett Sues over *Family Guy* Parody").
The suit came after MacFarlane had made the Charwoman
into a cleaning woman for a pornography store in one episode
of *Family Guy*. Burnett lost, but U.S. district judge Dean

Pregerson agreed that he could "fully appreciate how distasteful and offensive the segment [was] to Ms. Burnett" (qtd. in Grossberg).

I must admit, I can see how parts of the show might seem offensive if taken at face value. Look, for example, at the mock fifties instructional video that features in the episode "I Am Peter, Hear Me Roar."

> [*The screen becomes black and white. Vapid music plays in the background. The screen reads* "WOMEN IN THE WORKPLACE *ca. 1956," then switches to a shot of an office with various women working on typewriters. A businessman speaks to the camera.*]
>
> BUSINESSMAN: Irrational and emotionally fragile by nature, female coworkers are a peculiar animal. They are very insecure about their appearance. Be sure to tell them how good they look every day, even if they're homely and unkempt. [*He turns to an unattractive female typist.*] You're doing a great job, Muriel, and you're prettier than Mamie van Doren! [*She smiles. He grins at the camera, raising one eyebrow knowingly, and winks.*] And remember, nothing says "Good job!" like a firm open-palm slap on the behind. [*He walks past a woman bent over a file cabinet and demonstrates enthusiastically. She smiles, looking flattered. He grins at the camera again as the music comes to an end.*]

Laughing at something so blatantly sexist could cause anyone a pang of guilt, and before I thought more about the show this seemed to be a huge problem. I agreed with Dubner, and I failed to see how anyone could laugh at such jokes without feeling at least slightly ashamed.

Soon, though, I found myself forced to give *Family Guy* a chance. It was simply everywhere: my brother and many of my friends watched it religiously, and its devoted fans relentlessly proselytized for it. In case you have any doubts about its immense popularity, consider these facts. On Facebook, the universal forum for my generation, there are currently 23 separate *Family Guy* fan groups with a combined membership of 1,669 people (compared with only 6 groups protesting against *Family Guy*, with 105 members total). Users of the well-respected Internet Movie Database rate the show 8.8 out of 10. The box-set DVDs were the best-selling television DVDs of 2003 in the United States (Moloney). Among the public and within the industry, the show receives fantastic acclaim; it has won eight awards, including three primetime Emmys (IMDb). Most importantly, each time it was cancelled fans provided the brute force necessary to get it back on the air. In 2000, online campaigns did the trick; in 2002, devotees demonstrated outside Fox Studios, refused to watch the Fox network, and boycotted any companies that advertised on it (Moloney). Given the show's high profile, both with my friends and family and in the world at large, it would have been more work for me to avoid the Griffin family than to let myself sink into their animated world.

With more exposure, I found myself crafting a more positive view of *Family Guy*. Those who don't often watch the program, as Dubner admits he doesn't, could easily come to think that the cartoon takes pleasure in controversial humor just for its own sake. But those who pay more attention and think about the creators' intentions can see that *Family Guy* intelligently satirizes some aspects of American culture.

Some of this satire is actually quite obvious. Take, for instance, a quip Brian the dog makes about Stewie's literary choices in a fourth-season episode, "PTV." (Never mind that a dog and a baby can both read and hold lengthy conversations.)

[*The Griffins are in their car. Brian turns to Stewie, who sits reading in his car seat.*]

BRIAN: *East of Eden?* So you, you, you pretty much do whatever Oprah tells you to, huh?
STEWIE: You know, this book's been around for fifty years. It's a classic.
BRIAN: But you just got it last week. And there's a giant Oprah sticker on the front.
STEWIE: Oh—oh—oh, is that what that is? Oh, lemme just peel that right off.
BRIAN: So, uh, what are you gonna read after that one?
STEWIE: Well, she hasn't told us yet—damn!

Brian and Stewie demonstrate insightfully and comically how Americans are willing to follow the instructions of a celebrity blindly—and less willing to admit that they are doing so.

The more off-color jokes, though, those that give *Family Guy* 10 a bad name, attract a different kind of viewer. Such viewers are not "rats in a behaviorist's maze," as *Slate* writer Dana Stevens labels modern American television consumers in her article "Thinking Outside the Idiot Box." They are conscious and critical viewers, akin to the "screenagers" identified by Douglas Rushkoff in an essay entitled "Bart Simpson: Prince of Irreverence" (294). They are not—and this I cannot stress enough, self-serving as it may seem—immoral or easily manipulated people.

Rushkoff's piece analyzes the humor of *The Simpsons*, a show criticized for many of the same reasons as *Family Guy*. "The people I call 'screenagers,'" Rushkoff explains, " . . . speak the media language better than their parents do and they see through clumsy attempts to program them into submission" (294). He claims that gaming technology has made my generation realize that television is programmed for us with certain intentions; since we can control characters in the virtual world, we are more aware that characters on TV are similarly controlled. "Sure, [these 'screenagers'] might sit back and watch a program now and again," Rushkoff explains, "but they do so voluntarily, and with full knowledge of their complicity. It is not an involuntary surrender" (294). In his opinion, our critical eyes and our unwillingness to be programmed by the programmers make for an entirely new relationship with the shows we watch. Thus we enjoy *The Simpsons'* parodies of mass media culture since we are skeptical of it ourselves.

Rushkoff's argument about *The Simpsons* actually applies to *Family Guy* as well, except in one dimension: Rushkoff writes that *The Simpsons'* creators do "not comment on social issues as much as they [do on] the media imagery around a particular social issue" (296). MacFarlane and company seem to do the reverse. Trusting in their viewers' ability to analyze what they are watching, the creators of *Family Guy* point out the weaknesses and defects of U.S. society in a mocking and sometimes intolerant way.

Taken in this light, the "instructional video" quoted above becomes not only funny but also insightful. In its satire, viewers can recognize the sickly sweet and falsely sensitive sexism of the 1950s in observing just how conveniently self-serving the speaker of the video appears. The message of the clip denounces and ridicules sexism rather than condoning it. It is an excerpt that perfectly exemplifies the bold-faced candor of the show, from which it derives a lot of its appeal.

Making such comically outrageous remarks on the air also serves to expose certain prejudiced attitudes as outrageous themselves. Taking these comments at face value would be as foolish as taking Jonathan Swift's "Modest Proposal" seriously.

Furthermore, while they put bigoted words into the mouths of their characters, the show's writers cannot be accused of portraying these characters positively. Peter Griffin, the "family guy" of the show's title, probably says and does the most offensive things of all—but as a lazy, overweight, and insensitive failure of a man, he is hardly presented as someone to admire. Nobody in his or her right mind would observe Peter's behavior and deem it worth emulation.

Family Guy has its own responses to accusations of crudity. 15 In the episode "PTV," Peter sets up his own television station broadcasting from home and the Griffin family finds itself confronting the Federal Communications Commission directly. The episode makes many tongue-in-cheek jabs at the FCC, some of which are sung in a rousing musical number, but also sneaks in some of the creator's own opinions. The plot comes to a climax when the FCC begins to censor "real life" in the town of Quahog; officials place black censor bars in front of newly showered Griffins and blow foghorns whenever characters curse. MacFarlane makes an important point: that no amount of television censorship will ever change the harsh nature of reality—and to censor reality is mere folly. Likewise, he puts explicit arguments about censorship into lines spoken by his characters, as when Brian says that "responsibility lies with the parents [and] there are plenty of things that are much worse for children than television."

It must be said too that not all of *Family Guy*'s humor could be construed as offensive. Some of its jokes are more tame and insightful, the kind you might expect from the *New Yorker*. The following light commentary on the usefulness of high school algebra from "When You Wish Upon a Weinstein" could hardly be accused of upsetting anyone—except, perhaps, a few high school math teachers.

[*Shot of Peter on the couch and his son Chris lying at his feet and doing homework.*]

CHRIS: Dad, can you help me with my math? [My teacher] says if I don't learn it, I won't be able to function in the real world.

[*Shot of Chris standing holding a map in a run-down gas station next to an attendant in overalls and a trucker cap reading "*PUMP THIS.*" The attendant speaks with a Southern accent and gestures casually to show the different road configurations.*]

ATTENDANT: Okay, now what you gotta do is go down the road past the old Johnson place, and you're gonna find two roads, one parallel and one perpendicular. Now keep going until you come to a highway that bisects it at a 45-degree angle. [*Crosses his arms.*] Solve for x.

[*Shot of Chris lying on the ground next to the attendant in fetal position, sucking his thumb. His map lies abandoned near him.*]

In fact, *Family Guy* does not aim to hurt, and its creators take certain measures to keep it from hitting too hard. In an interview on *Access Hollywood*, Seth MacFarlane plainly states that there are certain jokes too upsetting to certain groups to go on the air. Similarly, to ensure that the easily misunderstood show doesn't fall into the hands of those too young to understand it, Fox will not license *Family Guy* rights to any products intended for children under the age of fourteen (Elliott).

However, this is not to say that MacFarlane's mission is corrective or noble. It is worth remembering that he wants only to amuse, a goal for which he was criticized by several of his professors at the Rhode Island School of Design (Weinraub). For this reason, his humor can be dangerous. On the one hand,

I don't agree with George Will's reductive and generalized statement in his article "Reality Television: Oxymoron" that "entertainment seeking a mass audience is ratcheting up the violence, sexuality, and degradation, becoming increasingly coarse and trying to be . . . shocking in an unshockable society." I believe *Family Guy* has its intelligent points, and some of its seemingly "coarse" scenes often have hidden merit. I must concede, though, that a few of the show's scenes seem to be doing just what Will claims; sometimes the creators do seem to cross— or, perhaps, eagerly race past—the line of indecency. In one such crude scene, an elderly dog slowly races a paraplegic and Peter, who has just been hit by a car, to get to a severed finger belonging to Peter himself ("Whistle While Your Wife Works"). Nor do I find it particularly funny when Stewie physically abuses Brian in a bloody fight over gambling money ("Patriot Games").

Thus, while *Family Guy* can provide a sort of relief by breaking down taboos, we must still wonder whether or not these taboos exist for a reason. An excess of offensive jokes, especially those that are often misconstrued, can seem to grant tacit permission to think offensively if it's done for comedy— and laughing at others' expense can be cruel, no matter how funny. Jokes all have their origins, and the funniest ones are those that hit home the hardest; if we listen to Freud, these are the ones that let our animalistic and aggressive impulses surface from the unconscious. The distinction between a shamelessly candid but insightful joke and a merely shameless joke is a slight but important one. While I love *Family Guy* as much as any fan, it's important not to lose sight of what's truly unfunny in real life—even as we appreciate what is hilarious in fiction.

The Griffin family watches TV.

Works Cited

"Carol Burnett Sues over *Family Guy* Parody." *CBC.com*. Canadian
  Broadcasting Centre, 16 Mar. 2007. Web. 14 July 2008.

Dubner, Stephen J. "Why Is *Family Guy* Okay When Imus Wasn't?" Web log
  post. *Freakonomics: The Hidden Side of Everything*, 3 Dec. 2007. Web. 14
  July 2008.

Elliott, Stuart. "Crude? So What! These Characters Still Find Work in Ads."
  New York Times. New York Times, 18 June 2008. Web. 14 July 2008.

Facebook. Search for *Family Guy* under "Groups." 14 July 2008.

Freud, Sigmund. *Jokes and Their Relation to the Unconscious*. 1905. Trans. James
  Strachey. New York: Norton, 1989. Print.

Grossberg, Josh. "Carol Burnett Can't Stop Stewie." *E! Online*. E!
  Entertainment Television, 5 June 2007. Web. 14 Jul. 2008.

"I Am Peter, Hear Me Roar." *Family Guy*. Prod. Seth MacFarlane. Twentieth Century Fox. 28 Mar. 2000. Web. 14 July 2008.

Internet Movie Database. *Family Guy*. Ed. unknown. Last update date unknown. Web. 14 July 2008.

MacFarlane, Seth. Interview. *Access Hollywood*. Online posting on YouTube. 8 May 2007. Web. 14 July 2008.

Moloney, Ben Adam. "*Family Guy*—The TV Series." British Broadcasting Corporation. 30 Sept. 2004. Web. 14 Jul. 2008.

"Patriot Games." *Family Guy*. Prod. Seth MacFarlane. Twentieth Century Fox. 29 Jan. 2006. Web. 22 July 2008.

"PTV." *Family Guy*. Prod. Seth MacFarlane. Twentieth Century Fox. 6 Nov. 2005. Web. 14 July 2008.

Rushkoff, Douglas. "Bart Simpson: Prince of Irreverence." *Leaving Springfield: The Simpsons and the Possibility of Oppositional Culture*. Ed. John Alberti. Detroit: Wayne State UP, 2004. 292–301. Print.

Stevens, Dana. "Thinking Outside the Idiot Box." *Slate*. Slate, 25 Mar. 2005. Web. 14 Jul. 2008.

Weinraub, Bernard. "The Young Guy of 'Family Guy': A 30-Year-Old's Cartoon Hit Makes an Unexpected Comeback." *New York Times*. New York Times, 7 Jul. 2004. Web. 14 July 2008.

"When You Wish Upon a Weinstein." *Family Guy*. Prod. Seth MacFarlane. Twentieth Century Fox. 9 Nov. 2003. Web. 22 July 2008.

"Whistle While Your Wife Works." *Family Guy*. Prod. Seth MacFarlane. Twentieth Century Fox. 12 Nov. 2006. Web. 14 July 2008.

Will, George F. "Reality Television: Oxymoron." *Washington Post* 21 June 2001: A25. Print.

Joining the Conversation

1. How would you characterize Antonia Peacocke's argument about the television cartoon *Family Guy*? What does she like about the show? What doesn't she like? What would you say is her overall opinion of *Family Guy*?

2. Find two places in the essay where Peacocke puts forward arguments that she herself disagrees with. Analyze what she

says about these arguments. What would you say are her reasons for including these opposing views?

3. While making a serious argument, Peacocke frequently uses humor to make her points. Identify two or three examples where she does so, and explain the role that such humor plays in helping her develop her argument.

4. Peacocke cites a number of authors in her essay. How does she weave their ideas in with her own ideas? How fairly does she represent their views?

5. Some might see Peacocke's essay as proof of Gerald Graff's argument in "Hidden Intellectualism" (pp. 380–86) that pop culture can be a subject for serious intellectual analysis. Write an essay on this topic, using Peacocke's essay either to support or to refute Graff's argument.

Small Change: Why the Revolution Will Not Be Tweeted

MALCOLM GLADWELL

———❧———

AT FOUR-THIRTY in the afternoon on Monday, February 1, 1960, four college students sat down at the lunch counter at the Woolworth's in downtown Greensboro, North Carolina. They were freshmen at North Carolina A. & T., a black college a mile or so away.

"I'd like a cup of coffee, please," one of the four, Ezell Blair, said to the waitress.

"We don't serve Negroes here," she replied.

The Woolworth's lunch counter was a long L-shaped bar that could seat sixty-six people, with a standup snack bar at one end. The seats were for whites. The snack bar was for blacks. Another employee, a black woman who worked at the

MALCOLM GLADWELL writes for the *New Yorker* and was one of *Time* magazine's 100 Most Influential People in 2005. His best-selling books include *The Tipping Point: How Little Things Make a Big Difference* (2000), *Blink: The Power of Thinking without Thinking* (2005), and *What the Dog Saw* (2009). He has also been a *Washington Post* reporter. This essay first appeared in the *New Yorker* on October 14, 2010.

steam table, approached the students and tried to warn them away. "You're acting stupid, ignorant!" she said. They didn't move. Around five-thirty, the front doors to the store were locked. The four still didn't move. Finally, they left by a side door. Outside, a small crowd had gathered, including a photographer from the Greensboro Record. "I'll be back tomorrow with A. & T. College," one of the students said.

By next morning, the protest had grown to twenty-seven 5 men and four women, most from the same dormitory as the original four. The men were dressed in suits and ties. The students had brought their schoolwork, and studied as they sat at the counter. On Wednesday, students from Greensboro's "Negro" secondary school, Dudley High, joined in, and the number of protesters swelled to eighty. By Thursday, the protesters numbered three hundred, including three white women, from the Greensboro campus of the University of North Carolina. By Saturday, the sit-in had reached six hundred. People spilled out onto the street. White teenagers waved Confederate flags. Someone threw a firecracker. At noon, the A. & T. football team arrived. "Here comes the wrecking crew," one of the white students shouted.

By the following Monday, sit-ins had spread to Winston-Salem, twenty-five miles away, and Durham, fifty miles away. The day after that, students at Fayetteville State Teachers College and at Johnson C. Smith College, in Charlotte, joined in, followed on Wednesday by students at St. Augustine's College and Shaw University, in Raleigh. On Thursday and Friday, the protest crossed state lines, surfacing in Hampton and Portsmouth, Virginia, in Rock Hill, South Carolina, and in Chattanooga, Tennessee. By the end of the month, there were sit-ins throughout the South, as far west as Texas. "I asked every student I met what the first day of the sitdowns had been like on his campus," the political theorist Michael Walzer wrote in *Dissent*. "The answer was always the same: 'It was like a fever. Everyone wanted to go.'" Some seventy thousand students eventually took part. Thousands were arrested and untold thousands more radicalized. These events in the early sixties became a civil-rights war that engulfed the South for the rest of the decade—and it happened without e-mail, texting, Facebook, or Twitter.

The world, we are told, is in the midst of a revolution. The new tools of social media have reinvented social activism. With Facebook and Twitter and the like, the traditional relationship between political authority and popular will has been upended, making it easier for the powerless to collaborate, coordinate, and give voice to their concerns. When ten thousand protesters took to the streets in Moldova in the spring of 2009 to protest against their country's Communist government, the action was dubbed the Twitter Revolution, because of the means by which the demonstrators had been brought together. A few months after that, when student protests rocked Tehran, the State Department took the unusual step of asking Twitter to suspend scheduled maintenance of its Web site, because the Administration didn't want such a critical organizing tool out of service at the height of the demonstrations. "Without Twitter the people of Iran would not have felt empowered and confident to stand up for freedom and democracy," Mark Pfeifle, a former national-security adviser, later wrote, calling for Twitter to be nominated for the Nobel Peace Prize. Where activists were once defined by their causes, they are now defined by their tools. Facebook warriors go online to push for change. "You are the best hope for us all," James K. Glassman, a former sen-

See Chapter 3 for tips on incorporating quotations.

ior State Department official, told a crowd of cyber activists at a recent conference sponsored by Facebook, A.T.&T., Howcast, MTV, and Google. Sites like Facebook, Glassman said, "give the U.S. a significant competitive advantage over terrorists. Some time ago, I said that Al Qaeda was 'eating our lunch on the Internet.' That is no longer the case. Al Qaeda is stuck in Web 1.0. The Internet is now about interactivity and conversation."

These are strong, and puzzling, claims. Why does it matter who is eating whose lunch on the Internet? Are people who log on to their Facebook page really the best hope for us all?

Social media can't provide what social change has always required.

As for Moldova's so-called Twitter Revolution, Evgeny Morozov, a scholar at Stanford who has been the most persistent of digital evangelism's critics, points out that Twitter had scant internal significance in Moldova, a country where very few Twitter accounts exist. Nor does it seem to have been a revolution, not least because the protests—as Anne Applebaum suggested in the *Washington Post*—may well have been a bit of stagecraft cooked up by the government. (In a country paranoid about Romanian revanchism, the protesters flew a Romanian flag over the Parliament building.) In the Iranian case, meanwhile, the people tweeting about the demonstrations were almost all in the West. "It is time to get Twitter's role in the events in Iran right," Golnaz Esfandiari wrote, this past summer, in *Foreign Policy*. "Simply put: There was no Twitter Revolution inside Iran." The cadre of prominent bloggers, like Andrew Sullivan, who championed the role of social media in Iran, Esfandiari continued, misunderstood the situation. "Western journalists who couldn't reach—or didn't bother reaching?—people on the ground in Iran simply scrolled through the English-language tweets post with tag #iranelection," she wrote. "Through it all, no one seemed to wonder why people trying to coordinate protests in Iran would be writing in any language other than Farsi."

Some of this grandiosity is to be expected. Innovators tend to be solipsists. They often want to cram every stray fact and experience into their new model. As the historian Robert Darnton has written, "The marvels of communication technology in the present have produced a false consciousness about the past—even a sense that communication has no history, or had nothing of importance to consider before the days of television and the Internet." But there is something else at work here, in the outsized enthusiasm for social media. Fifty years after one of the most extraordinary episodes of social upheaval in American history, we seem to have forgotten what activism is.

Greensboro in the early nineteen-sixties was the kind of place 10 where racial insubordination was routinely met with violence. The four students who first sat down at the lunch counter were terrified. "I suppose if anyone had come up behind me and yelled 'Boo,' I think I would have fallen off my seat," one of them said later. On the first day, the store manager notified the police chief, who immediately sent two officers to the store. On the third day, a gang of white toughs showed up at the lunch counter and stood ostentatiously behind the protesters, ominously muttering epithets such as "burr-head nigger." A local Ku Klux Klan leader made an appearance. On Saturday, as tensions grew, someone called in a bomb threat, and the entire store had to be evacuated.

The dangers were even clearer in the Mississippi Freedom Summer Project of 1964, another of the sentinel campaigns of the civil-rights movement. The Student Nonviolent Coordinating Committee recruited hundreds of Northern, largely white unpaid volunteers to run Freedom Schools, register black voters, and raise civil-rights awareness in the Deep South. "No one should go *anywhere* alone, but certainly not in an automobile and certainly not at night," they were instructed. Within days of arriving in Mississippi, three volunteers—Michael Schwerner, James Chaney, and Andrew Goodman—were kidnapped and killed, and during the rest of the summer, thirty-seven black churches were set on fire and dozens of safe houses were bombed; volunteers were beaten, shot at, arrested, and trailed by pickup trucks full of armed men. A quarter of those in the program dropped out. Activism that challenges the status quo—that attacks deeply rooted problems—is not for the faint of heart.

What makes people capable of this kind of activism? The Stanford sociologist Doug McAdam compared the Freedom Summer dropouts with the participants who stayed, and discovered that the key difference wasn't, as might be expected, ideological fervor. "*All* of the applicants—participants and withdrawals alike—emerge as highly committed, articulate supporters of the goals and values of the summer program," he concluded. What mattered more was an applicant's degree of personal connection to the civil-rights movement. All the volunteers were required to provide a list of personal contacts—the people they wanted kept apprised of their activities—and participants were far more likely than dropouts to have close friends who were also going to Mississippi. High-risk activism, McAdam concluded, is a "strong-tie" phenomenon.

This pattern shows up again and again. One study of the Red Brigades, the Italian terrorist group of the nineteen-seventies, found that seventy per cent of recruits had at least one good friend already in the organization. The same is true of the men who joined the mujahideen in Afghanistan. Even revolutionary actions that look spontaneous, like the demonstrations in East Germany that led to the fall of the Berlin Wall, are, at core, strong-tie phenomena. The opposition movement in East Germany consisted of several hundred groups, each with roughly a dozen members. Each group was in limited contact with the others: at the time, only thirteen per cent of East Germans even had a phone. All they knew was that on Monday nights, outside St. Nicholas Church in downtown Leipzig, people gathered to voice their anger at the state. And the primary determinant of who showed up was "critical friends"—the more friends you had who were critical of the regime the more likely you were to join the protest.

So one crucial fact about the four freshman at the Greensboro lunch counter—David Richmond, Franklin McCain, Ezell Blair, and Joseph McNeil—was their relationship with one another. McNeil was a roommate of Blair's in A. & T.'s Scott Hall dormitory. Richmond roomed with McCain one floor up, and Blair, Richmond, and McCain had all gone to Dudley High School. The four would smuggle beer into the dorm and talk late into the night in Blair and McNeil's room. They would all have remembered the murder of Emmett Till in 1955, the Montgomery bus boycott that same year, and the showdown in Little Rock in 1957. It was McNeil who brought up the idea of a sit-in at Woolworth's. They'd discussed it for nearly a month. Then McNeil came into the dorm room and asked the others if they were ready. There was a pause, and McCain said, in a way that works only with people who talk late into the night with one another, "Are you guys chicken or not?" Ezell Blair worked up the courage the next day to ask for a cup of coffee because he was flanked by his roommate and two good friends from high school.

The kind of activism associated with social media isn't like this at all. The platforms of social media are built around weak ties. Twitter is a way of following (or being followed by) people you may never have met. Facebook is a tool for efficiently managing your acquaintances, for keeping up with the people you would not otherwise be able to stay in touch with. That's why you can have a thousand "friends" on Facebook, as you never could in real life.

This is in many ways a wonderful thing. There is strength in weak ties, as the sociologist Mark Granovetter has observed.

Our acquaintances—not our friends—are our greatest source of new ideas and information. The Internet lets us exploit the power of these kinds of distant connections with marvelous efficiency. It's terrific at the diffusion of innovation, interdisciplinary collaboration, seamlessly matching up buyers and sellers, and the logistical functions of the dating world. But weak ties seldom lead to high-risk activism.

In a new book called *The Dragonfly Effect: Quick, Effective, and Powerful Ways to Use Social Media to Drive Social Change*, the business consultant Andy Smith and the Stanford Business School professor Jennifer Aaker tell the story of Sameer Bhatia, a young Silicon Valley entrepreneur who came down with acute myelogenous leukemia. It's a perfect illustration of social media's strengths. Bhatia needed a bone-marrow transplant, but he could not find a match among his relatives and friends. The odds were best with a donor of his ethnicity, and there were few South Asians in the national bone-marrow database. So Bhatia's business partner sent out an e-mail explaining Bhatia's plight to more than four hundred of their acquaintances, who forwarded the e-mail to their personal contacts; Facebook pages and YouTube videos were devoted to the Help Sameer campaign. Eventually, nearly twenty-five thousand new people were registered in the bone-marrow database, and Bhatia found a match.

But how did the campaign get so many people to sign up? By not asking too much of them. That's the only way you can get someone you don't really know to do something on your behalf. You can get thousands of people to sign up for a donor registry, because doing so is pretty easy. You have to send in a cheek swab and—in the highly unlikely event that your bone marrow is a good match for someone in need—spend a few hours at the hospital. Donating bone marrow isn't a trivial matter. But it doesn't involve financial or personal risk; it doesn't mean spending a summer being chased by armed men in pickup trucks. It doesn't require that you confront socially entrenched norms and practices. In fact, it's the kind of commitment that will bring only social acknowledgment and praise.

The evangelists of social media don't understand this distinction; they seem to believe that a Facebook friend is the same as a real friend and that signing up for a donor registry in Silicon Valley today is activism in the same sense as sitting at a segregated lunch counter in Greensboro in 1960. "Social networks are particularly effective at increasing motivation," Aaker and Smith write. But that's not true. Social networks are effective at increasing *participation*—by lessening the level of motivation that participation requires. The Facebook page of the Save Darfur Coalition has 1,282,339 members, who have donated an average of nine cents apiece. The next biggest Darfur charity on Facebook has 22,073 members, who have donated an average of thirty-five cents. Help Save Darfur has 2,797 members, who have given, on average, fifteen cents. A spokesperson for the Save Darfur Coalition told *Newsweek*, "We wouldn't necessarily gauge someone's value to the advocacy movement based on what they've given. This is a powerful mechanism to engage this critical population. They inform their community, attend events, volunteer. It's not something you can measure by looking at a ledger." In other words, Facebook activism succeeds not by motivating people to make a real sacrifice but by motivating them to do the things that people do when they are not motivated enough to make a real sacrifice. We are a long way from the lunch counters of Greensboro.

The students who joined the sit-ins across the South during the winter of 1960 described the movement as a "fever." But the civil-rights movement was more like a military campaign than like a contagion. In the late nineteen-fifties, there had been sixteen sit-ins in various cities throughout the South, fifteen of which were formally organized by civil-rights organizations like the N.A.A.C.P. and CORE. Possible locations for activism were scouted. Plans were drawn up. Movement activists held training sessions and retreats for would-be protesters. The Greensboro Four were a product of this groundwork: all were members of the N.A.A.C.P. Youth Council. They had close ties with the head of the local N.A.A.C.P. chapter. They had been briefed on the earlier wave of sit-ins in Durham, and had been part of a series of movement meetings in activist churches. When the sit-in movement spread from Greensboro throughout the South, it did not spread indiscriminately. It spread to those cities which had preexisting "movement centers"—a core of dedicated and trained activists ready to turn the "fever" into action.

The civil-rights movement was high-risk activism. It was also, crucially, strategic activism: a challenge to the establishment mounted with precision and discipline. The N.A.A.C.P. was a centralized organization, run from New York according to highly formalized operating procedures. At the Southern Christian Leadership Conference, Martin Luther King, Jr., was the unquestioned authority. At the center of the movement was the black church, which had, as Aldon D. Morris points out in his superb 1984 study, *The Origins of the Civil Rights Movement*, a carefully demarcated division of labor, with various standing committees and disciplined groups. "Each group was task-oriented and coordinated its activities through authority structures," Morris writes. "Individuals were held accountable for their assigned duties, and important conflicts were resolved by the minister, who usually exercised ultimate authority over the congregation."

This is the second crucial distinction between traditional activism and its online variant: social media are not about this kind of hierarchical organization. Facebook and the like are tools for building *networks*, which are the opposite, in structure and character, of hierarchies. Unlike hierarchies, with their rules and procedures, networks aren't controlled by a single central authority. Decisions are made through consensus, and the ties that bind people to the group are loose.

This structure makes networks enormously resilient and adaptable in low-risk situations. Wikipedia is a perfect example. It doesn't have an editor, sitting in New York, who directs and corrects each entry. The effort of putting together each entry is self-organized. If every entry in Wikipedia were to be erased tomorrow, the content would swiftly be restored, because that's what happens when a network of thousands spontaneously devote their time to a task.

There are many things, though, that networks don't do well. Car companies sensibly use a network to organize their hundreds of suppliers, but not to design their cars. No one believes that the articulation of a coherent design philosophy is best handled by a sprawling, leaderless organizational system. Because networks don't have a centralized leadership structure and clear lines of authority, they have real difficulty reaching consensus and setting goals. They can't think strategically; they are chronically prone to conflict and error. How do you make difficult choices about tactics or strategy or philosophical direction when everyone has an equal say?

The Palestine Liberation Organization originated as a network, and the international-relations scholars Mette Eilstrup-Sangiovanni and Calvert Jones argue in a recent essay in *International Security* that this is why it ran into such trouble as it grew: "Structural features typical of networks—the absence of central authority, the unchecked autonomy of rival groups, and the inability to arbitrate quarrels through formal mechanisms—made the P.L.O. excessively vulnerable to outside manipulation and internal strife."

In Germany in the nineteen-seventies, they go on, "the far more unified and successful left-wing terrorists tended to organize hierarchically, with professional management and clear divisions of labor. They were concentrated geographically in universities, where they could establish central leadership, trust, and camaraderie through regular, face-to-face meetings." They seldom betrayed their comrades in arms during police interrogations. Their counterparts on the right were organized as decentralized networks, and had no such discipline. These groups were regularly infiltrated, and members, once arrested, easily gave up their comrades. Similarly, Al Qaeda was most dangerous when it was a unified hierarchy. Now that it has dissipated into a network, it has proved far less effective.

The drawbacks of networks scarcely matter if the network isn't interested in systemic change—if it just wants to frighten or humiliate or make a splash—or if it doesn't need to think strategically. But if you're taking on a powerful and organized establishment you have to be a hierarchy. The Montgomery bus boycott required the participation of tens of thousands of people who depended on public transit to get to and from work each day. It lasted a *year*. In order to persuade those people to stay true to the cause, the boycott's organizers tasked each local black church with maintaining morale, and put together a free alternative private carpool service, with forty-eight dispatchers and forty-two pickup stations. Even the White Citizens Council, King later said, conceded that the carpool system moved with "military precision." By the time King came to Birmingham, for the climactic showdown with Police Commissioner

Eugene (Bull) Connor, he had a budget of a million dollars, and a hundred full-time staff members on the ground, divided into operational units. The operation itself was divided into steadily escalating phases, mapped out in advance. Support was maintained through consecutive mass meetings rotating from church to church around the city.

Boycotts and sit-ins and nonviolent confrontations—which were the weapons of choice for the civil-rights movement—are high-risk strategies. They leave little room for conflict and error. The moment even one protester deviates from the script and responds to provocation, the moral legitimacy of the entire protest is compromised. Enthusiasts for social media would no doubt have us believe that King's task in Birmingham would have been made infinitely easier had he been able to communicate with his followers through Facebook, and contented himself with tweets from a Birmingham jail. But networks are messy: think of the ceaseless pattern of correction and revision, amendment and debate, that characterizes Wikipedia. If Martin Luther King Jr. had tried to do a wiki-boycott in Montgomery, he would have been steamrollered by the white power structure. And of what use would a digital communication tool be in a town where ninety-eight per cent of the black community could be reached every Sunday morning at church? The things that King needed in Birmingham—discipline and strategy—were things that online social media cannot provide.

The bible of the social-media movement is Clay Shirky's *Here Comes Everybody.* Shirky, who teaches at New York University, sets out to demonstrate the organizing power of the Internet, and he begins with the story of Evan, who worked on Wall Street, and his friend Ivanna, after she left her smart phone, an expensive Sidekick, on the back seat of a New York City taxicab. The telephone company transferred the data on Ivanna's lost phone to a new phone, whereupon she and Evan discovered that the Sidekick was now in the hands of a teenager from Queens, who was using it to take photographs of herself and her friends.

When Evan e-mailed the teenager, Sasha, asking for the 30 phone back, she replied that his "white ass" didn't deserve to have it back. Miffed, he set up a Web page with her picture and a description of what had happened. He forwarded the link to his friends, and they forwarded it to their friends. Someone found the MySpace page of Sasha's boyfriend, and a link to it found its way onto the site. Someone found her address online and took a video of her home while driving by; Evan posted the video on the site. The story was picked up by the news filter Digg. Evan was now up to ten e-mails a minute. He created a bulletin board for his readers to share their stories, but it crashed under the weight of responses. Evan and Ivanna went to the police, but the police filed the report under "lost," rather than "stolen," which essentially closed the case. "By this point millions of readers were watching," Shirky writes, "and dozens of mainstream news outlets had covered the story." Bowing to the pressure, the N.Y.P.D. reclassified the item as "stolen." Sasha was arrested, and Evan got his friend's Sidekick back.

Shirky's argument is that this is the kind of thing that could never have happened in the pre-Internet age—and he's right. Evan could never have tracked down Sasha. The story of the Sidekick would never have been publicized. An army of people could never have been assembled to wage this fight. The police wouldn't have bowed to the pressure of a lone person who had misplaced something as trivial as a cell phone. The story, to Shirky, illustrates "the ease and speed with which a group can be mobilized for the right kind of cause" in the Internet age.

Shirky considers this model of activism an upgrade. But it is simply a form of organizing which favors the weak-tie connections that give us access to information over the strong-tie connections that help us persevere in the face of danger. It shifts our energies from organizations that promote strategic and disciplined activity and toward those which promote resilience and adaptability. It makes it easier for activists to express themselves, and harder for that expression to have any impact. The instruments of social media are well suited to making the existing social order more efficient. They are not a natural enemy of the status quo. If you are of the opinion that all the world needs is a little buffing around the edges, this should not trouble you. But if you think that there are still lunch counters out there that need integrating it ought to give you pause.

Shirky ends the story of the lost Sidekick by asking, portentously, "What happens next?"—no doubt imagining future waves of digital protesters. But he has already answered the question. What happens next is more of the same. A networked, weak-tie world is good at things like helping Wall Streeters get phones back from teenage girls. *Viva la revolución.*

Joining the Conversation

1. What claims about the power of social media to create large-scale social change is Malcolm Gladwell responding to? What does he say, and where in his text does he bring up the views he disagrees with?

2. What is Gladwell's view of the relationship between social media and social change? What are the main arguments he

presents to support his position? How does his discussion of the Woolworth's lunch counter sit-in of 1960, which he threads through his article, fit into his argument?

3. How does Gladwell define activism? How does he distinguish between "strong tie" and "weak tie" social activism? Explain this distinction and its relevance to Gladwell's argument.

4. Read Dennis Baron's blog post on the next page (p. 329). How do his views compare with Gladwell's—how are they similar, and how do they differ?

5. Write an essay responding to Gladwell, drawing on your own experience as a user of social media and framing your argument as a response to something specific that Gladwell says. (See Chapter 2 for templates for responding in this way.)

Reforming Egypt in 140 Characters?

DENNIS BARON

WESTERN OBSERVERS have been celebrating the role of Twitter, Facebook, smartphones, and the Internet in general in facilitating the overthrow of President Hosni Mubarak in Egypt last week. An Egyptian Google employee, imprisoned for rallying the opposition on Facebook, even became for a time a hero of the insurgency. The Twitter Revolution was similarly credited with fostering the earlier ousting of Tunisia's Ben Ali, and supporting Iran's green protests last year, and it's been instrumental in other outbreaks of resistance in a variety of totalitarian states across the globe. If only Twitter had been around for Tiananmen Square, enthusiasts retweeted one another. Not bad for a site that started as a way to tell your friends what you had for breakfast.

DENNIS BARON teaches at the University of Illinois at Urbana. He's written numerous books and articles on language, literacy, and the technologies of communication, most recently *A Better Pencil* (2009)—and has been a commentator for CNN, BBC, National Public Radio, and other television and radio shows discussing issues of language use. He is a regular blogger on language topics on his website, *The Web of Language*, where the piece included here was first published.

But skeptics point out that the crowds in Cairo's Tahrir Square continued to grow during the five days that the Mubarak government shut down the Internet; that only nineteen percent of Tunisians have online access; that while the Iran protests may have been tweeted round the world, there were few Twitter users actually in-country; and that although Americans can't seem to survive without the constant stimulus of digital multitasking, much of the rest of the world barely notices when the cable is down, being preoccupied instead with raising literacy rates, fighting famine and disease, and finding clean water, not to mention a source of electricity that works for more than an hour every day or two.

It's true that the Internet connects people, and it's become an unbeatable source of information—the Egyptian revolution

What if Tiananmen Square's "Tank Man" had a Twitter account?

INDEX LIBRORVM
PROHIBITORVM,
CVM REGVLIS CONFECTIS
per Patres a Tridentina Synodo delectos,
auctoritateSanctifs.D.N. Pij IIII,
Pont.Max. comprobatus.

VENETIIS, M. D. LXIIII.

For every eye-opening book there's an *index librorum prohibitonem*
—an official do-not-read list.

was up on Wikipedia faster than you could say Wolf Blitzer. The
telephone also connected and informed faster than anything
before it, and before the telephone the printing press was the
agent of rapid-fire change. All these technologies can foment
revolution, but they can also be used to suppress dissent.

You don't have to master the laws of physics to observe that
for every revolutionary manifesto there's an equal and opposite
volley of government propaganda. For every eye-opening book
there's an *index librorum prohibitorum*—an official do-not-read

list—or worse yet, a bonfire. For every phone tree organizing a protest rally there's a warrantless wiretap waiting to throw the rally-goers in jail. And for every revolutionary Internet site there's a firewall, or in the case of Egypt, a switch that shuts it all down. Cuba is a country well-known for blocking digital access, but responding to events in Egypt and the small but scary collection of island bloggers, El Lider's government is sponsoring a dot gov rebuttal, a cadre of official counterbloggers spreading the party line to the still small number of Cubans able to get online—about ten percent can access the official government-controlled 'net—or get a cell phone signal in their '55 Chevys.

All new means of communication bring with them an irre- 5 pressible excitement as they expand literacy and open up new knowledge, but in certain quarters they also spark fear and distrust. At the very least, civil and religious authorities start

Nobody believed Hosni Mubarak when he promised free and fair elections.

insisting on an *imprimatur*—literally, a permission to print—to license communication and censor content, channeling it all toward politically or spiritually desirable ends. And when pushed too far, they ban the books, shut down the phones, and pull the plug on the 'net.

It's no surprise that the uprising in Egypt took advantage of cutting-edge communications, and it is possible that without Facebook and Twitter, Hosni Mubarak might still be holed up in the Presidential Palace, planning free and fair one-party elections in September. But it's also likely that the civilization that brought us hieroglyphics, the riddle of the Sphinx, and the mummy's curse might have had a backup plan—after all, when the libraries are burning, the phone lines get cut, the newspaper is shuttered, tanks surround the television station, and the Internet goes down, there's always sneakernet to get the message out.

Joining the Conversation

1. Dennis Baron begins by summarizing a debate, noting various views about the role of Twitter, Facebook, and other social media in the recent uprisings in the Middle East. What are those views?

2. What's Baron's own view? How can you tell? Find one sentence that you think best states the argument he is making, and explain why you picked that particular sentence.

3. How does Baron use transitions to connect the parts of his text, and to help readers follow his train of thought? (See the discussions of transitions in Chapter 8 to help you think about how they help Baron develop his argument.)

4. What if Tiananmen Square's "Tank Man" had a Twitter account? What if Che Guevara had a Blackberry? What if

Napoleon had 20,000 Facebook friends? What if Romeo and Juliet could text? What if Lila Crane had read a review of the Bates Motel on TripAdvisor? What if your laptop could generate an answer to this question? Does technology change the course of history, or is that what people do? Write an essay developing your own argument about the larger effects of social media.

2b or Not 2b?

DAVID CRYSTAL

———◻———

LAST YEAR, in a newspaper article headed "I h8 txt msgs: How texting is wrecking our language," John Humphrys argued that texters are "vandals who are doing to our language what Genghis Khan did to his neighbours 800 years ago. They are destroying it: pillaging our punctuation; savaging our sentences; raping our vocabulary. And they must be stopped."

As a new variety of language, texting has been condemned as "textese," "slanguage," a "digital virus." According to John Sutherland of University College London, writing in this paper in 2002, it is "bleak, bald, sad shorthand. Drab shrinktalk. . . . Linguistically it's all pig's ear. . . . [I]t masks dyslexia, poor spelling and mental laziness. Texting is penmanship for illiterates."

DAVID CRYSTAL is a professor at the University of Wales and is known for his work in English language studies and linguistics. He has published more than 100 books, including *The Cambridge Encyclopedia of the English Language*, *A Little Book of Language* (2010), and *Begat: The King James Bible and the English Language* (2010). He also works on Internet applications and is the inventor of an app for searching databases. This essay first appeared in the *Guardian* on July 5, 2008, and then in his book *Txtng: The Gr8 Db8* (2008).

Ever since the arrival of printing—thought to be the invention of the devil because it would put false opinions into people's minds—people have been arguing that new technology would have disastrous consequences for language. Scares accompanied the introduction of the telegraph, telephone, and broadcasting. But has there ever been a linguistic phenomenon that has aroused such curiosity, suspicion, fear, confusion, antagonism, fascination, excitement, and enthusiasm all at once as texting? And in such a short space of time. Less than a decade ago, hardly anyone had heard of it.

The idea of a point-to-point short message service (or SMS) began to be discussed as part of the development of the Global System for Mobile Communications network in the mid-1980s, but it wasn't until the early 90s that phone companies started to develop its commercial possibilities. Text communicated by pagers were replaced by text messages, at first only 20 characters in length. It took five years or more before numbers of users started to build up. The average number of texts per GSM customer in 1995 was 0.4 per month; by the end of 2000 it was still only 35.

The slow start, it seems, was because the companies had 5 trouble working out reliable ways of charging for the new service. But once procedures were in place, texting rocketed. In the UK, in 2001, 12.2 billion text messages were sent. This had doubled by 2004, and was forecast to be 45 billion in 2007. On Christmas Day alone in 2006, over 205 million texts went out. World figures went from 17 billion in 2000 to 250 billion in 2001. They passed a trillion in 2005. Text messaging generated around $70 billion in 2005. That's more than three times as much as all Hollywood box office returns that year.

People think that the written language seen on mobile phone screens is new and alien, but all the popular beliefs about texting are wrong. Its graphic distinctiveness is not a new phenomenon, nor is its use restricted to the young. There is increasing evidence that it helps rather than hinders literacy. And only a very tiny part of it uses a distinctive orthography. A trillion text messages might seem a lot, but when we set these alongside the multi-trillion instances of standard orthography in everyday life, they appear as no more than a few ripples on the surface of the sea of language. Texting has added a new dimension to language use, but its long-term impact is negligible. It is not a disaster.

Although many texters enjoy breaking linguistic rules, they also know they need to be understood. There is no point in paying to send a message if it breaks so many rules that it ceases to be intelligible. When messages are longer, containing more information, the amount of standard orthography increases. Many texters alter just the grammatical words (such as "you" and "be"). As older and more conservative language users have begun to text, an even more standardised style has appeared. Some texters refuse to depart at all from traditional orthography. And conventional spelling and punctuation is the norm when institutions send out information messages, as in this university text to students: "Weather Alert! No classes today due to snow storm," or in the texts which radio listeners are invited to send in to programmes. These institutional messages now form the majority of texts in cyberspace—and several organisations forbid the use of abbreviations, knowing that many readers will not understand them. Bad textiquette.

Research has made it clear that the early media hysteria about the novelty (and thus the dangers) of text messaging was misplaced. In one American study, less than 20% of the text messages looked at showed abbreviated forms of any kind—

about three per message. And in a Norwegian study, the proportion was even lower, with just 6% using abbreviations. In my own text collection, the figure is about 10%.

People seem to have swallowed whole the stories that youngsters use nothing else but abbreviations when they text, such as the reports in 2003 that a teenager had written an essay so full of textspeak that her teacher was unable to understand it. An extract was posted online, and quoted incessantly, but as no one was ever able to track down the entire essay, it was probably a hoax.

There are several distinctive features of the way texts are 10 written that combine to give the impression of novelty, but none of them is, in fact, linguistically novel. Many of them were being used in chatroom interactions that predated the arrival of mobile phones. Some can be found in pre-computer informal writing, dating back a hundred years or more.

The most noticeable feature is the use of single letters, numerals, and symbols to represent words or parts of words, as with b "be" and 2 "to." They are called rebuses, and they go back centuries. Adults who condemn a "c u" in a young person's texting have forgotten that they once did the same thing themselves (though not on a mobile phone). In countless Christmas annuals, they solved puzzles like this one:

YY U R YY U B I C U R YY 4 ME
("Too wise you are . . .")

Similarly, the use of initial letters for whole words (n for "no," gf for "girlfriend," cmb "call me back") is not at all new. People have been initialising common phrases for ages. IOU is known from 1618. There is no difference, apart from the medium of communication, between a modern kid's "lol" ("laughing out loud") and an earlier generation's "Swalk" ("sealed with a loving kiss").

In texts we find such forms as msg ("message") and xlnt ("excellent"). Almst any wrd cn be abbrvted in ths wy—though there is no consistency between texters. But this isn't new either. Eric Partridge published his Dictionary of Abbreviations in 1942. It contained dozens of SMS-looking examples, such as agn "again," mth "month," and gd "good"—50 years before texting was born.

English has had abbreviated words ever since it began to be written down. Words such as exam, vet, fridge, cox, and bus are so familiar that they have effectively become new words. When some of these abbreviated forms first came into use, they also attracted criticism. In 1711, for example, Joseph Addison complained about the way words were being "miserably curtailed"—he mentioned pos (itive) and incog (nito). And Jonathan Swift thought that abbreviating words was a "barbarous custom."

What novelty there is in texting lies chiefly in the way it takes further some of the processes used in the past. Some of its juxtapositions create forms which have little precedent, apart from in puzzles. All conceivable types of features can be juxtaposed—sequences of shortened and full words (hldmecls "hold me close"), logograms and shortened words (2bctnd "to be continued"), logograms and nonstandard spellings (cu2nite), and so on. There are no less that four processes combined in iowan2bwu "I only want to be with you" full word + an initialism + a shortened word + two logograms + an initialism + a logogram. And some messages contain unusual processes: in iohis4u "I only have eyes for you," we see the addition of a plural ending to a logogram. One characteristic runs through all these examples: the letters, symbols, and words are run together, without spaces. This is certainly unusual in the history of special writing systems. But few texts string together long sequences of puzzling graphic units.

There are also individual differences in texting, as in any other linguistic domain. In 2002, Stuart Campbell was found guilty of the murder of his 15-year-old niece after his text message alibi was shown to be a forgery. He had claimed that certain texts sent by the girl showed he was innocent. But a detailed comparison of the vocabulary and other stylistic features of his own text messages and those of his niece showed that he had written the messages himself. The forensic possibilities have been further explored by a team at the University of Leicester. The fact that texting is a relatively unstandardised mode of communication, prone to idiosyncrasy, turns out to be an advantage in such a context, as authorship differences are likely to be more easily detectable than in writing using standard English.

Texters use deviant spellings—and they know they are deviant. But they are by no means the first to use such nonstandard forms as cos "because," wot "what," or gissa "give us a." Several of these are so much part of English literary tradition that they have been given entries in the *Oxford English Dictionary*. "Cos" is there from 1828 and "wot" from 1829. Many can be found in literary dialect representations, such as by Charles Dickens, Mark Twain, Walter Scott, DH Lawrence, or Alan Bleasdale ("Gissa job!").

Sending a message on a mobile phone is not the most natural of ways to communicate. The keypad isn't linguistically sensible. No one took letter-frequency considerations into account when designing it. For example, key 7 on my mobile contains four symbols, pqrs. It takes four key-presses to access the letter s, and yet s is one of the most frequently occurring letters in English. It is twice as easy to input q, which is one of the least frequently occurring letters. It should be the other way round. So any strategy that reduces the time and awkwardness of inputting graphic symbols is bound to be attractive.

Abbreviations were used as a natural, intuitive response to a technological problem. And they appeared in next to no time. Texters simply transferred (and then embellished) what they had encountered in other settings. We have all left notes in which we have replaced an and by an &, a three by a 3, and so on. Anglo-Saxon scribes used abbreviations of this kind.

But the need to save time and energy is by no means the whole story of texting. When we look at some texts, they are linguistically quite complex. There are an extraordinary number of ways in which people play with language—creating riddles, solving crosswords, playing Scrabble, inventing new words. Professional writers do the same—providing catchy copy for advertising slogans, thinking up puns in newspaper headlines, and writing poems, novels, and plays. Children quickly learn that one of the most enjoyable things you can do with language is to play with its sounds, words, grammar—and spelling.

The drive to be playful is there when we text, and it is hugely 20 powerful. Within two or three years of the arrival of texting, it developed a ludic dimension. In short, it's fun.

To celebrate World Poetry day in 2007, T-Mobile tried to find the UK's first "Txt laureate" in a competition for the best romantic poem in SMS. They had 200 entrants, and as with previous competitions the entries were a mixture of unabbreviated and abbreviated texts.

The winner, Ben Ziman-Bright, wrote conventionally:

The wet rustle of rain
can dampen today. Your text
buoys me above oil-rainbow puddles
like a paper boat, so that even
soaked to the skin
I am grinning.

The runner-up did not:

O hart that sorz
My luv adorz
He mAks me liv
He mAks me giv
Myslf 2 him
As my luv porz

(The author of the latter was, incidentally, in her late 60s.)

The length constraint in text-poetry fosters economy of expression in much the same way as other tightly constrained forms of poetry do, such as the haiku or the Welsh englyn. To say a poem must be written within 160 characters at first seems just as pointless as to say that a poem must be written in three lines of five, seven, and five syllables. But put such a discipline into the hands of a master, and the result can be poetic magic. Of course, SMS poetry has some way to go before it can match the haiku tradition; but then, haikus have had a head-start of several hundred years.

There is something about the genre which has no parallel elsewhere. This is nothing to do with the use of texting abbreviations. It is more to do with the way the short lines have an individual force. Reading a text poem, wrote Peter Sansom, who co-judged a *Guardian* competition in 2002, is "an urgent business . . . with a text poem you stay focused as it were in the now of each arriving line." The impact is evident even in one-liners, whose effect relies on the kind of succinctness we find in a maxim or proverb. U.A. Fanthorpe, Sansom's fellow judge, admired "Basildon: imagine a carpark." And they both liked "They phone you up, your mum and dad."

Several competitions have focussed on reworking famous 25 lines, titles, or quotations:

> txt me ishmael
> zen & 1 @ f m2 cycl mn10nc

The brevity of the SMS genre disallows complex formal patterning—of, say, the kind we might find in a sonnet. It isn't so easy to include more than a couple of images, such as similes, simply because there isn't the space. Writers have nonetheless tried to extend the potential of the medium. The SMS novel, for example, operates on a screen-by-screen basis. Each screen is a "chapter" describing an event in the story. Here is an interactive example from 2005, from an Indian website called "Cloakroom":

> Chptr 6: While Surching 4 Her Father, Rita Bumps In2 A Chai-walla & Tea Spills On Her Blouse. She Goes Inside Da Washroom, & Da Train Halts @ A Station.

In Japan, an author known as Yoshi has had a huge success with his text-messaging novel *Deep Love*. Readers sent feedback as the story unfolded, and some of their ideas were incorporated into it. He went on to make a film of the novel.

A mobile literature channel began in China in 2004. The "m-novel," as it is called, started with a love story, "Distance," by writer and broadcaster Xuan Huang. A young couple get to know each other because of a wrongly sent SMS message. The whole story is 1008 Chinese characters, told in 15 chapters, with one chapter sent each day.

Plainly, there are severe limits to the expressive power of the medium, when it is restricted to a screen in this way. So it is not surprising that, very early on, writers dispensed with the 160-character constraint, and engaged in SMS creative writing of any length using hard copy. Immediately there was a problem. By taking the writing away from the mobile phone screen, how could the distinctiveness of the genre be maintained? So the stylistic character of SMS writing changed, and texting abbreviations, previously optional, became obligatory.

Several SMS poets, such as Norman Silver, go well beyond 30 text-messaging conventions, introducing variations in line-shape, type-size, font, and colour that are reminiscent of the concrete poetry creations of the 1960s. They illustrate the way the genre is being shaped by the more powerful applications available on computers.

In 2007 Finnish writer Hannu Luntiala published *The Last Messages*, in which the whole 332-page narrative consists of SMS messages. It tells the story of an IT-executive who resigns his job and travels the world, using text messages to keep in touch with everyone. And the growing independence of the genre from its mobile-phone origins is well illustrated by the French novelist Phil Marso, who published a book in 2004 written entirely in French SMS shorthand, *Pas Sage a Taba vo SMS*—a piece of word-play intended to discourage young people from smoking. The next year he produced *L*, an SMS retelling of French poetic classics.

An extraordinary number of doom-laden prophecies have been made about the supposed linguistic evils unleashed by texting. Sadly, its creative potential has been virtually ignored. But five years of research has at last begun to dispel the myths. The most important finding is that texting does not erode children's ability to read and write. On the contrary, literacy improves. The latest studies (from a team at Coventry University) have found strong positive links between the use of text language and the skills underlying success in standard English in pre-teenage children. The more abbreviations in their messages, the higher they scored on tests of reading and vocabulary. The children who were better at spelling and writing used the most textisms. And the younger they received their first phone, the higher their scores.

Children could not be good at texting if they had not already developed considerable literacy awareness. Before you can write and play with abbreviated forms, you need to have a sense of how the sounds of your language relate to the letters. You need to know that there are such things as alternative spellings. If you are aware that your texting behaviour is different, you must have already intuited that there is such a thing as a standard. If you are using such abbreviations as lol and brb ("be right back"), you must have developed a sensitivity to the communicative needs of your textees.

Some people dislike texting. Some are bemused by it. But it is merely the latest manifestation of the human ability to be linguistically creative and to adapt language to suit the demands of diverse settings. There is no disaster pending. We will not see a new generation of adults growing up unable to write proper English. The language as a whole will not decline. In texting what we are seeing, in a small way, is language in evolution.

Joining the Conversation

1. David Crystal begins his article with some strong "they say" arguments, quoting writers who argue that text messaging is destroying the English language. At what point in the article do you begin to see that his own perspective is very different from that of such critics?

2. Summarize Crystal's arguments in favor of text messaging. In what ways have the dangers of this phenomenon been vastly overstated, in his opinion? How does he organize his argument? What are his main points, and what kinds of support does he offer?

3. Crystal wrote this article for a British newspaper read primarily by adults. What might he have done differently if the piece had been for, say, an audience of middle or high school students?

4. Reread the two text message poems on page 342. Which one do you prefer? In what ways do these poems support his argument?

5. Were you surprised by the research findings in paragraph 32 showing that texting improves literacy skills? Think about your own use of texting, and how it differs from more formal kinds of writing you do (including email). Try rewriting a couple text messages as email to see what you do differently—then revise some email as text messages. Finally, write a paragraph or two comparing your writing in texts and email and reflecting on the differences.

ROZ CHAST is a staff cartoonist for the *New Yorker*, where this cartoon first appeared in 2002. She is also the author or illustrator of many books, among them *Theories of Everything* (2006).

Joining the Conversation

1. What argument is Roz Chast making with this cartoon? That is, what larger point about young people's use of technology is she trying to make?

2. What assumption or position do you think Chast is responding to?

3. This is a visual text, though it includes words as well as pictures. Imagine you wanted to cite this cartoon in an essay about instant messaging. Write a paragraph about the point Chast makes, quoting from the cartoon for examples. Be sure to introduce any quotations and to follow them up with your own explanation.

4. Rewrite the dialogue between Romeo and Juliet using formal English. How does this change in language affect the way you read the cartoon? What sort of pictures should accompany your revision?

5. Take a passage from another classic literary text and rewrite it as Chast has here, as an instant message. You might try something from *The Odyssey*, *Pride and Prejudice*, *The Great Gatsby*, or any other text you have studied.

Extra Lives:
Why Video Games Matter

TOM BISSELL

—◻—

SOMEDAY MY CHILDREN will ask me where I was and what
I was doing when the United States elected its first black president. I could tell my children—who are entirely hypothetical;
call them Kermit and Hussein—that I was home at the time
and, like hundreds of millions of other Americans, watching
television. This would be a politician's answer, which is to say,
factual but inaccurate in every important detail. Because Kermit and Hussein deserve an honestly itemized answer, I will tell
them that, on November 4, 2008, their father was living in
Tallinn, Estonia, where the American Election Day's waning

TOM BISSELL teaches at Portland State University, and his writing has
appeared in the *New Republic* and the *Virginia Quarterly Review*, for
which he is a contributing editor. He has published both fiction and
nonfiction, including *God Lives in St. Petersburg and Other Stories* (2005)
and *The Father of All Things: A Marine, His Son, and the Legacy of Vietnam* (2007). This essay is taken from a chapter of his most recent book,
Extra Lives: Why Video Games Matter (2010). His Xbox Live gamertag
is T C Bissell, and his PlayStation Network gamertag is TCBissell.

hours were a cold, salmon-skied November 5 morning. My intention that day was to watch CNN International until the race was called. I will then be forced to tell Kermit and Hussein about what else happened on November 4, 2008.

The postapocalyptic video game *Fallout 3* had been officially released to the European market on October 30, but in Estponia it was nowhere to be found. For several weeks, Bethesda Softworks, *Fallout 3*'s developer, had been posting online a series of promotional gameplay videos, which I had been watching and rewatching with fetish-porn avidity. I left word with Tallinn's best game store: *Call me the moment Fallout 3 arrives.* In the late afternoon of November 4, they finally rang. When I slipped the game into the tray of my Xbox 360, the first polls were due to close in America in two hours. One hour of *Fall-*

Fallout 3 poster promoting the game's release.

out 3, I told myself. Maybe two. Absolutely no more than three. Seven hours later, blinking and dazed, I turned off my Xbox 360, checked in with CNN, and discovered that the acceptance speech had already been given.

And so, my beloved Kermit, my dear little Hussein, See Chapter 9
at the moment America changed forever, your father was on mixing collo-
wandering an ICBM-denuded wasteland, nervously mon- quial styles.
itoring his radiation level, armed only with a baseball bat, a 10mm pistol, and six rounds of ammunition, in search of a vicious gang of mohawked marauders who were 100 percent bad news and totally had to be dealt with. Trust Daddy on this one.

Fallout 3 was Bethesda's first release since 2006's *The Elder Scrolls IV: Oblivion*. Both games fall within a genre known by various names: the open-world or sandbox or free-roaming game. This genre is superintended by a few general conventions, which include the sensation of being inside a large and disinterestedly functioning world, a main story line that can be abandoned for subordinate story lines (or for no purpose at all), large numbers of supporting characters with whom meaningful interaction is possible, and the ability to customize (or pimp, in the parlance of our time) the game's player-controlled central character. The pleasures of the open world game are ample, complicated, and intensely private; their potency is difficult to explain, sort of like religion, of which these games become, for many, an aspartame form. Because of the freedom they grant gamers, the narrative- and mission-generating manner in which they reward exploration, and their convincing illusion of endlessness, the best open-world games tend to become leisure-time-eating viruses. As incomprehensible as it may seem, I have somehow spent more than two hundred hours playing *Oblivion*. I know this because the game keeps a running tally of the total time one has spent with it.

It is difficult to describe *Oblivion* without atavistic fears of being savaged by the same jean-jacketed dullards who in 1985 threw my *Advanced Dungeon & Dragons Monster Manual II* into Lake Michigan (That I did not even play D&D, and only had the book because I liked to look at the pictures, left my assailants unmoved.) As to what *Oblivion* is about, I note the involvement of orcs and a "summon skeleton" spell and leave it at that. So: two hundred hours playing *Oblivion*? How is that even possible? I am not actually sure. Completing the game's narrative missions took a fraction of that time, but in the world of *Oblivion* you can also pick flowers, explore caves, dive for treasure, buy houses, bet on gladiatorial arena fights, hunt bear, and read books. *Oblivion* is less a game than a world that best rewards full citizenship, and for a while I lived there and claimed it. At the time I was residing in Rome on a highly coveted literary fellowship, surrounded by interesting and brilliant people, and quite naturally mired in a lagoon of depression more dreadfully lush than any before or since. I would be lying if I said *Oblivion* did not, in some ways, aggravate my depression, but it also gave me something with which to fill my days other than piranhic self-hatred. It was an extra life; I am grateful to have had it.

When Bethesda announced that it had purchased the rights to develop *Fallout 3* from the defunct studio Interplay, the creators of the first two *Fallout* games, many were doubtful. How would the elvish imaginations behind *Oblivion* manage with the rather different milieu of an annihilated twenty-third-century America? The first *Fallout* games, which were exclusive to the personal computer, were celebrated for their clever satire and often freakishly exaggerated violence. *Oblivion* is about as satirical as a colonoscopy, and the fighting in the game, while not unviolent, is often weirdly inert.

Bethesda released *Fallout 3*'s first gameplay video in the summer of 2008. In it, Todd Howard, the game's producer, guides the player-controlled character into a disorientingly nuked Washington, DC, graced with just enough ravaged familiarities— among which a pummeled Washington Monument stands out— to be powerfully unsettling. Based on these few minutes, *Fallout 3* appeared guaranteed to take its place among the most visually impressive games ever made. When Bethesda posted a video showcasing *Fallout 3*'s in-game combat—a brilliant synthesis of trigger-happy first-person-style shooting and the more deliberative, turn-based tactics of the traditional role-playing video game, wherein you attack, suffer your enemy's counterattack,

The player-controlled character of *Fallout 3* in a futuristic Washington, D.C.

counterattack yourself, and so on, until one of you is dead—many could not believe the audacity of its cartoon-Peckinpah violence. Much of it was rendered in a slo-mo as disgusting as it was oddly beautiful: skulls exploding into the distinct flotsam of eyeballs, gray matter, and upper vertebrae; limbs liquefying into constellations of red pearls; torsos somersaulting through the air. The consensus was a bonfire of the skepticisms: *Fallout 3* was going to be fucking awesome.

Needless to say, the first seven hours I spent with the game were distinguished by a bounty of salutary things. Foremost among them was how the world of *Fallout 3* looked. The art direction in a good number of contemporary big-budget video games has the cheerful parasitism of a tribute band. Visual inspirations are perilously few: Forests will be Tolkienishly enchanted; futuristic industrial zones will be mazes of predictably grated metal catwalks; gunfights will erupt amid rubble- and car-strewn boulevards on loan from a thousand war-movie sieges. Once video games shed their distinctive vector-graphic and primary-color 8-bit origins, a commercially ascendant subset of game slowly but surely matured into what might well be the most visually derivative popular art form in history. *Fallout 3* is the rare big-budget game to begin rather than end with its derivativeness.

It opens in 2277, two centuries after a nuclear conflagration between the United States and China. Chronologically speaking, the world this Sino-American war destroyed was of late-twenty-first-century vintage, and yet its ruins are those of the gee-whiz futurism popular during the Cold War. *Fallout 3*'s Slinky-armed sentry Protectrons, for instance, are knowing plagiarisms of *Forbidden Planet*'s Robby the Robot, and the game's many specimens of faded prewar advertising mimic the nascent slickness of 1950s-era graphic design. *Fallout 3* bravely takes as its aesthetic foundation a future that is both six decades old and one of the least convincing ever conceptualized. The result is a fascinating past-future never-never-land weirdness that infects the game's every corner: *George Jetson Beyond Thunderdome*.

What also impressed me about *Fallout 3* was the buffet of 10 choices set out by its early stages. The first settlement one happens upon, Megaton, has been built around an undetonated nuclear warhead, which a strange religious cult native to the town actually worships. Megaton can serve as base of operations or be wiped off the face of the map shortly after one's arrival there by detonating its nuke in exchange for a handsome payment. I spent quite a while poking around Megaton and getting to know its many citizens. What this means is that the first several hours I spent inside *Fallout 3* were, in essence, optional. Even for an open-world game, this suggests an awesome range of narrative variability. (Eventually, of course, I made the time to go back and nuke the place.)

Fallout 3, finally, looks beautiful. Most modern games—even shitty ones—look beautiful. Taking note of this is akin to telling the chef of a Michelin-starred restaurant that the tablecloths were lovely. Nonetheless, at one point in *Fallout 3* I was running up the stairs of what used to be the Dupont Circle Metro station and, as I turned to bash in the brainpan of a radioactive ghoul, noticed the playful, lifelike way in which the high-noon sunlight streaked along the grain of my sledgehammer's wooden handle. During such moments, it is hard not to be startled—even moved—by the care poured into the game's smallest atmospheric details.

Despite all this, I had problems with *Fallout 3*, and a number of these problems seem to me emblematic of the intersection at which games in general currently find themselves stalled.

Take, for instance, *Fallout 3*'s tutorial. One feels for game designers: It would be hard to imagine a formal convention more inherently bizarre than the video-game tutorial. Imagine that, every time you open a novel, you are forced to suffer through a chapter in which the characters do nothing but talk to one another about the physical mechanics of how one goes about reading a book. Unfortunately, game designers do not really have a choice. Controller schemas change, sometimes drastically, from game to game, and designers cannot simply banish a game's relevant instructions to a directional booklet: That would be a violation of the interactive pact between game and gamer. Many games thus have to come up with a narratively plausible way in which one's controlled character engages in activity comprehensive enough to be instructive but not so intense as to involve a lot of failure. Games with a strong element of combat almost always solve this dilemma by opening with some sort of indifferently conceived boot-camp exercise or training round.

Fallout 3's tutorial opens, rather more ambitiously, with your character's birth, during which you pick your race and gender (if given the choice, I always opt for a woman, for whatever reason) and design your eventual appearance (probably this is the reason). The character who pulls you from your mother's birth canal is your father, whose voice is provided by Liam Neeson. (Many games attempt to class themselves up with early appearances by accomplished actors; Patrick Stewart's platinum larynx served this purpose in *Oblivion*.) Now, aspects of *Fallout 3*'s tutorial are brilliant: When you learn to walk as a baby, you are actually learning how to move within the game; you decide whether you want your character to be primarily strong, intelligent, or charismatic by reading a children's book; and, when the tutorial flashes forward to your tenth birthday party, you learn to fire weapons when you receive a BB gun as a gift. The tutorial flashes forward again, this time to a high school classroom, where your further define your character by answering ten aptitude-test-style questions. What is interesting about this is that it allows you to customize your character *indirectly* rather than directly, and many of the questions (one asks what you would do if your grandmother ordered you to kill someone) are morbidly amusing. While using an in-game aptitude test as a character-design aid is not exactly a new innovation, *Fallout 3* provides the most streamlined, narrratively economical, and interactively inventive go at it yet.

By the time I was taking this aptitude test, however, I was a dissident citizen of Vault 101, the isolated underground society in which *Fallout 3* proper begins. My revolt was directed at a few things. The first was *Fallout 3*'s dialogue, some of it so appalling ("Oh, James, we did it. A daughter. Our beautiful daughter") as to make Stephanie Meyer look like Ibsen. The second was *Fallout 3*'s addiction to trust-shattering storytelling redundancy, such as when your father announces, "I can't believe you're already ten," at what is clearly established as your tenth birthday party. The third, and least forgivable, was *Fallout 3*'s Jell-O-mold characterization: In the game's first ten minutes you exchange gossip with the spunky best friend, cower beneath the megalomaniacal leader, and gain the trust of the goodhearted cop. Vault 101 even has a resident cadre of hoodlums, the Tunnel Snakes, whose capo resembles a malevolent Fonz. Even with its backdrop of realized Cold War futurism, a greaser-style youth gang in an underground vault society in the year 2277 is the working definition of a dumb idea. During the tutorial's final sequence, the Tunnel Snakes' leader, your tormentor since childhood, requests your help in saving his mother from radioactive cockroaches (long story), a reversal of such tofu drama that, in my annoyance, I killed him, his mother, and then everyone else I could find in Vault 101, with the most perversely satisfying weapon I had on hand: a baseball bat. Allowing your decisions to establish for your character an in-game identity as a skull-crushing monster, a saint of patience, or some mixture thereof is another attractive feature of *Fallout 3*. These pretensions to morality, though, suddenly bored me, because they were occurring in a universe that had been designed by geniuses and written by Ed Wood Jr.

Had I really waited a year for this? And was I really missing a cardinal event in American history to keep playing it? I had, and I was, and I could not really explain why.

What I know is this: If I were reading a book or watching a film that, every ten minutes, had me gulping a gallon of aesthetic Pepto, I would stop reading or watching. Games, for some reason, do not have this problem. Or rather, their problem is not having this problem. I routinely tolerate in games crudities I would never tolerate in any other form of art or entertainment. For a long time my rationalization was that, provided a game was fun to play, certain failures could be overlooked. I came to accept that games were generally incompetent with almost every aspect of what I would call traditional narrative. In the last few years, however, a dilemma has become obvious. Games have grown immensely sophisticated in any number of ways while at the same time remaining stubbornly attached to aspects of traditional narrative for which they have shown little feeling. Too many games insist on telling stories in a manner in which some facility with plot and character is fundamental to—and often even determinative of—successful storytelling.

The counterargument to all this is that games such as *Fallout 3* are more about the world in which the game takes place than the story concocted to govern one's progress through it. It is a fair point, especially given how beautifully devastated and hypnotically lonely the world of *Fallout 3* is. But if the world is paramount, why bother with a story at all? Why not simply cut the ribbon on the invented world and let gamers explore it? The answer is that such a game would probably not be very involving. Traps, after all, need bait. In a narrative game, story and world combine to create an experience. As the game designer Jesse Schell writes in *The Art of Game Design*, "The game is not the experience. The game enables the experience, but it *is not the experience*." In a world as large as that of *Fallout 3*, which allows for an experience framed in terms of wandering and lonesomeness, story provides, if nothing else, badly needed direction and purpose. Unless some narrative game comes along that radically changes gamer expectation, stories, with or without Super Mutants, will continue to be what many games will use to harness their uniquely extravagant brand of fictional absorption.

I say this in full disclosure: The games that interest me the most are the games that choose to tell stories. Yes, video games have always told some form of story. PLUMBER'S GIRLFRIEND CAPTURED BY APE! is a story, but it is a rudimentary fairytale story without any of the proper fairytale's evocative nuances and dreads. Games are often compared to films, which would seem to make sense, given their many apparent similarities (both are scored, both have actors, both are cinematographical, and so on). Upon close inspection comparison falls leprously apart. In terms of storytelling, they could not be more different. Films favor a compressed type of storytelling and are able to do this because they have someone deciding where to point the camera. Games, on the other hand, contain more than most gamers can ever hope to see, and the person deciding where to point the camera is, in many cases, you—and you might never even see the "best part." The best part of looking up at a night sky, after all, is not any one star but the infinite possibility of what is between stars. Games often provide an approximation of this feeling, with the difference that you can find out what is out there. Teeming with secrets, hidden areas, and surprises that may pounce only on the second or third (or fourth) play-through—I still laugh to think of the time I made it to an isolated, hard-to-find corner of *Fallout 3*'s Wasteland and was greeted by the words FUCK YOU spray-painted on a rock—video games favor a form of storytelling that is, in many ways, completely unprecedented. The conventions of this form of storytelling are only a few decades old and were created in a formal vacuum by men and women who still walk among us. There are not many mediums whose Dantes and Homers one can ring up and talk to. With games, one can.

I am uninterested in whether games are better or worse than movies or novels or any other form of entertainment. More interesting to me is what games *can* do and how they make me feel while they are doing it. Comparing games to other forms of entertainment only serves as a reminder of what games are not. Storytelling, however, does not belong to film any more than it belongs to the novel. Film, novels, and video games are separate economies in which storytelling is the currency. The problem is that video-game storytelling, across a wide spectrum of games, too often feels counterfeit, and it is easy to tire of laundering the bills.

It should be said that *Fallout 3* gets much better as you play 20 through it. A few of its set pieces (such as stealing the Declaration of Independence from a ruined National Archives, which is protected by a bewigged robot programmed to believe itself to be Button Gwinnett, the Declaration's second signatory) are as gripping as any fiction I have come across. But it cannot be a coincidence that every scene involving human emotion (confronting a mind-wiped android who believes he is human, watching as a character close to you suffocates and dies) is at best unaffecting and at worst risible. Can it really be a surprise that deeper human motivations remain beyond the reach of something that regards character as the assignation of numerical values to hypothetical abilities and characteristics?

Viewed as a whole, *Fallout 3* is a game of profound stylishness, sophistication, and intelligence—so much so that every example of Etch A Sketch characterization, every stone-shoed narrative pivot, pains me. When we say a game is sophisticated, are we grading on a distressingly steep curve? Or do we need a new curve altogether? Might we really mean that the game in question only occasionally insults one's intelligence? Or is this kind of intelligence, at least when it comes to playing games, beside the point? How is it, finally, that I keep returning to a form of entertainment that I find so uniquely frustrating? To what part of me do games speak, and on which frequency?

Joining the Conversation

1. Why, according to Tom Bissell, are video games so appealing? What evidence does he provide?
2. Bissell begins with a self-mocking personal anecdote about playing video games. Why do you think he includes the story and places it in such a prominent location? How does it set the essay up as an argument that looks beyond the pros and cons of a particular video game?

3. Bissell says in paragraph 18 that the games that interest him the most are the ones that tell stories. How are they different from stories in films or novels?

4. So what? It's clear that Tom Bissell cares a lot about video games, but how does he make clear, as his title suggests, why they matter?

5. Bissell closes by asking, "How is it, finally, that I keep returning to a form of entertainment that I find so uniquely frustrating?" Write an essay about why you like video games—or if that's not the case, write about some other activity that you like a lot.

The Good, the Bad, and
The Daily Show

JASON ZINSER

———⊡———

IN RECENT YEARS an increasing number of Americans have turned away from mainstream media sources and tuned in to alternative, fake news programs such as *The Daily Show* with Jon Stewart. By cleverly blending comedy with coverage of news-worthy events, these programs create a hybrid form of enter-tainment-news. However, this new form of "infotainment" raises a number of unique ethical questions. Is it good to have large numbers of people getting their news from a comedian? What kind of information—or misinformation—do fake news programs impart to their audience? Might fake news like *The Daily Show* have a negative effect on the media and the culture at large?

Like most things, *The Daily Show* isn't all good or all bad. The question isn't whether Jon Stewart or the show's produc-

JASON ZINSER teaches at the University of North Florida. He received a Ph.D. in philosophy in 2007 from Florida State University, and he researches both evolutionary biology and environmental philosophies. This essay first appeared in *The Daily Show and Philosophy: Moments of Zen in the Art of Fake News* (2007), edited by Jason Holt.

ers and writers are morally corrupt people, but whether or not fake news is, on the whole, beneficial or damaging to society. What questions should we be asking about this apparent shift in journalism? What should we expect from the media? We wouldn't have to worry about such questions if fake news programs weren't influential, but their popularity requires us to examine them critically. As I will argue, *The Daily Show* exhibits both virtues and vices. The real challenge will be to assess the overall impact of fake news.

Before we can assess the news value of *The Daily Show*, we must first ask why we should care about where people get their news and whether it's important for them to be informed. The dissemination of news is extremely important for them to be informed. The dissemination of news is extremely important in a democratic state. Just think of the damaging effects state-controlled media have on North Korea, Iran, or Iraq under Hussein's regime. An informed public is the grease that keeps democracy running properly. Although foreign and domestic issues aren't settled by popular vote, an informed public wields great democratic power. An indirect test of this is the emphasis that politicians place on packaging their partisan messages, often in the form of a coordinated attack on the hearts and minds of the public. If our opinion didn't really matter, why would politicians go to such lengths? If our opinion does matter, then it seems we should be concerned with having the proper institutions in place to ensure that we're being properly informed.

Journalists like Tom Fenton have blamed the media for failing to anticipate the pre-9/11 threat posed by terrorism.[1] By reducing the number of foreign correspondents and cutting down on hard news stories, real foreign policy issues had been more or less remaindered to the periphery of the news. Threats like Al Qaeda were able to fly under the media's radar, even after the first World Trade Center bombing in 1993. Having a population concerned and informed about relevant facts and issues helps guide the future course of the country. Although the media is supposed to report stories "in the public interest," Fenton complained: "The networks are obsessed with the ratings race. Politicians and statesmen line up to appear on the ersatz news *Daily Show*, and bloggers seem to be breaking the real news. Even as the urgent problems of Iraq, Iran, North Korea, and a resurgent Russia compete for our attention, the news media fiddle while Rome burns" (p. x). Do fake news programs merely reflect this shift in media and culture, do they themselves change the journalistic landscape, or does the influence run both ways?

The Vices of Fake News

Ted Koppel, former host of ABC's *Nightline*, commented, "a lot of television viewers—more, quite frankly, than I'm comfortable with—get their news from the Comedy Channel on a program called *The Daily Show*."[2] What's the cause of Koppel's discomfort? I see two potential problems with so-called fake news programs: *deception* and *dilution*. Unlike dramatizations such as *The West Wing*, *The Daily Show* uses real events as a vehicle for comedy. Furthermore, the program's guest list would turn the head of any network news exec. Calling *The Daily Show* fake news is somewhat misleading (so we'll put the term in scare quotes—"fake"—from here on). At the same time, *The Daily Show* bills itself as a "nightly half-hour series unburdened by objectivity, journalistic integrity, or even accuracy." This leaves us with a tension: the show is "unburdened by objectivity," and yet "informs" large swaths of America about foreign and national news events. I'll call this the problem of deception—cloaking (even if it is unintentional) a real news program as entertainment. The second concern I'll call the problem of dilution. The success of *The Daily Show*, which attracts over 1.4 million for their daily dose,[3] may prompt traditional journalistic venues, such as nightly news programs on major broadcast networks, to infuse hard news with entertainment, which might dilute the news media at large. Each of these criticisms will be dealt with in turn.

The popularity of *The Daily Show* reflects its entertainment and comedic value. People tune in to watch Jon Stewart and his onscreen staff because they're funny. But laughs aren't the only thing viewers take away. The jokes and skits are based on, and peppered with, real news items and real stories. Whether people tune in to be entertained, to be informed, or both, the fact is that *The Daily Show* shapes people's perspective on the world. Once we realize this, we can and should question the quality of the information viewers are receiving.

Although the incidental imparting of news might be seen as a benefit (as I will discuss later), one could raise the complaint that, because of its use, because of how it functions, or is taken to function, *The Daily Show* should, but doesn't, hold itself to the same journalistic standards traditional news agencies do. Can a show "unburdened by objectivity" be expected to communicate news to the public accurately and responsibly? Can a program concerned with getting ratings through comedy be expected to provide objective and responsible coverage of world events? Of course "deception" means "the intentional imparting of false information to another," and it doesn't seem that *The Daily Show* fits this definition. For one thing, it's probably not meant to deceive anyone, and for another, it claims to be something other than a legitimate news source. However, is this claim fair? As already mentioned, the show's content and guest list suggest otherwise. Of course there are many purely entertaining, merely funny segments, but most of the show is centered on the news and newsworthy events. Furthermore, I'm not suggesting that viewers can't distinguish between the pure entertainment and the news-driven stories. I'm assuming that the audience is intelligent enough to thresh the wheat from the chaff. Even so, people might well think they're being fully or sufficiently informed when they watch *Daily Show* news segments. Can one be expected to get quality reporting from a comedy show? Does a comedian have the expertise or rigorous standards to communicate newsworthy events reliably?

Analogous arguments are often levied against violent video games and sexist music videos. Invariably, the creators of these perceived violent or offensive media claim that their products are fictional and not intended to be taken literally. Intentionally or not, if negative but predictable consequences result from particular media, the creators should, in some sense, be held accountable. Likewise, if people watch *The Daily Show* to become informed, either explicitly or implicitly, then the show may have obligations to provide a responsible product.[4]

A more pernicious form of deception occurs when entertainment is presented under the guise of unbiased, objective reporting. There are clear examples of this form of media deception emananting from both political parties and a variety of special interests. Anecdotally, I viewed Michael Moore's notorious film, *Fahrenheit 9/11*, at a university screening. While I cringed at many points during the screening, the undergraduate crowd erupted in cheers. My discomfort had little to do with my political leanings, and more to do with Moore's fallacious and rhetorical style, which is dangerous because many students likely took the film to be an unbiased retelling of events surrounding 9/11. The reasoning that leads to a conclusion is often as important as, if not in some ways more important than, the conclusion itself. There are a lot of unsound or invalid arguments that have true conclusions. You want an argument to yield a true conclusion, yes, but only when it has proper premises and strong reasoning to take you to that conclusion. Whatever the take-home message of *Fahrenheit 9/11* was, however justified it may be otherwise, it wasn't well argued for.

Although, unlike Moore's movie, which claimed to be a doc- 10 umentary, *The Daily Show* doesn't claim to be a news show, it may fall prey to similar criticism. While I find myself agreeing with many of the points made on the show, the path taken to these points is often short, even slight. Rather than prolonged discussion or detailed analysis of a particular topic, *Daily Show* news is, and must be, molded into joke form. The journey to a conclusion is often too quick, the answers too pat. When journalism is done well, it gives people enough information to make up their own minds. But substandard media tends to be pandering, not informing, often to the lowest common denominator, as Jon Stewart himself self-effacingly admits. Where *The Daily Show* falls on the continuum between substandard news media and good hard news remains an open question.

Another potential problem with "fake" news is the threat of dilution, undermining the integrity and substance of hard news. There are two ways that *The Daily Show* may be contributing to such dilution of the mass media. The first is that "fake" news, along with blogs and other alternative forms of media, fragments the face of journalism, making it difficult to decide which news sources to trust, perhaps unduly undermining audience confidence in news agencies. As such, *The Daily Show* may simply be part of a greater problem. For example, the internet has transformed research in a variety of ways, often for the worse. At my fingertips are staggering numbers of resources, an overwhelming amount of information. However, while the quantity and immediacy of access to information has certainly increased, it's not clear that the quality has. Practically anyone can put practically anything online whenever they want. Similarly, some have argued that the ever-increasing quantity of academic journals has reduced the quality of many of these journals. Not all sources or resources are created equal. If *The Daily Show* increases the dilution by adding another alternative to hard news, so much the worse.

A second form of dilution may be a result of the show's influence on the media at large. Make no mistake, like *The Daily Show*, mainstream media is part of the profit-driven corporate world. The pattern of mixing entertainment with news, mastered if not created by *The Daily Show*, might and perhaps already has spilled over into hard news, although whether *The Daily Show* is really to blame for this is another matter. Some see the hiring of Katie Couric as lead anchor of the *CBS Nightly News* as a nod to style over substance. Critics have noted that Couric clearly isn't being cast as a Walter Cronkite or Edward R. Murrow, but rather as an entertaining, engaging personality that can attract more viewers. The more popular "fake" news programs become, the more likely traditional media will continue to follow suit, softening hard news with mere and mixed entertainment. To echo Fenton, the fiddling becomes louder.

The Virtues of "Fake" News

Not all the news on "fake" news is bad. The criticisms raised in the previous section focused on the negative but unintended effects of "fake" news. If we can criticize *The Daily Show* for such consequences, then we should also be able to praise it for any unintentional, not to mention intentional, benefits. Matthew Baum argues that "fake" news imparts knowledge of certain issues (especially foreign policy) to an otherwise inattentive portion of the population.[5] Backed by extensive empirical data, Baum argues that regular viewers of "fake" news programming are more aware of foreign affairs than those who don't watch such programming. Like sneaking vegetables onto a pizza, The Daily Show delivers the news in a way better suited to our ever-shrinking attention spans. From this perspective, the show isn't "converting" viewers from traditional media venues, but rather informing an untapped segment of the population which would be uninformed otherwise. If true, this seemingly would be a genuine benefit, even if unintentional. In some ways Baum's view has been confirmed by a 2004 National Annenberg Election Study which found that Daily Show viewers could correctly answer more questions about the Presidential candidates than viewers of national television news or newspaper readers.[6] Unlike Baum, the authors of the Annenberg study were quick to point out that The Daily Show itself might not be responsible for raising the knowledge level of its viewers. Perhaps the show is simply more appealing to those who already happen to be informed.

Let's assume at least that Baum is correct in that The Daily Show attracts and informs an otherwise inattentive and uninformed segment of the public. Is this enough? Not necessarily. More than the content itself, the quality of the news is important. If The Daily Show simply informs viewers enough to be able to identify certain people, places, and events, and to know that certain things are going on in the world, it's not clear that the show provides a valuable public service. It isn't enough to simply report the facts or certain interpretations of them; news should be balanced and comprehensive, informing the audience in a useful, robust way. If viewers simply parrot what they happen to hear on *The Daily Show*, how can they be expected to make informed decisions about public policy? As the saying goes, "a little knowledge can be dangerous." To show that *The Daily Show's* imparting of minimal knowledge to an otherwise inattentive audience is really beneficial, something more is needed than what "fake" news usually provides. What's needed is for "fake" news to provide depth and insight, and not just make viewers aware, say, of where to locate Venezuela on a map. (This in itself would be no small feat, given Americans' poor knowledge of geography. But the news is supposed to do more than this.)

It would be truly beneficial to have *The Daily Show* impart 15 a kind of knowledge that traditional news can't. Surprisingly, this might be the show's greatest virtue, and perhaps also a significant reason for its success. Being "unburdened by objectivity," *The Daily Show* is unfettered by the typical constraints of traditional news. It has more freedom to comment on, and to counteract, the spin that so often accompanies news stories of the day. Through sarcasm, cynicism, parody, and irony, the show can impart a kind of information inappropriate and unavailable to conventional news outlets. Furthermore, *The Daily Show* isn't afraid to offend political parties, business concerns, religious (and other) groups, or individual people. To this extent, the news presented by *The Daily Show* is often more honest in certain respects than hard news is. Jon Stewart has the freedom to say the things that most anchors can only say off camera.

It's important to note that political and social changes are often initiated by a variety of means. Three stories come to mind. One fateful night at a campaign rally in Iowa, Howard Dean, in a moment of hyper-excitation, screamed into the microphone. This embarrassing moment was caught by the media, especially "fake" news. Shortly afterward, Dean's campaign ran out of steam—many think because of the "yawp heard round the world." It wouldn't be the first time that a presidential candidate fell due to an unfortunate turn of events. During his bid for the Presidency, Bob Dole fell off a stage during a campaign stop in Chico, California. Most commentary on the evening news concerned how many points Dole's fall would cost him in the polls, not whether such a cost would be in any way justified. What on earth could falling off a poorly constructed stage reveal about the quality of a Presidential candidate?

In contrast to these cases, consider the origin of the modern environmental movement in America. Rachel Carson's famous book, *Silent Spring*, brought to light the dangers of pesticides and their destructive effects on ecosystems. Consequently, DDT was banned and the environmental movement was born. Dean's scream and Dole's fall, although embarrassing, seem irrelevant to the qualifications of either as Presidential candidates. Carson, on the other hand, not a scientist but a nature writer, brought about significant change by raising relevant concerns in an innovative way. She didn't merely tell us that pesticides harm the environment, she made a strong case for why we should care about the environment.

See Chapter 8 on using transitions to help readers follow your train of thought.

The lesson here is that non-traditional news stories and non-traditional news outlets can be catalysts for political and social change, bad or good, the means relevant or irrelevant. As an unconventional outlet with a wide audience, *The Daily Show* is just the kind of vehicle that can, and often does, make a difference. Through amusing presentation of serious stories, *The Daily Show* humanizes them, imparting more than just facts, providing some perspective on them, reflecting and informing our concerns—exactly what good reporting ought to accomplish.

Teaching to the Top of the Class

To review, the potential hazards of "fake" news include deception and dilution, while the potential benefits include informing an otherwise inattentive audience and providing informed individuals with a different kind of information than that of traditional hard news. For these reasons, *The Daily Show* was both condemned and praised for being "unburdened by objectivity." Critically speaking, the lack of traditional journalistic standards doesn't require "fake" news to be especially thorough or impartial. Important but uninteresting news events may not be covered unless they can be made funny somehow. At the same time, the lack of journalistic standards allows "fake" news the liberty and the tools to inform the audience in ways unavailable to mainstream media. Can both of these be true? Yes. Although *The Daily Show* may be limited in the scope of events it covers, it often says insightful things about the stories it does cover. This is true not only of *The Daily Show*, but of a variety of "fake" news shows and other types of new media: blogs, quasi-documentaries, and cable news programming.

One important difference between *The Daily Show* and tra- 20 ditional media sources is that "fake" news typically doesn't gather the news, but rather comments on stories first reported by traditional news. As Aaron McKain puts it, traditional media acts as a "gatekeeper" for "fake" news.[1] So even when *The Daily Show* criticizes the traditional media, they may provide a different perspective on news content, but they don't provide a true *alternative* to it. McKain illustrates this problem by pointing to a particular episode: April 18, 2004. That day, mainstream media was focused on Michael Jackson's indictment, not on more newsworthy events like the Presidential election or the war in Iraq. When Jon Stewart is confronted by mainstream media criticism, his tactic is to claim that The Daily Show is comedy, not a news show. This seems at best rather convenient and at worst perhaps a bit hypocritical, and reinforces the charge of deception aired earlier. Nonetheless, the show can still be a useful foil to mainstream media. Even if The Daily Show is a little hypocritical in criticizing the media without offering a real alternative, it doesn't follow that the show is unreliable, or that its content is false. If a smoker tells his children not to smoke because it's bad for their health, he may be a hypocrite, but it doesn't follow that smoking isn't bad for one's health. To argue that because someone is a hypocrite, what they say is false, is an informal fallacy called ad hominem. To reject the advice simply because the advisor doesn't follow it is called tu quoque.[8]

The final verdict on The Daily Show seems to depend on its overall effects. How, for instance, would the mainstream media deal with the diluting effect of "fake" news? Reacting to "fake" news, conventional news could "harden," focusing more on breaking real news stories and less on sensationalism. That would be good. An unfortunate reaction would be for conventional news to follow The Daily Show's lead and become even more entertainment orientated. Mainstream media could drift more towards MTV than PBS, although certainly this might happen without "fake" news entering into the picture. Mainstream media could instead be unaffected by "fake" news programming. The thinking here would be exactly what was argued for by Baum, namely that people who watch The Daily Show aren't consumers of mainstream news to begin with, or they have their views reinforced rather than changed by "fake" news programming.

Assessing the overall impact of *The Daily Show* depends, then, not only on media reaction, but also on the net effect on the viewing audience. Here too there are several possibilities: good, bad, and indifferent. First, the show might provide, as said before, additional insight for already-informed individuals. Again, *The Daily Show*'s fresh perspective on stories attacks them from angles unavailable to mainstream media. Another possibility is that *The Daily Show* draws viewers who would typically go elsewhere, even though it's not a true alternative to conventional news and would, in that case, perform a public *disservice*. Finally, the show might minimally inform viewers who otherwise would be ignorant about newsworthy events. Although the information isn't up to hard news standards, it's perhaps better than nothing. Here, the benefit would be marginal, with some low-grade information getting through in *The Daily Show*'s less-than-comprehensive coverage.

Of course, these phenomena might well occur in combination. The empirical investigation discussed earlier seem to reflect both the good and the relatively indifferent scenarios. Baum's study suggests that "fake" news informs people who are previously uninformed, while the Annenberg study found that *Daily Show* viewers are well informed, thus supporting the "good" scenario. It's important to note that while Baum's study focused on "fake" news in general, including segments of shows such as *Late Night* with David Letterman and the *Tonight Show* with Jay Leno, the Annenberg study focused specifically on *Daily Show* viewers compared with control groups. Thus the Annenberg study seems to more accurately reflect the relationship between watching *The Daily Show* in particular and audience awareness, supporting the "good" scenario. Taken together, the studies suggest that we shouldn't treat all "fake" news the same way.

Again, due to *The Daily Show*'s emphasis on humor and constraints such as the gatekeeping function of mainstream media,
it's not a true alternative to mainstream news. The position of
Daily Show writers, producers, and performers is in a way analogous to the situation that often occurs for teachers, who frequently have to choose who to teach to. Do you try to get a
majority of students in a class involved? Do you teach only to
the bright kids? Or do you make sure that even the slower students make some progress? This choice is realized in the battle
between classroom content and students' interests and attention
spans. The more difficult the material, the drier and the less relevant it seems, the more students become uninterested. Some
teachers believe it's not their job to be entertaining, seeing themselves as professionals employed to impart knowledge, and students as responsible to motivate themselves. Others think that
a good teacher does both—grabbing students' attention, often
in entertaining ways, as a means of imparting information.

A few questions can be teased apart here. Is there a neces- 25
sary connection between entertainment value and informational content? Is there necessarily a trade-off when one teaches
to the majority, or when one focuses instead on the gifted or
the more challenged minority? What exactly is the educator's
responsibility? It's not obvious that there are clear, much less
known, answers to these questions. On a practical level, it's
often a matter of the educator's choice and personal teaching
style. Although the best teachers seem to strike an appropriate
balance between information and entertainment, it's tough to
say anything useful about how to find this balance.

Some might argue that because *The Daily Show* is entertainment, it's a paradigm case of teaching to the bottom of the class,
or at the very best, to the middle of the class. However, this judgment would be hasty. If the Annenberg study is correct, it seems

that the show's audience is composed of reasonably well-informed individuals, whether already informed or informed to some extent by the show. As I argued earlier, there's a unique and valuable kind of information that the show conveys to its audience. This means that *The Daily Show* actually teaches to the top of the class, imparting a higher form of information to those "in the know." Many of the jokes and skits on *The Daily Show* rely on sophisticated forms of humor and a sophisticated understanding of world events. There are, of course, gag skits which are simply entertaining. Perhaps *The Daily Show* teaches to the top of the class while providing entertainment for the rest.

Ultimately, it's each individual's responsibility to be informed. This only works when there are legitimate news sources available to choose from. It seems that as many legitimate media choices exist right now as existed before *The Daily Show* became a major cultural force, although sifting for these resources might be much harder now than it used to be. Who do you listen to? How can you distinguish between spin and fact? This is where *The Daily Show* can help. Rather than substituting for mainstream news, the show can *enhance* our understanding of mainstream media. To return to the teaching example, students must take an active role in their education. As the old saw goes, "you get out of it what you put into it." If you want to be an informed citizen, you must take some responsibility for seeking the truth in our increasingly foggy media landscape.

The Great Switcharoo

A solution to the problems described above is one which is wholly unlikely to occur. I believe that it would be best for *The Daily Show* and Rush Limbaugh to swap their respective audiences. Limbaugh fans should curl up on their couch and flip on Comedy Central every evening and *Daily Show* fans should listen to a portion of Limbaugh's radio broadcast (listening to the full three-hour broadcast would be beyond the pale). I advise this because both broadcasts are playing to the home crowd. *The Daily Show*, with its left slant, may just reinforce the views of its decidedly left-leaning audience, thus leaving them feeling superior and smug without really having engaged the other side on many issues. The same goes for "the right" and Rush. Listening to the opposition, instead of being continually congratulated for holding on to preexisting views, would press individuals to actively debate the arguments in question. Too often in the great debates of our time (for example, abortion, euthanasia, the war in Iraq, and stem cell research, to name a few) each side envisions a particular characterization of the opposition. In reality, the positions on either side of these debates are often well argued. The debates exist because the issues in question are complex. To ignore this complexity is to become a characterization yourself.[9]

NOTES

1. Tom Fenton, *Bad News: The Decline of Reporting, the Business of News, and the Danger to Us All* (New York: Harper Collins, 2005). Subsequent references will be made parenthetically in-text.

2. Lisa de Moraes, "Seriously: Kerry on Comedy Central," *Washington Post* (August 24, 2004), C1.

3. Thomas Goetz, "Reinventing Television," *Wired* 13 (09) (2005): www.wired.com/wired/archive/13.09/stewart.html.

4. Considering how, or if, we should hold them accountable would take us too far from the focus of this chapter.

5. Matthew Baum, "Sex, Lies, and War: How Soft News Brings Foreign Policy to the Inattentive Public," *American Political Science Review* 96 (1) (2002), pp. 91–109.

6. National Annenberg Election Survey" (press release), *Annenberg Public Policy Center* (September 21, 2004).

7. Aaron McKain, "Not Necessarily Not the News: Gatekeeping, Remediation, and *The Daily Show*," *Journal of American Culture* 28 (4) (2005), pp. 415–30. Subsequent references will be made parenthetically in-text.

8. For more on fallacies, see Liam Dempsey, "*The Daily Show*'s Exposé of Political Rhetoric," chapter 10 in *The Daily Show and Philosophy: Moments of Zen in the Art of Fake News*, ed. Jason Holt (Malden, MA: Blackwell, 2007).

9. Thanks to Jason Holt and Bill Irwin for helpful suggestions.

Joining the Conversation

1. Jason Zinser discusses positive and negative aspects of *The Daily Show*, considers the show's effects on its audience, and reaches a conclusion about the show's impact that is not entirely positive or negative. How would you summarize his argument?

2. The second paragraph of the essay contains a statement explaining why it matters whether *The Daily Show* is good or bad. What other reasons could Zinser have given?

3. In paragraph 15, Zinser argues that one of the primary strengths of *The Daily Show* is that it is "unburdened by objectivity." How might you use this same point to make a case *against* the value of the show?

4. Notice that Zinser includes almost no examples from *The Daily Show*. Help him out. Watch the show, looking for examples that support his argument. Transcribe them as Antonia Peacocke does on pp. 304 and 307 and explain what they demonstrate about the show.

Hidden Intellectualism

GERALD GRAFF

—◹—

EVERYONE KNOWS SOME young person who is impressively "street smart" but does poorly in school. What a waste, we think, that one who is so intelligent about so many things in life seems unable to apply that intelligence to academic work. What doesn't occur to us, though, is that schools and colleges might be at fault for missing the opportunity to tap into such street smarts and channel them into good academic work.

Nor do we consider one of the major reasons why schools and colleges overlook the intellectual potential of street smarts: the fact that we associate those street smarts with anti-intellectual concerns. We associate the educated life, the life of the mind, too narrowly and exclusively with subjects and texts that we consider inherently weighty and academic. We

GERALD GRAFF, one of the co-authors of this book, is a professor of English and education at the University of Illinois at Chicago. He was the 2008 President of the Modern Language Association, a U.S.-based professional association of scholars and teachers of English and other languages. This essay is adapted from his 2003 book, *Clueless in Academe: How Schooling Obscures the Life of the Mind.*

assume that it's possible to wax intellectual about Plato, Shakespeare, the French Revolution, and nuclear fission, but not about cars, dating, fashion, sports, TV, or video games.

The trouble with this assumption is that no necessary connection has ever been established between any text or subject and the educational depth and weight of the discussion it can generate. Real intellectuals turn any subject, however lightweight it may seem, into grist for their mill through the thoughtful questions they bring to it, whereas a dullard will find a way to drain the interest out of the richest subject. That's why a George Orwell writing on the cultural meanings of penny postcards is infinitely more substantial than the cogitations of many professors on Shakespeare or globalization.

See pp. 58–61 for tips on disagreeing, with reasons.

Students do need to read models of intellectually challenging writing—and Orwell is a great one—if they are to become intellectuals themselves. But they would be more prone to take on intellectual identities if we encouraged them to do so at first on subjects that interest them rather than ones that interest us.

I offer my own adolescent experience as a case in point. Until I entered college, I hated books and cared only for sports. The only reading I cared to do or could do was sports magazines, on which I became hooked, becoming a regular reader of *Sport* magazine in the late forties, *Sports Illustrated* when it began publishing in 1954, and the annual magazine guides to professional baseball, football, and basketball. I also loved the sports novels for boys of John R. Tunis and Clair Bee and autobiographies of sports stars like Joe DiMaggio's *Lucky to Be a Yankee* and Bob Feller's *Strikeout Story*. In short, I was your typical teenage anti-intellectual—or so I believed for a long time. I have recently come to think, however, that my preference for sports over schoolwork was not anti-intellectualism so much as intellectualism by other means.

In the Chicago neighborhood I grew up in, which had become a melting pot after World War II, our block was solidly middle class, but just a block away—doubtless concentrated there by the real estate companies—were African Americans, Native Americans, and "hillbilly" whites who had recently fled postwar joblessness in the South and Appalachia. Negotiating this class boundary was a tricky matter. On the one hand, it was necessary to maintain the boundary between "clean-cut" boys like me and working-class "hoods," as we called them, which meant that it was good to be openly smart in a book-ish sort of way. On the other hand, I was desperate for the approval of the hoods, whom I encountered daily on the play-ing field and in the neighborhood, and for this purpose it was not at all good to be book-smart. The hoods would turn on you if they sensed you were putting on airs over them: "Who you lookin' at, smart ass?" as a leather-jacketed youth once said to me as he relieved me of my pocket change along with my self-respect.

I grew up torn, then, between the need to prove I was smart and the fear of a beating if I proved it too well; between the need not to jeopardize my respectable future and the need to impress the hoods. As I lived it, the conflict came down to a choice between being physically tough and being verbal. For a boy in my neighborhood and elementary school, only being "tough" earned you complete legitimacy. I still recall endless, complicated debates in this period with my closest pals over who was "the toughest guy in the school." If you were less than negligible as a fighter, as I was, you settled for the next best thing, which was to be inarticulate, carefully hiding telltale marks of literacy like correct grammar and pronunciation.

In one way, then, it would be hard to imagine an adolescence more thoroughly anti-intellectual than mine. Yet in retrospect, I see that it's more complicated, that I and the 1950s themselves were not simply hostile toward intellectualism, but divided and ambivalent. When Marilyn Monroe married the playwright Arthur Miller in 1956 after divorcing the retired baseball star Joe DiMaggio, the symbolic triumph of geek over jock suggested the way the wind was blowing. Even Elvis, according to his biographer Peter Guralnick, turns out to have supported Adlai over Ike in the presidential election of 1956. "I don't dig the intellectual bit," he told reporters. "But I'm telling you, man, he knows the most."

Though I too thought I did not "dig the intellectual bit," I see now that I was unwittingly in training for it. The germs had actually been planted in the seemingly philistine debates about which boys were the toughest. I see now that in the interminable analysis of sports teams, movies, and toughness that my friends and I engaged in—a type of analysis, needless to say, that the real toughs would never have stooped to—I was already betraying an allegiance to the egghead world. I was practicing being an intellectual before I knew that was what I wanted to be.

It was in these discussions with friends about toughness and sports, I think, and in my reading of sports books and magazines, that I began to learn the rudiments of the intellectual life: how to make an argument, weigh different kinds of evidence, move between particulars and generalizations, summarize the views of others, and enter a conversation about ideas. It was in reading and arguing about sports and toughness that I experienced what it felt like to propose a generalization, restate and respond to a counterargument, and perform other intellectualizing operations, including composing the kind of sentences I am writing now.

Only much later did it dawn on me that the sports world was more compelling than school because it was *more intellectual than school,* not less. Sports after all was full of challenging arguments, debates, problems for analysis, and intricate statistics that you could care about, as school conspicuously was not. I believe that street smarts beat out book smarts in our culture not because street smarts are nonintellectual, as we generally suppose, but because they satisfy an intellectual thirst more thoroughly than school culture, which seems pale and unreal.

They also satisfy the thirst for community. When you entered sports debates, you became part of a community that was not limited to your family and friends, but was national and public. Whereas schoolwork isolated you from others, the pennant race or Ted Williams's .400 batting average was something you could talk about with people you had never met. Sports introduced you not only to a culture steeped in argument, but to a public argument culture that transcended the personal. I can't blame my schools for failing to make intellectual culture resemble the Super Bowl, but I do fault them for failing to learn anything from the sports and entertainment worlds about how to organize and represent intellectual culture, how to exploit its gamelike element and turn it into arresting public spectacle that might have competed more successfully for my youthful attention.

For here is another thing that never dawned on me and is still kept hidden from students, with tragic results: that the real intellectual world, the one that existed in the big world beyond school, is organized very much like the world of team sports, with rival texts, rival interpretations and evaluations of texts, rival theories of why they should be read and taught, and elaborate team competitions in which "fans" of writers, intellectual systems, methodologies, and -isms contend against each other.

To be sure, school contained plenty of competition, which became more invidious as one moved up the ladder (and has become even more so today with the advent of high-stakes testing). In this competition, points were scored not by making arguments, but by a show of information or vast reading, by grade-grubbing, or other forms of oneupmanship. School competition, in short, reproduced the less attractive features of sports culture without those that create close bonds and community.

And in distancing themselves from anything as enjoyable 15 and absorbing as sports, my schools missed the opportunity to capitalize on an element of drama and conflict that the intellectual world shares with sports. Consequently, I failed to see the parallels between the sports and academic worlds that could have helped me cross more readily from one argument culture to the other.

Sports is only one of the domains whose potential for literacy training (and not only for males) is seriously underestimated by educators, who see sports as competing with academic development rather than a route to it. But if this argument suggests why it is a good idea to assign readings and topics that are close to students' existing interests, it also suggests the limits of this tactic. For students who get excited about the chance to write about their passion for cars will often write as poorly and unreflectively on that topic as on Shakespeare or Plato. Here is the flip side of what I pointed out before: that there's no necessary relation between the degree of interest a student shows in a text or subject and the quality of thought or expression such a student manifests in writing or talking about it. The challenge, as college professor Ned Laff has put it, "is not simply to exploit students' nonacademic interests, but to get them to see those interests through academic eyes."

To say that students need to see their interests "through academic eyes" is to say that street smarts are not enough. Making students' nonacademic interests an object of academic study is useful, then, for getting students' attention and overcoming their boredom and alienation, but this tactic won't in itself necessarily move them closer to an academically rigorous treatment of those interests. On the other hand, inviting students to write about cars, sports, or clothing fashions does not have to be a pedagogical cop-out as long as students are required to see these interests "through academic eyes," that is, to think and write about cars, sports, and fashions in a reflective, analytical way, one that sees them as microcosms of what is going on in the wider culture.

If I am right, then schools and colleges are missing an opportunity when they do not encourage students to take their nonacademic interests as objects of academic study. It is self-defeating to decline to introduce any text or subject that figures to engage students who will otherwise tune out academic work entirely. If a student cannot get interested in Mill's *On Liberty* but will read *Sports Illustrated* or *Vogue* or the hip-hop magazine *Source* with absorption, this is a strong argument for assigning the magazines over the classic. It's a good bet that if students get hooked on reading and writing by doing term papers on *Source*, they will eventually get to *On Liberty*. But even if they don't, the magazine reading will make them more literate and reflective than they would be otherwise. So it makes pedagogical sense to develop classroom units on sports, cars, fashions, rap music, and other such topics. Give me the student anytime who writes a sharply argued, sociologically acute analysis of an issue of *Source* over the student who writes a lifeless explication of *Hamlet* or Socrates' *Apology*.

Joining the Conversation

1. Gerald Graff begins his essay with the view that we generally associate "book smarts" with intellectualism and "street smarts" with anti-intellectualism. Graff then provides an extended example from his early life to counter this viewpoint. What do you think of his argument that boyhood conversations about sports provided a solid foundation for his later intellectual life? What support does he provide, and how persuasive is it?

2. Graff argues in paragraph 13 that the intellectual world is much like the world of team sports, with "rival texts . . . , rival theories . . . , and elaborate team competitions." Can you think of any examples from your own experience that support this assertion? In what ways do you think "the real intellectual world" is different from the world of team sports?

3. Imagine a conversation between Graff and Antonia Peacocke (pp. 299–310) on how watching television shows like *Family Guy* can be "intellectual."

4. So what? Who cares? Graff does not answer these questions explicitly. Do it for him: write a brief paragraph saying why his argument matters, and for whom.

5. Graff argues that schools should encourage students to think critically, read, and write about areas of personal interest such as cars, fashion, or music—as long as they do so in an intellectually serious way. What do you think? Write an essay considering the educational merits of such a proposal, taking Graff's argument as a "they say."

Sixteen

Is Fast Food the New Tobacco?

———◻———

It is hard to live in the United States today and not have a taste for some fast foods—and at the same time, to feel one should not eat such foods. Whether one is looking at a chocolate doughnut or a bag of potato chips, it is almost impossible not to be pulled in two directions at once: to want the doughnuts or chips, but to fear how they will affect one's looks and health. The McDonald's billboard on the facing page captures this conflict well: A giant hamburger proclaiming "You Know You Want Me" seems to be addressing passersby who are determined to believe they *don't* want it. It is as if a battle is being waged among fast-food corporations, the diet and beauty industries, and the medical community over what we eat—and what we resist eating. The readings in this chapter offer various perspectives on this battle: who is responsible, what its causes are, and whether and how it should be addressed.

On the question of societal intervention versus personal responsibility, *Men's Health* magazine editor David Zinczenko blames the fast-food industry for the growing rate of obesity in the United States and argues that this industry should therefore be regulated by the government. In contrast, the libertarian commentator Radley Balko argues that what we eat should remain a matter of personal responsibility. Feminist author Susie Orbach believes that compulsive overeating and being overweight, particularly among women, can themselves be forms of rebellion against the expectations of a sexist, patriarchal society.

Other readings focus on the reasons people eat fast food and adopt sedentary lifestyles. Journalist Wil Haygood profiles residents of a small town in Kentucky as a way of showing the dangers of a fast-food diet and the reasons for its appeal. Media scholars Carrie Packwood Freeman and Debra Merskin show how fast-food advertisements specifically target men when marketing their products. First Lady Michelle Obama proposes a government-sponsored program to promote fitness and better eating in a campaign against childhood obesity. Author and food activist Michael Pollan argues for a diet of organic, plant-based foods.

Other writers are more skeptical about the effectiveness of any initiatives to change Americans' eating habits. Judith Warner agrees in theory with calls for healthier eating but suggests that persuading people to give up comfort foods could prove difficult. College student Mary Maxfield goes a step further, challenging the assumption that overeating is a problem at all and suggesting that critics are exaggerating the dangers.

Read on for a wide range of opinions on the matters of fast food and the so-called "obesity crisis." You'll likely find plenty to agree with, and just as much to disagree with. But whatever you think, this is a conversation that matters, and the pieces in this chapter will challenge you to respond—to see what others advocate, to think about what you believe and why—and then to add your own voice to the conversation.

Don't Blame the Eater

DAVID ZINCZENKO

––⊡––

IF EVER THERE WERE a newspaper headline custom-made for Jay Leno's monologue, this was it. Kids taking on McDonald's this week, suing the company for making them fat. Isn't that like middle-aged men suing Porsche for making them get speeding tickets? Whatever happened to personal responsibility?

I tend to sympathize with these portly fast-food patrons, though. Maybe that's because I used to be one of them.

I grew up as a typical mid 1980s latchkey kid. My parents were split up, my dad off trying to rebuild his life, my mom working long hours to make the monthly bills. Lunch and dinner, for me, was a daily choice between McDonald's, Taco Bell, Kentucky Fried Chicken or Pizza Hut. Then as now, these were

DAVID ZINCZENKO is the editor-in-chief of *Men's Health* magazine and the author of numerous best-selling books, including the *Eat This, Not That* and the *Abs Diet* series. He has contributed op-ed essays to the *New York Times*, the *Los Angeles Times*, and *USA Today* and has appeared on *Oprah*, *Ellen*, *20/20*, and *Good Morning America*. This piece was first published in the *New York Times* on November 23, 2002.

the only available options for an American kid to get an afford-able meal. By age 15, I had packed 212 pounds of torpid teenage tallow on my once lanky 5-foot-10 frame.

Then I got lucky. I went to college, joined the Navy Reserves and got involved with a health magazine. I learned how to man-age my diet. But most of the teenagers who live, as I once did, on a fast-food diet won't turn their lives around: They've crossed under the golden arches to a likely fate of lifetime obesity. And the problem isn't just theirs—it's all of ours.

For tips on saying why it matters, see Chapter 7.

Before 1994, diabetes in children was generally caused by a 5 genetic disorder—only about 5 percent of childhood cases were obesity-related, or Type 2, diabetes. Today, according to the National Institutes of Health, Type 2 diabetes accounts for at least 30 percent of all new childhood cases of diabetes in this country.

Not surprisingly, money spent to treat diabetes has sky-rocketed, too. The Centers for Disease Control and Prevention estimate that diabetes accounted for $2.6 billion in health care costs in 1969. Today's number is an unbelievable $100 billion a year.

Shouldn't we know better than to eat two meals a day in fast-food restaurants? That's one argument. But where, exactly, are consumers—particularly teenagers—supposed to find alter-natives? Drive down any thoroughfare in America, and I guarantee you'll see one of our country's more than 13,000 McDonald's restaurants. Now, drive back up the block and try to find someplace to buy a grapefruit.

Complicating the lack of alternatives is the lack of infor-mation about what, exactly, we're consuming. There are no calorie information charts on fast-food packaging, the way there are on grocery items. Advertisements don't carry warning labels the way tobacco ads do. Prepared foods aren't covered under Food and Drug Administration labeling laws. Some fast-food purveyors will provide calorie information on request, but even that can be hard to understand.

For example, one company's Web site lists its chicken salad as containing 150 calories; the almonds and noodles that come with it (an additional 190 calories) are listed separately. Add a serving of the 280-calorie dressing, and you've got a healthy lunch alternative that comes in at 620 calories. But that's not all. Read the small print on the back of the dressing packet and you'll realize it actually contains 2.5 servings. If you pour what you've been served, you're suddenly up around 1,040 calories, which is half of the government's recommended daily calorie intake. And that doesn't take into account that 450-calorie super-size Coke.

Make fun if you will of these kids launching lawsuits against 10 the fast-food industry, but don't be surprised if you're the next plaintiff. As with the tobacco industry, it may be only a matter of time before state governments begin to see a direct line between the $1 billion that McDonald's and Burger King spend each year on advertising and their own swelling health care costs.

And I'd say the industry is vulnerable. Fast-food companies are marketing to children a product with proven health hazards and no warning labels. They would do well to protect themselves, and their customers, by providing the nutrition information people need to make informed choices about their products. Without such warnings, we'll see more sick, obese children and more angry, litigious parents. I say, let the deep-fried chips fall where they may.

Joining the Conversation

1. Summarize Zinczenko's arguments (his "I say") against the practices of fast-food companies. How persuasive are these arguments?

2. One important move in all good argumentative writing is to introduce possible objections to the position being argued—what this book calls naysayers. What objections does Zinczenko introduce, and how does he respond? Can you think of other objections that he might have noted?

3. How does the story that Zinczenko tells in paragraphs 3 and 4 about his own experience support or fail to support his argument? How could the same story be used to support an argument opposed to Zinczenko's?

4. So what? Who cares? How does Zinczenko make clear to readers why his topic matters? Or, if he does not, how might he do so?

5. Write an essay responding to Zinczenko, using your own experience and knowledge as part of your argument. You may agree, disagree, or both, but be sure to represent Zinczenko's views near the beginning of your text, both summarizing and quoting from his arguments.

What You Eat Is Your Business

RADLEY BALKO

—⊡—

THIS JUNE, *Time* magazine and ABC News will host a three-day summit on obesity. ABC News anchor Peter Jennings, who last December anchored the prime-time special "How to Get Fat Without Really Trying," will host. Judging by the scheduled program, the summit promises to be a pep rally for media, nutrition activists, and policy makers—all agitating for a panoply of government anti-obesity initiatives, including prohibiting junk food in school vending machines, federal funding for new bike trails and sidewalks, more demanding labels on foodstuffs, restrictive

RADLEY BALKO is a senior editor at *Reason*, a monthly magazine that claims to stand for "free minds and free markets" and to provide an "alternative to right-wing and left-wing opinion magazines." Balko specializes in investigative writing on civil liberties and criminal justice issues. He is also a columnist for FoxNews.com and has contributed to such publications as the *Washington Post* and *Playboy*. At *The Agitator*, his personal blog, he describes himself as a "small-l" libertarian. This essay was first published on May 23, 2004, on Cato.org, a site sponsored by the Cato Institute, a foundation that aims to promote the principles of "limited government, individual liberty, free markets, and peace."

food marketing to children, and prodding the food industry into more "responsible" behavior. In other words, bringing government between you and your waistline.

Politicians have already climbed aboard. President Bush earmarked $200 million in his budget for anti-obesity measures. State legislatures and school boards across the country have begun banning snacks and soda from school campuses and vending machines. Senator Joe Lieberman and Oakland Mayor Jerry Brown, among others, have called for a "fat tax" on high-calorie foods. Congress is now considering menu-labeling legislation, which would force restaurants to send every menu item to the laboratory for nutritional testing.

This is the wrong way to fight obesity. Instead of manipulating or intervening in the array of food options available to American consumers, our government ought to be working to foster a sense of responsibility in and ownership of our own health and well-being. But we're doing just the opposite.

For decades now, America's health care system has been migrating toward socialism. Your well-being, shape, and condition have increasingly been deemed matters of "public health," instead of matters of personal responsibility. Our lawmakers just enacted a huge entitlement that requires some people to pay for other people's medicine. Senator Hillary Clinton just penned a lengthy article in the *New York Times Magazine* calling for yet more federal control of health care. All of the Democratic candidates for president boasted plans to push health care further into the public sector. More and more, states are preventing private health insurers from charging overweight and obese clients higher premiums, which effectively removes any financial incentive for maintaining a healthy lifestyle.

We're becoming less responsible for our own health, and 5 more responsible for everyone else's. Your heart attack drives up the cost of my premiums and office visits. And if the government is paying for my anti-cholesterol medication, what incentive is there for me to put down the cheeseburger?

This collective ownership of private health then paves the way for even more federal restrictions on consumer choice and civil liberties. A society where everyone is responsible for everyone else's well-being is a society more apt to accept government restrictions, for example— on what McDonald's can put on its menu, what Safeway or Kroger can put on grocery shelves, or holding food companies responsible for the bad habits of unhealthy consumers.

A growing army of nutritionist activists and food industry foes are egging the process on. Margo Wootan of the Center for Science in the Public Interest has said, "We've got to move beyond 'personal responsibility.'" The largest organization of trial lawyers now encourages its members to weed jury pools of candidates who show "personal responsibility bias." The title of Jennings's special from last December—"How to Get Fat Without Really Trying"—reveals his intent, which is to relieve viewers of responsibility for their own condition. Indeed, Jennings ended the program with an impassioned plea for government intervention to fight obesity.

For tips on distinguishing what you say from what others say, as Balko does here, see Chapter 5.

The best way to alleviate the obesity "public health" crisis is to remove obesity from the realm of public health. It doesn't belong there anyway. It's difficult to think of anything more private and of less public concern than what we choose to put into our bodies. It only becomes a public matter when we force the public to pay for the consequences of those choices. If policymakers want to fight obesity, they'll halt the creeping socialization of medicine, and move to return individual Americans' ownership of their own health and well-being back to individual Americans.

That means freeing insurance companies to reward healthy lifestyles, and penalize poor ones. It means halting plans to further socialize medicine and health care. Congress should also increase access to medical and health savings accounts, which give consumers the option of rolling money reserved for health care into a retirement account. These accounts introduce accountability into the health care system, and encourage caution with one's health care dollar. When money we spend on health care doesn't belong to our employer or the government, but is money we could devote to our own retirement, we're less likely to run to the doctor at the first sign of a cold.

We'll all make better choices about diet, exercise, and personal health when someone else isn't paying for the consequences of those choices. 10

Joining the Conversation

1. What does Radley Balko claim in this essay? How do you know? What position is he responding to? Cite examples from the text to support your answer.
2. Reread the last sentence of paragraph 1: "In other words, bringing government between you and your waistline." This is actually a sentence fragment, but it functions as metacommentary, inserted by Balko to make sure that readers see his point. Imagine that this statement were not there, and reread the first three paragraphs. Does it make a difference in how you read this piece?
3. Notice the direct quotations in paragraph 7. How has Balko integrated these quotations into his text—how has he introduced them, and what, if anything, has he said to explain them and tie them to his own text? Are there any changes

you might suggest? How do key terms in the quotations echo one another? (See Chapter 3 for advice on quoting, and pp. 114–16 for help on identifying key terms.)

4. Balko makes his own position about the so-called obesity crisis very clear, but does he consider any of the objections that might be offered to his position? If so, how does he deal with those objections? If not, what objections might he have raised?

5. Write an essay responding to Balko, agreeing, disagreeing, or both agreeing and disagreeing with his position. You might want to cite some of David Zinczenko's arguments (see pp. 391–93)—depending on what stand you take, Zinczenko's ideas could serve as support for what you believe or as one possible objection.

Junking Junk Food

JUDITH WARNER

—⌐◻⌐—

EARLIER THIS MONTH, Sarah Palin showed up in Bucks
County, Pa., with "dozens and dozens" of cookies, suggesting
that the state's schoolchildren risked losing the right to the
occasional classroom treat because of a high-minded anti-sugar
edict from the board of education. Pretty much everything
about the setup was wrong. Pennsylvania wasn't, as Palin
tweeted, in the midst of a "school cookie ban" debate. And the
school she turned into a photo op wouldn't have been subject
to such a ban had one existed; it wasn't a public school but a
private Christian academy. And while Palin might have been
seizing an opportunity to "intro kids 2 beauty of laissez-faire,"
she wasn't just visiting with schoolchildren but was delivering
a paid speech at a fund-raiser.

JUDITH WARNER writes the column "Domestic Disturbances" for the
New York Times and contributes to the *New York Times Magazine*,
where this article appeared on November 25, 2010. She is the author
of four books, including *Perfect Madness: Motherhood in the Age of Anxiety* (2005) and *We've Got Issues: Children and Parents in the Age of
Medication* (2010), as well as books on Hillary Clinton and Newt Gin-
grich. She has also served as a correspondent for *Newsweek* in Paris
and hosted *The Judith Warner Show* on XM satellite radio.

Still, however shaky its factual foundations, Palin's highly mediatized cookie showdown was a big rhetorical win. With her unerring feel for the message that travels straight to the American gut, she had come up with new and vivid imagery to make the case that the Obama "nanny state" is, essentially, snatching cookies—i.e., the pursuit of happiness—from the mouths of babes. Suddenly, Pennsylvania's suggestion that schools encourage alternatives to high-sugar sweets became an assault on the American way of life. On freedom and simple pleasures. On wholesome childhood delights and, of course, the integrity of the family.

Glenn Beck, too, has found a winning formula in mocking government efforts to lead Americans to live less fattening lives. His compendium of outrage on the topic waxes long—it includes reports of government health inspectors shutting down a 7-year-old's lemonade stand, for example—and his argument, like Palin's, is clear: the "choice architects" of the Obama administration, he says, believe "you're incapable of making decisions. . . . Left to your own devices, you're going to eat too much, you're going to be a big fat fatty."

At a time when more than two-thirds of American adults are indeed fat (overweight or obese) and 17 percent of children and adolescents are obese, declaring war on unhealthful eating, as the Obama administration has done to an unprecedented extent, could be fraught with political liability. Yet the administration has essentially tackled the problem as if it were a political no-brainer. Teaching Americans, and children in particular, healthier eating habits seemed so commonsensical a venture, so wholesome and safe, that Michelle Obama chose it for her apolitical personal project as first lady. She has succeeded in enlisting some bipartisan support, and some much-hyped cooperation from the food industry. But now, with antigovernment sentiment resurgent, the cookies are pushing back, like the return of the repressed. And as any homeowner who has ever been advised to bake cookies before showing a house for sale knows, their influence is irrational but real.

For in waging war on fat and sugar, what the administration 5 is doing is taking on central aspects of the American lifestyle. Eating too much, indiscriminately, anywhere, at any time, in response to any and all stimuli, is as central to our freewheeling, mavericky way of being as car cupholders and drivethroughs. You can't change specific eating behavior without addressing that way of life—without changing our culture of food. You need to present healthful eating as a new, desirable, freely chosen expression of the American way.

Perhaps the most successful government effort to regulate what and how much Americans consume—the food rationing programs of World War II—recognized this political-cultural-emotional scheme. Needing a number of foods, meat in particular, for the boys overseas, the government realized that it could successfully spread its message of "eat differently" only if it fought on two fronts: the nutritional and the psychological. And so it pursued a two-pronged campaign, with the Food and Nutrition Board handling the nutrition, and the psychology tasked to the Committee on Food Habits, led by the anthropologist Margaret Mead and charged by the National Research Council with "mobilizing anthropological and psychological insights as they bear upon the whole problem of changing food habits in order to raise the nutritional status of the people of the United States." Eating the way the government wanted you to eat—healthfully and with a mind to greater public welfare—was a way of displaying patriotism, adding to the war effort.

After the war, however, the work of the Committee on Food Habits was discontinued. But the government kept dissemi-

"OF COURSE I CAN!

I'm patriotic as can be—
And ration points won't worry me!"

A poster from the rationing program of the U.S. government in World War II.

nating nutritional advice, with the departments of agriculture and health and human services issuing nutritional guidelines that, in recent decades, have been revised every five years to reflect new and evolving scientific developments. There has, however, been no concerted parallel attempt to create more pointed and sophisticated approaches to changing how Americans think and feel about food. So we ended up with a wealth of knowledge about best nutritional practices but no cultural change to back it up.

And cultural change is what offers the best hope for transforming how and what Americans eat. As noted by David

Kessler, the former U.S. Food and Drug Administration commissioner and author of the 2009 book *The End of Overeating: Taking Control of the Insatiable American Appetite*, it was a shift in cultural attitudes, not laws or regulations, that led Americans to quit smoking. In the space of a generation, he says, cigarettes stopped being portrayed as "sexy and cool" and started to be seen as "a terribly disgusting, addictive product." Because of the unique emotional power of food, it's hard, if not impossible, to similarly stigmatize unhealthful eating. But it's not inconceivable, Kessler says, that social norms could change: that huge portions, or eating processed foods loaded with sugar, salt and fat, for example, could come to be seen as socially unacceptable.

See Chapter 2 for tips on when and how to paraphrase others' words.

The task is huge—and not just because of the predictable resistance there would be from the food industry. Largely, it's a question, Kessler says, of breaking old cycles of association: melt-in-the-mouth baked goods with home-safe happiness, for example, or fries with fulfillment—and replacing them with a new circuitry in which, somehow, eating healthfully is self-reinforcing. Can Michelle Obama make field greens and strawberries as comforting, satisfying, and heartwarmingly American as apple pie? She has her work cut out for her.

Joining the Conversation

1. Citing such influential figures as Michelle Obama, Sarah Palin, and Glenn Beck, Judith Warner suggests that changing people's eating habits could prove far more difficult than many imagine. Why does she think this change will be so challenging?

2. How are historical changes in public attitudes toward cigarette smoking, discussed in paragraph 8 of the essay, related to Warner's argument about Americans' eating habits?

3. How might Warner respond to the main points of Michelle Obama's campaign to promote healthy eating (pp. 417–33)?

4. Does Warner include any naysayers, possible objections to her argument? If not, do it for her. Insert a brief paragraph stating an objection to her argument and then responding to the objection as she might. (See Chapter 6 for examples and templates that will help.)

5. Warner seems to consider it unlikely that Americans will adopt a healthier diet anytime soon, despite efforts by Michelle Obama and others to promote better eating. Write a response to her in which you define the issue, consider her arguments carefully, and then say what you think (and why).

Kentucky Town of Manchester Illustrates National Obesity Crisis

WIL HAYGOOD

―◻―

THE BEAUTIFUL THING about this little town, the locals will tell you, is that everyone seems to know everyone. Where the children go to school, where the parents work. Who's engaged to be married, who's joining the military.

How Britney and Carlin—those would be Scott Robinson's girls—are doing in school.

Quite well, thank you.

"I just got my report card the other day. Wanna see it?" asks a smiling Carlin, 12. She shows off a row of A's. She's standing in her back yard, high on a hill overlooking a valley below.

Carlin Robinson is a large little girl. 5

WIL HAYGOOD has written for newspapers including the *Pittsburgh Post-Gazette*, the *Boston Globe*, and the *Washington Post*. He is the author of several books, including *Sweet Thunder: The Life and Times of Sugar Ray Robinson* (2009), *King of Cats: The Life and Times of Adam Clayton Powell Jr.* (2006), and *The Haygoods of Columbus: A Love Story* (1997). This article was first published in the *Washington Post* on July 12, 2010.

The people of Manchester take for granted knowing one another. "You never run into a stranger here," says Britney, Carlin's older sister.

Britney Robinson, 20, is a very large young woman.

Britney and Carlin: two sweet small-town girls, the pride of their dad.

Scott Robinson, 47, is a very large man.

The residents of this town of 2,100—95 miles southeast of Lex- 10 ington and deep in the Appalachian foothills—indeed appear to celebrate the joys of community closeness. The bake sales, the volunteering. But it's what goes uncelebrated, and even ignored, here that has become Manchester's defining feature: In an increasingly unhealthy country, it is one of the unhealthiest places of all.

The national obesity rate for adults is 24 percent; in Manchester and surrounding Clay County, it's been estimated to be as high as 52 percent. In a study of the healthiness of Kentucky's 120 counties, Clay County ranked dead last, with 41 percent of the population classified as in poor or fair health.

In Washington recently, first lady Michelle Obama presided over the unveiling of findings from an obesity task force. Highlights that she presented from the three-month study only deepened what many had come to fear: The number of overweight children is rising; there are not enough places to buy nutritious food in small towns; many places lack recreational venues.

It was as if she were talking about Manchester itself, a friendly town where little thought is given to what the health crisis might mean for its future, and the future of a country with Manchesters from coast to coast.

There is no YMCA or YWCA here.

There is no department of parks and recreation. 15

There is no fancy dues-paying gym with energy drinks and literature about healthful eating habits.

"I just don't know a lot about obesity," confesses Mayor Carmen Lewis. She ponders what unchecked obesity might mean to the future: "Until you realize it, you're blinded. Then you get to an age where you suddenly say, 'Oh, my God! What have I done to myself?'"

Scott Robinson was raised in Manchester, where coal mining provided him with steady work—that is, until the mines shut down or began to lay off large numbers of workers, including him. He took a job with the town of Manchester back in 1996. He does maintenance work. "Took a pay cut," he says, "but I needed a job with health insurance for me and my girls."

Around the time he got his new job, he and his wife split. She moved away. Scott raised the girls with the help of his mother and other relatives. "Wasn't easy," he allows.

Carlin and Britney are his only children. He confesses he 20 has begun to worry about Britney. Scott wonders whether the breakup of his marriage sent Britney into an emotional tailspin, and whether some of that pain manifested itself in her current behavior—overeating and secluding herself in her bedroom, where she spends hours on her computer.

"She is a borderline diabetic," says Pam Mathis, Scott's girlfriend. "She had to go to the doctor today. They told her she should lose up to 30 pounds."

Scott rubs his chin.

"She's a computer wiz, though," Pam goes on about Britney.

"Now, my little one, Carlin, she at least gets out and plays with the dog," Scott says. "But with Britney, it's all staying on the computer."

If the problem is a lack of exercise, Scott mentions that he 25 has tried to address that issue: "There's a basketball court out back of the house," he says.

"That's not for every child," Pam says. Pam would really like a bowling alley, but there's no bowling alley around.

"We also could use a bicycle trail," adds Scott. "Of course, we growed up riding our bicycles in the street."

The town has a retro, lived-in look. The downtown movie theater is gone, though the marquee is still visible. There has clearly been economic suffering. There is a medium-security federal prison on the edge of town, out past the gas stations that sell fried chicken and pizza.

"You don't have family cooking here in the restaurants," Pam says. "Mostly it's fast foods."

The intersection leading into town features a McDonald's, a Wendy's, an Arby's and a Subway.

And just beyond that, there's a Burger King, a Long John Silver's, a Lee's Famous Recipe Chicken and a Pizza Hut.

Not far from the Pizza Hut, there's a Wal-Mart. At the Wal-Mart, there are snacks—cotton candy and potato chips and caramel corn—sold in supersize helpings.

Manchester moments:

Half a dozen little kids are standing in line at the McDonald's. Four are clearly overweight.

A man and two kids emerge from a pickup, heading into the Arby's. The man is huge, the little girl is not, the little boy is. A little boy, overweight, balances his tray at the Wendy's. A burger. Big fries. Big soda.

At night, most of the lights glowing around town come from the fast-food places at that intersection.

The Pizza Hut seems to do a lively business.

Inside is Britney Robinson. She works at the Pizza Hut. She gets the employee discount.

Charlie Rawlins loathes every fast-food joint in Manchester.

An intersection in Manchester, Kentucky, sports a fast-food restaurant on nearly every corner with few options for anything else.

He might be the town apostate. He used to be "like, way 40 overweight, man," tipping the scales at 251 pounds. He's 5 feet 9 inches tall. He's 20 years old. The weight caused so much pain on his knees that he had to undergo several knee surgeries. Now he's down to 185 pounds, and could a person be any prouder of himself?

Charlie began speaking out about the fast-food places to friends a while ago. "I realized that no one was going to listen to me," he says. He educated himself about nutrition. "I started going in for the fruits, the asparagus, making my own salads." He realized he could live without the large boxes of sweets he used to load up on at Wal-Mart. "The kids around here, they'll eat cornbread and taters for lunch. They'll get a 20-piece chicken meal. It's killing them."

He knows these kids. He waits for them to come see him where he works. They don't. He is a personal trainer at Clay County Physical Therapy, a small space affiliated with a local hospital. It is not advertised as a gym, because it's mostly for physical therapy. He figures there's a reason that people don't come, a lack of resources. It costs $25 a month for individuals and $40 a month for families. "Which is a bargain," he proclaims. "I mean, look how much money these families around here spend on fast food!"

But they don't come.

If Charlie is the town apostate, Regina Stevens is the hard-boiled realist.

She's a pharmacist. She wants to be respectful of the towns- 45 folk. She says they are hugely unaware of the consequences of being overweight.

"A lot of our medications are for 'disease states,' such as Type 2 diabetes, hypertension, things that can be aversely affected by increased weight." Stevens says. As the town pharmacist, she knows how necessary she is to some people, and how unnecessary she could be to others.

"If many of my patients lost weight, they could be totally taken off some of these medications." The result, she says, could be profound: "They would have increased longevity in life."

Stevens thinks part of the problem may lie in a cultural feeling about the food that is set down in front of a child at home at mealtime here. "There is that feeling of 'clean you plate' in many of the homes around here. You don't throw food away. So the child has to eat all of the food, even if they are already full. I know I grew up with that very thing being said to me: 'Clean your plate.' "

When the budding scholar, home on break from the University of Kentucky in Lexington, looked around Manchester and saw the overweight kids and the overweight adults, and kept seeing them, it dawned on her: The problem would make an interesting academic study.

Jill Day grew up here. She knew the fear that locals harbor 50 about outsiders who come around with pencils and question-naires wanting to probe personal living habits. Maybe they wouldn't be willing to share confidences with an outsider, but she had her rural Kentucky roots, the familiar accent.

Day, who began studying for her doctorate in kinesiology and health promotion in 2005, got her advisers interested in her idea to conduct a study in Manchester and Clay County, but they cautioned her about the difficulty of getting people to talk about weight and obesity. Day typed out question-naires for the students and their parents. A good many of the parents—speaking for their children as well—wanted no part of the study. But 277 children, from seven elementary schools, did participate. Day's subjects were fourth- and fifth-graders.

Her study would prove to be the first of its kind undertaken in this region of Kentucky that focuses on the underlying causes that may lead to obesity. The students fell into categories of healthy, underweight, overweight, and obese. To measure activity—or in many cases inactivity—in the form of steps taken, Day equipped the students with pedometers.

"I was estimating in my head that one-third of the kids in Manchester would be overweight or obese," she recalls.

In fact, it was half of them.

Of the 277, eight of those fourth- and fifth-graders were 55 underweight, 135 were healthy, 49 were overweight and 85 were obese.

"It is discouraging to see statistics such as these," says Day, who is now an assistant professor of human development and kinesiology at Campbellsville University about 2 1/2 hours away. Also discouraging, she says, is the fear here of talking about obesity, a mind-set that can seem as thick and impenetrable as the morning fog in these foothills.

"It's a fear of knowing. A fear of knowing the truth. The families believe it's really not that bad. They believe the time to weigh yourself is when you go to the doctor. But they aren't going to the doctor!"

To those who would proclaim that obesity is largely hereditary, Day disagrees. "Since 1980, obesity has tripled in children, so we can't totally blame genetics for this increase."

By the study's end, the multilayered causes for the rise of obesity rates were clear to Day. "I hate to sound simplistic, but it is a lack of physical activity as well as poor eating habits," she says. She gives an example: "If you go to Wal-Mart, you will see someone circling the parking lot. And circling. They're looking for a closer spot to the front door so they won't have to walk. The attitude is we don't want to work as hard to get anyplace." The effects—"high blood pressure, heart disease, emotional and psychological issues in children, joint problems"—all crystallized for her. There were, as well, the issues of poverty and education. In Clay County, Day concluded, "the median per capita income is about $16,000 less than the national average, and less than 50 percent of the adults over 25 have graduated high school."

Day spent two years on her study, and she comes back home 60 occasionally for visits. She knows everyone, including Carlin Robinson, whom she ran into on a Sunday not long ago. She wouldn't dare tell little Carlin what she was really thinking. "I'm worried. She's leaning toward getting big."

Britney and Carlin are riding around, showing the town. The hills, the curves, the thick groves of trees, the jagged hillsides.

"We usually eat pizza at Pat's Pool Room," says Britney. "It's greasy food. It's a little shack where they grill hamburgers."

"It's very relaxing out here," Carlin says from the back seat, on a road curving up atop the town. "You don't have to listen to the cars."

They pass the little house where they lived with their dad a few years ago.

"Our dad and granny basically raised us," says Britney.   65

"Dad's really funny to be around," pipes up Carlin.

"Just real grounded," says Britney. "Our dad never whupped us."

Carlin spots another eatery out the window. "There's Mike's Quick Stop. They serve good hamburgers and hot dogs."

There's another restaurant. Carlin points it out. "My dad is a big steak fan," she says.

The sisters stop and eat. Chinese food. They clean their   70
plates.

Britney, who attends the Manchester branch of Eastern Kentucky University, wants to be an elementary school teacher. When it comes to activity, she likes sitting in the woods. She has friends, and they go into the woods and sit around and build a campfire. "Just like we did in high school," she says. "Basically, I work, sleep, hang out with my friends."

Later, at home, Carlin—her pretty braces gleaming—will talk about the food at her school. "Sometimes, I think they give us too much food." She says she has started to notice how much bigger she is than the other kids. "Sometimes you get picked on for your size."

Stepping away from Carlin, Britney admits she'd like to talk to her sister about the weight Carlin's been gaining, but she won't. "Talking about her weight just might push her buttons," she says. "You don't really want to bring it up, because you just don't know how the other person will feel. In a way it's uncomfortable. I know I should talk about it."

Instead, in the sweet sunshine out in front of their house, the girls show off Bella, their dog, who was found at an animal shelter with a broken jaw. Their dad is up in his little shed, 30 yards from the house, working his second job, which is packing corn for livestock to eat. "Just started this last December," he says. "Trying to make an extra dollar." Even from afar, his girth is noticeable.

Scott Robinson—who takes a blood pressure pill daily—has 75 no idea how much he weighs. "Lord, I couldn't tell you, he says. "Two-seventy, two-ninety. I don't remember the last time I weighed myself."

Carlin is at least 20 pounds overweight. "I won't weigh myself," she says. "No way. I ain't gonna embarrass myself. Why in the world would I want to do that?"

Britney Robinson is at least 30 pounds overweight. She doesn't weigh herself, either.

There are no full-length mirrors in the front rooms of their home that might reveal a full image of anyone.

But outside the house is a beautiful view of a valley, and a town at the edge of the valley, where so much of the population is a reflection of Scott, and Carlin and Britney.

Here is Britney now, taking in the view. "I just love it here," 80 she says.

Joining the Conversation

1. Wil Haygood begins this article by describing the small-town virtues of Manchester, Kentucky. Why does he start this way when the article actually has a much more negative

story to tell? What impressions do you think he wants to convey about the Robinson family's positive and negative qualities?

2. How does Haygood explain the serious increase in overweight and obese people in this town? What evidence does he provide? What attitudes does he say contribute to this problem?

3. So what? Who cares? How does Haygood show us why his topic matters? How might he make that point more persuasively?

4. Consider the situation Haygood depicts in light of the discussions of healthy living by Michelle Obama (pp. 417–33) and Judith Warner (pp. 400–04). How might Obama's plan to promote healthier eating and exercise be received in Manchester? How might Warner's concern about the potential difficulty of changing existing attitudes be reflected in the townspeople Haygood describes?

5. This article was written for a newspaper published in Washington, D.C. How might it be different if it were written for a newspaper in Manchester, Kentucky, the town Haygood writes about?

Remarks to the NAACP
National Convention

MICHELLE OBAMA

—◻—

WOW. O**H, MY** GOODNESS. (Applause.) Thank you all. Thank you so, so much. Everyone, please, please, please take your seats.

Thank you so much. It is such a pleasure and it is an honor to be here today for the 101st NAACP Convention. Yes! (Applause.)

I want to start by thanking Chairman Roslyn Brock, beautiful woman, for that very kind introduction. (Applause.) And I mentioned to her, I said, her mother's hot. She's gorgeous. Good genes. (Laughter.)

I also want to thank both her and your President and CEO Ben Jealous for their inspired leadership of this organization. Give them a round of applause. (Applause.)

MICHELLE OBAMA has been the assistant commissioner of planning and development in Chicago, the dean of student services at the University of Chicago, and vice president of community and external affairs for the University of Chicago Medical Center. This text comes from a speech she made to promote her Let's Move! campaign against childhood obesity at the NAACP national convention in Kansas City, Mo., on July 12, 2010.

I want to thank a few other people as well who are here. I want to thank Governor Nixon and the First Lady, Georgeanne Nixon, who are here. (Applause.) I want to thank Senator McCaskill, who was here, who's no longer here, but I wanted to say hello to her. Representatives Cleaver, Moore and Scott, who are here. (Applause.) And Mayor Funkhouser for all the outstanding work that all of you are doing for the people of this city and for this great state and for taking time to join us today. So let's give them all a round of applause. (Applause.)

And finally, I want to thank all of you. I want to thank you for a few things. First of all, thank you for being here today and thank you for the outstanding work that you've done in making this a great American institution. And also, I have to thank you for your prayers, for your support. I cannot tell you how much that means to me and my girls and my mom, and then my husband as well. (Applause.) Thank you all so, so much. It really keeps us going, and I am just thrilled to be here.

One hundred and one years ago, the NAACP was established in pursuit of a simple goal, and that was to spur this nation to live up to the founding ideals, to secure those blessings of liberty, to fulfill that promise of equality.

And since then, the work of this organization has been guided by a simple belief: that while we might not fully live out that promise or those blessings for ourselves, if we worked hard enough, and fought long enough, and believed strongly enough, that we could secure them for our children and for our grandchildren, and give them opportunities that we never dreamed of for ourselves. (Applause.)

So, for more than a century, the men and women of the NAACP have marched and protested. You have lobbied Presidents and fought unjust laws. You've stood up and sat in and risked life and limb so that African Americans could take their rightful places not just at lunch counters and on buses, but at universities and on battlefields—(applause)—and in hospitals and boardrooms; in Congress, the Supreme Court; and, yes, even the White House. (Applause.) Think about it—even the White House.

So I know that I stand here today, and I know that my hus- 10 band stands where he is today, because of this organization— (applause)—and because of the struggles and the sacrifices of all those who came before us.

But I also know that their legacy isn't an entitlement to be taken for granted. And I know it is not simply a gift to be enjoyed. Instead, it is an obligation to be fulfilled.

And when so many of our children still attend crumbling schools, and a black child is still far more likely to go to prison than a white child, I think the founders of this organization would agree that our work is not yet done. (Applause.)

When African American communities are still hit harder than just about anywhere by this economic downturn, and so many families are just barely scraping by, I think the founders would tell us that now is not the time to rest on our laurels.

When stubborn inequalities still persist—in education and health, in income and wealth—I think those founders would urge us to increase our intensity, and to increase our discipline and our focus and keep fighting for a better future for our children and our grandchildren. (Applause.)

And that's why I really wanted to come here today—because 15 I wanted to talk with you about an issue that I believe cries out for our attention—one that is of particular concern to me, not just as First Lady, but as a mother who believes that we owe it to our kids to prepare them for the challenges that we know lie ahead. And that issue is the epidemic of childhood obesity in America today.

Now, right now in America, one in three children is overweight or obese, putting them at greater risk of obesity-related conditions like diabetes and cancer, heart disease, asthma.

And we're already spending billions of dollars in this country a year to treat these conditions, and that number is only going to go up when these unhealthy children reach adulthood.

But it's important to be clear that this issue isn't about how our kids look. It's not about that. It's about how our kids feel. It's about their health and the health of our nation and the health of our economy.

And there's no doubt that this is a serious problem. It's one that is affecting every community across this country. But just like with so many other challenges that we face as a nation, the African American community is being hit even harder by this issue. (Applause.)

We are living today in a time where we're decades beyond 20 slavery; we are decades beyond Jim Crow, when one of the greatest risks to our children's future is their own health.

African American children are significantly more likely to be obese than are white children. Nearly half of African American children will develop diabetes at some point in their lives. People, that's half of our children.

And if we don't do something to reverse this trend right now, our kids won't be in any shape to continue the work begun by the founders of this great organization. (Applause.) They won't be in any condition to confront all those challenges that we know still remain.

So we need to take this issue seriously, as seriously as improving under-achieving schools, as seriously as eliminating youth violence or stopping the spread of HIV/AIDS or any of the other issues that we know are devastating our communities.

But in order to address this challenge, we also need to be honest with ourselves about how we got here, because we know that it wasn't always like this for our kids and our communities.

The way we live today is very different from even when I 25 was growing up. And I like to tell my kids I'm not that old. (Laughter.) They don't agree. (Laughter.)

Many of you probably grew up like I did—in a community that wasn't rich, not even middle class, but where people knew their neighbors, and they looked out for each other's kids.

In these kind of strong African American communities, we went to neighborhood schools around the corner. So many of us had to walk to and from school every day, rain or shine. I know you've told that story. (Laughter.) And in Chicago, where I was raised, we did it in the dead of winter. (Laughter.) No shoes on our feet—it was hard, but we walked! (Applause.)

And in school, we had recess twice a day and gym class twice a week, like it or not. (Applause.) And then when we got home in the afternoon, after school or in the summer, there was no way we'd be allowed to lie around the house watching TV. (Applause.) First of all, there wasn't that many channels. (Laughter.)

Our parents made us get up and play outside. Had to get up, get out, didn't have to—just couldn't be inside. And we would spend hours riding bikes, playing softball, freeze tag, jumping double-dutch. Kids nowadays don't even know how to jump double-dutch (Laughter and applause.)

We were constantly on the move, only stopping to eat or 30 what? When the streetlights came on, right? (Applause.)

And eating was a totally different experience back then. In my house, we rarely ate out—rarely. Even when both parents worked outside of the home, most families in my neighborhood sat down at the table together as a family for a meal. (Applause.) And in my house, Marian Robinson's house, we ate what we were served. (Laughter and applause.) My mother never cared whether me or my brother liked what was on our plates. (Laughter.) We either ate what was there or we didn't eat. It was as simple as that. (Laughter.)

We never ate anything fancy, but the portion sizes were reasonable and there were rarely seconds—maybe for your father, but not for you. (Laughter.) And there was always a vegetable on the plate. (Applause.)

And many of our grandparents tended their own gardens or they relied on, as my father told me, "The Vegetable Man" who brought fresh produce. That was how people got by back then— they had fresh fruits and vegetables in their own backyards, and in jars in their cellar during the winter. And that wasn't just being thrifty—that was healthy too, little did we know.

And unless it was Sunday, or somebody's birthday, there was no expectation of dessert after our meals. And we didn't dream of asking for soda or pop. That was for special occasions.

Now, if you were lucky, you might get a quarter or two to 35 take to the corner store and get some penny candy. But you did not eat it all at once because you never knew when you'd see another piece of candy. (Laughter.) So you saved it in that little brown bag under your bed. (Laughter and applause.) That bag would be all worn out and sweaty. (Laughter.) You'd hold on to that bag, take out a half a piece of candy every other day. (Laughter.)

Back then, without any expert advice and without spending too much money, we managed to lead pretty healthy lives.

But things are a little different today, and many kids these days aren't so fortunate.

So many kids can't attend neighborhood schools or don't, so instead of walking to school, they ride in a car or they're in a bus. And in too many schools, recess and gym class have been slashed because of budget cuts. Fears about safety mean that those afternoons outside have been replaced by afternoons inside with TV, video games, the Internet.

In fact, studies have found that African American children spend an average of nearly six hours a day watching TV—and that every extra hour of TV they watch is associated with the consumption of an additional 167 calories.

For many folks, those nutritious family meals are a thing of the past, because a lot of people today are living in communities without a single grocery store, so they have to take two, three buses, a taxi, walk for miles just to buy a head of lettuce for a salad or to get some fresh fruit for their kids.

Most folks don't grow their own food the way many of our parents and grandparents did. A lot of folks also just don't have the time to cook at home on a regular basis. So instead, they wind up grabbing fast food or something from the corner store or the mini-mart—places that have few, if any, healthy options.

And we've seen how kids in our communities regularly stop by these stores on their way to school—buying themselves sodas and pop and chips for breakfast. And we've seen how they come right back to those same stores after school to buy their afternoon snack of candy and sugary drinks.

According to one study, on average, a trip to the corner store, a child will walk out of that store with more than 350 calories worth of food and beverage   this is on average. So if they're going two and three times a day, that can really add up.

And taken together, all of these things have made for a perfect storm of bad habits and unhealthy choices—a lifestyle that's dooming too many of our children to a lifetime of poor health and undermining our best efforts to build them a better future.

See, we can build our kids the best schools on earth, but if they don't have the basic nutrition they need to concentrate, they're still going to have a challenge learning. (Applause.) And we can create the best jobs in the world—we must—but that won't mean that folks will have the energy and the stamina to actually do those jobs.

We can offer people the best health care money can buy, 45 but if they're still leading unhealthy lives, then we'll still just be treating those diseases and conditions once they've developed rather than keeping people from getting sick in the first place. (Applause.)

See, and the thing is, is that none of us wants that kind of future for our kids or for our country.

And surely the men and women of the NAACP haven't spent a century organizing and advocating and working day and night only to raise the first generation in history that might be on track to live shorter lives than their parents.

And that's why I've made improving the quality of our children's health one of my top priorities.

As many of you may know, my efforts began with the planting of a garden on the South Lawn of the White House. (Applause.) But it's important to understand that this garden symbolizes so much more than just watching beautiful things grow. It's become a way to spark a broader conversation about the health and well-being not just of our kids but of our communities.

And in an effort to elevate that conversation nationally, we 50 launched "Let's Move." It's a nationwide campaign to rally this country around a single, ambitious goal, and that is to solve childhood obesity in a generation so that children born today reach adulthood at a healthy weight.

And through this initiative, we are bringing together governors and mayors, businessess and community groups, educators, parents, athletes, health professionals, you name it, because it is going to take all of us, working together, to help our kids lead healthier lives right from the beginning.

"Let's Move," the campaign, has four components.

The first, we're working to give parents the information they need to make healthy decisions for their families.

For example, we're working with the FDA and the food industry to provide better labeling, something simple, so folks don't have to spend hours squinting at labels, trying to figure out whether the food they're buying is healthy or not.

Our new health care legislation requires chain restaurants 55 to post the calories in the food they serve so that parents have the information they need to make healthy choices for their kids in restaurants. (Applause.)

And we're working with doctors and pediatricians to ensure that they routinely screen our children for obesity. And I can personally attest to the value of these screenings based on my own personal experiences, because it wasn't that long ago when the Obamas weren't exactly eating as healthy as we should have been. And it was our daughter's pediatrician who actually pulled us aside and suggested that I think about making some changes to our family's diet. And it made a world of differences.

But we also know that giving better information to parents is not enough, because with 31 million American children participating in federal school meal programs, many of our kids are consuming as many as half their daily calories at school.

That's why the second part of "Let's Move" is to get healthier food into our schools. (Applause.)

And we're working to reauthorize our child nutrition legislation that will make significant new investments to revamp our school meals and improve the food that we offer in those school vending machines, so that we're serving our kids less sugar, salt and fat, and more vegetables, fruits and whole grains.

This is bipartisan legislation and it is critically important for the health and success of our children, and we are hoping that Congress will act swiftly to get this passed. (Applause.) 60

But we also know that healthy eating is only half the battle. Experts recommend at least 60 minutes a day of activity. That's at least the bare minimum, and many of our kids aren't even close.

So the third part of "Let's Move" is to help our kids get moving, to find new ways for them to get and stay active and fit. And we're working to get more kids participating in daily physical education classes and to get more schools offering recess for their students.

We've set a goal of increasing the number of kids who walk or ride their bikes to school by 50 percent in the next five years.

And we've recruited professional athletes—they've been fantastic—from different sports leagues to inspire our kids to get up off that couch and to get moving.

But we know that even if we offer the most nutritious school meals, and we give kids every opportunity to be fit and we give parents the information they need to prepare healthy food for their families, all that won't mean much if our families still live 65 in communities where that healthy food simply isn't available in the first place.

And that brings me to the fourth and final component of the campaign, and that is to ensure that all families have access to fresh, affordable food in their communities where they live. (Applause.)

And one of the most shocking statistics for me in all of this is that right now, 23.5 million Americans, including 6.5 million children, live in what we call "food deserts"—areas without a single supermarket. This is particularly serious in African American communities where folks wind up buying their groceries at places like gas stations and bodegas and corner stores where they often pay higher prices for lower-quality food. (Applause.)

But the good news is that we know that this trend is reversible, because when healthier options are available in our community, we know that folks will actually take advantage of those options.

One study found that African Americans ate 32 percent more fruits and vegetables for each additional supermarket in their community. So we know the kind of difference that we can make with some changes. We know that when we provide the right incentives—things like grants and tax credits, and help securing permits and zoning—businesses are willing to invest and lay down roots in our communities.

And many grocers are finding that when they set up shop in high-need areas, they can actually make a decent profit. They're learning that they can do well by doing good. ⁷⁰

So as part of "Let's Move," we've proposed a Healthy Food Financing Initiative—a $400 million a year fund that we'll use to attract hundreds of millions of more dollars from the private and non-profit sectors to bring grocery stores and other healthy food retailers to underserved areas across the country.

And our goal is ambitious—we want to eliminate food deserts in this country within seven years, and create jobs and revitalize neighborhoods along the way. (Applause.)

So, I know these goals are ambitious, and there are many, many more. And as First Lady, I am going to do everything that I can to ensure that we meet them.

But I also know that at the end of the day, government can only do so much.

I have spoken to so many experts about this issue, and not 75 a single one of them said that the solution is to have government tell people what to do. It's not going to work. Instead, this is about families taking responsibility and making manageable changes that fit with their budgets and their needs and their tastes. That's the only way it's going to work.

It's about making those little changes that can really add up—simple things like taking the stairs instead of the elevator, walking instead of riding in a car or bus, even something as simple as turning on the radio and dancing with your children in the middle of your living room for hours. That will work up a sweat. (Applause.)

How about replacing all of that soda and those sugary drinks with water? (Applause.) Kids won't like it as first, trust me. But they'll grow to like it. Or deciding that they don't get dessert with every meal. As I tell my kids, dessert is not a right. (Laughter.) Or they don't get it every day.

Or just being more thoughtful about how we prepare our food—baking instead of frying. I know. (Laughter.) Don't shoot me. (Applause.) And cutting back on those portion sizes.

Look, no one wants to give up Sunday meal. No one wants to say goodbye to mac and cheese and fried chicken and mashed potatoes—oh, I'm getting hungry—(laughter)—forever. No one wants to do that. Not even the Obamas, trust me.

But chefs across the country are showing us that with a few 80 simple changes and substitutions, we can find healthy, creative solutions that work for our families and our communities.

And that's why I am excited about our new "Let's Cook" video series, which we're launching on our "Let's Move" website at letsmove.gov.

This is a great series featuring Sam Kass, who a lot of people think is cute—I don't know if that helps. (Laughter.) But this series features some of the country's top chefs, who will be demonstrating how folks can prepare simple, affordable, nutritious meals for their families.

The first guest chef is a guy by the name of Marvin Woods, who's known for his cuisine based in North Africa, the Caribbean, South America, the Low Country. He's demonstrating how to prepare a week of healthy and tasty dinners for a family of four on a tight budget. And he provides recipes, shopping lists, so that folks can do it all themselves at home.

And finally, it's one thing we can think about, is working to make sure that our kids get a healthy start from the beginning, by promoting breastfeeding in our communities. (Applause). One thing we do know is that babies that are breastfed are less likely to be obese as children, but 40 percent of African American babies are never breastfed at all, not even during the first week of their lives.

And we know this isn't possible or practical for some moms, 85 but we've got a WIC [Women, Infants, and Children] program that's providing new support to low-income moms who want to try so that they get the support they need.

And under the new health care legislation, businesses will now have to accommodate mothers who want to continue breastfeeding once they get back to work. (Applause.) Now, the men, you may not understand how important that is. (Laughter.) But trust me, it's important to have a place to go.

But let's be clear, this isn't just about changing what our kids are eating and the lifestyles they're leading—it's also about changing our own habits as well. Because believe it or not, if you're obese, there's a 40 percent chance that your kids will be obese as well. And if you both you and the child's other parent are obese, that number jumps to 80 percent.

And this is more than just genetics at work. The fact is, we all know we are our children's first and best teachers and role models. We teach them healthy habits not just by what we say but by how we live. Shoot, I can't tell Malia and Sasha to eat their vegetables if I'm sitting around eating french fries—trust me, they will not let that happen. And I can't tell them to go run around outside if I'm spending all my free time on the couch watching TV.

And this isn't just about the example that we set as individuals and as families, but about the lifestyle we're promoting in our communities as well.

It's about the example we set in our schools. It's about 90 schools like the Kelly Edwards Elementary School in Williston, South Carolina. It's a Bronze Award winner in our USDA Healthier U.S. School Challenge. This is a school where students have planted their own garden so that they can taste all kinds of fresh vegetables; they can stay active because they've got their own dance team.

And it's about establishing strong community partnerships that involve folks from every sector and every background.

There's a Fresh Food Financing Initiative in Pennsylvania— it's a great example. This initiative is a collaboration between business, non-profit and government that's funded more than

80 supermarket projects, bringing nutritious food to hundreds of thousands of people in underserved communities.

These are just a couple of the thousands of programs and projects that are making a difference in communities across the country already.

So if there's anybody here, after all this talking I've done, who feels a little overwhelmed by this challenge—because it can be overwhelming—if there is anyone here who might even already be losing hope thinking about how hard it will be to get going, or giving up, I just want you to take a look around at all the things that are already being accomplished, because I want folks to learn from each other and to be inspired by each other, because that's what we've always done.

That is exactly what happened here in this city half a cen- 95 tury ago. See, because back in 1958, folks right here in Kansas City saw what folks down in Montgomery had achieved with their bus boycott. So they were inspired by all those men and women who walked miles walked miles home each day on aching feet because they knew there was a principle at stake.

So folks here organized their own boycott of department stores that refused to serve African Americans. (Applause.) Handbills publicizing their meetings stated, and this is a quote: "They stopped riding in Montgomery, so let's stop buying in Kansas City." (Applause.)

A local music teacher even composed a song that became the anthem for their efforts. It was entitled "Let's take the walk that counts."

And then, as you know, a few years later, in April of 1964, folks turned out in droves to pass a public accommodations law mandating that all residents, regardless of their skin color, be served in restaurants, hotels and other public places. Even folks who were too sick to walk showed up to vote. (Applause.)

One organizer recalled that they used wheelchairs to get people to the polls and even brought one man in on a stretcher. So think about that—being carried to the ballot box on a stretcher. (Applause.) Those folks didn't do all that just for themselves. They did it because they wanted something better for their children and for their grandchildren. That's why they did it.

And in the end, that's what has driven this organization 100 since its founding.

It is why Daisy Bates endured hate mail and death threats to guide those nine young men and women who would walk through those schoolhouse doors in Little Rock.

It is why Thurgood Marshall fought so hard to ensure that children like Linda Brown, and children like my daughters and your sons and daughters, would never again know the cruel inequality of separate but equal.

It is why so many men and women—legends and icons and ordinary folks—have faced down their doubts, their cynicism and their fears, and they've taken that walk that counts.

So we owe it to all those who've come before us to ensure that all those who come after us—our children and our grandchildren—that they have the strength and the energy and the enduring good health that they need to continue and complete that journey. (Applause.)

So I'm asking you, NAACP, will you move with me? 105 (Applause.) Let's move! I'm going to need you, NAACP. (Applause.) This is not an endeavor that I can do by myself. We cannot change the health of our community alone. I'm going to need each and every single one of you to work together for this campaign for our children's future. If we do this together, we can change the way our children think about their health forever.

So I want to thank you all in advance, again, for your prayers and your thoughts and your support. The struggle continues.

Thank you all. God bless you, God bless this organization, and God bless America. Thank you all so much. (Applause.)

Joining the Conversation

1. Michelle Obama gave this speech at the annual convention of the NAACP, the largest African American organization in the country. What is her main point, and how does she support her argument?

2. Obama compares today's eating and exercise habits with those from when she was a child. What are the main differences, and how does she explain the reasons for the changes?

3. This text was delivered as a speech. As you read it, how can you tell that it was written to be heard rather than read? How might it have been different as a piece of writing rather than as a speech?

4. How might Obama respond to Radley Balko's argument that choices about eating and lifestyle are matters of personal responsibility, especially where children are concerned?

5. Write an article reporting on Obama's speech. Assume the article will be published in your college newspaper and write for an audience of students. You'll need to summarize Obama's main points and quote some of what she said.

Escape from the Western Diet

MICHAEL POLLAN

—◻—

THE UNDERTOW OF NUTRITIONISM is powerful. . . . Much nutrition science qualifies as reductionist science, focusing as it does on individual nutrients (such as certain fats or carbohydrates or antioxidants) rather than on whole foods or dietary patterns. . . . But using this sort of science to try to figure out what's wrong with the Western diet is probably unavoidable. However imperfect, it's the sharpest experimental and explanatory tool we have. It also satisfies our hunger for a simple, one-nutrient explanation. Yet it's one thing to entertain such explanations and quite another to mistake them for the whole truth or to let any one of them dictate the way you eat.

[And] many of the scientific theories put forward to account for exactly what in the Western diet is responsible for Western diseases conflict with one another. The lipid hypothesis cannot

MICHAEL POLLAN has written six books, including *The Omnivore's Dilemma: A Natural History of Four Meals* (2006), *Food Rules: An Eater's Manual* (2010), and *In Defense of Food: An Eater's Manifesto* (2008), from which this essay was excerpted. He was named one of *Time* magazine's top 100 Most Influential People in 2010 and teaches at the University of California at Berkeley.

be reconciled with the carbohydrate hypothesis, and the theory that a deficiency of omega-3 fatty acids (call it the neolipid hypothesis) is chiefly to blame for chronic illness is at odds with the theory that refined carbohydrates are the key. And while everyone can agree that the flood of refined carbohydrates has pushed important micronutrients out of the modern diet, the scientists who blame our health problems on deficiencies of these micronutrients are not the same scientists who see a sugar-soaked diet leading to metabolic syndrome and from there to diabetes, heart disease, and cancer. It is only natural for scientists no less than the rest of us to gravitate toward a single, all-encompassing explanation. That is probably why you now find some of the most fervent critics of the lipid hypothesis embracing the carbohydrate hypothesis with the same absolutist zeal that they once condemned in the Fat Boys. In the course of my own research into these theories, I have been specifically warned by scientists allied with the carbohydrate camp not to "fall under the spell of the omega-3 cult." *Cult?* There is a lot more religion in science than you might expect.

So here we find ourselves . . . lost at sea amid the crosscurrents of conflicting science.

Or do we?

Because it turns out we don't need to declare our allegiance 5 to any one of these schools of thought in order to figure out how best to eat. In the end, they are only theories, scientific explanations for an empirical phenomenon that is not itself in doubt: People eating a Western diet are prone to a complex of chronic diseases that seldom strike people eating more traditional diets. Scientists can argue all they want about the biological mechanisms behind this phenomenon, but whichever it is, the solution to the problem would appear to remain very much the same: *Stop eating a Western diet.*

In truth the chief value of any and all theories of nutrition, apart from satisfying our curiosity about how things work, is not to the eater so much as it is to the food industry and the medical community. The food industry needs theories so it can better redesign specific processed foods; a new theory means a new line of products, allowing the industry to go on tweaking the Western diet instead of making any more radical change to its business model. For the industry it's obviously preferable to have a scientific rationale for *further* processing foods— whether by lowering the fat or carbs or by boosting omega-3s or fortifying them with antioxidants and probiotics—than to entertain seriously the proposition that processed foods of any kind are a big part of the problem.

For the medical community too scientific theories about diet nourish business as usual. New theories beget new drugs to treat diabetes, high blood pressure, and cholesterol; new treatments and procedures to ameliorate chronic diseases; and new diets organized around each new theory's elevation of one class of nutrient and demotion of another. Much lip service is paid to the importance of prevention, but the health care industry, being an industry, stands to profit more handsomely from new drugs and procedures to treat chronic diseases than it does from a wholesale change in the way people eat. Cynical? Perhaps. You could argue that the medical community's willingness to treat the broad contours of the Western diet as a given is a reflection of its realism rather than its greed. "People don't want to go there," as Walter Willett responded to the critic who asked him why the Nurses' Health Study didn't study the benefits of more alternative diets. Still, medicalizing the whole problem of the Western diet instead of working to overturn it (whether at the level of the patient or politics) is exactly what you'd expect from a health care community that is sympathetic to nutritionism as a matter of temperament, philosophy, and economics. You would not expect such a medical community to be sensitive to the cultural or ecological dimensions of the food problem—and it isn't. We'll know this has changed when doctors kick the fast-food franchises out of the hospitals.

So what would a more ecological or cultural approach to the food problem counsel us? How might we plot our escape from nutritionism and, in turn, from the most harmful effects of the Western diet? To Denis Burkitt, the English doctor stationed in Africa during World War II who gave the Western diseases their name, the answer seemed straightforward, if daunting. "The only way we're going reduce disease," he said, "is to go backwards to the diet and lifestyle of our ancestors." This sounds uncomfortably like the approach of the diabetic Aborigines who went back to the bush to heal themselves. But I don't think this is what Burkitt had in mind; even if it was, it is not a very attractive or practical strategy for most of us. No, the challenge we face today is figuring out how to escape the worst elements of the Western diet and lifestyle *without* going back to the bush.

In theory, nothing could be simpler: To escape the Western diet and the ideology of nutritionism, we have only to stop eating and thinking that way. But this is harder to do in practice, given the treacherous food environment we now inhabit and the loss of cultural tools to guide us through it. Take the question of whole versus processed foods, presumably one of the simpler distinctions between modern industrial foods and older kinds. Gyorgy Scrinis, who coined the term "nutritionism," suggests that the most important fact about any food is not its nutrient content but its degree of processing. He writes that "whole foods and industrial foods are the only two food groups I'd consider including in any useful food 'pyramid.'" In other words, instead of worrying about nutrients, we should simply avoid any food that has been processed to such an extent that it is more the product of industry than of nature.

This sounds like a sensible rule of thumb until you realize 10 that industrial processes have by now invaded many whole foods too. Is a steak from a feedlot steer that consumed a diet of corn, various industrial waste products, antibiotics, and hormones still a "whole food"? I'm not so sure. The steer has itself been raised on a Western diet, and that diet has rendered its meat substantially different—in the type and amount of fat in it as well as its vitamin content—from the beef our ancestors ate. The steer's industrial upbringing has also rendered its meat so cheap that we're likely to eat more of it more often than our ancestors ever would have. This suggests yet another sense in which this beef has become an industrial food: It is designed to be eaten industrially too—as fast food.

So plotting our way out of the Western diet is not going to be simple. Yet I am convinced that it can be done, and in the course of my research, I have collected and developed some straightforward (and distinctly unscientific) rules of thumb, or personal eating policies, that might at least point us in the right direction. They don't say much about specific foods—about what sort of oil to cook with or whether you should eat meat. They don't have much to say about nutrients or calories, either, though eating according to these rules will perforce change the balance of nutrients and amount of calories in your diet. I'm not interested in dictating anyone's menu, but rather in developing what I think of as eating algorithms—mental programs that, if you run them when you're shopping for food or deciding on a meal, will produce a great many different dinners, all of them "healthy" in the broadest sense of that word.

And our sense of that word stands in need of some broadening. When most of us think about food and health, we think in fairly narrow nutritionist terms—about our personal physical health and how the ingestion of this particular nutrient or rejection of that affects it. But I no longer think it's possible to separate our bodily health from the health of the environment from which we eat or the environment in which we eat or, for that matter, from the health of our general outlook about food (and health). If my explorations of the food chain have taught me anything, it's that it is a food chain, and all the links in it are in fact linked: the health of the soil to the health of the plants and animals we eat to the health of the food culture in which we eat them to the health of the eater, in body as well as mind. [So you will find rules here] concerning not only what to eat but also how to eat it as well as how that food is produced. Food consists not just in piles of chemicals; it also comprises a set of social and ecological relationships, reaching back to the land and outward to other people. Some of these rules may strike you as having nothing whatever to do with health; in fact they do.

Many of the policies will also strike you as involving more work—and in fact they do. If there is one important sense in which we do need to heed Burkitt's call to "go backwards" or follow the Aborigines back into the bush, it is this one: In order to eat well we need to invest more time, effort, and resources in providing for our sustenance, to dust off a word, than most of us do today. A hallmark of the Western diet is food that is fast, cheap, and easy. Americans spend less than 10 percent of their income on food; they also spend less than a half hour a day preparing meals and little more than an hour enjoying them.[1] For most people for most of history, gathering and preparing food has been an occupation at the very heart of daily life. Traditionally people have allocated a far greater proportion of their income to food—as they still do in several of the countries where people eat better than we do and as a consequence are healthier than we are.[2] Here, then, is one way in which we would do well to go a little native: backward, or perhaps it is forward, to a time and place where the gathering and preparing and enjoying of food were closer to the center of a well-lived life.

[I'd like to propose] three rules—"*Eat food. Not too much. Mostly plants.*"—that I now need to unpack, providing some elaboration and refinement in the form of more specific guidelines, injunctions, subclauses, and the like. Each of these three main rules can serve as category headings for a set of personal policies to guide us in our eating choices without too much trouble or thought. The idea behind having a simple policy like "avoid foods that make health claims" is to make the process simpler and more pleasurable than trying to eat by the numbers and nutrients, as nutritionism encourages us to do.

So under "Eat Food," I propose some practical ways to separate, and defend, real food from the cascade of foodlike products that now surround and confound us, especially in the supermarket. Many of the tips under this rubric concern shopping and take the form of filters that should help keep out the sort of products you want to avoid. Under "Mostly Plants," I'll dwell more specifically, and affirmatively, on the best types of foods (not nutrients) to eat. Lest you worry, there is, as the adverb suggests, more to this list than fruits and vegetables. Last, under "Not Too Much," the focus shifts from the foods themselves to the question of how to eat them—the manners, mores, and habits that go into creating a healthy, and pleasing, culture of eating.

NOTES

1. David M. Cutler, et al., "Why Have Americans Become More Obese?," *Journal of Economic Perspectives*, Vol. 17, No. 3 (Summer, 2003), pp. 93–118. In 1995 Americans spent twenty-seven minutes preparing meals and four minutes cleaning up after them; in 1965 the figure was forty-four minutes of preparation and twenty-one minutes of cleanup. Total time spent eating has dropped from sixty-nine minutes to sixty-five, all of which suggests a trend toward prepackaged meals.

2. Compared to the 9.9 percent of their income Americans spend on food, the Italians spend 14.9 percent, the French 14.9 percent, and the Spanish 17.1 percent.

Joining the Conversation

1. What does Michael Pollan mean when he refers to the "Western diet"? Why does he believe Americans need to "escape" from it?

2. Pollan begins with a "they say," citing a variety of scientific theories known as nutritionism. Summarize his response to these views. What is his objection to such views, and to the business and research interests that promote them?

3. If Pollan were to read Mary Maxfield's response to this article (pp. 442–47), how might he, in turn, respond to her?

4. Write an essay that begins where Pollan's piece ends, perhaps by quoting from paragraph 14: "*Eat food. Not too much. Mostly plants.*" You'll need to explain his argument, and then respond with your own views.

Food as Thought:
Resisting the Moralization of Eating

MARY MAXFIELD

——◻——

HOW DO FRENCH PEOPLE eat so unhealthily—famously indulging in cheese, cream, and wine—but stay, on average, healthier than Americans? Journalist Michael Pollan offers readers a simple solution: quit obsessing over this French paradox and start obsessing over the french fry. Pointing to what he considers the American paradox—"a notably unhealthy population preoccupied with . . . the idea of eating healthy" (9)—Pollan contends that our definition of healthy eating is driven by a well-funded corporate machine. According to Pollan, the food industry, along with nutrition science and journalism, is capitalizing on our confusion over how to eat.

MARY MAXFIELD graduated from Fontbonne University in December 2010 with a degree in creative social change and minors in sociology, American culture studies, and women's and gender studies. Her academic interests include bodies, gender, sexuality, politics, and rhetoric. Read her blog at missmarymax.wordpress.com, or follow her on Twitter @missmarymax.

While Pollan implicates his own profession in this critique, he simultaneously contributes to our cultural anxiety over food. The same critic who argues that "any and all theories of nutrition [serve] not the eater [but] the food industry," nevertheless proposes his own theory: the elimination of processed foods (141). Likewise, even after noting that the connections between diet and health that we take as gospel apparently *aren't*, Pollan nevertheless adheres to contemporary common-sense science, making assumptions about diet, health, and weight that underpin the very food industry he critiques.

Thus as he attempts to dismantle one paradox, Pollan embodies another: he's a critic of nutrition and food science who nevertheless bolsters the American investment in those industries. After publishing *In Defense of Food* (and its equally successful predecessor, *The Omnivore's Dilemma*), Pollan released *Food Rules*, a pocket-sized manual for better eating. Of course, Pollan contends that *his* guidelines function differently than the prescriptions (and proscriptions) of food scientists, because his rules function as "eating algorithms" that "produce many different dinners" (144) rather than specifying a concrete menu. Yet no matter how many meals fit Pollan's formula—"Eat food, not too much, mostly plants" (1)—it remains a dictate provided by an expert to those who apparently can't properly nourish themselves.

Pollan and other like-minded nutrition hawks consistently back up their claims with concerns over American health. Although acknowledging that eating primarily for health represents a departure from the historical purpose of food—fuel for our bodies—these gastronomical philosophers nevertheless position themselves as protectors of health. Americans need this protection, we are told, because we're a nation stricken by heart disease, diabetes, and cancer. According to this line of thought, each of these maladies is tied to our diet and essentially to our weight. As a culture, we no longer discuss healthy eating without also discussing unhealthy weights. Linking nutrition and body type, voices like Pollan's warn us against eating too much—often without any parallel warnings against eating too little. Pollan himself insists that overeating constitutes "the greatest threat" to our survival (7), and our government concurs, pouring resources into a fight against the obesity epidemic, that plague of fatness that supposedly threatens our national health.

The problem is that our understanding of health is as based 5 in culture as it is in fact. Despite some doubt in academic circles over connections between diet, health, and weight, common-sense reportage continues to presume that they are directly connected. Pollan, for example, twice notes that our diet of processed foods makes us "sick and fat" (10), and then— without evidence to support that claim—conflates health with weight and condemns fatness out of hand. Later, he refers to obesity as a Western disease (11)—again presuming a correlation between weight and health—and even cites statistics on eating habits from a study entitled "Why Have Americans Become More Obese?" (145).

A growing group of academics who have examined the research on obesity at length have discovered fundamental flaws behind perceptions of fatness, diet, and health. Law professor and journalist Paul Campos notes that "lies about fat, fitness, and health . . . not coincidentally serve the interests of America's $50-billion-per-year diet industry," and fat-acceptance activist Kate Harding elaborates on this point, observing that "if you scratch an article on the obesity crisis, you will almost always find a press release from a company that's developing a weight loss drug—or from a 'research group' . . . funded by such companies" ("Don't You Realize"). Harding and Campos both belong to a school that has repeatedly challenged the validity of the body mass index (BMI), a tool that uses height and weight measurements to calculate body fat. Originally developed by a mathematician as a purely statistical tool, the BMI has become medicine's go-to means for predicting heart disease and other maladies, despite research that suggests a low BMI presents a greater mortality risk than a high one and that, in general, BMI cannot accurately predict one's health (Campos).

Culturally, however, we resist these scientific findings in favor of a perspective that considers fatness fatal and thinness immortal. Our skewed views of fatness then facilitate skewed views of food. We continue to believe in a "right" or "healthy" way of eating that involves eating less and eating differently than we instinctively would, despite evidence to the contrary provided both by scholars like Harding and Campos, and by Health at Every Size (HAES) nutritionists like Michelle Allison. HAES advocates challenge our cultural misconceptions, suggesting that—outside of specific medical conditions like celiac disease and anorexia—"what a person eats [rarely] takes primacy over how they eat it" (Allison, "Eating"). In essence, we can eat as we always have—which includes eating for emotional and social reasons—and still survive or even thrive.

Few of us, however, manage to think about eating this way. As Allison notes, "there are a lot of pressures and barriers in this world that get in our way, that confuse us, that distract us and attempt to control us in counterproductive ways" ("Rules vs. Trust"). In this context, "health" functions moralistically. It results from making decisions like choosing fresh mozzarella over spray cheese, the "right" foods over the "wrong" ones.

Experts offer science to substantiate those designations, yet science—as Campos, Harding, and Allison show—does not actually support these systems. Instead, as even Pollan notes, there remains "a lot [of] religion in science" (140).

That "religion" presents itself in the moralizing of food, the attempt—in how we eat—to rise above our beastly natures. As a culture, when we imagine eating like animals, we visualize a feeding frenzy. Allison observes that when she says "Adult human beings are allowed to eat whatever and however much they want," what people actually hear is: "Go out and cram your face with Twinkies!" ("Eat Food"). (Indeed, for Pollan, the total elimination of American anxiety about food translates to a laissez-faire policy of "let them eat Twinkies" [9].) Yet Allison and other HAES nutritionists suggest that adult humans will eat in a way that is good for them, given the opportunity ("Eat Food"). When we attempt to rise above our animal nature through the moralization of food, we unnecessarily complicate the practice of eating. Food—be it french fry or granola bar, Twinkie or brown rice—isn't moral or immoral. Inherently, food is ethically neutral; notions of good and bad, healthy and unhealthy are projected onto it by culture. Staying mindful of that culture (and critical of the hidden interests that help guide it) can free us each to follow a formula we have long known but recently forgotten: Trust yourself. Trust your body. Meet your needs.

WORKS CITED

Allison, Michelle. "Eat Food. Stuff You Like. As Much As You Want." *The Fat Nutritionist*. n.pag., 15 Feb. 2010. Web. 19 Jan. 2011.
---. "Eating—the WHAT or the HOW?" *The Fat Nutritionist*. n.pag., 17 Aug. 2010. Web. 19 Jan. 2011.

---. "Rules vs. Trust in Eating." *The Fat Nutritionist*. n.pag., 15 Dec. 2009.
    Web. 19 Jan. 2011.

Campos, Paul. "Being Fat Is OK." *Jewish World Review*. Jewish World Review,
    23 Apr. 2001. Web. 25 Mar. 2011.

Harding, Kate. "Don't You Realize Fat Is Unhealthy?" *Shapely Prose*.
    Wordpress, 20 June 2007. Web. 19 Jan. 2011.

Pollan, Michael. *In Defense of Food: An Eater's Manifesto*. New York: Penguin,
    2008. Print.

Joining the Conversation

1. In what ways does Mary Maxfield disagree with Michael
   Pollan (pp. 434–41) and other critics of the Western diet?
   What is her "they say," and what does she say?

2. What supporting evidence does Maxfield offer to counter
   the views of Michael Pollan and other critics?

3. Read Wil Haygood's article (pp. 406–15), and compare
   what he says with what Maxfield says. Which is more convincing and why?

4. Mayfield concludes by offering a formula for eating: "Trust
   yourself. Trust your body. Meet your needs." This formula
   contrasts with Michael Pollan's "Eat food. Not too much.
   Mostly plants." Write an essay responding to these arguments and presenting your own formula for eating.

Fat Is a Feminist Issue

SUSIE ORBACH

—◫—

OBESITY AND OVEREATING have joined sex as central issues in the lives of many women today. In the United States, 50 percent of women are estimated to be overweight. Every women's magazine has a diet column. Diet doctors and clinics flourish. The names of diet foods are now part of our general vocabulary. Physical fitness and beauty are every woman's goals. While this preoccupation with fat and food has become so common that we tend to take it for granted, being fat, feeling fat and the compulsion to overeat are, in fact, serious and painful experiences for the women involved.

SUSIE ORBACH is chair of the Relational School in the United Kingdom and is involved with Anybody, an organization "that campaigns for body diversity." She has published several books on women's health and emotional well-being, including *Bodies* (2009), *On Eating* (2002), and *Fat Is a Feminist Issue* (1978), from which this piece is taken. Orbach has worked extensively, as both an author and a therapist, on women's weight issues, and she served as an adviser to Princess Diana when she was suffering from bulimia. She appears frequently on British television and radio and is now a consultant to the British National Health Service.

Being fat isolates and invalidates a woman. Almost inevitably, the explanations offered for fatness point a finger at the failure of women themselves to control their weight, control their appetites and control their impulses. Women suffering from the problem of compulsive eating endure double anguish. feeling out of step with the rest of society, and believing that it is all their own fault. . . .

Here's the "they say." For tips on starting with that move, see Chapter 1.

A feminist perspective to the problem of women's compulsive eating is essential if we are to move on from the ineffective blame-the-victim approach.[1] . . . Feminism insists that those painful personal experiences derive from the social context into which female babies are born, and within which they develop to become adult women. The fact that compulsive eating is overwhelmingly a woman's problem suggests that it has something to do with the experience of being female in our society. Feminism argues that being fat represents an attempt to break free of society's sex stereotypes. Getting fat can thus be understood as a definite and purposeful act; it is a directed, conscious or unconscious, challenge to sex-role stereotyping and culturally defined experience of womanhood.

Fat is a social disease, and fat is a feminist issue. Fat is *not* about lack of self-control or lack of willpower. Fat *is* about protection, sex, nurturance, strength, boundaries, mothering, substance, assertion and rage. It is a response to the inequality of the sexes. Fat expresses experiences of women today in ways that are seldom examined and even more seldom treated. . . . What is it about the social position of women that leads them to respond to it by getting fat?

The current ideological justification for inequality of the sexes has been built on the concept of the innate differences between women and men. Women alone can give birth to and breast-feed their infants and, as a result, a primary dependency relationship develops between mother and child. While this biological capacity is the only known genetic difference between men and women,[2] it is used as the basis on which to divide unequally women and men's labor, power, roles and expectations. The division of labor has become institutionalized. Women's capacity to reproduce and provide nourishment has relegated her to the care and socialization of children.

The relegation of women to the social roles of wife and mother has several significant consequences that contribute to the problem of fat. First, in order to become a wife and mother, a woman has to have a man. Getting a man is presented as an almost unattainable and yet essential goal. To get a man, a woman has to learn to regard herself as an item, a commodity, a sex object. Much of her experience and identity depends on how she and others see her. As John Berger says in *Ways of Seeing:* "Men *act* and women *appear*. Men look at women. Women watch themselves being looked at. This determines not only most relations between men and women, but also the relation of women to themselves."[3]

This emphasis on presentation as the central aspect of a woman's existence makes her extremely self-conscious. It demands that she occupy herself with a self-image that others will find pleasing and attractive—an image that will immediately convey what kind of woman she is. She must observe and evaluate herself, scrutinizing every detail of herself as though she were an outside judge. She attempts to make herself in the image of womanhood presented by billboards, newspapers, magazines and television. The media present women either in a sexual context or within the family, reflecting a woman's two prescribed roles, first as a sex object, and then as a mother. She is brought up to marry by "catching" a man with her good looks and pleasing manner. To do this she must look appealing, earthy, sensual, sexual, virginal, innocent, reliable, daring, mysterious, coquettish and thin. In other words, she offers her self-image on the marriage marketplace. As a married woman, her sexuality will be sanctioned and her economic needs will be looked after. She will have achieved the first step of womanhood.

Since women are taught to see themselves from the outside as candidates for men, they become prey to the huge fashion and diet industries that first set up the ideal images and then exhort women to meet them. The message is loud and clear— the woman's body is not her own. The woman's body is not satisfactory as it is. It must be thin, free of "unwanted hair," deodorized, perfumed and clothed. It must conform to an ideal physical type. Family and school socialization teaches girls to groom themselves properly. Furthermore, the job is never-ending, for the image changes from year to year. In the early 1960s, the only way to feel acceptable was to be skinny and flat chested with long straight hair. The first of these was achieved by near starvation, the second, by binding one's breasts with an ace bandage and the third, by ironing one's hair. Then in the early 1970s, the look was curly hair and full breasts. Just as styles in clothes change seasonally, so women's bodies are expected to change to fit these fashions. Long and skinny one year, petite and demure the next, women are continually manipulated by images of proper womanhood, which are extremely powerful because they are presented as the only reality. To ignore them means to risk being an outcast. Women are urged to conform, to help out the economy by continuous consumption of goods and clothing that are quickly made unwearable by the next season's fashion styles in clothes and body shapes. In the background, a ten billion dollar industry waits to remold bodies to the latest fashion. In this way, women are caught in an attempt to conform to a standard that is *externally* defined and constantly changing. But these models of femininity are experienced by women as unreal, frightening and unattainable. They produce a picture that is far removed from the reality of women's day-to-day lives.

The one constant in these images is that a woman must be thin. For many women, compulsive eating and being fat have become one way to avoid being marketed or seen as the ideal woman: "My fat says 'screw you' to all who want me to be the perfect mom, sweetheart, [and] maid. Take me for who *I* am, not for who I'm supposed to be. If you are really interested in *me,* you can wade through the layers and find out who I am." In this way, fat expresses a rebellion against the powerlessness of the woman, against the pressure to look and act in a certain way and against being evaluated on her ability to create an image of herself.

NOTES

1. William Ryan, *Blame the Victim* (New York, 1971). This book shows how we come to blame the victims of oppression rather than its perpetrators.

2. Dorothy Griffiths and Esther Saraga, "Sex Differences in a Sexist Society," International Conference on Sex-role Stereotyping, British Psychological Society, Cardiff, Wales, July 1977.

3. John Berger et al., *Ways of Seeing* (London, 1972) 47.

Joining the Conversation

1. Susie Orbach begins by citing what others say about obesity as an issue among women in the United States, noting in paragraph 2 that "almost inevitably, the explanations offered for fatness point a finger at the failure of women themselves to control their weight." That's her "they say"; what then does *she* say? Cite lines from her text in your answer.

2. In paragraphs 3 and 4, Orbach describes a feminist perspective on compulsive eating and obesity. Summarize that perspective.

3. Orbach focuses on weight and body image as a women's issue, but men too face pressures concerning diet and body image. What are some of those pressures?

4. Does Orbach introduce any naysayers, any objections or possible objections to her own position? If so, what are they? If not, what objections might she have considered, and how do you think she would have dealt with them?

5. Orbach says that being overweight is a way for many women to rebel against social pressures to be thin. What do you think? Write an essay in which you agree, disagree, or both agree and disagree with her position, but be sure to summarize or quote Orbach's views before you offer your own.

Having It His Way:
The Construction of Masculinity
in Fast-Food TV Advertising

CARRIE PACKWOOD FREEMAN
AND DEBRA MERSKIN

—⬚—

AN ATTRACTIVE twenty-something guy buying organic tofu
and produce at a grocery checkout counter looks sheepishly at
the man behind him who is buying about half a pig's worth of
ribs. The healthy shopper's masculinity is in question when he
looks over his choice of wimpy health food. Not to worry. Help
is on the way when he spies a Hummer ad in the magazine rack.
It is clear what he must do in order to restore his manhood; he
leaves the produce and buys the SUV.

Why does this humorous Hummer TV advertisement about
meat and masculinity make sense to American viewers? Clearly,

CARRIE PACKWOOD FREEMAN teaches at Georgia State University and
studies how the media portrays veganism and animal food production.
She has written for *Eugene Weekly* on vegan issues and is active in
animal rights groups. DEBRA MERSKIN teaches at the University of
Oregon and does research on the media's portrayal of women and
minorities. This essay first appeared in *Food for Thought: Essays on Eating and Culture* (2008).

advertisers trust we believe that a traditional American male does not eat organic, plant-based proteins—he primarily eats meat, which would also explain the prominence of masculine themes in advertisements for meat products, like burgers and subs.

Anthropologists have documented the historical connection between males and domination of nature and other animals, such as evidenced by humans' traditional role as animal hunters.[1] These historical relations contribute to food remaining a highly gendered cultural object in America today, particularly the gendering of meat as masculine food. Even though most women also eat meat, females are more closely associated with cultivation and consumption of plant-based foods, whereas males are more heavily associated with the killing, grilling, and consuming of animals.[2]

Ecofeminism has critiqued this patriarchal domination of animals and nature as being linked to sexist oppression of women, contributing to a larger environmental and animal rights discourse that seeks to reduce humanity's role in the destruction of other species. Yet, despite these critiques, the masculine identity of man as defined by meat-eating is still celebrated by media in the twenty-first century, particularly in fast-food advertisements. To examine how this identity is often reinforced insted of challenged in American culture, this study conducts a semiotic analysis of representations of masculinity in a small selection of television advertisements for various fast-food restaurants in 2006–2007.

Advertising doesn't just sell things, it articulates values and builds meaning, sometimes through constructing stereotypes that simplify a complex trait such as gender.[3] If largely unchallenged, these carefully cultivated constructions of gender become normalized as a "regime of truth" in the American popular imagination. This analysis of American television fast-food advertising critically explores the techniques used by advertisers to exploit and perpetuate a perceived connection between masculinity and meat. We unpack the connotative messages within these commercials in order to read what they tell us about masculine identity and values in America. As we evaluate what this means for society in the twenty-first century, our analysis is influenced by our roles as feminists, vegetarians, and environmentalists. Thus, we argue that the heteronormative, sex-role stereotypes promoted in fast-food commercials are as unhealthy as the fast food itself.

To begin, we contextualize social problems surrounding the promotion of both masculinity and meat by expanding on: man's anthropological association with meat, ecofeminist perspectives on patriarchy and meat, issues with the fast-food and meat industries, and the construction of masculinity in advertising.

Human Anthropological Connections with Eating Meat

In *An Unnatural Order*, Mason explains that the human practices of killing and eating animals are "virtual sacraments in our culture" because many theories have promoted the belief that humans have been natural hunters throughout our entire evolution.[4] But new evidence suggests that, for millions of years of evolution, we humans were largely vegetarian.[5] Organized hunting of large animals, primarily by men, did not begin until approximately 20,000 years ago. Multiple anthropologists theorize that men created rituals around hunting, most of which excluded women, to gain status for themselves, as previously women had been the more revered sex for their roles as food-gatherers and procreators. As the primary foragers, women likely invented plant agriculture, which accounts for women's association with plant food as well as their importance in early agrarian societies, where many gods were female.

The domestication of animals about 11,000 years ago created a transition for many human societies to a more sedentary, agricultural way of life that included surpluses and a division of wealth. In order to protect this wealth, patriarchal warrior cultures developed, creating oppressive systems of control labor such as slavery and imperialism. Herdsmen of larger, fast-moving animals like cows had to be most warlike herders, which accounts for the later masculine mystique around cowboys and beef. According to Mason, while forager societies often viewed other animals with wonder, respect, and partnership, herder/agrarian societies disempowered animals in order to control and demystify them.[6] Thus, many human groups came to view domesticated animals as commodities and wild animals as competition and pests. Religion was often used to justify this newfound domination over nature.

In the book *Beyond Beef*, Rifkin traces the connection between meat, masculinity, and religion to ancient Egypt, where the first universal religion was bull worship, based on the bull god, Apis, who represented strength, virility and a masculine passion for war and subjugation. To mark the year's end, the Apis bull would be ritually sacrificed and fed to the king so he could incorporate the bull's fierce strength and power. More recently, in American culture, cowboys tamed the "Wild West" (and all its inhabitants), reducing millions of acres to a vast cattle grazing area, forever associating red meat with this supposedly brave and tough category of American men. Meat is further linked to masculinity by its historic association with war and male aggression, as in the practice of reserving meat for warriors.[7] In fact, the Vedic word for "war" means "desire for cows," and the Sanskrit word for "battle," *gavisti*, means "desire for cattle."

Ecofeminist Perspectives on Meat and Patriarchy

In *The Sexual Politics of Meat*, Adams promotes an ecofeminist-vegetarian theory, asserting that "women and animals are similarly positioned in a patriarchal world, as objects rather than subject,"[8] both enduring a "cycle of objectification, fragmentation, and consumption."[9] This actuality is reinforced through media images where men "consume" women and other animals like pieces of meat. She concludes that "eating animals acts as a mirror and representation of patriarchal values. Meat-eating is the reinscription of male power at every meal."[10]

Adams highlights men's historical role in hunting animals and its perceived high social value in many cultures. "Meat was a valuable economic commodity; those who controlled this commodity achieved power."[11] Sanday found that when economies relied on plant food women held more status, and the society tended to be egalitarian, while meat-based cultures were more patriarchal.[12] Leakey and Lewin similarly found "women's social standing is roughly equal to men's only when society itself is not formalized around roles for distributing meat."[13]

Because of this history of men as meat-eaters, the men of today who eschew meat often face the stigmatization of being labeled effeminate. Adams cites nutritionist Jean Mayer, who believes that in modern society "the more men sit at their desks all day, the more they want to be reassured about their maleness in eating those large slabs of bleeding meat which are the last symbols of machismo."[14]

There is a gendered dichotomy in America's association with certain types of food for men versus women. Adams describes this dichotomy:

> Meat is king: this noun describing meat is a noun denoting male power. Vegetables . . . have become as associated with women as

meat is with men, recalling on a subconscious level the days of Woman the Gatherer. Since women have been made subsidiary in a male-dominated, meat-eating world, so has our food.[15]

Furthermore, nutritional scientist Sobal found this gendering of food persists in modern marriages, "men and women 'do gender' by consuming gender appropriate foods. Men emphasize meat."[16]

Issues with the Meat and Fast-Food Industries

Popular media such as *Fast Food Nation* and *Super Size Me* call attention to problems with the fast-food industry, such as low pay for workers, marketing to children, and unhealthy, and sometimes unsafe, food.[17] Many of their menu items are low in fiber and high in fat, sodium, cholesterol and simple carbohydrates, which can contribute to obesity and disease, especially when consumed in the extra-large portion sizes that are common.[18] Also, fast-food companies are the chief financial supporter of the meat industry, a problematic industry which is associated with labor exploitation (especially of immigrants),[19] mass animal cruelty and death,[20] and environmental destruction, including being a leading cause of global warming.[21] In addition, people who consume large amounts of animal products, and less whole grains and produce, may be at increased risk of contracting diseases like cancer, heart disease, and diabetes, as animal products are devoid of fiber yet contain cholesterol and saturated fat.[22] This is why the American Dietetic Association (ADA) suggests a plant-based diet prevents disease.

But since only 2.5 percent of Americans claim to be vegetarian, the average American is consuming meat, approximately 211 pounds of animal flesh a year, half of which is red

15

meat.[23] While census data on meat consumption are not segmented by gender, at least one study proves the common belief that men tend to eat more meat than women.[24] Also, physician Emily Senay contends that despite the health risks red meat remains a staple of the masculine diet: "If they had their druthers, many men would eat a big steak and a baked potato every night for dinner."[25]

Constructions of Masculinity in Advertising

Script theory helps explain manly characters in media stories.[26] The "macho personality constellation" is comprised of three behavioral dispositions: entitlement to callous sex, propensity toward violence, and danger as exciting. When it comes to advertising specifically, research conducted in the 1970s, which has yet to be rebuked, described the basic aspects and attributes of men.[27] In relation to women, men are shown as more autonomous, employed in more occupations, used more often than women as voices of authority in voice-overs, and more often located in the public sphere (offices and outdoors).

Katz claims that today's advertisers are challenged to maintain historical heteronormative gender differences in a more progressive era "characterized by a loosening of rigid gender distinctions," so advertising masculinity must be constructed in direct opposition to femininity.[28] One way modern advertisers accomplish this is to "equate masculinity with violence, power, and control (and femininity with passivity).[29]

Beer advertising is one genre that clearly demonstrates heteronormative male behaviors, attitudes, and beliefs. Strate's study of beer commercials found men seek acceptance among their male peers and use beer as a reward that "function as a symbol of initiation and group membership."[30] Generally, men monopolize activity in beer commercials, although occasionally women enter the story, typically as decorative objects or as the symbolic "other woman."

The marketing of meat also often relies on gender. As there 20 is a dearth of literature specifically addressing meat and masculinity in advertising, Adams' *Pornography of Meat* stands out. Her analysis shows how animals are feminized and women are animalized and both are often sexualized, to their ultimate detriment. The provocative title is an accusation that the dominant perspective of our advertising culture is the "pleasurable consumption of consumable beings," where Adams explains "how someone becomes a piece of meat."[31] She claims male dominance over women and all other animals virtually "disappears as a privilege and is experienced as 'desire,' as 'appetite,' as 'pleasure.'"[32]

Meating Men

To examine meat's association with masculinity in male-targeted fast-food television advertisements, we conducted an interpretive textual analysis of approximately 17 ads, using Hall's theory of representation and Barthes' method of semiotic analysis. In selecting texts, we sought fast-food television commercials that appeared to be targeted to males. The following types of codes indicated a male focus: men had the lead parts and did most of the talking, women were used primarily as objects of the male gaze, men hung out with other men and outnumbered women, and/or the narrator mentioned men specifically. In addition, while we cannot prove that other fast-food ads do not associate meat with femininity, a rudimentary perusal of most fast-food ads fails to suggest that the industry is constructing an association between meat and women as specifically and frequently as it is between meat and men.

We included ads from Burger King, Carl's Jr., Jack in the Box, Arby's, Quizno's, and Subway. Marketing experts confirm the Burger King and Carl's Jr. campaigns are specifically targeted toward young men.[33] We initially included Subway's 2006 diet campaign with Jared as a counterexample of a more positive and less hypermasculinized approach than that used by Carl's Jr. or Burger King; however, in 2007, even Subway began to exemplify masculinity by using athletes to emphasize the meatiness of its subs.

To analyze the texts, we watched the advertisements multiple times while taking detailed notes. We then analyzed each according to common semiotic signifier including: location, music, slogans, narration, colors, gender roles, gender relations, demographics, bodily appearance, power level by gender, violent acts, food types and descriptions, relationship between food and gender, and values. Taking all the ads into consideration, we looked for themes, patterns, and anomalies across all these signifying elements.

The following are brief descriptions of the ads we included in our analysis, all of which appeared on television in the Pacific Northwest in 2006 and early 2007.

Burger King (slogan "Have It Your Way")

BK Manthem (Texas Double Whopper)—A man inspires a crowd of men to march in the streets to reclaim their right to eat meat instead of "chick food." The narrative follows an over-the-top, male-themed remake of Helen Reddy's feminist song, "I Am Woman Hear me Roar." Tagline "Eat like a man, man."

BK Stacker Construction (Double, Triple or Quadruple "Stacker" Burgers)—A boss on a mock burger construction site angrily instructs another worker, both played by little people, not to include any veggies on the stacker, as it only contains meat and cheese. He sexually harasses a full-size female employee who flicks him into a bulldozer. Tagline "Stack it high, tough guy."

Hootie Country Song (Tender Crisp Bacon Cheddar Ranch)—The lead singer from the rock group Hootie and the Blowfish sings a country song about a male fantasy land set around the sandwich. It is located on a colorful, theatrical, Western-themed set with cheerful cowboys and sexualized cowgirls—including Dallas Cowboy Cheerleaders.

Whopper Senior and Junior—A series of humorous commercails where a dad, wearing a large whopper costume, tries to teach life lessons to his rebellious teenage son, wearing the whopper junior costume. It is set in the home with female relatives playing non-burger background characters. Tagline "Whopper Jr. for a buck."

Carl's Jr.

Wings (Buffalo Chicken Sandwich)—A young man chomping on chicken wings stares at a voluptuous, flirty, blond waitress. Then we see his girlfriend giving him a reproachful look, as he innocently asks "What?" The announcer tells us it is more fun to eat wings when out with the guys.

Series of at least four commercials featuring a young woman 30 acting seductively while eating a juicy burger. 1. Paris Hilton wears a leather bathing suit while washing a luxury car, 2. Woman rides a mechanical bull in a warehouse, 3. Woman models lingerie, and 4. Woman in an office almost drips sauce on her white suit while her male coworkers watch from afar. The latter is the only ad in this series in which men appear. None of the women have speaking roles, as male narrators inform us about the sandwiches.

Jack in the Box

Test Marketing (Diner Melt Combo)—Jack (company spokesman) and another executive stand behind a two-way mirror watching a group of male test subjects prove men prefer fast food over other variables meant to capture their attention, such as a motorcycle, a keg of beer, TV with sports, and women having a pillow fight. The executive informs Jack that with these findings they can rule the world. Tagline "Indulge."

Arby's

Construction Workers (Reuben sandwich)—Three male construction workers on a break stare silently at two attractive women walking by. They only start catcalling when a balding man in a suit walks by carrying an Arby's bag. Guitar music and slow motion lead the viewer to see the man in the unexpected role of a sex object. Tagline "I'm thinking Arby's."

Quizno's

Testimonials (Submarine sandwiches)—A man displaying a sub next to a Quizno's sub interviews at least seven men on the street who all testify that the Quizno's subs are better because they are meatier. No females are interviewed in this version.

Subway (slogan "Eat Fresh")

Low-fat Subs—Jared, a male spokesman who is known for losing lots of weight on a diet of low-fat Subway sandwiches, informs us that Subway has eight sandwiches with six grams of fat or less (a veggie sub is seen as one of them but is farthest from the camera). He compares this to the BK Stacker that has 54 grams of fat, saying, "That's more fat than in all eight of these subway sandwiches combined."

Athletes say "More Meat" (Foot-long Subway Club)—A series of at least three ads featuring Jared continuing in his role of promoting the low-fat benefit of the subs while a professional athlete promotes its meatiness. The athletes include a large male football player, a large male wrestler, and a petite female ice-skater. Jared proclaims, "A foot-long subway club is half the fat of a McDonald's Big Mac but twice the meat." Reminiscent of the old Miller Lite commercials, the athletes repeat "more meat" while Jared repeats "less fat" until Jared gives in to the athlete's side of the debate. The males use a more bullying approach to convince Jared to agree with their "more meat" argument, while the female uses a coy and sweet approach.

Coding Masculinity

This section begins with a description of the codes used to signify masculinity in these advertisements, followed by a discussion of the major themes uncovered regarding meat's role in representing freedom from constraints and loyalty to the heterosexual male group identity.

The commercials analyzed for this study illustrate a strong connection between meat and masculinity. These fast-foods ads share basic gendered codes that reinforce lessons of heterosexual male socialization. For example, all of the voice-overs and the lead actors with speaking roles are men. In fact, in all but a few ads women are presented as silent and willing objects of the male gaze. Rather than the pastel tones of female targeted advertising, the colors in these ads are grays, neutrals, with some bright primary colors. When music is used, it is either sung by a male lead or is a growling rock guitar riff meant to emphasize a female character's sexuality. While most slogans are gender neutral, Burger King specifically targets men with instructions to "stack it high, tough guy," and "eat like a man, man."

In addition, action in the commercials takes place in groups of men in the public sphere such as outdoors on city streets, reinforcing the traditional locations most advertising situates males instead of female.[34] Only a few scenes take place inside an office, demonstrating a general sense of freedom from responsibility at home or at work. An exception is Burger King, which uses home and family as a setting to emphasize the father/son relationship of its Whopper Senior and Junior.

Of Mosher and Anderson's three macho personality character traits, sex is emphasized more explicitly than are violence and danger in these food ads.[35] Most ads avoid denotatively demonstrating *violent* acts, with the exception of the BK Manthem's humorous scenes of property destruction and fighting. However, connotatively, violence is implied because animals are killed to produce the meat used in the sandwiches. Whether stated outright or implied, all of the male characters implicitly seek meat sandwiches as prey, and the hunting ground is fast-food restaurants. Third, the only aspect of *danger* demonstrated in these ads is men's overall disregard of health, as the food's unhealthy nutritional content goes unmentioned by all companies except Subway, and no company overtly promotes any vegetarian sandwiches.

The following section provides a discussion of the primary 40 themes found in the ads where men's consumption of meat, and often women, enable them to (1) seek freedom from personal and social constraints and (2) remain loyal to the (heterosexual) male group.

Freedom via Food: Having It His Way

Consistent with Burger King's mandate to "Have It Your Way," fast-food ads promote a narcissistic focus on fulfilling individual short-term desires free from concerns over the consequences to oneself or society. Subway is the only advertiser who raises a rational concern, in this case health, by using Jared to promote low-fat sandwich choices. But most fast-food commercials show a general irreverence to long-term health issues, favoring immediate gratification instead, such as is indicated by Jack in the Box's tagline "indulge." Food becomes just a tool for satisfying desires, even gluttonous ones. Thus size does matter in the burger battles, as Subway brags its sandwiches have twice the meat of burgers, while Quizno's brags its subs are even meatier than Subway's. And Burger King's slogan instructs men to "stack it high, tough guy," emphasizing how customers can choose three or four layers of beef and cheese. Commercials create a sense of plenty by constructing sandwiches that bulge and overflow with condiments literally dripping onto tables and fingers.

Plentitude is part of the male fantasyland that Burger King creates in its Hootie ad, where a guy can get anything he wants, as much as he wants, and when he wants it. In this ad, meat grows on trees, ranch dressing overflows the maidens' buckets, and the streets are paved with cheese. While the basis for this fantasy is abundance of fast food, one also sees an abundance of sexually available females—attractive, young, Daisy Duke "country" women wear low-cut tops and/or short skirts and dance happily around the Western-themed set. The ad demonstrates how men's "wildest fantasies" come true by having Dallas Cowboys cheerleaders shave them.

Hootie's lyric also list several kinds of freedoms found in its fantasy land—financial freedom ("all the lotto tickets pay") and freedom from work and obligation (being able to "veg all day"). In this paradise, guys "never get in trouble, never need an excuse" and "no one tells you to behave." Most fast-food commercials do not show men on the job or dressed for work, preferring to emphasize leisure.

Ads also imply freedom from another constraint, women: nagging wives, girlfriends, and mothers. The annoyance of obligation to women is avoided, as committed or familial relationships between men and women are rarely shown. In fact, besides the Burger King Whopper Senior/Junior commercials showing a wife and daughter in the background, only two other commercials feature a man in a committed relationship with a woman. In both cases, the girlfriends are portayed as restricting a man's freedom. First, a Carl's Jr. buffalo wing commercial reveals a woman giving her a boyfriend a disdainful and accusing look after catching him staring at an attractive waitress. The announcer emphasizes that men should only go out with other guys to eat wings if they want to have any fun. Second, the BK Manthem singer walks out on his sophisticated girlfriend because he is sick of her dictating that he eat small-portioned gourmet meals that appear more leafy than meaty.

The Manthem ad states men have been so nutritionally con- 45 strained and emasculated by the modern woman, that guys should unite in revolution to regain control over their ability to eat meat. It openly mocks the women's rights movement by satirizing Helen Reddy's feminist song "I am woman hear me roar" and showing men burning their underwear in the streets to make fun of alleged "bra burnings" by feminist activists in the 1960s. Similarly, many ads show a preference for disempowered women by either symbolically annihilating them or concentrating on sexualized female body parts instead of female partnership, intelligence, speech, or social contributions. By disempowering women in these commercials, men gain more freedom and control to have it their way.

Loyalty to Male Group: Bonding over Beef and Babes

While the first theme of freedom may seem contradictory to the second theme of group loyalty, they are actually complementary as being "one of the guys" is made to seem effortless and natural. Two commercials in particular strongly emphasize stereotypes of straight, meat-eating men as if they are a homogenous group with a pack mentality. The first is the Jack in the Box ad demonstrating guys being drawn in packs to a combo meal more so than to other stereotypical male temptations such as motorcycles, kegs of beer, televised sports, and young women pillow-fighting. Second, in the BK Manthem, men's fervor over their right to eat meat causes them to act out "typical" male exploits, such as flexing muscles, punching each other, chopping cement blocks, destroying property, and playing with big machinery.

In many ways, fast-food commercials stereotype men most according to their gender, rather than by other human characteristics such as age, race, body type, or class. For example, although white is the most common race, the men in these ads are often shown in racially mixed groups, are a wide range of ages, and have a variety of body types. Class, however, is a category where there is some stereotyping, as working- and middle-class men are more common than upper-class, yet when jobs are shown we see both blue and white collar represented. But what most commonly unites all these men in fast-food commercials is their gender identity as heterosexual males who share a desire to communally consume animal meat and symbolically consume the "flesh" of sexualized and objectified women.

Objectification of Women

Commercials sometimes show the meat becoming conflated with the flesh of women as mutual objects of male desire. Burger King's male fantasy commercial, starring Hootie, refers to products on the sandwich while showing related parts of female actresses. For example, chicken breasts equate with breasts of a woman and ranch dressing overflows like milk from a woman's breast. Burger King's stacker commercial has a guy implying that a woman's rear end is a "bun." The Carl's Jr. plastic surgeon commercial equates naturally large chicken breasts with women wanting breast augmentation. In addition, in the series of Carl's Jr. commercials that focus on a lone, sexualized woman doing something seductive while also eating a burger, the flesh of both humans and nonhumans become objects of the camera's implied heterosexual male gaze.

Meat as the Supreme Male Identity Trait

As the Jack in the Box commercial indicated, a desire for meat is the quintessential factor defining a homogenous male identity, even more so than other temptations, like women. For example, Arby's assumes it is humorous, yet believable, that construction workers would get more excited by a Reuben sandwich, even when carried by a man, than they would by attractive women. And Burger King's Manthem considers red meat's allure so powerful that it can serve as the sole motivating factor inspiring hundreds of men to unite into a spontaneous men's movement. This ad constructs red meat as distinctly male, in direct opposition to "chick food," such as tofu and quiche. In fact, the lyrics "I will eat this meat, until my innie turns into an outie" tells men that if they have become sissies by giving in to women and eating too many vegetables, meat can literally transform them back into a man. Men must stand up in defiance, presumably against women, for their right to "eat like a man" and have meat.

Guys are the presumed experts when it comes to finding meat, 50 as demonstrated by Quizno's man-on-the-street testimonials asking only men about the meatiness of subs. This mirrors most commercials, where meat is a man's food and women need not be consulted.[36] So, perhaps it is no surprise when Burger King went looking for people to portray its Whoppers in costume, who seemed more natural to personify its burgers than guys?

Conclusion

In this chapter we have identified some recent commercials which illustrate the American fast-food industry's propensity for equating meat with heterosexual masculinity. Many common elements reveal the presumed target audience to be straight males, in accordance with male advertising stereotypes: male characters dominate and do all the speaking; locations are in the public and avoid the domestic sphere; and the male gaze objectifies women, who are relegated to secondary, often mute, status. The ads connote meat is used by men to both experience freedom from constraints and remain loyal to their group identity as heterosexual males.

Despite their health benefits, plant foods are derided as feminine and not as satisfying as meat. The ads suggest men should seek immediate gratification of their hunger by eating meat, often in large quantities, without being hindered by notions of social responsibility, sustainability or health, as may be dictated by women. Even Subway, which shows some respect for women and health, still reinforces some male stereotypes by associating muscular athletes with meat and using Jared, a wimpier "smart" guy, to represent the more feminine concern of dieting; Cebrzynski observed that, in all its ads, Subway uses only Jared to promote health while it uses other men, both athletes and comedians, to promote other food traits. Subway's use of a football player and a pro wrestler to emphasize the meatiness of low-fat subs bolsters Katz' contention that advertising uses "violent male athletes to help sell products . . . that have historically been gendered female."[37] Fast food is part of a hedonistic male fantasy where men have plenty of meat, women, money, and leisure time and are free from responsibility. Men are stereotyped as a homogenous group whose most central feature is a shared desire for the consumption of meat, including that of women as silent sexual objects. In cases where human and animal flesh are conflated, as in "breast" meat, it bolsters Adams' contention that advertising often sexualizes animals and animalizes females. In some cases, men's temptations for both kinds of flesh can be enjoyed simultaneously, as in the Carl's Jr. assertion that guys go out to eat wings together so they can ogle waitresses. In other cases (Arby's and Jack in the Box), meat consumption is privileged as being even more tempting to men than looking at women's bodies.

While aspects of these advertisements seem like harmless commercial entertainment, we suggest a concern that the overall message of hedonism is detrimental to social justice (for human and nonhuman animals) and ecological sustainability. To the extent that it perpetuates stereotypes of men in one-dimensional terms as self-indulgent, womanizing carnivores, fast-food advertising lowers society's expectations for the positive contributions men should be and often are making to promoting equality and social responsibility. Many of these commercials urge men to behave in self-interested ways that disregard the social consequences of their actions and prioritize an individualistic sense of taking over a more community-oriented sense of giving.

Another disturbing outcome of using gender stereotypes to sell fast food is the resulting reinforcement of the male/female dichotomy that has been the basis for patriarchal oppression. The ads construct the ideal woman as a silent, passive, meat-eating, agreeable stranger who is young, pretty, thin, and fair-skinned with long hair and a voluptuous body willingly put on display for the male viewer. The objectification of women in many of these commercials may in fact be a backlash against the empowerment American women have achieved in the centuries' old struggle for women's rights. And, while we admit that it is challenging to market products which are not particularly socially responsible, we hope that it could be done in a way that does not continue to sacrifice the rights of traditionally oppressed groups in order to further empower a dominant social group such as heterosexual American men. When fast-food companies insist on telling men to "have it your way" in the twenty-first century, they might as well be telling them to turn back the clock on social progress.

Drawing on Strate's study of beer commercials, "the myth of masculinity does have a number of redeeming features (facing challenges and taking risks are valuable activities in many contexts), but the unrelenting one-dimensionality of masculinity as presented by," in this case fast-food commercials, "is clearly anachronistic, possible laughable, but without a doubt," too filling.[38]

NOTES

1. See Jim Mason, *An Unnatural Order: Why We Are Destroying the Planet and Each Other* (New York: Continuum, 1993), and Jeremy Rifkin, *Beyond Beef* (New York: Plume, 1992).

2. See Carol Adams, *The Pornography of Meat* (New York: Continuum, 2003), and Carol Adams, *The Sexual Politics of Meat: A Feminist-Vegetarian Critical Theory* (New York: Continuum, 1990).

3. See Stuart Hall, *Representation: Cultural Representations and Signifying Practices* (London: Sage, 1997); Stuart Hall, "Introduction," in *Paper Voices: The Popular Press and Social Change, 1935–1965*, ed. Anthony Charles Smith (London: Chatto & Windus, 1975), 11–24; Judith Williamson, *Decoding Advertisements: Ideology and Meaning in Advertising* (New York: Marion Boyaars, 1978).

4. Mason, 81.

5. Ibid.

6. Ibid.

7. See Carol Adams, *Sexual Politics.*

8. Adams, *Sexual Politics,* 168.

9. Ibid.

10. Ibid., 187.

11. Ibid., 34.

12. See Peggy Sanday, *Female Power and Male Dominance: On the Origins of Sexual Inequality* (Cambridge and New York: Cambridge University Press, 1981).

13. Richard E. Leakey and Roger Lewin, *People of the Lake: Mankind and Its Beginnings* (New York: Doubleday, 1978). x.

14. Adams, *Sexual Politics,* 34.

15. Ibid., 33.

16. Jeffery Sobal, "Men, Meat, and Marriage: Models of Masculinity," Food & Foodways 13 (2005): 135.

17. See Eric Schlosser, *Fast-Food Nation: The Dark Side of the All-American Meal* (New York: Harper Collins, 2002), and Morgan Spurlock (Prod., Dir., and Writer), *Super Size Me.* Film. (Culver City, CA: Columbia TriStar Home Entertainment, 2004).

18. See also Alex Jamieson, *The Great American Detox Diet: Feel Better, Look Better, and Lose Weight by Cleaning up Your Diet* (New York: Rodale, 2005).

19. Schlosser.

20. See also David Fraser, "Farm Animal Production: Changing Agriculture in a Changing Culture," *Journal of Applied Animal Welfare Science* 4 (2001): 3, and Peter Singer and Jim Mason, *The Way We Eat: Why Our Food Choices Matter* (New York: Rodale, 2006).

21. Kathy Freston, "Vegetarian Is the New Prius," *Common Dreams*, January 20, 2007). Online: http://www.commondreams.org/views07/0120-20.htm (accessed March 31, 2007), and Sierra Club, (2006), "Clean Water and Factory Farms. Report and Fact Sheets from the Sierra Club. Online: http://www.sierraclub.org/factoryfarms/factsheets/ (accessed April 1, 2007).

22. See also Neal Barnard, *Food for Life: How the New Four Food Groups Can Save Your Life* (New York: Three Rivers Press, 1993), and Howard Lyman, *No More Bull! The Mad Cowboy Targets America's Worst Enemy: Our Diet* (New York: Scribner, 2005).

23. See also Katrina Arabe, "Eat, Drink, Man, Woman," February, 2003. Thomasnet. Online: http://news.thomasnet.com/IMT/archives/2003/02/eat_drink_man_w.html (accessed March 29, 2007).

24. Alison McCook, "Men: I'll Take Meat and Hold the Veggies, Starch," *Reuter's Health.* Online: http://preventdisease.com/news/articles/men_take_meat.shtm. (accessed March 29, 2007).

25. Emily Senay and Rob Waters, *From Boys to Men: A Woman's Guide to the Health of Husbands, Partners, Sons, Fathers, and Brothers* (New York: Simon & Schuster, 2004), 297.

26. See Donald L. Mosher, and Ronald D. Anderson, "Macho Personality, Sexual Aggression, and Reactions to Guided Imagery of Realistic Rape," *Journal of Research in Personality* 18 (1986): 150–63.

27. Joseph R. Dominick and Gail E. Rauch, "The Image of Women in Network TV Commercials," *Journal of Broadcasting* 16 (1972): 259-65; Kenneth Schneider and Sharon Schneider, "Trends in Sex Roles in Television Commercials," *Journal of Marketing* 43 (1979): 79-84.

28. Jackson Katz, "Advertising and the Construction of Violent White Masculinity," in *Gender, Race, and Class in Media*, ed. Gail Dines and J. Humez (Thousand Oaks, CA: Sage, 2003), 351.

29. Ibid., 352.

30. Lance Strate, "Beer Commercials: A Manual on Masculinity," in *Men, Masculinity, and the Media*, ed. Steve Craig (Newbury Park, CA: Sage, 1992), 85.

31. Adams, *The Pornography of Meat*, 13.

32. Ibid., 171.

33. See also Gregg Cebrzynski, "Please rise-if you're a guy-for singing of national 'Manthem,'" *Nation's Restaurant News* 40, no. 21(2006a): 18, available Online at: Business Source Premier database (accessed March 31, 2007); Gregg Cebrzynski, "Creepy King, "Whopperheads' Give BK Ads an Edge They Never Had," *Nation's Restaurant News* 38 (2004): 14, available Online at: Business Source Premier database (accessed March 30, 2007); Marianne Paskowski, "Paris Hilton to the Rescue," *Multichannel News* 26, no. 22: 50, available Online at: Business Source Premier database (accessed March 30, 2007); Randi Schmelzer and Axel Koester, "Raunchy Ranch," *Adweek* 46, no. 7 (2005): 24, available Online at: Business Source Premier database (accessed March 30, 2007).

34. See Dominick and Rauch; Schneider.

35. See Mosher and Anderson.

36. With the one exception of Subway's use of a female athlete.

37. See Katz, 356.

38. See Strate, 92.

WORKS CITED*

Adams, Carol. *The Pornography of Meat*. New York: Continuum, 2003.
———. *The Sexual Politics of Meat: A Feminist-Vegetarian Critical Theory*. New York: Continuum, 1990.
American Dietetic Association. "Position Paper on Vegetarianism," available online at http://www.eatright.org/cps/rde/xchg/ada/hs.sxl/advocacy_933_ENU_HTML.htm (accessed March 31, 2007).
———. "Research Says Fast Food Intake May Affect Children's Nutrition," available online at http://www.eatright.org/cps/rde/xchg/ada/hs.xsl/home_4400_ENU_HTML.htm (accessed March 31, 2007).
Arabe, Katrina. "Eat, Drink, Man, Woman." February, 2003. Available online at Thomas-net.http://news.thomasnet.com/IMT/archives/2003/02/eat_drink_man_w.html (accessed March 29, 2007).
Barnard, Neal. *Food for Life: How the New Four Food Groups Can Save Your Life*. New York: Three Rivers Press, 1993.
Barthes, Roland. *Mythologies*. New York: Hill and Wang, 1972.

*Based on a variation of the *Chicago* style of documentation.

Bussey, Kay, and Albert Bandura. "Social Cognitive Theory of Gender Development and Differentiation." *Psychological Review* 106 (1999): 676–713.

Cebrzynski, Gregg. "Creepy King, 'Wopperheads' Give BK Ads an Edge They Never Had." *Nations's Restaurant News* 28 (2004): 14–30.

———. "Jared Fogle Goes on the Attack for Subway's Low-Fat Sandwiches." *Nation's Restaurant News* 40 (2006): 16-31.

———. "Please rise-if you're a guy-for singing of national 'Manthem.'" *Nation's Restaurant News* 40 (2006): 18.

Coombes, Rosemary J. *The Cultural Life of Intellectual Properties: Authorship, Appropriation, and the Law.* Durham: Duke University Press, 1998.

Craig, Steve. "Considering Men and the Media." In *Men, Masculinity, and the Media,* ed. S. Craig, 1-7. Newbury Park, CA: Sage, 1992

DeFleur, Melvin L., and Everette E. Dennis. *Understanding Mass Communication.* Boston: Houghton Mifflin, 1998.

Dominick, Joseph R., and G. E. Rauch. "The Image of Women in Network TV Commercials." *Journal of Broadcasting* 16 (1972): 259–65.

Fraser, David. "Farm Animal Production: Changing Agriculture in a Changing Culture." *Journal of Applied Animal Welfare Science* 4 (2001): 3.

Freston, Kathy. "Vegetarian Is the New Prius." *Common Dreams,* January 20, 2007. Available online at http://www.commondreams.org/view07/0120-20.htm (accessed March 32, 2007).

Hall, Stuart. Introduction In *Paper Voices: The Popular Press and Social Change, 1935-1965,* ed. Anthony Charles Smith, 11-24. London: Chatto & Windus, 1975.

———. *Representation: Cultural Representations and Signifying Practices.* London: Sage, 1997.

Jamieson, Alex. *The Great American Detox Diet: Feel Better, Look Better, and Lose Weight by Cleaning up Your Diet.* New York: Rodale, 2005.

Katz, Jackson. "Advertising and the Construction of Violent White Masculinity." In *Gender, Race, and Class in Media,* edited by G. Dines and J. Humez, 349–58. Thousand Oaks, CA: Sage, 2003.

Leakey, Richard F., and Roger Lewin. *People of the Lake: Mankind and Its Beginnings.* New York: Doubleday, 1978.

Lyman, Howard. *No More Bull! The Mad Cowboy Targets America's Worst Enemy: Our Diet.* New York: Scribner, 2005.

Mason, Jim. *An Unnatural Order: Why We Are Destroying the Planet and Each Other.* New York: Continuum, 1993.

McCook, Alison. "Men: I'll Take Meat and Hold the Veggies, Starch." *Reuter's Health*. Available online at http://preventdisease.com/news/ articles/men_take_meat.shtml (accessed March 29, 2007).

Mosher, Donald L., and Ronald D. Anderson. "Macho Personality, Sexual Aggression, and Reactions to Guided Imagery of Realistic Rape." *Journal of Research in Personality* 18 (1986): 150–63.

Parasecoli, Fabio. "Feeding Hard Bodies: Food and Masculinities in men's Fitness Magazines." *Food & Foodways* 13 (2005): 17–37.

Paskowski, Marianne. "Paris Hilton to the Rescue." *Multichannel News* 26, no. 22 (2005): 50. Available online at Business Source Premier data base (accessed March 30, 2007).

Rifkin, Jeremy. *Beyond Beef*. New York: Plume, 1992.

Sanday, Peggy. *Female Power and Male Dominance: On the Origins of Sexual Inequality*." Cambridge, UK, and New York: Cambridge University Press, 1981.

Schlosser, Eric. *Fast-Food Nation: The Dark Side of the All-American Meal*. New York: Harper Collins, 2002.

Schmelzer, Randi, and Axel Koester. "Raunchy Ranch." *Adweek* 46, no. 7 (2005): 24. Available at Business Source Premier database (accessed March 30, 2007).

Schneider, Kenneth, and Sharon Schneider. "Trends in Sex Roles in Television Commercials." *Journal of Marketing* 43 (1979): 79–84.

Senay, Emily, and Rob Waters. *From Boys to Men: A Woman's Guide to the Health of Husbands, Partners, Sons, Fathers, and Brothers*. New York: Simon & Schuster, 2004.

Sierra Club. "Clean Water and Factory Farms. Report and Fact Sheets from the Sierra Club." 2006. Available online at http://www.sierraclub .org/factoryfarms/factsheets/ (accessed April 1, 2007).

Singer, Peter and Jim Mason. *The Way We Eat: Why Our Food Choices Matter*. New York: Rodale, 2006.

Sobal, Jeffrey. "Men, Mear, and Marriage: Models of Masculinity." *Food & Foodways* 13 (2005): 135–58.

Strate, Lance. "Beer Commercials: A Manual on Masculinity." In *Men, Masculinity, and the Media*, edited by Steve Craig, 79–92. Newbury Park, CA: Sage, 1992.

Super Size Me. Written, produced and directed by Morgan Spurlock. Film. Culver City, CA: Columbia TriStar Home Entertainment, 2004.

Van Dijk, Teun Adrianus. *Discourse, Racism, and Ideology.* La Laguna, Mexico: RCEI Ediciones, 1996.

Williamson, Judith, *Decoding Advertisements: Ideology and Meaning in Advertising.* New York: Marion Boyars, 1978.

Joining the Conversation

1. Carrie Packwood Freeman and Debra Merskin argue that fast-food advertisements portray eating meat as an important part of masculine behavior and male bonding. How are women generally depicted in these ads? Why do the authors find the stereotypes reinforced by such ads problematic and disturbing?

2. Think of a commercial for a different type of product that displays the stereotypical macho behaviors and attitudes of fast-food commercials. Describe the commercial and compare it with the fast-food ads discussed by the authors. What do such ads reveal about what advertisers think will be persuasive to male (and female) viewers? Do you think such views are accurate? Why or why not?

3. So what? How do the authors make the case that their argument is important?

4. Imagine Freeman and Merskin having a conversation with Susie Orbach. Would they be likely to agree that food can be a symbol of rebellion for both men and women? Why or why not?

5. Examine one of the ads analyzed in this essay. What do Freeman and Merskin say about it? Summarize their analysis of this ad, and then suggest what else might be said about it. What do *you* think about the ad, and why?

SEVENTEEN

WHY DOES IT MATTER WHO WINS THE BIG GAME?

—⌐—

SPORTS ARE NOT only big business but big news as well. Tens of millions of fans attend professional, college, and high school games around the country, while even more people follow sports on TV, on the Internet, in newspapers, and in magazines. When a team makes it to the top—be it the Super Bowl, World Series, NBA finals, World Cup, or NCAA finals, it's a major story nationally (even internationally) and a huge event locally. The comments and projections of players, coaches, and pundits are endlessly dissected in the media. Stories appear in major media venues about the frenzy of interest among hometown fans. When a college's football or basketball team is successful, applications to the school increase significantly.

The outcome of a major sporting event can affect the moods of serious and even not-so-serious fans: elation and celebration over a victory, depression and anger over a loss. Entire cities get caught up in the hoopla. In Pittsburgh, for example, the decline of the steel industry crippled the local economy for several decades, starting in the 1970s. As unemployment raged and the population plummeted, the successes of the Steelers, winners of six Super Bowls, are credited by most analysts with helping maintain pride and hope among residents as the city worked, with considerable success, to reinvent itself as a high-tech corporate center. A team can thus come to represent the aspirations of an entire region or people.

The readings in this chapter offer a variety of perspectives exploring the appeal and significance of sports. Maya Angelou, in an excerpt from her autobiography *I Know Why the Caged Bird Sings* depicts the intense identification of a group of poor African Americans in 1930s Arkansas with heavyweight boxer Joe Louis, a successful black man fighting his way to the top in a segregated country. Novelist and critic Wilfrid Sheed examines the wider importance of sports in society with examples from across the globe. Felisa Rogers writes about her utter lack of interest in football until she fell in love with a passionate fan, and now appreciates the bonds it can create across gender and class boundaries.

Other authors in the chapter write about the motivations that can lead ambitious athletes to use performance-enhancing drugs and the responses of passionate fans and the general public to this drug use. Blogger William Moller equates Yankee great Alex Rodriguez's much-publicized steroid use with his own use of Ritalin to stay awake all night and study during school. Sportswriter Joe Posnanski argues against those who criticize today's athletes for drug use while simultaneously celebrating the stars of the past, who themselves often took amphetamines and found other ways to cheat in order to gain a competitive advantage.

Three readings in this chapter focus on women and their increasing role in the sports world—both as athletes and as fans. Michael Kimmelman writes about the evolution of women's tennis into a widely publicized international sport complete with star players from all over the world, television coverage, and substantial prize money. Jennie Yabroff takes up the cause of cheerleading, arguing that it is as demanding and competitive as any sport and therefore deserves to be considered a sport in its own right. Student writer Sara Maratta proclaims her interest in ice hockey but decries the treatment of women and sports in the media.

As you read this chapter's discussions of the role of sports in our lives and in our imaginations, you will have the opportunity to look more deeply into these issues and to contribute your own perspective to the larger conversation.

Champion of the World

MAYA ANGELOU

—◈—

THE LAST INCH of space was filled, yet people continued to wedge themselves along the walls of the Store. Uncle Willie had turned the radio up to its last notch so that youngsters on the porch wouldn't miss a word. Women sat on kitchen chairs, dining-room chairs, stools, and upturned wooden boxes. Small children and babies perched on every lap available and men leaned on the shelves or on each other.

The apprehensive mood was shot through with shafts of gaiety, as a black sky is streaked with lightning.

"I ain't worried 'bout this fight. Joe's gonna whip that cracker like it's open season."

MAYA ANGELOU is a poet and author whose many books include *I Know Why the Caged Bird Sings* (1970), *Phenomenal Woman* (2000), and *Letter to My Daughter* (2008). She was San Francisco's first African American woman to serve as a cable car conductor and worked for the Southern Christian Leadership Conference during the civil rights era. She has received multiple awards, including the Presidential Medal of the Arts, and read her poem "On the Pulse of Morning" at the 1993 inauguration of President Bill Clinton. This text is an excerpt from *I Know Why the Caged Bird Sings*.

"He gone whip him till that white boy call him Momma."

At last the talking finished and the string-along songs about 5 razor blades were over and the fight began.

"A quick jab to the head." In the Store the crowd grunted. "A left to the head and a right and another left." One of the listeners cackled like a hen and was quieted.

"They're in a clinch, Louis is trying to fight his way out."

Some bitter comedian on the porch said, "That white man don't mind hugging that niggah now, I betcha."

"The referee is moving in to break them up, but Louis finally pushed the contender away and it's an uppercut to the chin. The contender is hanging on, now he's backing away. Louis catches him with a short left to the jaw."

A tide of murmuring assent poured out the door and into 10 the yard.

"Another left and another left. Louis is saving that mighty right. . . ." The mutter in the store had grown into a baby roar and it was pierced by the clang of a bell and the announcer's "That's the bell for round three, ladies and gentlemen."

As I pushed my way into the Store I wondered if the announcer gave any thought to the fact that he was addressing as "ladies and gentlemen" all the Negroes around the world who sat sweating and praying, glued to their "Master's voice."*

There were only a few calls for RC Colas, Dr Peppers, and Hires root beer. The real festivities would begin after the fight. Then even the old Christian ladies who taught their children and tried themselves to practice turning the other cheek would buy soft drinks, and if the Brown Bomber's victory was

---

* **"Master's voice"** A reference to RCA's advertising campaign featuring a dog listening to a phonograph.

a particularly bloody one they would order peanut patties and Baby Ruths also.

Bailey and I laid the coins on top of the cash register. Uncle Willie didn't allow us to ring up sales during a fight. It was too noisy and might shake up the atmosphere. When the gong rang for the next round we pushed through the near-sacred quiet to the herd of children outside.

"He's got Louis against the ropes and now it's a left to the body and a right to the ribs. Another right to the body, it looks like it was low. . . . Yes, ladies and gentlemen, the referee is signaling but the contender keeps raining the blows on Louis. It's another to the body, and it looks like Louis is going down."

My race groaned. It was our people falling. It was another lynching, yet another Black man hanging on a tree. One more woman ambushed and raped. A Black boy whipped and maimed. It was hounds on the trail of a man running through slimy swamps. It was a white woman slapping her maid for being forgetful.

The men in the Store stood away from the walls and at attention. Women greedily clutched the babes on their laps while on the porch the shufflings and smiles, flirtings and pinchings of a few minutes before were gone. This might be the end of the world. If Joe lost we were back in slavery and beyond help. It would all be true; the accusations that we were lower types of human beings. Only a little higher than apes. True that we were stupid and ugly and lazy and dirty and unlucky and worst of all, that God himself hated us and ordained us to be hewers of wood and drawers of water, forever and ever, world without end.

We didn't breathe. We didn't hope. We waited.

"He's off the ropes, ladies and gentlemen. He's moving towards the corner of the ring." There was no time to be relieved. The worst might still happen.

"And now it looks like Joe is mad. He's caught Carnera with 20 a left hook to the head and a right to the head. It's a left jab to the body and another left to the head. There's a left cross and a right to the head. The contender's right eye is bleeding and he can't seem to keep his block up. Louis is penetrating every block. The referee is moving in, but Louis sends a left to the body and it's an uppercut to the chin and the contender is dropping. He's on the canvas, ladies and gentlemen."

Babies slid to the floor as women stood up and men leaned toward the radio.

"Here's the referee. He's counting. One, two, three, four, five, six, seven. . . . Is the contender trying to get up again?"

All the men in the store shouted, "NO."

" . . . eight, nine, ten." There were a few sounds from the audience, but they seemed to be holding themselves in against tremendous pressure.

"The fight is all over, ladies and gentlemen. Let's get the 25 microphone over to the referee . . . . Here he is. He's got the Brown Bomber's hand, he's holding it up . . . Here he is. . . ."

Then the voice, husky and familiar, came to wash over us—"The winnah, and still heavyweight champeen of the world . . . Joe Louis."

Champion of the world. A Black boy. Some Black mother's son. He was the strongest man in the world. People drank Coca-Colas like ambrosia and ate candy bars like Christmas. Some of the men went behind the Store and poured white lightning in their soft-drink bottles, and a few of the bigger boys followed them. Those who were not chased away came back blowing their breath in front of themselves like proud smokers.

It would take an hour or more before the people would leave the Store and head for home. Those who lived too far had made arrangements to stay in town. It wouldn't be fit for a Black man and his family to be caught on a lonely country road on a night when Joe Louis had proved that we were the strongest people in the world.

Joining the Conversation

1. Maya Angelou shows vividly how much it mattered to the people at the Store that Joe Louis win. What are some of the details that make us understand how important it was? Why did it matter so much?
2. How does this essay answer the question about why sports matter?
3. Angelou wrote this essay as a narrative, so there's no explicit thesis statement. If it had a thesis statement, what do you think it would be?
4. At one level, Angelou wrote this essay to describe a memorable event. But she clearly cared about more than who won a boxing match. What do you think motivated her to write the piece as she did?
5. Write your own brief account of an event when you had strong emotions about the outcome—winning a game, getting an A on an exam, getting married, or something else. Try to convey your emotions vividly, as Angelou does.

Why Sports Matter

WILFRID SHEED

—⬚—

IT'S HARD TO SAY exactly when the new era began, but at some point lost in the smog of the 19th century, sports went from being officially a bad thing to being a very good thing indeed, virtually a pillar of state. England, where it all began, was coming into its maturity as an imperial power and the Industrial Revolution was turning country boys into city boys overnight, and society's guardians began to look at all forms of entertainment in the light of these developments, but especially at sports.

Thus preachers, who had previously considered sports the devil's work, open invitations to brutishness and gambling (how times have changed!), gradually perceived that they might be

WILFRID SHEED (1930–2011) wrote many books, both fiction and nonfiction, including *The House That George Built with a Little Help from Irving, Cole and a Crew of Fifty* (2007), *In Love with Daylight: A Memoir of Recovery* (1995), *My Life as a Fan* (1993), and *Baseball and Lesser Sports* (1991). This essay was published in the Winter 1995 issue of *The Wilson Quarterly*, a periodical published by the Woodrow Wilson International Center for Scholars.

rescued and cleaned up in the service of the Lord—and what was good for God was good for England; likewise schoolteachers, who had once punished idle play, decided to join, not resist, and they began to enforce organized sports with such severity that some children grew to loathe and fear the very word "recreation."

And finally the last, because they had the most to lose, holdouts—Dickens's mythic factory owners, along with more humane businessmen—came round too, on the understanding that if the workers must have some time off, there were worse ways to spend it than in a rule-bound, open-air, referee-dominated contest of skill and strength.

But perhaps the greatest benefit of all, to judge from the fuss that would be made about it, was that sports not only outlawed cheating but drilled its devotees to detect and despise it in each other and by extension in themselves. This was crucial. A nation on the verge of great transactions—a nation also in the midst of a population explosion that might have reduced it to Third-World, or at least downtown–Los Angeles, status overnight—needed a citizenry it could trust. Indeed, the English would go on to make such a fetish of fair play that it became an international joke. Yet the empire was sustained by this fetish at least as much as by force, and the British sportsman's knack of combining slyness and decency continued to baffle and frustrate more cynical nations right to the end.

But in promoting sport so zestfully, the powers that be had 5 unwittingly unleashed a small monster of their own, albeit a wholesome one. By the '90s of this century, sports worship had grown and taken on a life of its own, beyond the wildest dreams of Thomas Arnold (1795–1842), the English public school headmaster who might be considered the founding father of the

A YMCA workout, circa 1900. The idea that sports build character owes much to the 19th-century "muscular Christianity" movement and the Young Men's Christian Association, founded in 1844

Sports and Character movement. And the educational establishment, having faithfully drummed sports into its charges, must now pause at some point to tell them—and itself—that "it's only a game," and prove it to them, or else watch sports grow and grow until they bury both the establishment and its schools: a force that can take on Sex can easily roll over Education. The president of a major university, writing in the *New York Times* op-ed page a few years ago, said that he wanted academics to be on a par with athletics at his place, a strangled cry which suggested that the monster was already standing on his chest close to his windpipe.

Thus, too, the clergy must worry about idolatry and the sin of False Worship, and the business community about the sheer waste of time and emotional energy committed to sport. A fan, perhaps even more than an athlete, who gets some of his obsessive energy out of his system by playing—can become so psychologically enmeshed in sports that the rest of life seems like a rather boring dream that must be gotten through somehow. Thus transfixed, one can sleepwalk one's way through anything from a dull job to an oppressive regime to a marriage that could possibly use some attention.

The good and the bad of sports are exquisitely balanced even at the best of times. Victory and defeat induce respectively a joy and despair way beyond the run of normal human experience. When a politician says he hates something viscerally— whether it's John Major* on terrorism or Senator Windbag on flag-burning—one doubts his insides are much disturbed: as Dr. Johnson might say, he will eat his dinner tonight.

But a sports fan who has seen a sure victory slip away in the bottom of the ninth, or the work of a whole season obliterated by a referee's call in overtime, is disconsolate beyond the power of description, although Sophocles comes close. This author experienced such grief over the defeat of the Dodgers by the Cardinals in 1942 as an 11-year-old should not be asked to bear. An adult inflicting such pain on a child would be thrown in jail.

Yet I got over it, and was all the better for it, recovering sufficiently to root for the Cardinals over the hated Yankees in the World Series. This cycle of make-believe deaths and

*John Major Former Prime Minister of the United Kingdom and Leader of the Conservative Party (1990–1997).

rebirths can actually be the healthiest thing about sports, or the most dangerous, depending on how you handle it. At its worst, it can cause riots and death, but at its best the pain of defeat is cleansing and instructive, a very good rehearsal for life.

Upon reading the second volume of William Manchester's life of Churchill, *The Last Lion* (1988), I was struck by the fact that the lion in question was splendidly imperturbable about such matters as the rise of Hitler and the fall of Poland, but was completely unstrung by any blow to his vanity, such as losing a by-election or failing to get a cabinet appointment. But if sports teaches you anything, it is that less important things can hurt more than important ones—but that they *are* less important, and that there are tricks for dealing with them: absorbing the pain and putting it in perspective, almost reflexively.

One of the glories of the human imagination is its capacity for alternative realities and its ability to live other people's lives to the emotional full, whether they be Oedipus or the Chicago Cubs (and that's another distinction for the civilized individual—art and sports). But if you don't learn that crying over something doesn't make it important—if you forget which reality is which for too long, or can't find your mental way out of Wrigley Field when the game is over—you might be better off if you'd never heard about sports to begin with.

"Meeting with triumph and disaster" (Rudyard Kipling would have made a, well, interesting football coach: "I want you men to go out there *and treat those two impostors just the same*, do you hear me?") is only one of several things that sports teach, and teach better than anything else. The problem is that in school, where many of the lessons of sports are learned, sports increasingly interfere with other lessons that must be learned.

A coach's discipline is different in kind from a regular teacher's, because the coach wants the same thing the class wants—to win. There is no such clear goal for a regular teacher. Whether a student pays attention in class is pretty much up to him. It's a one-on-one affair between student and authority figure, with the student, if anything, holding the edge, surrounded by allies, most of whom have no special desire to go where the teacher is going and are only too happy to keep the pace slow.

But the coach starts out with his class already at white heat: these kids will work for him to a degree unimaginable in a classroom, and with an eagerness and excitement that only creative kids in school ever experience. An English teacher looking at a football drill or a pep rally must overflow with envy: if he could capture just one ounce of such energy for his poetry class, his students would be the wonder of the nation. But in the classroom, the teacher is the only one who works as hard as that—like a coach doing solitary pushups and kneebends, while the students look on idly, waiting for something to interest them.

Yet sports don't have to be the teacher's enemy. At least the young athletes have learned discipline from *somewhere*, and there are no harder workers than jocks or ex-jocks if they can be made to see the point of it as clearly as they see the point of sports. Arthur Ashe, the great African American tennis player, once suggested that if making the team were made to depend entirely on one's grades, the grades would be achieved somehow or other by these highly competitive spirits.

Above all, every kind of athlete knows what many other students never will, that nothing can be learned without discipline. The words are synonymous. And in the pursuit of what they want, athletes are already used to policing themselves and, if necessary, each other.

So all that seems to be required now is for the schools to show that they think that an education is as desirable as winning, if only by granting the student-athletes sufficient time to study and get one. The games themselves need not be a problem, providing as they do a God-given carrot, a natural incentive to cooperate with whatever the school really wants. The real problem, and it keeps coming back like a toothache, is that there is no such thing as moderation or cool judgment once you sign on for a big-time sports program. You must either keep growing helplessly with the others, or pull the plug on the whole thing, as Robert M. Hutchins did at the University of Chicago more than 50 years ago when he took his school out of the Big 10 for keeps, to a flourish of headlines. The lonely grandeur of that gesture tells you how unreal it would be to expect many more of them.

If it was hard to leave the table back in 1939, when you had nothing to lose but a few alumni contributions, it would be just about impossible to do so today with so much TV money floating around. And the TV money has also made it that much more difficult to slip any real moral wisdom or spiritual balance into the student-athlete's regimen. Since the players tend to have the impression that the school is already making a lot of money off their backs without paying them for it, except in devalued degrees, the school is the last place they are going to turn to for moral guidance.

Many years ago, a famous Yale coach told his team that playing in the Yale-Harvard game that day was the most important thing they would ever do in their lives, and he has been laughed at for it ever since. But subjectively he was right: in the make-believe part of one's psyche that thinks games are important enough to work and suffer for, it was the most important thing and always would be. Until the next Big Game.

But any way you read it, no story could tell one more about 20 the difference between sports then and sports now. In the old days, the players were paid in nothing but glory, so the authorities laid on the glory with a shovel. But no up-to-the-minute coach today would dream of telling his team to do or die for Old State U. since he knows that some of them are barely on speaking terms with the place, and it's a bit much to ask someone to die for an institution where he hasn't completed a single serious course, or made one civilian friend, or even had time for the glee club.

If all that the new athletes are getting out of a college is the privilege of wearing its colors—and presumably making them look good—simple justice demands that they get paid real money for their pains, as many people are suggesting these days. If the Big Game is just another payday, and if the most important thing about it is the scout in the stands, and if the fight song just sounds like bad music—pay the man.

But this is a counsel of despair. Outside of the mare's nest of pay scales and competitive bidding and other uncollegiate games it would open up, professionalization would also make the athlete's isolation official: whether he would henceforth be looked up to as a professional or down on as a hired hand (it would probably depend on his value to the team), the one thing he would never again be is a regular member of the student body, which emphatically does not get paid for what it does between classes. The class distinctions that universities usually try so hard to keep outside come back with a rush the moment you institute a payroll.

To which, of course, a critic might retort that the athlete hasn't been a regular member of the student body for some time now and isn't about to become one, so calling him a student-athlete just provides a hypocritical cover for not paying him his share of the proceeds. And the critic may be right. But if so, and if we follow his lead and give up on the very possibility of scholar-athletes, we should be clear about just what it is we're giving up.

The school that pays its students to play games for it not only loses some of its integrity as a school (i.e. as a self-sufficient exchange center for academic goods and services, ideas, and values), it is also saying some very peculiar things about the nature of games themselves and their relationship to other college activities across the board.

It is saying, for instance, that playing in the band at half 25 time is still fun (no one has ever suggested paying the band), but that throwing and catching a ball is work—and that even this depends on what kind of ball you're using. A football equals work, a volleyball is only play. Appearing on television is obviously work, but even here distinctions are made: players work, cheerleaders have fun. Shooting baskets is work, helping to clean up afterward is its own reward.

The greatest chasm of all would open up between sports and the whole outside world of student activity, including such strenuous matters as staying up all night for a month to put the yearbook to bed, rehearsing the class play till your eyes cross, or working overtime in the lab. All of these tortures are considered so much part of the college experience that you actually pay the place to let you undergo them. But basketball is different. For basketball, the college pays you.

I have lingered over this hypothetical threat not simply because some strong voices are urging it but because it is so close to being here already. Collegiate athletes are already a quite distinct caste leading a charmed but precarious life not unlike that of commandos in wartime, who live both better and worse than the regular army, but always apart. College athletes already have in many cases a potentially adversarial relationship with management. It doesn't take much to turn a sports team into a trade union, complete with grievance committee and perpetual chip on shoulder, and the latest TV packages would seem very close to being enough to do it.

Under the circumstances, it seems quixotic to talk about moral instruction at all—except that moral instruction is inevitable. Sports teach, it is their nature. They teach fairness or cheating, teamwork or selfishness, compassion or coldness. A coach who runs up the score against a weak opponent has taught his team plenty. And so did the much maligned Lou Holtz when he jerked two useful players out of Notre Dame's lineup on the eve of an Orange Bowl because, in his view, they had shown contempt for the team by skipping practice. Of course, the players may have wanted the time to study. (I didn't say the lessons were simple.)

Schools and colleges also teach something by their very natures, which is that you are now playing for a whole community and not just yourself, and that if you win, the community will join you in experiencing a kind of crazy collective joy that used to more than make up for not getting paid. Although even to talk about such things now sounds anachronistic and sentimental, over the years this particular experience has helped to define the American style of sports as much as any single factor—the simple fact that even the superstars once played in front of and in the name of cheering friends whom they saw in class the next day.

To the extent that we are losing this, if we are, we are los- 30
ing a real natural resource and killing a lot of fun. But the possibility of plunging the athletes back into the community without disturbing the college sports juggernaut too much edges

us somewhat beyond sports and into race relations. On many campuses, blacks apparently want no part of the white community anyway, sports or no sports, and in fact the sports teams are probably the most integrated thing on campus. So the logical next move would be for the *athletes* to teach the student body the values they've learned from sports—but I doubt if the juggernaut could spare them long enough for that.

Anyhow, whatever the academics may add or subtract, the sports lesson goes on like a machine that can't be turned off, affecting the whole style of the society around it in ways the society may not even be aware of. Concerning which, I call upon my first overseas witness.

A few years back, I flew to Port of Spain, Trinidad, with my father to watch a cricket match between Australia and the West Indies. (My father would have flown to Mars if the mood was on him.) The match was over early and we found ourselves with three days left to kill, so we decided to spend them at the law courts where an acquaintance of ours happened to be presiding as judge.

The weather inside was stifling, and the ceiling fans only seemed to make things worse as they dragged the wet air slowly round and round the room. Yet both the judge and the lawyers wore wigs and winter-weight gowns, and the law they practiced hour after sweltering hour was as fiendishly sharp and serpentine as anything you'd hear at the Old Bailey on a cold day in London. And one couldn't help making the connection between the decorous aggressiveness of the law court and the figures in white we'd seen the day before playing cricket in the same heat with their own brand of courteous savagery. The surface of cricket is as silky smooth as the rules of court or the opening of a classic detective story: voices are subdued, clothes are immaculate. But at the center, the atmosphere is murder-ously intense. Where Americans prefer to intimidate with noise and rudeness, the English and their erstwhile colonials go for silence and tyrannical politeness, such that the incoming bats-man feels he is on trial for his life.

Obviously the connection is no accident: it is one of the great imperial clichés. First we'll show you our games (says Colonel Blimp), and then perhaps you'll understand our other institutions. What was striking about the above scenes was that Trinidad had triumphantly thrown off British rule several years before, yet maintained both the game and the institution more wholeheartedly than ever.

Anyone who has encountered Trinidadians, or Jamaicans, 35 or Barbadians, will recognize a distinctive style—polite, ironic, tough—a style that has nothing to do with race and everything to do with culture. And while only a fanatic would attribute the style totally to cricket, only an equal and oppo-site fanatic would ignore altogether an activity to which the area's small fry have devoted more time than they have ever spent in church and more attention than they have ever paid in school. When a local Muslim ran amuck a few years ago and tried to stage one of those hostage-holding protests common to the rest of the world, a local professor observed, "We don't do things like that in Trinidad. We are a cricket-playing nation"—a remark no Englishman has made in 50 years.

In a sense, cricket was the demonstration sport of the whole Victorian ethos: the game that instilled the most patience and the most discipline and was, for long stretches at a time, the least like fun and the most like work. The fact that it is now played best and most authentically in the lands of calypso and sun is proof positive of the power of a sport to make its own way and impose its own style anywhere it takes root unless another sport got there first.

This last fact, in its turn, has recently taken on a global significance, as markets open up everywhere like spring flowers, and in each of them thousands of new TV sets are turned on to find out what the rest of us have been up to all this time and what interests us. And the latest word from America these days is sports, to an extent that might astonish the non-sports-minded, who probably think it's still things like movies, rock music, and fast food.

Each of these has served a turn at selling America, for better or worse, but our movies have been around so long by now that foreigners half-think they made them themselves. Rock music can be more or less produced locally, and McDonald's is already a cliché. (The real breakthrough will be enough food, never mind the speed.) American culture has triumphed so thoroughly that people scarcely know it's American any more.

But what's still new and different out of America is the Super Bowl, which, thanks to the extraordinary telegenic charms of American football, has swept the globe with the force of a new art movement, or at least a new dance craze: people stay up all night to watch it in Europe and Australia, and London betting parlors make book on it.

For another kind of corruption closer to home, witness the 40 ecstatic savagery of British soccer crowds, riding a violence high into Europe and getting banned from the Continent for their pains during the late 1980s, like a disease or a rabid animal. This, from the mother of parliaments, and of cricket, gives one special pause and is worth a longer look, because it shows where another strand of the great Victorian sports adventure led.

Sports hooliganism is actually not so much a new development as a regression or atavism. According to legend, the original game from which soccer, rugby, and, by extension, American football all derive was a primeval affair in which one village attempted by fair means or foul—legend says nothing about rules—to move an object (nothing so fancy as a ball, I imagine) to the far end of another: it was total war, with everyone pitching in, and while it sounds kind of jolly now, we know from records that the earliest English school games were just plain bloody, and had to be toned down again and yet again—from kicking allowed above the knee, to kicking allowed *below* the knee, to no kicking at all—before they could begin to do the godly work that Thomas Arnold had in mind for them. (If the Battle of Waterloo really was won "on the playing fields of Eton," it must have been as much thanks to the brutality learned there as to the sportsmanship.)

Soccer, born in Britain, spread rapidly around the world at the end of the 19th century. This painting depicts a soccer game in Rio de Janeiro.

Interestingly enough, Charles Dickens's description of a village election in *Pickwick Papers* (1837) makes the politics of the period sound like a not-too-distant cousin of the mythic village Game: rough, corrupt, and of course jolly, always jolly.

At that stage cricket was actually more refined than voting, as a match described in the same book indicates. It was the country sport, in ethos, as football was the town one, but throughout the century both sports would grow side by side with elections in both sophistication and popularity, matching strides and suiting each other very well, with sports teaching the democratic virtues of fairness and team spirit, and democracy feeding back its own lessons: whatever the rest of life says to you, this game belongs to you, the players. The rules, however mystifying at times, have not been imposed on you from above, but have grown out of the sport itself and are designed to give you the best possible game each time out, so it's in your simple best interests to obey them. (The idea of shaping the rules to suit the spectators, and eventually the TV cameras, was far in the future.)

One can exaggerate the usefulness of sports to democracy, and many people have. Nothing could better illustrate how the same game can produce radically different effects in different settings than to compare India with the West Indies. When Rudyard Kipling wrote about "flanneled fools at the wicket and muddied oafs at the goal," he may to some extent have been voicing the exasperation of a myopic, sportless man, but he was also quite legitimately aiming at the smug insularity of the English, buffered on all sides by their playthings, their cricket and football and the rest. Kipling's first experience of this must have been in India, where members of the British Raj were wont to set up their wickets and disappear into cricket for years on end. Presumably, their servants would learn democracy by fielding for them.

In Barbados, which inch for inch has probably produced the finest cricket talent in the world, the game actually served to introduce the slaves to their masters, and to keep them on speaking terms through the squalls of emancipation, and leave them friendly afterward. A retired schoolmaster whom I met at the Bridgetown Cricket Club, surrounded entirely by blacks, assured me that the transition from white to black rule was as painless as it could be and that if there is such a thing as a color-blind society, Barbados is it. And both sides agree that cricket had at least something to do with it.

This is further proof, if proof is still needed, that sports 45 should not be left on automatic pilot, but require intelligence and breadth of vision at every turn to be of any use at all. In Barbados, the white minority has learned its lesson well over the years: a society that plays together had better do a few other things together as well, whether that society be a former colony or an American university.

But finally, it comes down to what a society wants its games to do for it. The English who settled in Barbados *wanted* a stake in their new country, so the Game became a sort of preliminary town meeting; the Anglo-Indians, contrariwise, were perched on the fringe of a vast country, doing their damnedest *not* to get sucked in too far: a colonial officer who Indianized was no use at all. So the Game was just a transaction, a handshake, a one-afternoon stand, if you will. Afterward one withdrew to the club to reorganize one's Englishness.

So when the roof finally fell in on them in the 1940s, many Anglo-Indians knew almost as little about the country they had been infesting as they had on arrival. Sports, if pursued too exclusively, can narrow the imagination and sap the curiosity. At the end of a good day, one feels drained and satisfied, and certainly in no mood to learn anything, let alone reform it, and the Anglo-Indian cricketers had hardly even had time to see the countryside, let alone talk to it.

It was in this sort of sense that sports failed even Mother England. (Sports can do only so much.) The British ruling class thought it knew its own people the way colonial officers thought they knew the natives, because they had played with them. But they had only played with some of their own people, and they had only played in a certain way.

Cricket reflected neither the rest of England nor even the century it was in. With exceptions, British working-class boys didn't consider cricket their game at all, but if anything, a symbol in the class war. When I lived in Britain in the early 1950s, the crowds at Lord's cricket ground seemed as different in tone from the crowds at the Queen's Park and Fulham soccer grounds as a first-class railway carriage was from third class, or the saloon bar from the public one. (The English could divide *anything* into classes.) Sports did not resolve the class problem but if anything hardened it, and soccer remains, vestigially, the sport of resentment, the outsiders' sport.

A sports team is a tiny parliament operating on a war footing. 50 And what holds it together and makes it work is the much maligned cult of winning. An interviewer once asked Senator Bill Bradley (D.-N.J.), late of the New York Knicks, whether he didn't think we rather overdid our mania for winning, obviously expecting the liberal Bill to agree with him heartily. But Bradley knew too much, he had been in the trenches himself where false pieties are as useless as they are in real warfare, and he said in effect "No—if you don't emphasize winning over everything else, players tend to become selfish."

A team trying to win will clean itself like a cat of anything that slows it down. So the athlete who wants to show off must find ways to do it between plays, or between games, and in such a way that he doesn't hog the limelight totally and leave his teammates, who may also want to show off, in shadow. Thus we arrive at a breed of disciplined exhibitionists, affable egotists who like nothing better than to be photographed congratulating their *teammates*, or to be interviewed in the same capacity ("I guess I knew the Babe* better than anybody")—a mixed bag indeed.

But these players are interspersed among perfectly normal young people who will probably represent their country in the sports era as attractively and accurately as anything the world has seen of ours since the GIs of World War II—who were also a mixed bag. But what is attractive about them will be precisely their unspoiled pre-money, pre-television essence, or whatever remains of it, a folk quality that sports keep alive against the odds, like an old religion in a modern country. TV may change the look of it, and the cost of it, and even the way some of the athletes feel about it, but if you were lucky enough to see the American ice hockey team upsetting the Russians at Lake Placid in 1980, with the achievement gradually dawning and settling on the players' and fans' faces, you saw a sporting print of America as it was a hundred years ago and will be tomorrow if we don't mess up, next to which a political convention seems by now utterly contrived and synthetic, and untrue to its own nature.

While it is tempting to say that what an athlete gets out of his sport and his life is his own affair and no special business of anyone else's, it is in fact a matter of considerable public interest that he get as much out of both as possible, because the gap between what a fulfilled athlete can get out of life and the

---

***Babe** Babe (George Herman) Ruth, a baseball player for the Boston Red Sox (1914–19) and the New York Yankees (1920–34).

blinkered world of the hacker is dangerously wide, and there are more young citizens playing around on the edge of it right now than ever before in history—ours or anybody else's.

A player who is simply going through the motions is a loose cannon even within his sport. Since he isn't quite sure why he's doing this, he leans towards the primary explanation: it must be for the money. And why not? That's why the coach is doing it, with his contract on the side with the shoe company, whose products our guy has to play in every night. And that's why the school is doing it, as it angles to get into the big-bucks tournaments and appear on TV, cutting his class time to nothing, if need be, in order to do so.

Fortunately for everyone, the best way that he, the player, can make some money too is to play the game as well as he can. And this is why the system seems to work despite itself. But, as I say, a player thus motivated is a loose cannon. Because if he doesn't get that money, or some kind of payoff outside of the sheer joy of playing, the best you can hope for is a malcontent, the worst a cheat, and the usual, a dropout.

American sports are more and more geared to make it seem that everything you do is aimed toward something else—the game toward the tournament; the tournament toward a better tournament next year; toward a better high school, college, pro team, winning pro team, more money with the pro team or I'll go to another one, never mind which; endorsements; agents; job opportunities—so that it's hard to say at any one point that *this* is what it's for. The American dream as currently construed is more like an order to keep moving until you fall off the continent and don't you dare stop dreaming.

One constant throughout this is, of course, money, which appears in every chapter like Woody Allen's mysterious character Zelig, reassuring the dreamer of some continuity at least. The psychological significance of this character may be judged by the intensity with which ballplayers bargain for meaningless additions to already vast salaries in order to make the most money at their particular position: if money is what you've always played for, you can't stop now, even though who gets the most depends on whose contract has come up most recently, so you can never rest there.

The other constant through every phase of the sports branch of the American dream is the game itself—baseball, football, whatever—which, like some improbable 18th-century heroine, has usually come reeling through this maze of temptation and corruption with its virtue more or less intact, if only because no one has yet thought of a profitable way of corrupting it. Unlike movies and the other arts, games are never more commercial than when they are played exactly as they should be. Of course, if any little thing can be done to make the contests even *more* commercial—eliminating this, shortening that, a designated hitter here and a 24-second clock there—it will be, but the heart of sports remains pure. An athlete shinnying up the greasy pole will find a recognizably similar game at the top to the one he played as a child—and this will be the guarantor of his innocence up there if anything can be.

What it guarantees for women is a brand new question for most of us—too fresh to answer though never too fresh to talk about. To wit, if certain sports are in some sense an apprenticeship for, and escape from, the world of politics and business, it stands to reason that great numbers of women will want to play them too, however much the games themselves seem to have been designed exclusively by men for men, for example football, whose weekly injury list seems like a benign version of a war memorial.

So maybe we can expect some new rules shortly, or even a 60 whole new game—but if so along what lines? Women have not succeeded so far in making either business or politics "kinder and gentler" because the material itself won't permit it: you can't be kind with shareholders' money or gentle with Saddam Hussein, or even with Margaret Thatcher, if her country needs something.

But will sports prove that much more malleable? How much reform can they stand without losing their original point? The evidence so far suggests that the tide usually runs the other way, and that the sport changes the players long before they can change it. Most games, whether played in boardrooms or stadiums, have a way of dictating not only exactly how they should be played but with what attitude, so that the mildest of citizens may suddenly find his engorged face parked in that of an umpire without being quite sure how it got there. And this goes apparently whether one's name is Andre Agassi or Martina Navratilova.

But these matters of protocol may conceivably be negotiable at that. What isn't is the other thing that sports dictate, which is that you will always play them as hard as possible, since violence is the inevitable and often exhilarating by-product of taking your foot off the brake and seeing just what your body is capable of. And this is an element of sports that can't be compromised with without losing the point for sure. You can, if you like, put helmets on the boxers to reduce the damage, and you can bench your star quarterback to keep down the score, but what you can't do is tell either of them to take it easy, or to "have a heart."

And this, not the physical pain, will surely be the hardest aspect of competitive sports for many women to swallow: their sheer implacability and ice-cold legalism, which could break your heart even if you were playing touch football in a suit of armor. Sports are in fact as unfeeling as life itself. The ref still calls penalties against you even when you're down 50–0, and the scoreboard won't be adjusted afterward to make you feel better. Nowhere does self-esteem take a worse pounding than on a sports field—unless maybe it's at a chess board where "checkmate in three" can hurt worse than a blind-side tackle that breaks both legs. What you get in exchange for these ritual humiliations is a thimbleful of self-knowledge, a small but precious sense of how reality works, and all the self-esteem you can earn with your own muscle and sweat—and here, sports relents a little: it rewards duffers who try hard with almost as much self-satisfaction as it gives to champions.

This, for the last 150 years, is how men in the modern world have prepared themselves for life. If women decide to take this route too in significant numbers, and indications are that they are doing so, it will, if nothing else, test the sturdiest of all truisms, that men naturally are just and women merciful. Men are, it seems fair to assume, not really born just, but usually have it thrust upon them the first time they try to cheat someone, or someone tries to cheat them, and they realize that justice is the most kindness you can give to two people at the same time, if their interests differ. Any kindness you have left after you've played games long enough will be solid indeed— and of course, the generosity of athletes to teammates is legendary, and to foes only slightly less so. What one might hope women, or *somebody*, might effect is an opening up of this parochialism to let the rest of the world in.

If this should ever happen, I can only say the blessings of 65 sports would be infinitely easier to argue than they have been in this essay.

Joining the Conversation

1. In paragraph 5, Wilfrid Sheed points out that "By the '90s of this century, sports worship had grown and taken on a life of its own," at times overwhelming other parts of life such as education. This position serves as a naysayer to the author's argument about the value of sports. What examples can you come up with of this overemphasis on sports that Sheed describes? What in your view are some of its negative effects?

2. How does the author support his views on the wider importance of sports? What evidence and arguments does he provide? How convincing are they to you and why?

3. Joe Posnanski ends his essay on p. 559 by saying that baseball "is as beautiful now as it ever was." Applying this statement to U.S. sports in general, do you think Sheed would agree with Posnanski, disagree, or agree but with a difference? What evidence do you find in Sheed's essay to support your answer?

4. Sheed wrote this essay for an audience of intellectuals and published it in an academic journal in 1995. Find five places in the text that reflect the intended audience. How might Sheed have presented his ideas differently if he had been writing for, say, an audience of first-year college students?

5. Using Sheed's arguments on the positive role that sports play in society as your "they say," write an essay discussing both the positive and negative effects of sports.

Women Who Hit Very Hard
and How They've Changed Tennis

MICHAEL KIMMELMAN

—◻—

ON THE DAY BEFORE Wimbledon started, when the club grounds had not yet opened to the public, Justine Henin, the diminutive Belgian tennis great, stepped onto practice court No. 3, then still an emerald patch of unspoiled grass. The sun had just come out after several cloudy days, and all around, players, their coaches and families, yammering in various languages, exchanged greetings like veteran bunkmates on the first day at summer camp. Not Henin. Having unretired last year as suddenly as she quit 16 months earlier—saying she had got all she wanted from the sport—she remained absorbed with her coach, Carlos Rodriguez, in their warm-up routine.

MICHAEL KIMMELMAN writes for the *New York Times* and the *New York Review of Books*. He has written a blog on tennis, and his books include *Portraits: Talking with Artists at the Met, the Modern, the Louvre, and Elsewhere* (1998), *The Accidental Masterpiece: On the Art of Life and Vice Versa* (2005), *More Things Like This* (2009), and *Oscar Niemeyer* (2009). This article first appeared in the *New York Times* on August 25, 2010.

She began exchanging ground strokes, forehands and backhands, slowly then harder, with a hitting partner, one of the men that the top women hire to practice with, a tall, powerful young Briton, Scott Sears, who missed a few shots, apologized and began to sweat. Henin missed nothing, ever. Most eyes now turned toward her, drawn by the silence of the practice, which was interrupted only when Rodriguez, to whom Henin kept turning for assurance, issued a gentle "*marche*" every once in a while.

In Henin, the line between an expression of vulnerability and a devouring stare of slightly sour competitiveness can be fuzzy. Venus and Serena Williams, the game's longtime dominant sisters, tend to look more abstracted, in a world closed onto themselves. Until they're threatened. Then the array of weapons—the fist pumps, the drive to win, the sheer, overwhelming athleticism—emerge. Henin, "the sister of no mercy," as she is called, is a more elegant player but no less unrelentingly obsessed with crushing her opponents.

Finished, she gathered up her belongings, leaving Sears in a pool of sweat, then walked off, head down so as not to catch anyone's eye, trying to preserve, it seemed, like breath on glass, the focus she had on court. Even practicing, she made an argument for promoters who claim that women's tennis has never been better off.

Women have certainly never hit harder and not just on account of improved equipment. They're stronger, bigger, faster, better trained and pushed above all by the example of the Williams sisters. Serena, glorious and musclebound, and Venus, long-limbed and tall, have redefined the sport around power. Years ago, tennis writers used to call Martina Navratilova, listed at 5-foot-8 and lean, a giantess with popping veins because other women seemed weaklings by comparison. Now most tour players would dwarf her. In large part what makes Henin, at 5-foot-5, such an exception on the tour and such fun to watch is that she's nearly always David against the rising tide of Goliaths.

"When I started, all the top players thought the Grand Slams began in the quarterfinals, because the early rounds were so easy and we only had to give 50 percent to get through them," Kim Clijsters, Belgium's other tennis superstar, told me when we sat down to talk one day at Wimbledon. "Now I have to be at least 85 to 90 percent at my best from the beginning of a tournament. Venus and Serena raised the bar for everyone. We

Serena Williams

all had to go back to the gym. Younger players saw that, and now they're hitting harder and harder."

This is a basic truth about the Williamses, held among professional watchers of the sport as well as players. Venus says it herself: "Serena and I did change the game, and it's interesting to see people on court now trying to do all our moves. To be that person, the one who changed the game, wow, that's too good to be true." For guidance in using and introducing quotations, see Chapter 3.

Lately, it has been Serena, the top-ranked woman, who has dominated the field, but a foot injury forced her to withdraw from the United States Open, the last major tournament of the year. Pretenders have come and gone in recent years, capitalizing on the sisters' irregular schedules, as well as on Henin's absence, before succumbing to injury or nerves or simply retiring. When, for a while, both Henin and Clijsters, who quit in 2007 to have a baby, were gone, the game looked bereft of its only serious challengers.

Clijsters is now back, defending her United States Open title in New York beginning this week. That, so shortly after coming out of retirement, she could have won at all last year (Serena crashed out in their semifinal over a foot-fault call she profanely protested) signaled to some skeptics how thin on the ground are the women capable of actually winning majors. With Henin suffering a partial ligament fracture to her right elbow in a match against Clijsters at Wimbledon and now out of commission for the rest of the year, one of those few women is missing, again.

It's not common these days to find women with their range: 10 with the defensive skills to neutralize the big serves, or an accomplished net game or a good second serve. Many women's matches get bogged down with baseline exchanges—a criticism that might be leveled at the men's matches except that, as Federer put it after losing to Andy Murray in the final of the Rogers Cup in Toronto earlier this month, the men, in general, are more evenly matched. They "don't have the margins like maybe exist in women's tennis," whereby players like the Williamses "can just come out and maybe dominate an opponent every single time," Federer said. "That doesn't happen in the men's game."

Does that matter? "When Chrissie and Martina were winning 36 majors," Billie Jean King, the tennis legend, talking pure performance, not personality, recalled of the Chris Evert versus Martina Navratilova rivalry of the late '70s and early '80s, "everyone was complaining about only two good players, no depth. Now, that was supposedly the golden age, and there's no depth and only the Williams sisters today? Give me a break. My lord, what I would give to hit one ball like them."

It's true, there is more depth now, meaning more women beyond the top 10 or 20 or even top 100 who can smack a given forehand or backhand harder than King ever dreamed of doing, although consistency is another question. Ana Ivanovic, who looked to be the next Maria Sharapova after she won the French Open in 2008 and rose to No. 1, is beautiful, charming and talkative. She was called the future of tennis until she slumped, her serve and forehand betrayed by nerves. This month in Cincinnati, she lost in a semifinal to Clijsters, withdrawing in tears after hurting her foot. She wrestled in the first round at Wimbledon with her service toss against Shahar Peer, from Israel. Tennis is a game; but it can be heartbreaking to watch sometimes. One set down, scrambling to stay alive in the second, Ivanovic slammed her racquet in frustration. She kept making mistakes, defeating herself. Her talent escaped her. Afterward, snatching up her belongings, she hurried through the crowd toward the locker room, struggling not to break down in public.

"I think it's sort of cyclical," said Bud Collins, the legendary tennis commentator, when I asked him about the ups and downs of the women's tour over the years. But, he added, "when they talk about depth today, I snicker."

Depth means more talent, more players who can knock the bejesus out of a ball. But there's a difference between more good tennis players and more great ones. Stacey Allaster, chairwoman and chief executive of the Women's Tennis Association, says that there are more great ones. One morning, she delivered the tour's basic message. "Our underlying mission and values remain as strong as they were in 1973," she said, "plus we have greater responsibility now in going to places like China and the Middle East, showing the world that women are strong and deserve to be treated equally." Feminist missionary work aside, tour executives see global outreach as critical to the bottom line, especially as fewer top players are from the United States, traditionally the sport's biggest market.

"I have no doubt that there will be a Chinese No. 1," says 15 David Shoemaker, president of the W.T.A., who oversees the association's efforts in that country. "People say the Chinese don't know how to develop players, that they're too rigid, but they're wrong," he says. "Part of the beauty of the game is how unpredictable it has always been. What we've got today is in fact what everyone always said they wanted. There are eight different Grand Slam champions playing at Wimbledon, and a bunch more who have been No. 1."

Success can mean millions in prize money and endorsements. When the women's tour started in the early 1970s, the total annual prize money was $300,000. Today it's $86 million, counting the Grand Slams, which (and this remains one of the most contested topics behind the scenes) pay men and women equally. Wimbledon and the French Open lagged behind until

Venus Williams wrote an article for the *Times of London* a few years ago claiming she felt like a second-class citizen. Tournament officials got the message.

King, whose straight-set victory over Bobby Riggs in the so-called Battle of the Sexes in 1973 attracted some 50 million television viewers around the world and gave the tour its initial publicity boost, reflected the other day on how players back then "were activists, ours was totally a political movement, and today the tour is so much more important than most of the young players realize. They forget that a woman could not get a credit card on her own."

King earned $1,800 for winning Wimbledon in the late 1960s, Navratilova, $18,000 in the '70s. Now the winner takes home $1.6 million. In the tour's early days, women had to barnstorm the globe to make a decent living, and the best players aimed to be ranked No. 1 when the season ended. Grand Slam trophies figured less in their calculations. Today stars construct their careers around the slams, picking and choosing among other tour events, which vie for their participation, creating a delicate and complicated ecosystem. The system demands a broad cast of supporting players, a bit like the expendable crew members on the old *Star Trek* series.

Costs are high. At Grand Slams like Wimbledon and the U.S. Open, top players may pay to take along a coach, a trainer, a practice partner and an assistant. A single slam can set a star back between $30,000 and $50,000, according to Carlos Fleming, an agent for I.M.G., the management firm with the largest stable of tennis players. A year on tour, Fleming estimated, can require an outlay of hundreds of thousands or more in travel expenses. For journeywomen, flying economy and sharing trainers and coaches, a Grand Slam can still cost $10,000, and annual costs can run as high as $150,000. Unlike players on a professional baseball team, whose contracts basically guarantee their salaries, pros on the tennis circuit must earn that money back by winning. And when their skills decline, so do their nest eggs, if they ever had them. Players end up playing to please themselves; it's a privilege, or a lark, to be on tour if you're not highly ranked, but rarely a gold mine.

Allaster likes to call touring pros "independent contractors," 20 because they work for themselves. And this has consequences aside from having to earn a living with each game. Since 2001, the Williams sisters have boycotted the tournament at Indian Wells, in California, one of the tour's biggest events. Venus withdrew from the semifinals that year, and Serena was roundly booed afterward. Richard Williams, their father, claimed that he heard racist slurs. Despite being cajoled, fined, penalized and begged, they haven't returned. They're young, rich, profoundly gifted African-American women who operate as they wish, in a tennis world that's still overwhelmingly white, conformist and reluctant to acknowledge that race is even an issue. The Indian Wells boycott, a matter of principle or a show of power or both, underscores the tour's impotence. "The business is ultimately not sustainable on the backs of two players," Allaster acknowledged at one point, finessing what Bud Collins later put more bluntly. The W.T.A., he said, is dependent on the Williams sisters even as it's hopeful that new champions will come along to supplant them.

So where are they? The top-ranked women today are, conspicuously, not getting any younger. Serena is about to turn 29, Venus is 30. The women's tour used to turn out a steady stream of teen idols. But new strength training and equipment have made it harder for teenagers to compete against grown women, and the tour is now wary of encouraging them to try. In 1979,

Tracy Austin won the U.S. Open at age 16, reached No. 1 the next year, but fell out of the Top 10 by 22. A shoulder injury in 1985 did in Andrea Jaeger, who reached No. 2, also while a teenager. During the late '90s, Martina Hingis won five Grand Slams in her teens, then retired in 2003 at 22, returning to the tour three years later only to be expelled after testing positive for cocaine. And this summer, Jennifer Capriati, who reached the Top 10 at 14, in 1990, landed in a Florida hospital after an overdose of prescription drugs.

While there are young talents on tour, like Wozniacki and Melanie Oudin, the 18-year-old American right-hander, ranked No. 44, they're few. The casualty list prompted W.T.A. officials some years ago (the Williams sisters, who began playing as teenagers in the mid-1990s, were already around) to impose restrictions on whether and how much teenagers could play. "I will listen to doctors more than to agents," is how Allaster puts it. Most insiders endorse the policy.

Others, like Mary Joe Fernandez, a retired American player, now a television commentator, contend that by protecting the many, the tour may be holding back that rare precocious player—the next rival to the Williams sisters, perhaps—who, like Hingis and Capriati, may happen to peak as a teenager. "I understand the age rule, but I turned pro at 14—I missed my prom and graduation because I played the French Open—and while not everybody is ready then, some are," Fernandez says. "At the same time I don't entirely buy the argument about power, since the same thing was said years ago, whether it was that Navratilova hit harder than anyone, or Monica Seles or Capriati or now Serena. The game needs young stars. And it may be that some women develop younger."

This view is seconded by Tom Perrotta, editor at large at *Tennis* magazine. "Why does it matter if you start your career at 16 and end it at 25?" he asked. "Skeptics on the development side of the game will tell you that the women's tour has become more monotonous, that there's a missing generation. Some blame parents, some blame the academies turning out robot players, some the age rule. Maybe it's just that the Williams sisters have set the bar too high or that all the money spoils players' appetites for getting to the very top. I don't know. But I do know that while you have a bigger pool of good players from more countries, having many more good players doesn't substitute for having a few more icons."

Maybe she's out there now, some 10-year-old girl preparing to raise the women's game another notch and prove the skeptics wrong. Meanwhile there's Serena to carry the sport on her broad shoulders. Only Zvonareva stood between her and the Wimbledon title everyone had expected her to win from the beginning. Heavy ground strokes nipping the lines kept the Russian in the fight for a while. At 3-3 in the first set, the crowd cheering, it looked as if it might be a contest. Then Williams found another gear, moving inside the baseline to receive even Zvonareva's first serves, pushing the Russian onto her heels, wearing her down. Zvonareva played well. But she was totally outgunned.

"Come back!" one fan called out.

"All is forgiven," joked another. Then someone yelled, "Come on, Serena," and Bud Collins, in the seat next to mine, shook his head.

"Sadist," he said.

At the end, Williams never even faced a break point. Zvonareva thanked her surgeon during the postmatch ceremony. Williams teased King, watching from the stands, because with the victory she passed King's total of 12 Grand Slam singles titles.

People worrying about the game today will probably be the 30 same ones, years from now, who boast about having seen Serena in her prime, along with Henin and Venus and Sharapova and Clijsters.

There's nothing like it, they'll say. Those were the days.

Joining the Conversation

1. When Michael Kimmelman writes that "power" has transformed women's tennis, he is ostensibly referring to the hardhitting style, with its booming serves and powerful baseline shots. Through what other developments in the sport is "power" changing women's tennis?

2. In paragraph 10, Kimmelman quotes tennis player Roger Federer, who says that men's tennis is "more evenly matched," whereas the Williams sisters "dominate an opponent every time." Why, in your view, does he bring up this naysayer, or possible objection to his argument, and how does he respond to it?

3. Where in the essay do you find a "so what?" That is, how does Kimmelman try to make clear that this topic—and his perspective on it—are important?

4. Wilfrid Sheed, at the end of his essay on pp. 508–10, poses questions about women and sports: both how the sports industry might be difficult for women and how the industry might change because of women's increasing involvement. How might Kimmelman use evidence from women's professional tennis to respond to Sheed?

5. In his conclusion, Kimmelman predicts that the same people who complain about women's tennis today will eventually glorify it: "There's nothing like it, they'll say. Those were the days." Could this comment apply to other sports? Using Kimmelman's words as a "they say," write an essay assessing the current state of a sport about which you are knowledgeable.

In Defense of Cheering

JENNIE YABROFF

———□———

THE TEAM is in bad shape. One member has a broken rib. The other, a possible concussion from a nasty fall. A third wraps a compression bandage around a sprained ankle. They've been practicing day and night, focusing on their sport to the exclusion of most everything else, and the strain is showing. Their coach is screaming at them from the sidelines. What they could really use is a nice, peppy cheerleader to raise their spirits. The only thing is, these *are* the cheerleaders.

Bring it on? Modern cheerleaders do, with a vengeance. There's a lot more to cheering than short skirts and "fight, fight, fight!" says Kate Torgovnick, author of *Cheer*. Torgovnick spent a year following three groups—a four-time championship team, an all-girls squad and an all-African American team—none of which fit the stereotype of vapid blondes doing splits on the sidelines. Instead, she discovered, competitive cheerleaders are more like extreme athletes: daredevil adrenaline junkies who

JENNIE YABROFF, a freelance writer and blogger, has written for *Newsweek*, the *New York Times*, Salon.com, and the *San Francisco Chronicle*. This article first appeared on March 15, 2008, in *Newsweek*.

often perform exhausted or hurt and love their sport with an addict's devotion. And unlike more-revered athletes—such as football players or even gymnasts—cheerleaders have to contend with lack of respect from their peers and frequent mockery (think of Will Ferrell and Cheri Oteri's cheerleading skit on *Saturday Night Live*). The truth, says Torgovnick, is that cheerleading has a long, distinguished history—five American presidents did it—is a demanding sport, and deserves to be taken seriously. So make some noise!

Cheerleaders have been around since the 1890s, egging on Princeton in its first football game against Rutgers, but they looked a lot different. For one thing, they were all men. For another, they didn't do much, besides using megaphones to pump up the crowd. Over the years the guys incorporated backflips and handsprings in their routines, and, during World War II, women joined the squads. Around the same time, the president of Kilgore College caught students drinking in the parking lot during halftime, so he asked the cheer team to take the field between quarters to keep students in their seats. And thus, Torgovnick writes, modern cheerleading was born.

Today, there's a split between the stunt-heavy, gymnastic-style teams, whose routines are filled with flying bodies and physics-defying contortions, and the more traditional, pompom-shaking "spirit squads." At the University of Oregon and the University of Maryland, the competitive cheerleaders don't even cheer for the athletic teams—they save their backflips for big-time competitions such as the World Cheerleading Championships—which makes you wonder how far we are from the day when cheerleaders get their due as athletes. Torgovnick says the biggest surprise in writing her book was learning how popular the sport is with men again. After becoming

female-dominated in the 1950s and 1960s, college cheerleading is now 50 percent male. "I assumed if you were a guy cheerleader you're gay," says the writer, "but it's this culture of manly men who come from football, wrestling, baseball, and get pulled into this world." If they get static about their activities, they can always point to their forefathers in cheer: before leading the country, FDR led the crowd at Harvard, and Eisenhower, sidelined from football by a knee injury, wielded the megaphone at West Point. Ronald Reagan played football as the Gipper on film, but in real life he rooted on the basketball team at Eureka College as a cheerleader. And both Bushes had that rah-rah spirit at Yale; George W. cheered for Andover as well.

Though the sport continues to evolve, most people's per- 5
ception of it remains rooted in 1950s stereotypes, says Torgovnick. "The image of the cheerleader straddles the virgin/whore

line," she says. "She's either the straight A's prom queen, or the short skirt, slutty, queen-bee kind of girl." This misconception is perpetuated by stories about cheerleaders run amok, such as the self-proclaimed "fab five" high-school cheerleaders in Texas who harassed their teachers and posted dirty photos of themselves on the Internet, or the Carolina Panthers cheerleaders who were arrested after a bar fight. "Cheerleaders have such a wholesome, all-American, uncorruptible image, the idea of them being corrupted really appeals to people," Torgovnick says. But she admits that there is something about the sport that attracts drama queens: "To be a cheerleader you have to want to be the center of attention," she says. "The women do like wearing that uniform." And the men like it, too.

Joining the Conversation

1. Jennie Yabroff argues that cheerleaders are in many ways comparable to the athletes they cheer for. What view of cheerleading is she arguing against? Where do you find that view in the essay?
2. What reasons and evidence does Yabroff provide to support her view in defense of cheerleading? What, in her opinion, is valuable about the activity? Can you come up with other examples that either support or oppose her position?
3. Paragraph 3 provides some background on the history of cheerleading. How does this information contribute to the essay? Does it support the argument? What, if anything, does it add?
4. Cheerleading is usually seen as an activity dominated by girls and women, but according to Yabroff, cheerleading squads were originally all-male, and recent years have seen a trend

of increasing male involvement. How, in your view, are gender issues related to arguments about the value of cheerleading?

5. What do you think? Respond to Yabroff's argument. Start by summarizing her views, and then agree with them, disagree, or both. Remember: if you agree, you still need to add something new to the conversation; if you disagree, you need to explain why.

How I Learned to Love Football

FELISA ROGERS

RICH LIKES to tell me about football. When we first got married, a picture of Brett Favre hung in his office. I learned about Favre's battle with alcohol and Vicodin, his propensity for throwing interceptions, and his improvisational gusto, exemplified by his stumbling underhanded pass to tight end Donald Lee for a first down in the snowbound 2007 NFC division game against the Seattle Seahawks.

After a while (about 15 seconds) my eyes would glaze over, and I'd find myself thinking about Thursday's dinner plans or perhaps Alexander Hamilton. "You're not listening to me, again," Rich would say, sounding wounded. And then my inevitable reply: "You're talking about *football!*"

FELISA ROGERS is a freelance writer who lives in Oregon. A graduate of Evergreen State College and former teacher, she has contributed to ehow.com, USAToday.com, and Peoplesguide.com on subjects including family and travel. She is also a blogger and a frequent contributor to Salon.com, where this article first appeared on February 5, 2011.

My family never cared much for sports. My dad was a nerd, and my mom was a beatnik. They raised me to believe that football and baseball were the province of Neanderthal types who didn't know the difference between Carl Jung and Carlos Castaneda. I don't think I can blame my parents for my complete athletic incompetence, but the game was never on at our house and maybe I missed some crucial early indoctrination that allows the average American to understand the parameters of an inning or the meaning of "second down."

I attended school in a small redneck town in Oregon called Mapleton, where sports were the ticket to popularity. My social status suffered: The mere mention of football or softball awakened a paralyzing dread in me. PE was akin to the Roman Coliseum: I was dumped onto a field and someone was chasing me and I had no idea what the rules were and people were *watching* me. My fearful lack of coordination was so obvious that even my parents became concerned and gave me a softball for my birthday one year. "How about we play catch?" my dad said awkwardly, looking at the ball like it was a severed head. We didn't get too far.

Eventually my incompetence hardened into an intense dislike for playing sports, watching sports, or even hearing about sports. In school, I kept this distaste to myself; I didn't want to be a complete pariah. I pretended to know what people were talking about when they brought up the Seahawks, and I engaged in sports-related activities that required minimal contact with the ball, such as being the scorekeeper for our middle school volleyball team.

Freshman year, I played second clarinet in the pep band, which meant I had to go to every home football game. I didn't mind that much. The games, with their bonfires and

5

hot cider, had a certain appeal. I understood ritual, after all:
Majestic in their blue and white jerseys, our boys tore across
the frosted fields like fleeting gods; my cousin made out under
the bleachers; and on the homecoming bonfire, we roasted
effigies of our opponents. I felt a certain awe, but I still had
no idea what was going on.

Sophomore year I moved to a bigger town and attended
South Eugene High School, home of the Axemen. South was
a large school, and there were hundreds of students who never
seemed to know whether our team had won or lost. For the
first time in my life, I didn't have to pretend to be interested
in sports. It was liberating. My extracurricular activities were
writing bad poetry and imitating Winona Ryder, and people
still liked me. It was actually cool to hate football. From that
point on, I ignored sports completely.

Sadly, I was not destined to live out the rest of my years in
the contemplation of poetry. In my twenties I accidentally
dated an Atlanta Falcons fan. And while I didn't exactly
develop a magical love for football, four years with Josh taught
me what the majority of Americans know instinctively: Watching sports, particularly football, is a good excuse to sit around
with friends, drinking beer and eating nachos. (The key word
being beer.) As soon as the TV clicked off and the bottles of
Rainier disappeared, my focus vanished: I hadn't escaped from
Mapleton only to revert to pretending to care about football
just because some guy I liked was a fan. Josh would try to tell
me about the Falcons, and I'd roll my eyes: "I'm sorry, but I
don't get it. It doesn't matter how many times you try to explain
it to me. I hate sports. It's, like, genetic."

Those four years in no way prepared me for the harsh reality of dating and then marrying a Green Bay Packers fan. When

I first met Rich, I told my friend Becky: "I can't believe it, it's like we have everything in common. He loves the Rolling Stones, and presidential history and vans. He even knows how to play John Prine songs on the guitar."

You think you know someone. Then you discover that he 10 squanders 80 percent of his available brain power thinking about Brett Favre.

Rich's love for Brett Favre was real, and almost touching. When he talked about Favre, his eyes would sparkle and exuberance would infect his diction, his normal quiet mutter giving way to a braying crescendo. It drove me crazy, and it began to cause a serious rift in our relationship: I stopped listening when he opened his mouth.

"You're not listening to me," he'd say.

"You're talking about football," I'd say.

"No I wasn't," he'd say hotly.

And my weak reply: "Well I thought you might be going to 15 talk about football."

Football wasn't our only problem. A few months after we got married, Rich got laid off from his job and my major contract dried up. Finances were tight, and garden-variety misfortune eclipsed our happiness: Our beloved cat got hit by a car, my grandmother died, our aged Honda broke down, Rich's mom and grandmother suffered from serious health problems, we kept getting closer to broke. Though I never expected him to take care of me, Rich felt an old-fashioned pressure to be the breadwinner, and when things were going bad, he didn't see it as our problem, so much as his. When he could get work he would take it, but those jobs always seemed to mean lower pay for longer hours and a long commute. He was stretched to the breaking point, constantly worried and frequently terse. Except when he talked about the Green Bay Packers.

Rich sounded happy when he talked about the Packers. Even when he was bemoaning the dark saga that culminated in Favre signing with the Minnesota Vikings, he had that light in his eyes. I began to notice that his monologues about the Packers could be tightly crafted and inspired. As a lit major and linguistic stickler, he latched onto the theme of Favre as a tragic hero, in the classical sense of the word. "A lot of people misuse the word *tragic*, which technically implies someone undone by hubris. Like Hamlet, Favre is a perfect example," he'd say seriously.

And it wasn't just Favre: I was treated to the inspiring life stories of wide receiver Donald Driver (grew up in a U-Haul!) and (former) Packers cornerback Al Harris (recovered from a ruptured spleen in record time and returned to finish the season!). And I soaked in the mythology of Green Bay: the legacy of Vince Lombardi, and the Packers' unique status as the only NFL team that's owned by its town, not by a rich guy or a corporation.

I started listening to Rich when he talked about football, because it was a lifeline between who he had become and who he used to be. And the more I actually listened, the more I actually understood. Rich's love for the Packers made me realize that football was more than just a bunch of jocks bashing into each other to demonstrate their unfathomable understanding of an elaborate and mysterious code of rules. Though Rich's interpretation of the game and players might be a touch more academic than most, he mirrors millions of other Americans. Football fandom is a source of comfort, common ground where one can meet with friends and rivals alike, an equalizing arena where your opinion is just as valid as the next guy's, economics or expertise be damned. Simply watching the game gives you the right to believe, wholeheartedly and without reservation, that your team deserves to win.

I noticed football fandom gives Rich something to talk about 20 with huge segments of the population, something he actually finds interesting. I began imagining what it would be like to live in a world where half the population had an avid and serious interest in American presidential history. I'd never be bored at a party again.

Philosophical revelations aside, I also began to get some understanding of the mechanics of the game: "So wait, the team has four chances to advance the ball 10 yards? And they're heading toward the opponents' end zone?" Light dawned in my eyes this time.

It sounds stupid, but things got better for us from there. We were still broke, but Rich seemed to spend fewer hours staring into the abyss. It was as though by listening I was affirming some part of him that was safe from the cold realities of survival.

Today, of course, we are an Aaron Rodgers house. (Never, ever get Rich started on Packers fans who defected when Favre left the team.) Over coffee in the morning, I can expect to be enlightened on Rodgers' latest quarterback ranking. Rich also periodically interrupts my work to remind me of small facial expressions and gestures that indicate that Rodgers is a stand-up guy.

"I'm glad we like Rodgers," I found myself saying one day. "I mean it would be terrible if the Packers had replaced Favre with someone with a bad personality, like Roethlisberger." I stopped in my tracks. Would it be terrible? Really? Did I actually have an opinion about this? Did I care?

I thought about it. Yep. The suspicion that I cared about a 25 football team was confirmed when I learned that the Packers had beaten the Falcons and thus advanced to the NFC Championship Game. "I can't believe they did it!" I exclaimed to my friend Mizu, who looked confused, probably remembering a dour poetry-writing teenager of yesteryear.

I still don't really understand football. Some obscure rule pops just at the moment I think I've grasped a play. (The stereotype of the dumb football player amazes me. No one who could remember all this crap could possibly be dumb.) Compared with your average zealous Green Bay Packers fan (and yes, the average Packers fan is zealous), I'm an ignorant dilettante. But I'm learning. I'm sure there are a million Steelers fans who have also had a rough year and who also deserve happiness, but I won't be thinking about them on Sunday. As an American football fan it's my prerogative to believe in the worthiness of the Green Bay Packers and Packers fans everywhere. One in particular.

Joining the Conversation

1. Perhaps surprisingly, this essay focuses to a large extent on relationships—particularly Felisa Rogers' relationship with her husband and the important role that a shared interest in the Green Bay Packers plays in it. How did her learning about football and developing an interest in the Packers help their marriage and their lives in general?

2. How does Rogers use humor to discuss the development of her attitude about football—and to let us see that following a football team is in some ways a serious matter?

3. In paragraph 19, Rogers says that "Football fandom is a source of comfort, common ground where one can meet with friends and rivals alike, an equalizing arena where your opinion is just as valid as the next guy's, economics or

expertise be damned." What support does she offer for this view? Is her argument persuasive? Why or why not?

4. Compare Maya Angelou's depiction on pp. 484–88 of African American fans of boxer Joe Louis in the 1930s South with Felisa Rogers' description of how she came to appreciate football. What does each author say about the bonding powers of sports?

5. Write an essay about the benefits of being a fan—of a team, a player, a singer, an author, anything. Be sure to answer the "so what" question and to make clear to your readers why your subject matters to you.

Move Over Boys,
Make Room in the Crease

SARA MARATTA

AT THE AWKWARD AGE OF 14, I caught a fever of an unknown origin. It hit me fast and has had a profound impact on my life to this day. It has helped me become fluent in a new lingo, cost me an enormous amount of money, exposed me to an eccentric circle of passionate people who enjoy sub-zero temperatures, and kept my evenings occupied from October until April.

Symptoms of this fever became noticeable on a blustery February night six years ago. On a quest for a dose of mind-

SARA MARATTA is studying journalism and political science at the University of Cincinnati and is interested in a career in journalism or politics. In her free time, she reads Jane Austen, watches Columbus Blue Jacket hockey games, plays golf. She writes for the independent student-run newspaper at her university and works as an intern at *Cincinnati Magazine*, and she's been published in *It All Changed in an Instant: More Six-Word Memoirs by Writers Famous & Obscure* (2010).

less television, I sashayed into our family room to see what intellectual programming my father was consuming. I anticipated something along the lines of *Iron Chef*, or possibly *American Choppers*, but to my surprise he was entranced by a hockey game.

At a loss for other means of amusement, I decided to see if this cold-weather sport appealed to my fancy. I listened carefully to the color analyst and play-by-play announcer as they animatedly provided second-by-second intel on the action on the ice. I heard words that did not exist in my lexicon, such as *five-hole, hat-trick, slashing, shootout,* and *power play.* Their raw enthusiasm was addicting, and my heart began to beat wildly as I followed the puck back and forth between the blue lines and into the crease. (In case you're not a hockey admirer, the crease is the area in front of the net, right before the goal line, which the goalie must guard with his life in order to prevent goals from being scored.) I actually found myself cheering when brawls broke out between the competing players, secretly hoping for a knockout; I can only describe what I felt as unadulterated exhilaration. What kind of primitive people could condone such brutal, yet thrilling fighting? I needed to infiltrate this rare breed to discover what fed their zeal.

I never would have surmised that the cult-like world of ice hockey would be the place where my ardent affection for sports would be seen as legitimate and where I would be recognized as a knowledgeable aficionada. I am a devout fan who attends games with my family and friends, and stays up into the early morning hours watching away games on TV. I don my Blue Jackets gear as proudly as a patriot would. Although I was welcomed with cordiality into the NHL fan clique of the Columbus Blue Jackets hockey franchise, those outside this group did not and have not accepted me as a true enthusiast who has a real comprehension and love for what goes on in the crease. Why? Because I am a woman.

In the year 2010, women are becoming more accepted into the sports world—not just as fans and players, but also as voices in sports journalism. However, men still dominate. Who cares, you ask? How does a male-dominated sports world affect women's acceptance as serious fans and professionals? Ultimately, what is at stake here is the awareness that sports are not exclusively male-oriented; therefore, females can and should be involved and have the opportunity to provide insightful opinions about these pastimes.

In sports, there are only a handful of professional female athletes who possess clout and are known by the majority of the populace as quasi-celebrities. Although the excellence they have achieved labels them as the faces of their sports, they receive less attention and ultimately have smaller followings than most males in the same shoes. Female athletes are just as capable and accomplished as the men, yet fans do not give them the chance to prove that they deserve to be admired and followed.

The women's tennis circuit has been plagued by ubiquitous gendered coverage, with greater attention being given to the way women physically look on the tour, compared to men. Therefore, female players struggle with the pressure to look feminine while lobbing a shot over the net or crushing an ace right down the center of the court. Jelena Jankovic, a Serbian player, admits that embracing and enhancing her femininity is part of developing her brand, saying, "Face it, there are fans who like to look at girls in nice tennis dresses" (as cited in Kimmelman, 2010).

Similarly, in the successful 1999 Women's World Cup for soccer, players faced a double standard. In "Two Kicks Forward, One Kick Back," Neal Christopherson, Michelle Janning, and Eileen Diaz McConnell state that these female soccer players, in order to be accepted, had to "exhibit qualities of male athletes, yet retain their femininity" (2002, p. 173). Do you think male players have to consider their looks when preparing for a match? Although things have gotten better and gradually more women are acknowledged as serious contenders, the glass ceiling has yet to be broken; it has only cracked a bit. Female players, although most likely as fit and as talented as most men, must constantly monitor and tailor their persona to fit the stereotypical mold of what a female athlete should look like in the eyes of the image-conscious fans.

Negative stereotypes about women's participation in sports are even more rampant in cheerleading. Most individuals typecast cheerleaders as dumb blond pompom-pushers, attention-hogs with a 1950s veneer who cannot be classified as true athletes. In her 2008 *Newsweek* article "In Defense of Cheering," Jennie Yabroff reports that "unlike more-revered athletes—such as football players or even gymnasts—cheerleaders have to contend with lack of respect from their peers and frequent mockery" (2008). Like other women in sports, cheerleaders are perceived as illegitimate wannabes in short skirts, rather than as athletes. In actuality, 21st-century cheerleaders are "more like extreme athletes: daredevil adrenaline junkies who often perform exhausted or hurt," writes Yabroff. College squads have come a long way since that 1950s stereotype: a good number include men, and some teams perform their feats of midair gymnastics and dance solely in competition (Yabroff, 2008). Yet cheerleaders experience the same intolerance that all women athletes do.

Although it is true that the media's coverage of women's 10 sports has increased, there is a plethora of evidence that male perspectives still dominate American media coverage, leading to less treatment of women's sports. If men and women are competing in sports of the same caliber with the same degree of finesse, then the only fair type of reportage would have to be equal and unbiased accounts. In fact, newspapers' treatment of the 1999 Women's World Cup "contained gendered commentary about women's status in society and focused on the soccer players as women" (Christopherson et al., 2002, p. 175). Christopherson, Janning, and McConnell concluded that this focus on femininity was an effort on the media's part to market the Women's World Cup "to resonate and appeal to men" (2002, p. 184). The authors point out that interest in and coverage of women's participation in "male-appropriate" (i.e., physical and aggressive) sports reached an all-time high at the time of the Cup, surpassing even the popularity of women's basketball (2002, p. 171). However, they also recognize that media coverage of female sporting events is flawed, criticizing "the repeated and somewhat inaccurate framing of the games as a new era for women and women's empowerment" (2002, p. 171). In other words, the media spent more time discussing the event in terms of feminist progress than focusing on the game in and of itself.

Not only is there bias against women's sports in the media, there are also some who believe that women cannot offer valuable insights and opinions when it comes to reporting sports. Female professional sports reporters are often considered nothing more than talking heads who get paid to look pretty. Erin Andrews, an intelligent and well-versed sports journalist, has been constantly objectified throughout her career. Just Google her name and you will be overwhelmed with pictures of her breasts and backside—even nude photos and videos taken through a hotel peephole. It doesn't seem to matter that she can dissect a complicated game of football with the grace of a seasoned pro.

Take it from Andrea Kremer, an NBC football sideline reporter and ESPN's first female correspondent, who has received her share of criticism as a woman commenting on a man's game. In an NPR interview, she asserted, "women have earned their positions. I've always maintained there's not a sports gene that only men possess . . . . It should be, in my opinion, about what do they contribute to a telecast or to a broadcast" (2011). When questioned about the perception that you have to play the game to know it, she told listeners,

> Believe me, there are plenty of male commentators who have never played the game, as well. As far as I'm concerned, you can learn about sports. I mean, when I was a child, God bless my parents. They didn't think it was funny for this little blonde to love football. They were buying me books. They were supporting my interest. And believe me, . . . I hear this all the time. Oh, did you have brothers? Is that why you like sports? No, I like sports because I just have loved it my whole life. (2011)

But not every female sports fan is lucky enough to have sympathetic parents, as Kremer and I do. Although we were born in different decades, we both have had to face the same ominous glass ceiling that stands between us and the world of sports. As a woman, I identify with all women who have been discouraged, disregarded, or disinvited from pursing a passion for sports. Women who are fans, players, and journalists still are the minority group struggling for recognition. We are still lacking a general awareness that sports are not solely male-dominated: Women should be active in sports, and their astute commentary about sports should be given as much clout as that of men.

I go to hockey games for the pure enjoyment of them, so why should I be treated any differently than the men in the arena? I don't travel two hours to a Blue Jackets game and pay an exorbitant amount for a ticket just to spite the men who don't desire my presence. I consider myself a devoted fan; a casual fan would not brave the elements for two hours to get her favorite player's autograph. I get a thrill out of seeing an action-packed period of penalty-filled four-on-four play, dancing to "Tick, Tick, Tick Boom" during intermissions, buying overpriced paraphernalia, eating Skyline cheese conies, and just taking in the ambiance of camaraderie and sportsmanship. I go to hockey games because I love them, and I say that love is reason enough to justify what we do in life. It shouldn't matter who is on the rink, track, or field—what should matter is that they are there because they love the sport just as much as I do.

REFERENCES

Christopherson, N., Janning, M., & McConnell, E. D. (2002). Two kicks forward, one kick back: A content analysis of media discourse on the 1999 Women's World Cup Soccer Championship. *Sociology of Sport Journal*, 19(2), 170–188.

Kimmelman, M. (2010, April 25). How power has transformed women's tennis. *The New York Times Magazine*. Retrieved from www.nytimes.com

Kremer, A. (2011, January 7). Journalist on challenges facing female sports reporters [Radio interview]. In M. Block (Host), *All Things Considered*. Washington, DC: National Public Radio. Retrieved from www.npr.org

Yabroff, J. (2008, March 15). In defense of cheering. *Newsweek*. Retrieved from http://www.newsweek.com

Joining the Conversation

1. According to Sara Maratta, "men still dominate" in the world of sports. What evidence does she provide to support this view?
2. Where does Maratta acknowledge naysayers, and how does she address their views as a way of developing her argument?
3. Felisa Rogers' description of her interest in football (pp. 529–35) provides a contrast to Maratta's discussion of her interest in hockey. How do their views of fandom and the importance of sports differ? Can you find any common ground in their arguments? Which author do you find more persuasive, and why?
4. Do you agree with Sara Maratta? Disagree? Agree *and* disagree? Write an essay setting forth what you think, being careful to frame your argument as a response to what Maratta says.

We, the Public,
Place the Best Athletes on Pedestals

WILLIAM MOLLER

I SPENT MY HIGH SCHOOL YEARS at a boarding school hidden among the apple orchards of Massachusetts. Known for a spartan philosophy regarding the adolescent need for sleep, the school worked us to the bone, regularly slamming us with six hours of homework. I pulled a lot more all-nighters (of the scholastic sort) in my years there than I ever did in college. When we weren't in class, the library, study hall, or formal sit-down meals, we were likely found on a sports field. We also had school on Saturday, beginning at 8 AM just like every other non-Sunday morning.

Adding kindling to the fire, the students were not your laid-back types; everyone wanted that spot at the top of the class,

WILLIAM MOLLER, a financial analyst, contributes regularly to sports blogs dedicated to his hometown team, the New York Yankees, including "It's about the Money" and "The Yankees Dollar," where this article first appeared in May 2009, soon after Yankee Alex Rodriguez had admitted to steroid use. In the original blog post, Moller used hyperlinks to let readers see his sources directly; they appear as footnotes here.

and social life was rife with competition. The type A's that fill the investment banking, legal, and political worlds—those are the kids I spent my high school years with.

And so it was that midway through my sophomore year, I found myself on my third all-nighter in a row, attempting to memorize historically significant pieces of art out of E. H. Gombrich's *The Story of Art*. I had finished a calculus exam the day before, and the day before that had been devoted to world history. And on that one cold night in February, I had had enough. I had hit that point where you've had so little sleep over such a long time that you start seeing spots, as if you'd been staring at a bright light for too long. The grade I would compete for the next day suddenly slipped in importance, and I began daydreaming about how easy the real world would be compared to the hell I was going through.

But there was hope. A friend who I was taking occasional study breaks with read the story in the bags beneath my eyes, in the slump of my shoulders, the nervous drumming of my fingers on the chair as we sipped flat, warm Coke in the common room. My personal *deus ex machina*,* he handed me a small white pill.

I was very innocent. I matured way after most of my peers, 5 and was probably best known for being the kid who took all the soprano solos away from the girls in the choir as a first-year student. I don't think I had ever been buzzed, much less drunk. I'd certainly never smoked a cigarette. And knowing full well that what I was doing could be nothing better than against the rules (and *less* importantly, illegal), I did what I felt I needed

---

*__deus ex machina__ Term from ancient Greek drama (literally, "god from the machine"), referring to an actor playing a god who was mechanically lowered onto the stage in order to intervene on a character's behalf.

to do, to accomplish what was demanded of me. And it worked. I woke up and regained focus like nothing I'd ever experienced. Unfortunately, it also came with serious side effects: I was a hypersensitized, stuffed-up, sweaty, wide-eyed mess, but I studied until the birds started chirping. And I aced my test.

Later I found out the pill was Ritalin, and it was classified as a class 3 drug.* I did it again, too—only a handful of times, as the side effects were so awful. But every time it was still illegal, still against the rules. And as emphasized above, I was much more worried about the scholastic consequences if I were discovered abusing a prescription drug than the fact that I was breaking the law. Though I was using it in a far different manner than the baseball players who would later get caught with it in their systems, it was still very clearly a "performance-enhancing drug."

Just like every other person on this planet, I was giving in to the incentive scheme that was presented to me. The negative of doing poorly on the test was far greater than the negative of getting caught, discounted by the anesthetic of low probability.

I imagine that the same dilemma must have occurred in Alex Rodriguez's subconscious before he made the decision to start taking steroids. Alex has been a phenom in every sense of the word since he was old enough to be labeled an athlete. Who knows if he took steroids in high school—and who cares, really? He did take them in the major leagues, he almost certainly took them before moving to Texas, and there's really no compelling argument that he hasn't been taking them since he moved to New York.

What it really comes down to is that the reason Alex did steroids is you and me. We, the public, place the best athletes

---

*class 3 drug   A drug that is illegal to possess without a prescription.

on pedestals, gods on high. And Alex is a prime candidate for such treatment. He's an archetype, carrying the look of someone who will one day be cast in bronze. He's a physical monstrosity, capable of knocking the ball out of Yankee Stadium with only one hand on the bat. And at the deepest level Alex Rodriguez wants, *craves*, fame. More than that, really, he wants to be loved. He came to New York wanting to erase the memories of Mantle and DiMaggio and Berra.* He wanted to be beautiful and powerful and funny and philanthropic and every other positive adjective he could find.

Really, it was no question whether Alex would take steroids 10 once they were offered. They promised wealth and fame above his wildest dreams. Let's be clear: A-Rod could have been a good player without steroids, maybe even a great player. But he didn't want that. He wanted to be *A-Rod*.

And now the cat is out of the bag. Now that we have a test showing us that A-Rod used, we finally stop turning a blind eye to what was patently obvious before. But only for Alex.

The entire steroid outcry is pure hypocrisy. Look, you and I both understand that the majority of the best players in baseball are steroid users. And so are a good portion of the less-than-best. And when I say that, I do so without adding the negative connotation added by the self-righteous media types who make a living by drumming up indignation from the masses. If it came out that Mariano Rivera and Derek Jeter† were on some sort of designer steroid, I'd be surprised and disappointed, but by no means amazed.

*Mantle and DiMaggio and Berra   All record-breaking Yankees players.
†Mariano Rivera and Derek Jeter   Current Yankees stars.

It's why I wasn't surprised in the slightest when Andy Pettitte admitted to using HGH.* My only disgust with that situation is that he certainly didn't use it once and then get rid of it, as he said. When Pettitte used HGH (which isn't proven to do anything for athletes, by the way) he did it because he didn't think he'd get caught, not because he thought it was acceptable. And there's no reason to believe he really would have stopped after one use.

This all reeks of the attitude taken toward marijuana by politicians until Barack Obama came around. When asked about marijuana use, Bill Clinton's response was typical: "I didn't inhale." When later asked about marijuana in the context of Clinton's response, Obama replied, "Yes, I did . . . The point was to inhale, that was the point."

Just as the vast majority of people try marijuana at some point in their lives, the vast majority of baseball players have used steroids, be it HGH, Stanozolol, the cream, the clear, or any other BALCO creation.[†] This game is all about getting an edge—whether it be the front offices using BABIP[‡] to pick the right players, Sammy Sosa corking a bat, Johnny Damon using

---

*Pettitte and HGH In 2007, after allegations were leaked to the press following a federal investigation, Yankees pitcher Andy Pettitte (b. 1972) admitted to using human growth hormone (HGH) to enhance his athletic performance.

†BALCO The Bay Area Laboratory Cooperative is a San Francisco-based company that was at the center of the Major League Baseball drug scandal. Stanozolol is an anabolic steroid (see http://en.wikipedia.org/wiki/Stanozolol). The cream and the clear are steroids created and distributed by BALCO (see http://en.wikipedia.org/wiki/BALCO_Scandal) [Moller's note].

‡BABIP Batting average on balls in play, one statistic used to gauge a player's abilities.

Baseball Cards 2011

I'LL TRADE YOU ONE OF BARRY BONDS' LAWYER FOR TWO OF HIS GIRLFRIENDS...

MY BASEBALL CAR[D]

DANZIGER
NYTS/CWS Mar 30 2011 (4726)

maple instead of ash bats, K-Rod putting resin on his baseball cap, Pete Rose mixing Adderall* in with a cup of coffee, or Mark McGwire's unabashed andro use. Heck, after Ritalin was outlawed in MLB, the number of baseball players being diagnosed with ADD† (for which Ritalin happens to be prescribed)

---

*Adderall   Until 2006, no rules existed to prevent players from using amphetamines such as Adderall to cause a spike in focus and energy level, and such use was rampant. "Corking a bat": hollowing out a bat and replacing the core with a lighter material, to bring the bat beneath regulation weight and gain an advantage. "Maple instead of ash bats": In 2008, the use of maple bats, which tend to shatter rather than splinter, came under scrutiny for the danger they posed to fielders and fans alike. "Resin": Pitchers are known to sometimes use the brim of their baseball caps to hide banned substances such as pine tar, vasoline, or resin, which affect the movement of the ball [Moller's note].

†ADD   Attention deficit disorder; symptoms include difficulty with staying focused and controlling one's behavior.

jumped significantly! Is it okay, since they have a doctor's script? There's a lot of money and fame at stake, and it skews that all-important incentive scheme.

Each and every general manager in the game shares at least three attributes: They're very smart, and they know exactly what's going on—but act as if they don't. And we the public let ourselves be fooled. What's worse, when enough information comes out that we can no longer ignore that a player used, we demonize them relative to their "untainted" peers. By all accounts, Barry Bonds is a real jerk—which is plenty of reason to dislike him. But don't hate him because he's a "cheater." In that sense, he's just one of the gang.

Back in February of 2000, I got to choose between breaking the rules and breaking my grades. I chose the rules, and it wasn't a tough decision. And I'd wager that the lure of being A-Rod is a bit more seductive than an A on that art history test.

Joining the Conversation

1. William Moller begins his essay on steroid use by telling about his own experiences taking Ritalin to meet the rigorous academic demands of his school. How effective do you find this opening? How does this anecdote relate to the main point of the essay?

2. What reasons and evidence does Moller offer to justify Rodriguez's use of steroids? Does he bring in any naysayers, possible objections to his argument, and attempt to counter them?

3. Moller is identified as the author of a blog about the New York Yankees, his hometown team. How do you think the argument and use of evidence might be different if the essay

were written by a doctor specializing in the effects of medications on the human body?

4. In his concluding paragraph, Moller writes, "I got to choose between breaking the rules and breaking my grades. I chose the rules, and it wasn't a tough decision. And I'd wager that the lure of being A-Rod is a bit more seductive than an A on that art history test." He makes this point to explain and, to some extent, defend the use of performance-enhancing drugs by athletes. Take this same paragraph and rewrite it to support the opposite argument.

5. Moller argues that "the reason Alex did steroids is you and me." How responsible are sports fans for the behavior of professional athletes? Using Moller's position as a "they say," write your own essay in response. Whatever position you take, acknowledge (and answer) objections to what you say.

Cheating and CHEATING

JOE POSNANSKI

—▣—

Above all, the story of Willie Mays reminds us of a time when the only performance-enhancing drug was joy.
　　　　　　　　　　　　　　　　　　　　—*Pete Hamill*

THE ABOVE SENTENCE—which concluded Pete Hamill's *New York Times* review of James Hirsch's excellent Willie Mays book—has been batted around a bit on the Internet the last few days. It has been batted around mainly because, well, with all due respect, it's ridiculous. As more than one person cynically has written, and more than a few hundred cynically have thought: "I didn't know that joy was another word for amphetamines."

Up front, I should say that I love Pete Hamill. He's another writing hero of mine. He, more than almost anyone else I've

JOE POSNANSKI is a senior writer for *Sports Illustrated*. He has twice won the best sports columnist award from the Associated Press Sports Editors. His books include *The Machine: The Story of the 1975 Cincinnati Reds* (2009), *The Soul of Baseball: A Road Trip through Buck O'Neil's America* (2007), and *The Good Stuff: Columns about the Magic of Sports* (2001). This article first appeared in his "Curiously Long Posts" blog on SI.com on March 1, 2010.

read, has a knack for capturing the whiff of smoke and black-and-white charm of a certain time and place and occasion—New York in the 1960s, a rainy night out with Frank Sinatra, the violence and beauty of a Sugar Ray Robinson fight. A Pete Hamill essay on Willie Mays was exactly what I wanted to read on a cold Sunday morning as the days begin to lengthen.

And, sure, I expected romance. That's Hamill. That's Mays. This was going to be a love story, the author never hid from that. He hits you square between the eyes with the first sentence: "A long time ago in America, there was a beautiful game called baseball." Yes. Well. This time was, of course, when men were men, when pitchers finished what they started, when the World Series ended before the chill of autumn turned harsh, when the good teams were all in New York and none were in that vast wasteland west of St. Louis. This was that time, Hamill writes, "long before the innocence of game was permanently stained by the filthy deception of steroids."

And then: "In that vanished time, there was a ballplayer named Willie Mays."

Right. Romance. Well, I think Mays is one of those players ⁵ worthy of myth—he really could do everything. Bill James called him the third greatest player ever—behind only Ruth and Wagner, who played in an era that is hard to compare to our own. Mays's era feels much closer. He could crush long home runs, he could run, he could throw, he could hit, he could field. It's hard to pick one favorite Mays season. It certainly could be 1954, just after he returned from the army, when he led the league in hitting (.345) and slugging (.667—the highest slugging percentage of his career), won the MVP award, and made the most famous catch in World Series history.

But, then again, it could be 1956 when he became the second player—the first since Ken Williams in 1922—to hit 30 homers and steal 30 bases. Thirty-thirty wasn't even a thing then (Mays has often said that if he had known people would have made a big deal out of 40-40, he would have done it a few times), but it came natural to Mays. Then, the best year could be 1957 when Mays hit .333, banged 26 doubles, 20 triples, 35 home runs, stole 38 bases and won the first center field Gold Glove award. Or, the year could involve the slightly older Mays of 1965—he was 34 that year—and he hit 52 home runs (nobody else hit even 40), led the league in on-base percentage, slugging percentage, total bases, and runs created. He won the Gold Glove again that year, the ninth time in a row.

The point is that throughout his career, Willie Mays shook the imagination. I have little doubt that if I had grown up to

Willie Mays

the baseball music of Willie Mays, he would have been a hero. I have little doubt that if I was 20 or 25 years older, I might have written an essay with the sentence "In that vanished time, there was a ballplayer named Willie Mays."

So, no, it wasn't the goo-goo-eyed romance of the essay that got me. I wanted that. No, it was the willful self-deception. Surely, Pete Hamill knows that baseball was never innocent, that America was never innocent, that innocence itself was never innocent.

Baseball in Willie Mays's time, like baseball in every time, was rife with cheating and racism and alcoholism and small-mindedness. You know, people love to talk about the players of the steroid era cheating the game. But did anyone in baseball history more willfully and brashly cheat the game than Leo Durocher and the 1951 Giants, who rigged an elaborate sign-stealing system that undoubtedly helped the Giants catch the Dodgers and win the pennant, win the pennant, win the pennant?

In Hirsch's book, Mays explains away this organized and pre- 10 meditated bit of cheating by saying that stealing signs was "always part of the game—everyone did it." And that if he did steal signs that "they sure didn't help me."

Everyone did it. The cheating didn't help me. Wow, does that sound familiar?

Then there's amphetamines. I have never understood why many people are so outraged about baseball players' steroid use and so unperturbed by amphetamine use. I guess it makes some sense on a gut level—injecting yourself with steroids seems so much more villainous than popping a couple of greenies to get a boost. Steroids seemed much more in our faces as fans. The players unapologetically got bigger. A few of them hit an unnatural number of home runs. There seemed a much more direct cause and effect . . . steroids = bigger muscles = more home runs. And maybe the cause and effect did not seem quite as obvious with the widespread use of amphetamines.

BUT is any of that true? Best I can tell, amphetamines (like steroids) were illegal without prescription in American society but were just a part of the baseball culture. Best I can tell, amphetamines are performance-enhancing drugs that, many people feel, sharpen focus and increase energy levels and help an athlete overcome exhaustion. Best I can tell, amphetamines can have terrible side effects and can be difficult to quit (and can be extremely dangerous to quit).

In other words, it seems more or less the same level of cheating and more or less the same level of wrong. As far as whether amphetamines had a huge effect on the game . . . I don't know. I don't want to throw names out there, but there are records and performances—consecutive games played and huge stolen bases totals just as a for instance—that you could logically connect to amphetamine use. I remember having a conversation with a baseball insider about a player who was quite good for one year and then descended into an abyss.

"What happened?" I asked. 15

"He stopped taking greenies," he said. "He just doesn't have the same spark."

In 1985, John Milner testified that there was some sort of "red juice" in Willie Mays's locker when they both played for the Mets. Milner said that was a liquid amphetamine. Mays would say he got it from a doctor, and the doctor said it was actually cough syrup. There really isn't any more clarity on that issue, but Mays does not deny that he may have used amphetamines as a player. In the book, his quote is as follows:

"My problem was if I could stay on the field. I would go to the doctor and would say to the doctor, 'Hey, I need something to keep me going. Could you give me some sort of vitamin?' I don't know what they put in there, and I never asked a question about anything."

Well . . . there you go. I don't think there's much question based on that quote that Mays used amphetamines in his day. Shoot, just about every player did. Pete Rose did. Hank Aaron admitted trying it. Hirsch, in his own words, believes there's a big difference between steroids and amphetamines—the former, he says, builds muscle mass and enhances performance while the latter "restores energy and allows someone to perform at full strength." That seems to be the argument.

But I think there's a much bigger difference: Steroids were 20 not readily available when Willie Mays played ball.

This is not meant in any way to diminish the great Willie Mays or cheapen the wonderful time when he played baseball. Mays was wonderful. Baseball was wonderful. But they weren't playing baseball on a higher plane of morality in the 1950s or the 1930s or the 1910s. Players were always looking for an edge and more money. Owners were always trying to milk the fans for whatever they could get. There was always a "if you ain't cheating, you ain't trying," vibe in baseball.

And there have always been players who lift us higher. Honus Wagner did, Ty Cobb did, Pete Alexander did, Joe Jackson did, Rogers Hornsby did, Babe Ruth did, Lefty Grove did, Joe DiMaggio did, Ted Williams did, Stan Musial did, Bob Feller did, Jackie Robinson did, Willie Mays did, Sandy Koufax did, Mickey Mantle did, Hank Aaron did, Pete Rose did, Reggie Jackson did, George Brett did, Ozzie Smith did, Greg Maddux did, Barry Bonds did, Mark McGwire did, Roger Clemens did, Pedro Martinez did, Albert Pujols did. They used different bits of motivation. They took advantage of their specific time and place. Some plainly cheated. Some quietly pushed the edge.

Some were self-destructive. Some played it as square as they could.

But when it comes down to it, I guess my big issue with Pete Hamill's romantic essay is there never really was a long-ago time in America when there was a beautiful game called baseball. The game, for better and worse, is as beautiful now as it ever was.

Joining the Conversation

1. Joe Posnanski introduces his essay with a "they say," a position that he discusses in more detail throughout the essay and with which he clearly disagrees. In two or three sentences, summarize the view he is arguing against.
2. Posnanski is highly critical of a position expressed by fellow writer Pete Hamill, yet he states in paragraph 2, "Up front, I should say that I love Pete Hamill. He's another writing hero of mine." What effect does this praise have on how you read the critical comments that follow, and why?
3. This essay does not so much take a position on the ethics of performance-enhancing drugs as it does on attitudes toward baseball's past as opposed to its present. What does Posnanski believe is wrong about the view he is criticizing? Does he agree with it in any sense?
4. In reflecting on the willingness of ballplayers in different eras to gain an edge any way they could, Posnanski echoes a point made by William Moller in the previous piece. Write an essay in which you respond to their views with your own position on this controversial topic.

An aerial view of a new suburban development in 1958.

EIGHTEEN

WHAT'S UP WITH
THE AMERICAN DREAM?

—▱—

IT IS HARD TO IMAGINE anything more fundamental to most Americans than the belief that we are the authors of our own fate—that we are in the driver's seat, particularly when it comes to our economic success. We go to school, study, get jobs, and work hard, all with the assumption that doing so will allow us to achieve financial security, buy that house in the suburbs with the white picket fence, and perhaps even attain great wealth. This faith in the American Dream, in the United States as a land of opportunity, dates back to a claim made in the eighteenth century by the French writer J. Hector St. John de Crevecoeur. He thought that what made the "new American" unique, in contrast to the oppressed classes in monarchical societies, was the opportunity to reap "the rewards of [one's] industry" in direct proportion to "the progress of [one's] labor." Take away this faith that we will be justly rewarded for our hard work, and it might become difficult for many of us to get up in the morning and do our best.

According to several writers in this chapter, this faith in the American Dream has been undermined by a combination of global economic developments and government policies that have perilously widened the gulf between the very rich and the rest of us. Op-ed writer Bob Herbert, journalist Robert Frank, and economist Paul Krugman each highlight how income for the wealthiest Americans has increased while middle and lower incomes have remained stagnant. These writers offer policy recommendations to increase opportunities for all. Cultural studies scholars Constance M. Ruzich and A. J. Grant examine the collapse of the real estate market and the increasing difficulties of obtaining home ownership for less wealthy Americans, while also considering the role of language and the creation of terms such as "predatory lending" in public perceptions of the crisis. Though these writers question whether the dream of equal opportunity ever came true for most Americans in the way that de Crevecoeur suggested, they agree that the last few decades have so shifted the balance of wealth and power to large corporations and the privileged few that even the modest financial security that average Americans dream about is becoming just that: a dream with little chance of realization.

Columnist Cal Thomas, in contrast, replies that these alarmist critiques are unwarranted and that the American Dream is as alive and well as ever. Student Brandon King responds to the pessimistic scenarios by arguing that opportunities for advancement still exist and that economic advancement for the average person will actually increase if only taxes are lowered and government spending is reduced.

A touchstone case of this economic debate is the controversy surrounding the mega-chain Wal-Mart. Journalist Karen Olsson critiques the retail giant for keeping employees' salaries and benefits low in its quest for high profits, while economist Sebastian Mallaby argues that Wal-Mart is only doing what it must to survive in a difficult economy, that Americans want and benefit from the store's low prices, and that its salaries and benefits are better than people may think.

Finally, Barack Obama, in a highly acclaimed speech on race and opportunity delivered during his presidential campaign, argues for the importance of ensuring the continued existence of the American Dream for all despite differences in race, class, and education. As you read this chapter, you will find a variety of perspectives on this vital issue, and you will have a chance to make your own contribution to the ongoing discussion.

Hiding from Reality

BOB HERBERT

—◰—

HOWEVER YOU WANT to define the American dream, there is not much of it that's left anymore.

Wherever you choose to look—at the economy and jobs, the public schools, the budget deficits, the nonstop warfare overseas—you'll see a country in sad shape. Standards of living are declining, and American parents increasingly believe that their children will inherit a very bad deal.

We're in denial about the extent of the rot in the system, and the effort that would be required to turn things around. It will likely take many years, perhaps a decade or more, to get employment back to a level at which one could fairly say the economy is thriving.

BOB HERBERT was an op-ed columnist for the *New York Times* from 1993 until 2011. His column, dedicated to issues such as race and poverty in the United States, was syndicated in many other newspapers. Herbert has taught at Brooklyn College and the Columbia University Graduate School of Journalism. This article first appeared in the *New York Times* on November 19, 2010, and sparked a response by Cal Thomas, which appears on pp. 568–70.

Consider this startling information from the Pew Hispanic Center: in the year following the official end of the Great Recession in June 2009, foreign-born workers in the U.S. gained 656,000 jobs while native-born workers lost 1.2 million. But even as the hiring of immigrants picked up during that period, those same workers "experienced a sharp decline in earnings."

What this shows is not that we should discriminate against foreign-born workers, but that the U.S. needs to develop a full-employment economy that provides jobs for all who want to work at pay that enables the workers and their families to enjoy a decent standard of living. In other words, a resurrection of the American dream.

Right now, nothing close to that is happening.

The human suffering in the years required to recover from the recession will continue to be immense. And that suffering will only be made worse if the nation embarks on a misguided crash program of deficit reduction that in the short term will undermine any recovery, and in the long term will make true deficit reduction that much harder to achieve.

The wreckage from the recession and the nation's mindlessly destructive policies in the years leading up to the recession is all around us. We still don't have the money to pay for the wars that we insist on fighting year after year. We have neither the will nor the common sense to either raise taxes to pay for the wars, or stop fighting them.

State and local governments, faced with fiscal nightmares, are reducing services, cutting their work forces, hacking away at health and pension benefits, and raising taxes and fees. So far it hasn't been enough, so there is more carnage to come. In many cases, the austerity measures are punishing some of the most vulnerable people, including children, the sick and the disabled.

For all the talk about the need to improve the public schools 10
and get rid of incompetent teachers, school systems around the
country are being hammered with dreadful cutbacks and teachers are being let go in droves, not because they are incompetent, but strictly for budget reasons. There was a time when the
United States understood the importance of educating its young
people and led the way in compulsory public schooling. It also
built the finest higher education system in the world. Now,
although no one will admit it publicly, we've decided to go in
another direction.

In New York City, for example, Mayor Michael Bloomberg's
choice to run the public school system is Cathleen Black, a
wealthy corporate executive with no background in education
whose children attended expensive private schools. Mr.
Bloomberg has asserted that Ms. Black's management expertise will be a boon to the city's public school children. But the
truth is that Ms. Black, if she gets a necessary waiver for her
new job, will be presiding over budget cuts that can only hurt
the schools. As part of a proposed austerity budget, the mayor
is planning to eliminate the jobs of thousands of public school
teachers over the next two years. Take that, kids.

We've become a hapless, can't-do society, and it's, frankly,
embarrassing. Public figures talk endlessly about "transforma-
tive changes" in public education, but the years go by and we
see no such thing. Politicians across the spectrum insist that
they are all about job creation while the employment situation
in the real world remains beyond pathetic.

All we are good at is bulldozing money to the very wealthy.
No wonder the country is in such a deep slide.

We don't even seem to realize how deep a hole we're in. If
student test scores jumped a couple of points or the jobless rate
fell by a point and half, the politicians and the news media

would crow as if something great had been achieved. That's how people behave when they're in denial.

America will never get its act together until we recognize 15 how much trouble we're really in, and how much effort and shared sacrifice is needed to stop the decline. Only then will we be able to begin resuscitating the dream.

Joining the Conversation

1. Bob Herbert provides a number of examples of the dismal reality that he wants Americans to focus on. What, in his view, do these examples all have in common?

2. Herbert does not indicate a "they say" in this piece. Think about the topic he writes about. Why would he not state an explicit agrument he's responding to? Would it strengthen his argument to do so?

3. In the next reading in this chapter (pp. 568–70), Cal Thomas responds directly to this piece. If Herbert were to post a comment to Thomas's article on Townhall.com, what might he say?

4. Can you find any naysayers, or possible objections, to Herbert's argument anywhere in his text? If not, try to come up with two or three and figure out where you could introduce them appropriately in his essay.

5. Construct an argument of your own that responds to Herbert's charges and to his call for "a resurrection of the American dream," agreeing with him, disagreeing, or both agreeing and disagreeing. Whatever stand you take, be sure to consider other positions as well as your own, including some of the views expressed in this chapter— Herbert's, Thomas's, Brandon King's, or others.

Is the American Dream Over?

CAL THOMAS

—▭—

FOR GENERATIONS, parents have told their children about
"the American dream." Basically it has meant building a life
based on the foundational principles that created and have
sustained America for more than 200 years. By doing so, one
might reasonably expect a new generation to achieve a better life than their parents and grandparents experienced. But
what defines "better"? In modern times it has been defined as
achieving greater prosperity and consuming more material
goods.

At least one liberal writer is channeling Jimmy Carter,
implying our best days are behind us and this version of the
American dream is over. Writing recently in the *New York
Times*, columnist Bob Herbert says: "However you want to

CAL THOMAS serves as a panelist on *Fox News Watch*, a media criticism program on Fox News. His eleven books include *Blinded by Might:
Can the Religious Right Save America?* (1999), written with Ed Dobson,
and *Common Ground: How to Stop the Partisan War That Is Destroying
America* (2007), written with Bob Beckel. This column, which first
appeared on Townhall.com on November 23, 2010, responds directly
to Bob Herbert's "Hiding from Reality," on pp. 564–67.

define the American dream, there is not much of it that's left anymore. Wherever you choose to look—at the economy and jobs, the public schools, the budget deficits, the nonstop warfare overseas—you'll see a country in sad shape. Standards of living are declining, and American parents increasingly believe that their children will inherit a very bad deal."

Herbert does not assess blame for this, so I will. His version of the American dream—as opposed to the original dream, which remains for those who would embrace it—is over for a very good reason. Setting aside war, which was imposed on America, the eclipse of liberalism's American dream has been largely caused by expanding, encroaching, over-taxing, over-spending, and over-regulating government. This has produced a country of government addicts with an entitlement mentality. These twin maladies have eroded self-reliance, individual initiative, and personal accountability. A monopolistic government school system keeps the poor from achieving their dreams, as many remain locked (thanks to Democrats and their union supporters) in failing government schools, producing graduates (if in fact they do graduate) who lag behind other nations in subjects that matter.

Herbert claims, "We have become a hapless, can't-do society." He says it's "embarrassing." Is it not the politicians who lead a people increasingly dependent on them who are responsible for this? The liberals among them and their policies are leading us down a path to economic and cultural insolvency.

The creation of a government that is out of control, and thus out of touch robs every citizen, preventing fulfillment of the original American dream. 5

Anyone who thinks dysfunctional government is going to help achieve their dreams is putting their faith in the wrong place. People who believe a politician of whatever party or persuasion can make their life better than individual initiative are doing more than dreaming; such persons are displaying cult-like faith, which can never be fulfilled.

The rules for achieving the American dream may no longer be taught in and supported by culture, but that doesn't mean they don't work. The rules are known to previous generations: studying and staying in school; achieving at least an undergraduate degree; avoiding drugs that harm your mind and body; getting married before you have children and working hard to stay married as an example to those children and to benefit society; saving and investing for retirement so as not to burden taxpayers and relatives; living within one's means; demonstrating personal honesty and professional integrity, which comes from character developed in one's youth, usually with a sense of right and wrong once imposed by parents and affirmed by culture.

"America will never get its act together until we recognize how much trouble we're really in," writes Herbert. That's true, but more than acknowledging the obvious is needed. We must also understand what got us here and the path that leads upward. What got us here is unrestrained liberalism. What will get us back on the right path is . . . (see above).

Joining the Conversation

1. Cal Thomas responds directly to the essay by Bob Herbert (pp. 564–67). What is it exactly that Herbert says, and how fairly does Thomas represent that position?
2. Thomas and Herbert have opposing viewpoints on the economy and the American dream. Compare the arguments and evidence each author presents. What if anything do they agree about?

3. Thomas lists "rules for achieving the American dream" in paragraph 7. What obstacles might stand in the way of someone following all these rules? How might Bob Herbert respond to them? Can you think of other rules to add to the list?

4. Thomas poses a question in his title: Is the American dream over? How does he answer that question? What is the main point of his essay?

5. Write an essay summarizing the arguments made by Cal Thomas and Bob Herbert and then saying what you think and why.

The American Dream:
Dead, Alive, or on Hold?

BRANDON KING

—◻—

WHAT IS THE TRUE STATE of the so-called "American Dream" today? Is it still around, waiting to be achieved by those who work hard enough, or is it effectively dead, killed off by the Great Recession and the economic hardships that many Americans have come to face? Statistics reveal alarming facts, including trillions of dollars lost in the stock market (Paradis, 2009). While these losses, combined with admittedly high unemployment in the past few years, have contributed to seemingly dismal prospects for prosperity in the United States, I believe that the ideals and values of the American Dream are still very much alive. In fact, the original term "American Dream" was coined during the Great Depression by James Truslow Adams, who wrote that the American dream "is that

BRANDON KING is studying political science at the University of Cincinnati and plans to attend law school. He has always enjoyed writing pieces related to his major, particularly on the topics of economic inequality and political structures in the United States. He eventually hopes to enter a career in public service. King wrote this essay in 2011, for this book.

dream of a land in which life should be better and richer and fuller for everyone, with opportunity for each according to ability and achievement, regardless of social class or circumstances of birth" (1931). I would redefine the American Dream today as the potential to work for an honest, secure way of life and save for the future. Many liberal economists and activists say that the American Dream is dead, but I say that it's more alive and important than ever—and that it is the key to climbing out of the Great Recession, overcoming inequality, and achieving true prosperity.

Despite the harshness of the Great Recession, a 2009 *New York Times* survey found that 72 percent of Americans still believed it was possible to start poor, work hard, and become rich in America (Seelye, 2009). In the same survey, Americans were also asked questions about what they believed constituted being "successful," with the majority naming things such as a steady job, financial security for the future, being able to retire without struggling, and having a secure place of residence. Less common were responses about owning a home or car and being able to buy other expensive goods, implying a subtle shift from the American Dream of the past to a more modest one today. In many ways, the American Dream of today is a trimmed down version of its former self. The real sign of success in our society used to be owning expensive items, namely cars and homes, and acquiring more material wealth. Living the American Dream meant going from dirt poor to filthy rich and becoming more than you could have ever imagined. Today, most people do not strive for a rags-to-riches transition, and instead prefer a stable, middle-class lifestyle, one in which they can focus on saving money for the future and having secure employment. For example, more and more people now rent their homes instead of buying; a recent study showed a decrease in home ownership from 69% in 2005 to about 66.5% in 2010, and an increase in renter households of 1.1 million (Hoak, 2011). Americans are scrutinizing their spending habits more intensely, as shown in a survey completed in 2009 showing that approximately two-thirds of Americans have permanently changed their spending habits as a result of the Great Recession and that one-fourth hope to save more money for the future (Frietchen, 2009).

Looking at the fragile economy today, it is tempting to focus on the unevenness of the recovery: the stock market has made impressive rebounds in recent months, but the unemployment rate remains high. Thanks to bailouts for large corporations and stimulus measures intended to generate growth, economic activity seems to be on its way towards pre-recession levels, but the economy remains fragile. Weak national real estate markets, sluggish job growth, and the slow recovery of liquid assets lost during the recession are obstacles to a full recovery.

To many, the most worrisome problem is inequality: that wealth is concentrated into the hands of a rich minority. One economist, Robert Reich, even says that "As long as income and wealth keep concentrating at the top, and the great divide between America's have-mores and have-lesses continues to widen, the Great Recession won't end, at least not in the real economy" (Reich, 2009). The essence of Reich's argument is that Wall Street will effectively deter any meaningful recovery on Main Street. Another economist, Paul Krugman, holds a similar position, writing that "The lion's share of economic growth in America over the past thirty years has gone to a small, wealthy minority," and that "the lack of clear economic progress for lower and middle income families is in itself an important reason to seek a more equal distribution of income" (2007). Krugman believes that the American Dream is no longer possible for most Americans, and that the government should enact policies to close the income gap.

We may have genuine inequality issues and a sizable divide 5 between the rich and poor, and we might have an economy that is recovering too slowly for public interest. The American Dream, however, is based on perception, on the way someone *imagines* how to be successful. How can anyone claim that because there are more poor people than rich, or more power and wealth concentrated at the top, that the entire premise of the American Dream is dead? In fact, the safeguards of the welfare system, including the minimum wage and unemployment benefits, were long ago put in place to protect the poorest Americans. During the Great Recession, the federal government decided that raising the minimum wage would stimulate worker productivity and help close the income gap. In reality, however, it has done little to make the poor richer. In fact, raising the minimum wage, which makes labor more expensive, could force companies to cut back and hire fewer workers.

With a different approach to fixing the economy, some economists and politicians argue that supporting the richest sectors of the American economy will bring economic stability and a full recovery. They claim that a sizable income gap does not necessarily prevent individuals in the lower and middle classes from achieving the American Dream. I agree: government funding for Wall Street and struggling businesses makes the economy healthier. I believe that we should keep in mind the ways in which large businesses and financial institutions enable many others to attain economic stability and security. For example, providing money to businesses may encourage them to hire more people, thereby increasing job opportunities. Just last year, President Obama presented a proposal, later passed by Congress, establishing a $33 billion tax credit to provide incentives for businesses to hire more work-ers and increase existing wages (Gomstyn, 2010). Increased sup-port for Wall Street could in this way make the overall economy healthier so that everyone has increased opportunities.

Some, however, argue that raising taxes on the rich and on America's wealthy businesses is an effective means of closing the income gap. For *New York Times* columnist Bob Herbert, our economic problems are the result of bad policy decisions that have led to the rapid migration of American jobs overseas, the degradation of the American education system, and continuous costly wars. His primary point in a recent *New York Times* col-umn was that America "does not have the common sense to raise taxes," his solution to solving inequality issues and achiev-ing greater economic security (2010). Robert Reich and Paul Krugman concur with Herbert's analysis and recommend raising taxes (Krugman, 2007). My question for Herbert is, "Given the Great Recession and the tough economic climate that we con-tinue to live in, would raising taxes still be the prudent thing to do?" Maybe Herbert believes that higher taxes for the rich would help solve the issue of inequality, but in reality, it would not help people achieve the American Dream at all. According to writer Dana Golden (2009), the more wealth the rich accumu-late, the more they will spend it, thereby stimulating the econ-omy. She also points out that the creation of wealth and its subsequent use is one way jobs are created, even in difficult eco-nomic times. Taxing the rich only decreases their spending potential and thus their ability to stimulate the economy.

In contrast to Herbert's bleak view, economist Cal Thomas responds to arguments about inequality issues by arguing that "The rules for achieving the American Dream may no longer be taught and supported by culture, but that doesn't mean that they don't work" (2010). Indeed, the media inundate us with countless images and stories of struggling workers and the growing ranks of the poor while suggesting that the American Dream is simply beyond the grasp of the vast majority of Americans. Thomas's response is that only because of "unrestrained liberalism" are the true means of realizing the American Dream being more and more eroded in our society. Despite the recent recession, Thomas and others like him have faith that as long as people believe they have a chance of becoming better off than they are today, then the American Dream is intact. Instead of trying to interfere with the enterprise that creates jobs and growth, we should rely on the values of the American Dream: that anybody can climb out of hardship and achieve success. Only then will the American Dream remain alive for future generations.

Just last year, a newspaper editor in Atlanta stated that, "the Great Recession didn't kill the American Dream. But the promise of a good life in exchange for hard, honest work has been bruised and frayed for millions of middle class Americans" (Chapman, 2010). The idea of the American Dream has in fact suffered in recent years, although it is my belief that this is not new. As a nation, we have dealt with economic downturns in the past, and the American Dream has faced trials and tests before. The economic panics of the late 1970s and after the 9/11 terrorist attacks are both prime examples. Even since the height of the Great Recession, however, we have adapted the values contained within the American Dream to meet new challenges. Of course, some will be quick to say that these changes have only come about as a result of the greed and corruption of the rich and powerful. Like laissez-faire economists and Wall Street supporters, however, I believe that it is necessary and imperative to continue supporting the business mechanisms that sustain our economy. The American Dream will continue to exist as part of the American psyche, not artificially stimulated by government regulations to change income distribution. If the Great Recession has taught us anything, it is that planning for the future by saving more and enacting policies that sustain economic growth are what will keep the American Dream alive.

REFERENCES*

Adams, J. T. (1931). *Epic of America.* Boston: Little, Brown.

Chapman, D. (2010, December 10). American dream deferred, not dead. *Atlanta Journal-Constitution.* Retrieved from http://www.ajc.com/

Frietchen, C. (2009, October 24). Imagining yourself post-recession: Survey shows spending-habit changes [Web log post]. *Productopia: A World Without Buyer's Remorse.* Retrieved from http://www.consumersearch. com/blog/imagining-yourself-post-recession-survey-shows-spending-habit-changes#

Golden, D. (2009, January 10). The economy, credit and trickle down economics (the ripple effect). *EzineArticles.* Retrieved from http://ezinearticles.com/?The-Economy,-Credit-and-Trickle-Down-Economics-(The-Ripple-Effect)&id=1865774

Gomstyn, A. (2010, January 29). Obama announces $33B hiring tax credit. *ABC News.* Retrieved from http://abcnews.go.com/

Herbert, B. (2010). Hiding from reality. *The New York Times.* Retrieved from http://www.nytimes.com/

Hoak, A. (2011, February 8). More people choosing to rent, not buy, their home. *MarketWatch.* Retrieved from http://www.marketwatch.com/

Krugman, P. (2007). *The conscience of a liberal.* New York, NY: Norton.

Paradis, T. (2009, October 10). The statistics of the great recession. *Huffington Post.* Retrieved from http://www.huffingtonpost.com/

Reich, R. (2009, December 27). 2009: The year Wall Street bounced back and Main Street got shafted. *Huffington Post.* Retrieved from http://www.huffingtonpost.com/

*Based on the APA style of documentation.

Seelye, K. (2009, May 7). What happens to the American Dream in a
    recession? *The New York Times.* Retrieved from http://www.nytimes.com/
Thomas, C. (2010, November 23). Is the American Dream over? *Townhall.*
    Retrieved from http://townhall.com/columnists/CalThomas/2010/11/23/
    is_the_american_dream_over

Joining the Conversation

1. How does Brandon King redefine the American Dream? How does the redefinition affect his argument?
2. Summarize King's argument in this essay. What reasons and evidence does he use to support his views? How persuasive do you find his argument?
3. How does King connect the various parts of his essay? Look in particular at the beginnings and endings of paragraphs. What sorts of transitions and other connecting devices does King use? If you find places where he needs a transition or other device, supply it and explain why you think it improves the essay.
4. How well does King introduce and explain Paul Krugman's views on inequality and taxation? How thoroughly does he respond?
5. Write an essay responding to King's argument about the American Dream from your own perspective—as a student, as a worker, or both.

Income Inequality:
Too Big to Ignore

ROBERT H. FRANK

———◙———

PEOPLE OFTEN REMEMBER the past with exaggerated fondness. Sometimes, however, important aspects of life really were better in the old days.

During the three decades after World War II, for example, incomes in the United States rose rapidly and at about the same rate—almost 3 percent a year—for people at all income levels. America had an economically vibrant middle class. Roads and bridges were well maintained, and impressive new infrastructure was being built. People were optimistic.

By contrast, during the last three decades the economy has grown much more slowly, and our infrastructure has fallen into

ROBERT H. FRANK teaches at Cornell University and writes monthly columns on economic issues for the *New York Times*. His books include *The Economic Naturalist's Field Guide: Common Sense Principles for Troubled Times* (2009), *Falling Behind: How Rising Inequality Harms the Middle Class* (2007), and many economics textbooks. This essay appeared in the *New York Times* on October 16, 2010.

grave disrepair. Most troubling, all significant income growth has been concentrated at the top of the scale. The share of total income going to the top 1 percent of earners, which stood at 8.9 percent in 1976, rose to 23.5 percent by 2007, but during the same period, the average inflation-adjusted hourly wage declined by more than 7 percent.

For tips on using transitions to connect the details of an argument, see Chapter 8

Yet many economists are reluctant to confront rising income inequality directly, saying that whether this trend is good or bad requires a value judgment that is best left to philosophers. But that disclaimer rings hollow. Economics, after all, was founded by moral philosophers, and links between the disciplines remain strong. So economists are well positioned to address this question, and the answer is very clear.

Adam Smith,* the father of modern economics, was a pro- 5 fessor of moral philosophy at the University of Glasgow. His first book, "A Theory of Moral Sentiments," was published more than 25 years before his celebrated "Wealth of Nations," which was itself peppered with trenchant moral analysis.

Some moral philosophers address inequality by invoking principles of justice and fairness. But because they have been unable to forge broad agreement about what these abstract principles mean in practice, they've made little progress. The more pragmatic cost-benefit approach favored by Smith has proved more fruitful, for it turns out that rising inequality has created enormous losses and few gains, even for its ostensible beneficiaries.

Recent research on psychological well-being has taught us that beyond a certain point, across-the-board spending

---

*Adam Smith Scottish economist (1723–90).

increases often do little more than raise the bar for what is considered enough. A C.E.O. may think he needs a 30,000-square-foot mansion, for example, just because each of his peers has one. Although they might all be just as happy in more modest dwellings, few would be willing to downsize on their own.

People do not exist in a social vacuum. Community norms define clear expectations about what people should spend on interview suits and birthday parties. Rising inequality has thus spawned a multitude of "expenditure cascades," whose first step is increased spending by top earners.

The rich have been spending more simply because they have so much extra money. Their spending shifts the frame of reference that shapes the demands of those just below them, who travel in overlapping social circles. So this second group, too, spends more, which shifts the frame of reference for the group just below it, and so on, all the way down the income ladder. These cascades have made it substantially more expensive for middle-class families to achieve basic financial goals.

In a recent working paper based on census data for the 100 [10] most populous counties in the United States, Adam Seth Levine (a postdoctoral researcher in political science at Vanderbilt University), Oege Dijk (an economics Ph.D. student at the European University Institute), and I found that the counties where income inequality grew fastest also showed the biggest increases in symptoms of financial distress.

For example, even after controlling for other factors, these counties had the largest increases in bankruptcy filings.

Divorce rates are another reliable indicator of financial distress, as marriage counselors report that a high proportion of couples they see are experiencing significant financial problems. The counties with the biggest increases in inequality also reported the largest increases in divorce rates.

Another footprint of financial distress is long commute times, because families who are short on cash often try to make ends meet by moving to where housing is cheaper—in many cases, farther from work. The counties where long commute times had grown the most were again those with the largest increases in inequality.

The middle-class squeeze has also reduced voters' willingness to support even basic public services. Rich and poor alike endure crumbling roads, weak bridges, an unreliable rail system, and cargo containers that enter our ports without scrutiny. And many Americans live in the shadow of poorly maintained dams that could collapse at any moment.

Economists who say we should relegate questions about inequal- 15
ity to philosophers often advocate policies, like tax cuts for the
wealthy, that increase inequality substantially. That greater
inequality causes real harm is beyond doubt.

But are there offsetting benefits?

There is no persuasive evidence that greater inequality bolsters economic growth or enhances anyone's well-being. Yes,
the rich can now buy bigger mansions and host more expensive parties. But this appears to have made them no happier.
And in our winner-take-all economy, one effect of the growing inequality has been to lure our most talented graduates to
the largely unproductive chase for financial bonanzas on Wall
Street.

In short, the economist's cost-benefit approach—itself long
an important arrow in the moral philosopher's quiver—has
much to say about the effects of rising inequality. We need not
reach agreement on all philosophical principles of fairness to
recognize that it has imposed considerable harm across the
income scale without generating significant offsetting benefits.

No one dares to argue that rising inequality is required in
the name of fairness. So maybe we should just agree that it's a
bad thing—and try to do something about it.

Joining the Conversation

1. This article, from the *New York Times* Sunday Business Section, makes an argument about the increasingly unequal
   income levels of Americans. What is Robert Frank's claim,
   and how does he show that the topic is important?
2. Frank invokes Adam Smith, the eighteenth-century founder
   of the modern field of economics, in discussing income

inequality. Why does he bring up Smith, and how do the ideas of this classic economist support the author's own argument?

3. In paragraph 8, Frank discusses what he calls "expenditure cascades." What does he mean by this term, and why does he believe that the phenomenon he is describing plays an important role in the nation's financial crisis?

4. Compare Frank's argument with that of Constance Ruzich and A. J. Grant, on pp. 624–45 of this chapter. In what ways do Frank's views differ from Ruzich and Grant's? Can you find any points on which these authors would be likely to agree?

5. The author cites statistics in paragraph 3 showing that the share of total income going to the top 1 percent of earners tripled from 1976 to 2007, while average wages declined (when adjusted for inflation) during this same period. Take the perspective of a person in that top 1 percent, and write an essay arguing against the view that the increasing disparity in Americans' incomes is a bad thing.

Confronting Inequality

PAUL KRUGMAN

—⌐⌐—

THE AMERICA I GREW UP IN was a relatively equal middle-class society. Over the past generation, however, the country has returned to Gilded Age levels of inequality. In this chapter I'll outline policies that can help reverse these changes. I'll begin with the question of values. Why should we care about high and rising inequality?

One reason to care about inequality is the straightforward matter of living standards. The lion's share of economic growth in America over the past thirty years has gone to a small, wealthy minority, to such an extent that it's unclear whether the typical family has benefited at all from technological progress and the rising productivity it brings. The lack of clear economic progress for lower- and middle-income families is in itself an important reason to seek a more equal distribution of income.

PAUL KRUGMAN teaches economics at Princeton and writes an op-ed column in the *New York Times*. He was awarded the Nobel Prize in Economics in 2008. Krugman is the author of many books, among them *The Age of Diminished Expectations* (1989) and *The Great Unraveling: Losing Our Way in the New Century* (2003). "Confronting Inequality" is a chapter from his 2007 book, *The Conscience of a Liberal*.

Beyond that, however, is the damage extreme inequality does to our society and our democracy. Ever since America's founding, our idea of ourselves has been that of a nation without sharp class distinctions—not a leveled society of perfect equality, but one in which the gap between the economic elite and the typical citizen isn't an unbridgeable charm. That's why Thomas Jefferson wrote, "The small landholders are the most precious part of a state."[1] Translated into modern terms as an assertion that a broad middle class is the most precious part of a state, Jefferson's statement remains as true as ever. High inequality, which has turned us into a nation with a much-weakened middle class, has a corrosive effect on social relations and politics, one that has become ever more apparent as America has moved deeper into a new Gilded Age.

The Costs of Inequality

One of the best arguments I've ever seen for the social costs of inequality came from a movement conservative trying to argue the opposite. In 1997 Irving Kristol, one of the original neoconservative intellectuals, published an article in the *Wall Street Journal* called "Income Inequality Without Class Conflict." Kristol argued that we shouldn't worry about income inequality, because whatever the numbers may say, class distinctions are, in reality, all but gone. Today, he asserted,

> income inequality tends to be swamped by even greater social equality. . . . In all of our major cities, there is not a single restaurant where a CEO can lunch or dine with the absolute assurance that he will not run into his secretary. If you fly first class, who will be your traveling companions? You never know. If you go to

Paris, you will be lost in a crowd of young people flashing their credit cards.[2]

By claiming that income inequality doesn't matter because See p. 60 on using someone else's evidence to support your position. we have social equality, Kristol was in effect admitting that income inequality *would* be a problem if it led to social inequality. And here's the thing: It does. Kristol's fantasy of a world in which the rich live just like you and me, and nobody feels socially inferior, bears no resemblance to the real America we live in.

Lifestyles of the rich and famous are arguably the least important part of the story, yet it's worth pointing out that Kristol's vision of CEOs rubbing shoulders with the middle class is totally contradicted by the reporting of Robert Frank of the *Wall Street Journal*, whose assigned beat is covering the lives of the wealthy. In his book *Richistan* Frank describes what he learned:

A couple and their two dogs board a private jet in Aspen, Colorado.

Today's rich had formed their own virtual country. . . . [T]hey had built a self-contained world unto themselves, complete with their own health-care system (concierge doctors), travel network (Net Jets, destination clubs), separate economy. . . . The rich weren't just getting richer; they were becoming financial foreigners, creating their own country within a country, their own society within a society, and their economy within an economy.[3]

The fact is that vast income inequality inevitably brings vast social inequality in its train. And this social inequality isn't just a matter of envy and insults. It has real, negative consequences for the way people live in this country. It may not matter much that the great majority of Americans can't afford to stay in the eleven-thousand-dollar-a-night hotel suites popping up in luxury hotels around the world.[4] It matters a great deal that millions of middle-class families buy houses they can't really afford, taking

Crowds of passengers at O'Hare International Airport in Chicago.

on more mortgage debt than they can safely handle, because they're desperate to send their children to a good school—and intensifying inequality means that the desirable school districts are growing fewer in number, and more expensive to live in.

Elizabeth Warren, a Harvard Law School expert in bankruptcy, and Amelia Warren Tyagi, a business consultant, have studied the rise of bankruptcy in the United States. By 2005, just before a new law making it much harder for individuals to declare bankruptcy took effect, the number of families filing for bankruptcy each year was five times its level in the early 1980s. The proximate reason for this surge in bankruptcies was that families were taking on more debt—and this led to moralistic pronouncements about people spending too much on luxuries they can't afford. What Warren and Tyagi found, however, was that middle-class families were actually spending *less* on luxuries than they had in the 1970s. Instead the rise in debt mainly reflected increased spending on housing, largely driven by competition to get into good school districts. Middle-class Americans have been caught up in a rat race, not because they're greedy or foolish but because they're trying to give their children a chance in an increasingly unequal society.[5] And they're right to be worried: A bad start can ruin a child's chances for life.

Americans still tend to say, when asked, that individuals can make their own place in society. According to one survey 61 percent of Americans agree with the statement that "people get rewarded for their effort," compared with 49 percent in Canada and only 23 percent in France.[6] In reality, however, America has vast inequality of opportunity as well as results. We may believe that anyone can succeed through hard work and determination, but the facts say otherwise.

There are many pieces of evidence showing that Horatio 10 Alger stories are very rare in real life. One of the most striking comes from a study published by the National Center for Education Statistics, which tracked the educational experience of Americans who were eighth graders in 1988. Those eighth graders were sorted both by apparent talent, as measured by a mathematics test, and by the socioeconomic status of their parents, as measured by occupations, incomes, and education.

The key result is shown in Table 1. Not surprisingly, both getting a high test score and having high-status parents increased a student's chance of finishing college. But family status mattered more. Students who scored in the bottom fourth on the exam, but came from families whose status put them in the top fourth—what we used to call RDKs, for "rich dumb kids," when I was a teenager—were more likely to finish college than students who scored in the top fourth but whose parents were in the bottom fourth. What this tells us is that the idea that we have anything close to equality of opportunity is clearly a fantasy. It would be closer to the truth, though not the whole truth, to say that in modern America, class—inherited class—usually trumps talent.

Isn't that true everywhere? Not to the same extent. International comparisons of "intergenerational mobility," the extent to which people can achieve higher status than their parents, are tricky because countries don't collect perfectly

TABLE 1. PERCENTAGE OF 1988 EIGHTH GRADERS FINISHING COLLEGE

	SCORE IN BOTTOM QUARTILE	SCORE IN TOP QUARTILE
Parents in Bottom Quartile	3	29
Parents in Top Quartile	30	74

Source: National Center for Education Statistics, *The Condition of Education 2003*, 47.

comparable data. Nonetheless it's clear that Horatio Alger has moved to someplace in Europe: Mobility is highest in the Scandinavian countries, and most results suggest that mobility is lower in the United States than it is in France, Canada, and maybe even Britain. Not only don't Americans have equal opportunity, opportunity is less equal here than elsewhere in the West.

It's not hard to understand why. Our unique lack of universal health care, all by itself, puts Americans who are unlucky in their parents at a disadvantage: Because American children from low-income families are often uninsured, they're more likely to have health problems that derail their life chances. Poor nutrition, thanks to low income and a lack of social support, can have the same effect. Life disruptions that affect a child's parents can also make upward mobility hard—and the weakness of the U.S. social safety net makes such disruptions more likely and worse if they happen. Then there's the highly uneven quality of U.S. basic education, and so on. What it all comes down to is that although the principle of "equality of opportunity, not equality of results" sounds fine, it's a largely fictitious distinction. A society with highly unequal results is, more or less inevitably, a society with highly unequal opportunity, too. If you truly believe that all Americans are entitled to an equal chance at the starting line, that's an argument for doing something to reduce inequality.

America's high inequality, then, imposes serious costs on our society that go beyond the way it holds down the purchasing power of most families. And there's another way in which inequality damages us: It corrupts our politics. "If there are men in this country big enough to own the government of the United States," said Woodrow Wilson in 1913, in words that would be almost inconceivable from a modern president, "they are going to own it."[7] Well, now there are, and they do. Not completely, of course, but hardly a week goes by without the disclosure of a case in which the influence of money has grotesquely distorted U.S. government policy.

As this book went to press, there was a spectacular exam- 15 ple: The way even some Democrats rallied to the support of hedge fund managers, who receive an unconscionable tax break. Through a quirk in the way the tax laws have been interpreted, these managers—some of whom make more than a billion dollars a year—get to have most of their earnings taxed at the capital gains rate, which is only 15 percent, even as other high earners pay a 35 percent rate. The hedge fund tax loophole costs the government more than $6 billion a year in lost revenue, roughly the cost of providing health care to three million children.[8] Almost $2 billion of the total goes to just twenty-five individuals. Even conservative economists believe that the tax break is unjustified, and should be eliminated.[9]

Yet the tax break has powerful political support—and not just from Republicans. In July 2007 Senator Charles Schumer of New York, the head of the Democratic Senatorial Campaign Committee, let it be known that he would favor eliminating the hedge fund loophole only if other, deeply entrenched tax breaks were eliminated at the same time. As everyone understood, this was a "poison pill," a way of blocking reform without explicitly saying no. And although Schumer denied it, everyone also suspected that his position was driven by the large sums hedge funds contribute to Democratic political campaigns.[10]

The hedge fund loophole is a classic example of how the concentration of income in a few hands corrupts politics. Beyond that is the bigger story of how income inequality has reinforced the rise of movement conservatism, a fundamentally undemocratic force. Rising inequality has to an important extent been caused by the rightward shift of our politics, but the causation also runs the other way. The new wealth of the rich has increased their influence, sustaining the institutions of movement conservatism and pulling the Republican Party even further into the movement's orbit. The ugliness of our politics is in large part a reflection of the inequality of our income distribution.

More broadly still, high levels of inequality strain the bonds that hold us together as a society. There has been a long-term downward trend in the extent to which Americans trust either the government or one another. In the sixties, most Americans agreed with the proposition that "most people can be trusted"; today most disagree.[11] In the sixties, most Americans believed that the government is run "for the benefit of all"; today, most believe that it's run for "a few big interests."[12] And there's convincing evidence that growing inequality is behind our growing cynicism, which is making the United States seem increasingly like a Latin American country. As the political scientists Eric Uslaner and Mitchell Brown point out (and support with extensive data), "In a world of haves and have-nots, those at either end of the economic spectrum have little reason to believe that 'most people can be trusted' . . . social trust rests on a foundation of economic equality."[13]

The Arithmetic of Equalization

Suppose we agree that the United States should become more like other advanced countries, whose tax and benefit systems do much more than ours to reduce inequality. The next question is what that decision might involve.

In part it would involve undoing many of the tax cuts for 20 the wealthy that movement conservatives have pushed through since 1980. Table 2 shows what has happened to three tax rates that strongly affect the top 1 percent of the U.S. population, while having little effect on anyone else. Between 1979 and 2006 the top tax rate on earned income was cut in half; the tax rate on capital gains was cut almost as much; the tax rate on corporate profits fell by more than a quarter. High incomes in America are much less taxed than they used to be. Thus raising taxes on the rich back toward historical levels can pay for part, though only part, of a stronger safety net that limits inequality.

The first step toward restoring progressivity to the tax system is to let the Bush tax cuts for the very well off expire at the end of 2010, as they are now scheduled to. That alone would raise a significant amount of revenue. The nonpartisan Urban-Brookings Joint Tax Policy Center estimates that letting the Bush tax cuts expire for people with incomes over two hundred thousand dollars would be worth about $140 billion a year starting in 2012. That's enough to pay for the subsidies needed to implement universal health care. A tax-cut rollback of this kind, used to finance health care reform, would significantly reduce inequality. It would do so partly by modestly reducing incomes

TABLE 2. THREE TOP RATES (PERCENTAGE)

	TOP TAX ON EARNED INCOME	TOP TAX ON LONG-TERM CAPITAL GAINS	TOP TAX ON CORPORATE PROFITS
1979	70	28	48
2006	35	15	35

Source: Urban-Brookings Tax Policy Center <http://taxpolicycenter.org/taxfacts/ tfdb/tftemplate.cfm>.

at the top: The Tax Policy Center estimates that allowing the Bush tax cuts to expire for Americans making more than two hundred thousand dollars a year would reduce the aftertax incomes of the richest 1 percent of Americans by about 4.5 percent compared with what they would be if the Bush tax cuts were made permanent. Meanwhile middle- and lower-income Americans would be assured of health care—one of the key aspects of being truly middle class.[14]

Another relatively easy move from a political point of view would be closing some of the obvious loopholes in the U.S. system. These include the rule described earlier that allows financial wheeler-dealers, such as hedge fund managers, to classify their earnings as capital gains, taxed at a 15 percent rate rather than 35 percent. The major tax loopholes also include rules that let corporations, drug companies in particular, shift recorded profits to low-tax jurisdictions overseas, costing billions more; one recent study estimates that tax avoidance by multinationals costs about $50 billion a year.[15]

Going beyond rolling back the Bush cuts and closing obvious loopholes would be a more difficult political undertaking. Yet there can be rapid shifts in what seems politically realistic. At the end of 2004 it seemed all too possible that Social Security, the centerpiece of the New Deal, would be privatized and effectively phased out. Today Social Security appears safe, and universal health care seems within reach. If universal health care can be achieved, and the New Deal idea that government can be a force for good is reinvigorated, things that now seem off the table might not look so far out.

Both historical and international evidence show that there is room for tax increases at the top that go beyond merely rolling back the Bush cuts. Even before the Bush tax cuts, top tax rates in the United States were low by historical standards—

the tax rate on the top bracket was only 39.6 percent during the Clinton years, compared with 70 percent in the seventies and 50 percent even *after* Reagan's 1981 tax cut. Top U.S. tax rates are also low compared with those in European countries. For example, in Britain, the top income tax rate is 40 percent, seemingly equivalent to the top rate of the Clinton years. However, in Britain employers also pay a social insurance tax— the equivalent of the employer share of FICA* here—that applies to all earned income. (Most of the U.S. equivalent is levied only on income up to a maximum of $97,500.) As a result very highly paid British employees face an effective tax rate of almost 48 percent. In France effective top rates are even higher. Also, in Britain capital gains are taxed as ordinary income, so that the effective tax rate on capital gains for people with high income is 40 percent, compared with 15 percent in the United States.[16] Taxing capital gains as ordinary income in the United States would yield significantly more revenue, and also limit the range of tax abuses like the hedge fund loophole.

Also, from the New Deal until the 1970s it was considered normal and appropriate to have "super" tax rates on very-high-income individuals. Only a few people were subject to the 70 percent top bracket in the 70s, let alone the 90 percent plus top rates of the Eisenhower years. It used to be argued that a surtax on very high incomes serves no real purpose other than punishing the rich because it wouldn't raise much money, but that's no longer true. Today the top 0.1 percent of Americans, a class with a minimum income of about $1.3 million and an average income of about $3.5 million, receives more than 7 percent of

*FICA   Federal Insurance Contributions Act, an employment tax that helps fund Social Security and Medicare.

all income—up from just 2.2 percent in 1979.[17] A surtax on that income would yield a significant amount of revenue, which could be used to help a lot of people. All in all, then, the next step after rolling back the Bush tax cuts and implementing universal health care should be a broader effort to restore the progressivity of U.S. taxes, and use the revenue to pay for more benefits that help lower- and middle-income families.

Realistically, however, this would not be enough to pay for social expenditures comparable to those in other advanced countries, not even the relatively modest Canadian level. In addition to imposing higher taxes on the rich, other advanced countries also impose higher taxes on the middle class, through both higher social insurance payments and value-added taxes—in effect, national sales taxes. Social insurance taxes and VATs are not, in themselves, progressive. Their effect in reducing inequality is indirect but large: They pay for benefits, and these benefits are worth more as a percentage of income to people with lower incomes.

As a political matter, persuading the public that middle-income families would be better off paying somewhat higher taxes in return for a stronger social safety net will be a hard sell after decades of antitax, antigovernment propaganda. Much as I would like to see the United States devote another 2 or 3 percent of GDP* to social expenditure beyond health care, it's probably an endeavor that has to wait until liberals have established a strong track record of successfully using the government to make peoples' lives better and more secure. This is one reason health care reform, which is tremendously important in itself, would have

---

*GDP Gross domestic product. One measure of income and output for a country's economy.

further benefits: It would blaze the trail for a wider progressive agenda. This is also the reason movement conservatives are fiercely determined not to let health care reform succeed.

Reducing Market Inequality

Aftermarket policies can do a great deal to reduce inequality. But that should not be our whole focus. The Great Compression[†] also involved a sharp reduction in the inequality of market income. This was accomplished in part through wage controls during World War II, an experience we hope won't be repeated. Still, there are several steps we can take.

The first step has already been taken: In 2007 Congress passed the first increase in the minimum wage within a decade. In the 1950s and 1960s the minimum wage averaged about half of the average wage. By 2006, however, the purchasing power of the minimum wage had been so eroded by inflation that in real terms it was at its lowest point since 1955, and was only 31 percent of the average wage. Thanks to the new Democratic majority in Congress, the minimum is scheduled to rise from its current $5.15 an hour to $7.25 by 2009. This won't restore all the erosion, but it's an important first step.

There are two common but somewhat contradictory objec- 30 tions often heard to increasing the minimum wage. On one hand, it's argued that raising the minimum wage will reduce employment and increase unemployment. On the other it's argued that raising the minimum will have little or no effect in raising wages. The evidence, however, suggests that a minimum wage increase will in fact have modest positive effects.

[†]See paragraph 40.

On the employment side, a classic study by David Card of Berkeley and Alan Krueger of Princeton, two of America's best labor economists, found no evidence that minimum wage increases in the range the United States has experienced led to job losses.[18] Their work has been furiously attacked both because it seems to contradict Econ 101 and because it was ideologically disturbing to many. Yet it has stood up very well to repeated challenges, and new cases confirming its results keep coming in. For example, the state of Washington has a minimum wage almost three dollars an hour higher than its neighbor Idaho; business experiences near the state line seem to indicate that, if anything, Washington has gained jobs at Idaho's expense. "Small-business owners in Washington," reported the *New York Times*, "say they have prospered far beyond their expectation. . . . Idaho teenagers cross the state line to work in fast-food restaurants in Washington."

All the empirical evidence suggests that minimum wage increases *in the range that is likely to take place* do not lead to significant job losses. True, an increase in the minimum wage to, say, fifteen dollars an hour would probably cause job losses, because it would dramatically raise the cost of employment in some industries. But that's not what's on—or even near—the table.

Meanwhile minimum wage increases can have fairly significant effects on wages at the bottom end of the scale. The Economic Policy Institute estimates that the worst-paid 10 percent of the U.S. labor force, 13 million workers, will gain from the just-enacted minimum wage increase. Of these, 5.6 million are currently being paid less than the new minimum wage, and would see a direct benefit. The rest are workers earning more than the new minimum wage, who would benefit from ripple effects of the higher minimum.

The minimum wage, however, matters mainly to low-paid workers. Any broader effort to reduce market inequality will have to do something about incomes further up the scale. The most important tool in that respect is likely to be an end to the thirty-year tilt of government policy against unions.

The drastic decline in the U.S. union movement was not, 35 as is often claimed, an inevitable result of globalization and increased competition. International comparisons show that the U.S. union decline is unique, even though other countries faced the same global pressures. Again, in 1960 Canada and the United States had essentially equal rates of unionization, 32 and 30 percent of wage and salary workers, respectively. By 1999 U.S. unionization was down to 13 percent, but Canadian unionization was unchanged. The sources of union decline in America lie not in market forces but in the political climate created by movement conservatism, which allowed employers to engage in union-busting activities and punish workers for supporting union organizers. Without that changed political climate, much of the service economy—especially giant retailers like Wal-Mart—would probably be unionized today.

A new political climate could revitalize the union movement—and revitalizing unions should be a key progressive goal. Specific legislation, such as the Employee Free Choice Act, which would reduce the ability of employers to intimidate workers into rejecting a union, is only part of what's needed. It's also crucial to enforce labor laws already on the books. Much if not most of the antiunion activity that led to the sharp decline in American unionization was illegal even under existing law. But employers judged, correctly, that they could get away with it.

The hard-to-answer question is the extent to which a newly empowered U.S. union movement would reduce inequality.

International comparisons suggest that it might make quite a lot of difference. The sharpest increases in wage inequality in the Western world have taken place in the United States and in Britain, both of which experienced sharp declines in union membership. (Britain is still far more unionized than America, but it used to have more than 50 percent unionization.) Canada, although its economy is closely linked to that of the United States, appears to have had substantially less increase in wage inequality—and it's likely that the persistence of a strong union movement is an important reason why. Unions raise the wages of their members, who tend to be in the middle of the wage distribution; they also tend to equalize wages among members. Perhaps most important, they act as a countervailing force to management, enforcing social norms that limit very high and very low pay even among people who aren't union members. They also mobilize their members to vote for progressive policies. Would getting the United States back to historical levels of unionization undo a large part of the Great Divergence? We don't know—but it might, and encouraging a union resurgence should be a major goal of progressive policy.

A reinvigorated union movement isn't the only change that could reduce extreme inequalities in pay. A number of other factors discouraged very high paychecks for a generation after World War II. One was a change in the political climate: Very high executive pay used to provoke public scrutiny, congressional hearings, and even presidential intervention. But that all ended in the Reagan years.

Historical experience still suggests that a new progressive majority should not be shy about questioning private-sector pay when it seems outrageous. Moral suasion was effective in the past, and could be so again.

Another Great Compression?

The Great Compression, the abrupt reduction in economic 40
inequality that took place in the United States in the 1930s
and 1940s, took place at a time of crisis. Today America's state
is troubled, but we're not in the midst of a great depression or
a world war. Correspondingly, we shouldn't expect changes as
drastic or sudden as those that took place seventy years ago.
The process of reducing inequality now is likely to be more of
a Great Moderation than a Great Compression.

Yet it is possible, both as an economic matter and in terms
of practical politics, to reduce inequality and make America a
middle-class nation again. And now is the time to get started.

NOTES

1. Thomas Jefferson, letter to James Madison, 28 Oct. 1785 <http://press-pubs.uchicago.edu/founders/documents/v1ch15s32.html>.

2. Irving Kristol, "Income Inequality Without Class Conflict," *Wall Street Journal* 18 Dec. 1997: A22.

3. Robert Frank, *Richistan: A Journey Through the American Wealth Boom and the Lives of the New Rich* (Crown, 2007) 3–4.

4. "Suites for the Sweet," *Newsweek International* July 2–9 <http://www.msnbc.msn.com/id/19388720/site/newsweek>, part of a special report on "Secret Habits of the Super Rich."

5. Elizabeth Warren and Amelia Warren Tyagi, "What's Hurting the Middle Class," *Boston Review* (Sept./Oct. 2005) <http://bostonreview.net/BR30.5/warrentyagi.html>.

6. Tom Hertz, *Understanding Mobility in America* (Center for American Progress, 2006) <http://www.americanprogress.org/issues/2006/04/b1579981.html>.

7. Woodrow Wilson, *The New Freedom* (Doubleday, 1913), Project Gutenberg <http://www.gutenberg.org/files/14811/14811-h/14811-h.htm>.

8. "Tax Breaks for Billionaires," Economic Policy Institute Policy Memorandum no. 120 <http://www.epi.org/content.cfm/pm120>.

9. See, for example, Jessica Holzer, "Conservatives Break with GOP Leaders on a Tax Bill," *The Hill* 18 July 2007 <http://thehill.com/leading-the-news/conservatives-break-with-gop-leaders-on-a-tax-bill-2007-07-18.html>.

10. "In Opposing Tax Plan, Schumer Supports Wall Street Over Party," *New York Times* 30 July 2007: A1.

11. Eric M. Uslaner and Mitchell Brown, "Inequality, Trust, and Civic Engagement," *American Politics Research* 33.6 (2005): 868–94.

12. *The ANES Guide to Public Opinion and Electoral Behavior*, table 5A.2 <http://electionstudies.org/nesguide/toptable/tab5a_2.htm>.

13. Uslaner and Brown, "Inequality, Trust, and Civic Engagement."

14. Tax Policy Center, "Options to Extend the 2001–2006 Tax Cuts, Static Impact on Individual Income and Estate Tax Liability and Revenue ($ billions), 2008–17," Table T07-0126 <http://taxpolicycenter.org/TaxModel/tmdb/Content/PDF/T07-0126.pdf>.

15. Kimberly A. Clausing, "Multinational Firm Tax Avoidance and U.S. Government Revenue" (working paper, Wellesley College, Wellesley, MA, 2007).

16. OECD Tax Database <http://www.oecd.org/ctp/taxdatabase>.

17. Piketty and Saez, 2005 preliminary estimates <http://elsa.berkeley.edu/~saez/TabFig2005prel.xls>.

18. David Card and Alan B. Krueger, "Minimum Wages and Employment: A Case Study of the Fast-Food Industry in New Jersey and Pennsylvania," *American Economic Review* 84.4 (1994): 772–93.

Joining the Conversation

1. Krugman begins by asking the "so what?" question in paragraph 1: "Why should we care about high and rising inequality?" How does he answer this question?

2. What evidence does Krugman provide for the prevalence of economic inequality in U.S. society? How convincing is this evidence to you?

3. Notice how many direct quotations Krugman includes. Why do you think he includes so many? What, if anything, do

the quotations contribute that a summary or paraphrase would not?

4. In paragraph 4 Krugman quotes someone whose views he does not agree with, but then uses those views to support his own argument. How do you know he is quoting a view that he disagrees with?

5. Write an essay responding to Krugman, agreeing with him on some points and disagreeing with him on others. Start by summarizing his arguments before moving on to give your own views. See guidelines on pp. 64–66 that will help you to agree and disagree simultaneously.

Up Against Wal-Mart

KAREN OLSSON

—▱—

JENNIFER MCLAUGHLIN IS 22, has a baby, drives a truck, wears wide-leg jeans and spiky plastic chokers, dyes her hair dark red, and works at Wal-Mart. The store in Paris, Texas—Wal-Mart Supercenter #148—is just down the road from the modest apartment complex where McLaughlin lives with her boyfriend and her one-year-old son; five days a week she drives to the store, puts on a blue vest with "How May I Help You?" emblazoned across the back, and clocks in. Some days she works in the Garden Center and some days in the toy department. The pace is frenetic, even by the normally fast-paced standards of retailing; often, it seems, there simply aren't enough people around to get the job done. On a given shift McLaughlin might

KAREN OLSSON is a senior editor at *Texas Monthly* and has also written for *Slate*, the *Washington Post*, and the *New York Times Magazine*. She is the author of the novel *Waterloo* (2005) and has won awards from the Association of Alternative Newsweeklies for her investigative reporting and feature stories. "Up Against Wal-Mart" appeared in the March/April 2003 issue of *Mother Jones*, a nonprofit magazine with a commitment to social justice that boasts of a tradition of "smart, fearless" investigative reporting.

man a register, hop on a mechanical lift to retrieve something from a high shelf, catch fish from a tank, run over to another department to help locate an item, restock the shelves, dust off the bike racks, or field questions about potting soil and lawn mowers. "It's stressful," she says. "They push you to the limit. They just want to see how much they can get away with without having to hire someone else."

Then there's the matter of her pay. After three years with the company, McLaughlin earns only $16,800 a year. "And I'm considered high-paid," she says. "The way they pay you, you cannot make it by yourself without having a second job or someone to help you, unless you've been there for 20 years or you're a manager." Because health insurance on the Wal-Mart plan would deduct up to $85 from her biweekly paycheck of $550, she goes without, and relies on Medicaid to cover her son, Gage.

Complaints about understaffing and low pay are not uncommon among retail workers—but Wal-Mart is no mere peddler of saucepans and boom boxes. The company is the world's largest retailer, with $220 billion in sales, and the nation's largest private employer, with 3,372 stores and more than 1 million hourly workers. Its annual revenues account for 2 percent of America's entire domestic product. Even as the economy has slowed, the company has continued to metastasize, with plans to add 800,000 more jobs worldwide by 2007.

Given its staggering size and rapid expansion, Wal-Mart increasingly sets the standard for wages and benefits throughout the U.S. economy. "Americans can't live on a Wal-Mart paycheck," says Greg Denier, communications director for the United Food and Commercial Workers International Union (UFCW). "Yet it's the dominant employer, and what they pay will be the future of working America." The average hourly worker at Wal-Mart earns barely $18,000 a year at a company that pocketed $6.6 billion in profits last year. Forty percent of employees opt not to receive coverage under the company's medical plan, which costs up to $2,844 a year, plus a deductible. As Jennifer McLaughlin puts it, "They're on top of the Fortune 500, and I can't get health insurance for my kid." Angered by the disparity between profits and wages, thousands of former and current employees like McLaughlin have started to fight the company on a variety of fronts. Workers in 27 states are suing Wal-Mart for violating wage-and-hour laws; in the first of the cases to go to trial, an Oregon jury found the company guilty in December of systematically forcing employees to work overtime without pay. The retailer also faces a sex-discrimination lawsuit that accuses it of wrongly denying promotions and equal pay to 700,000 women. And across the country, workers have launched a massive drive to organize a union at Wal-Mart, demanding better wages and working conditions. Employees at more than 100 stores in 25 states—including Supercenter #148 in Paris—are currently trying to unionize the company, and in July the UFCW launched an organizing blitz in the Midwest, hoping to mobilize nearly 120,000 workers in Michigan, Kentucky, Ohio, and Indiana.

Wal-Mart has responded to the union drive by trying to stop 5 workers from organizing—sometimes in violation of federal labor law. In 10 separate cases, the National Labor Relations Board has ruled that Wal-Mart repeatedly broke the law by interrogating workers, confiscating union literature, and firing union supporters. At the first sign of organizing in a store, Wal-Mart dispatches a team of union busters from its headquarters in Bentonville, Arkansas, sometimes setting up surveillance cameras to monitor workers. "In my 35 years in labor relations, I've never seen a company that will go to the lengths that Wal-Mart goes to, to avoid a union," says Martin Levitt, a management consultant who helped the company develop its anti-union tactics before writing a book called *Confessions of a Union Buster*. "They have zero tolerance."

The retaliation can be extreme. In February 2000, the meat-cutting department at a Wal-Mart in Jacksonville, Texas, voted to join the UFCW—the only Wal-Mart in the nation where workers successfully organized a union. Two weeks after the vote, the company announced it was eliminating its meat-cutting departments in all of its stores nationwide. It also fired four workers who voted for the union. "They held a meeting and said there was nothing we could do," recalls Dotty Jones, a former meat cutter in Jacksonville. "No matter which way the election went, they would hold it up in court until we were old and gray."

If you've seen one Wal-Mart, you've seen the Paris store, more or less: a gray cinder-block warehouse of a building, with a red stripe across the front, flags on the roof, WAL-MART spelled in large capitals in the center, and the company credos ("We Sell for Less" and "Everyday Low Prices") to the left and the right. Inside, the cavernous store is bathed in a dim fluorescent light that makes the white walls and linoleum look dingy, and on a Friday shortly before Christmas, the merchandise is everywhere: not only in bins and on shelves, but in boxes waiting to be unloaded, or just stationed in some odd corner, like the pine gun cabinets ($169.87) lined up by the rest rooms. Television monitors advertise thermometers and compact discs. Christmas carols play over the audio system, and yet there's a kind of silence to the place, a suspension of ordinary life, as shoppers in their trances drift through the store and fill carts with tubs of popcorn, a microwave, a chess set, dog biscuits. Here Protestant thrift and consumer wants are reconciled, for the moment anyway, in carts brimming with bargains.

Wal-Mart's success story was scripted by its founder, Sam Walton, whose genius was not so much for innovation as for picking which of his competitors' innovations to copy in his own stores. In 1945, Walton bought a franchise variety store in Newport, Arkansas. The most successful retailers, he noticed, were chains like Sears and A&P, which distributed goods to stores most efficiently, lowered prices to generate a larger volume of sales, and in the process generated a lot of cash to finance further expansion. These, in turn, would serve as basic principles of Walton's business. As he explains in his autobiography, *Sam Walton, Made in America,* he drove long distances to buy ladies' panties at lower prices, recognizing that selling more pairs at four for a dollar would bring greater profits than selling fewer pairs at three for a dollar. The women of northeastern Arkansas were soon awash in underwear, and a discounter was born. Walton opened his first Wal-Mart Discount City in 1962 and gradually expanded out from his Arkansas base. By 1970 Wal-Mart owned 32 outlets; by 1980 there were 276; by 1990, 1,528 in 29 states.

The company grew, in no small part, by dint of its legendary frugality—a habit that started with Sam Walton himself, who drove an old pickup truck and shared hotel rooms on company trips and insisted on keeping the headquarters in Arkansas as plain as possible. Payroll, of course, tends to be a rather larger expense than hotel rooms, and Walton kept that as low as he could, too. He paid his first clerks 50 to 60 cents an hour—substantially below minimum wage at the time—by taking questionable advantage of a small-business exemption to the Fair Labor Standards Act. In 1970, Walton fended off an organizing push by the Retail Clerks Union in two small Missouri towns by hiring a professional union buster, John Tate, to lecture workers on the negative aspects of unions. On Tate's advice, he also took steps to win his workers over, encouraging them to air concerns with managers and implementing a profit-sharing program.

A few years later, Wal-Mart hired a consulting firm named 10 Alpha Associates to develop a "union avoidance program." Martin Levitt, the consultant who worked on the program, says that Wal-Mart does "whatever it takes to wear people down and destroy their spirit." Each manager, he says, is taught to take union organizing personally: "Anyone supporting a union is slapping that supervisor in the face." The company also encouraged employees to believe in the good intentions of "Mr. Sam," who peppered his autobiography with tributes to his "associates": "If you want to take care of the customers you have to make sure you're taking care of the people in the stores."

Yet many Wal-Mart workers allege that the company Walton left behind when he died in 1992 is anything but a benevolent caretaker. "We're underpaid, and I'm worried about my retirement," says an overnight stocker in Minnesota who asked not to be identified. "I imagine I'll be working until I'm 90." Her daughter works as a stocker, too, but after nine years she doesn't make enough to support her children. "She's had to go down to the food bank, and I've sent stuff over for them," her mother says. "They just can't do it." On the job, she adds, workers are forced to scramble to make up for understaffing. "We're short—we have a skimpy crew at night. We've got pallets stacked over our heads, and we can't get caught up with all of it."

A quick look around at the store in Paris makes clear what an employee is up against: thousands of items (90,000 in a typical Wal-Mart) that customers are constantly removing from the shelves and not putting back, or putting back in the wrong place, or dropping on the floor—the store a kind of Augean stable,* with a corps of blue-vested Herculeses trying to keep things clean. (When I mention this to Jennifer McLaughlin, she tells me that's why no one likes to work the 2 a.m. to 11 a.m. shift, because "all it is, is putting stuff back.") To get the job done, according to the dozens of employee lawsuits filed against the company, Wal-Mart routinely forces employees to work overtime without pay. In the Oregon wage-and-hour case, a former personnel manager named Carolyn Thiebes testified that supervisors, pressured by company headquarters to keep payroll low, regularly deleted hours from time records and rep-

*__Augean stable__ In Greek mythology, a huge stable belonging to King Augeas that Hercules cleaned in a single day as part of his Twelve Labors.

rimanded employees who claimed overtime. In 2000, Wal-Mart settled similar lawsuits involving 67,000 workers in New Mexico and Colorado, reportedly paying more than $50 million.

Wal-Mart blames unpaid overtime on individual department managers, insisting that such practices violate company policy. "We rely on our associates," says spokesman Bill Wertz. "It makes no business sense whatsoever to mistreat them." But Russell Lloyd, an attorney representing Wal-Mart employees in Texas, says the company "has a pattern throughout all stores of treating their workers the same way." Corporate headquarters collects reams of data on every store and every employee, he says, and uses sales figures to calculate how many hours of labor it wants to allot to each store. Store managers are then required to schedule fewer hours than the number allotted, and their performance is monitored in daily reports back to Bentonville. To meet the goals, supervisors pressure employees to work extra hours without pay.

"I was asked to work off the clock, sometimes by the store manager, sometimes by the assistant manager," says Liberty Morales Serna, a former employee in Houston. "They would know you'd clocked out already, and they'd say, 'Do me a favor. I don't have anyone coming in—could you stay here?' It would be like four or five hours. They were understaffed, and they expected you to work these hours."

When Judy Danneman, a widow raising three children, 15 went to work as an hourly department manager, in West Palm Beach, Florida, she quickly realized that she would have to climb the management ladder in order to survive—because, as she puts it, "my kids had this bad habit of eating." The only way to do that, she says, was to work off the clock: "Working unpaid overtime equaled saving your job." When she finally became an assistant manager, Danneman knew she had to enforce the same policy: "I knew for my department managers to get their work done, they had to work off the clock. It was an unwritten rule. The majority of them were single mothers raising children, or else married women with children. It was sad, and it was totally demanding and very draining and very stressful."

In fact, more than two-thirds of all Wal-Mart employees are women—yet women make up less than 10 percent of top store managers. Back when she was first lady of Arkansas, Hillary Clinton became the first woman appointed to the Wal-Mart board, and tried to get the company to hire more women managers, but that effort apparently went the way of national health insurance. Wal-Mart today has the same percentage of women in management that the average company had in 1975.

Attorneys representing workers contend that Wal-Mart is too tightly controlled from headquarters in Arkansas to claim ignorance of what's happening in its stores. "In Bentonville they control the air conditioning, the music, and the freezer temperature for each store," says Brad Seligman, a lawyer with the Impact Fund, a nonprofit legal organization in Berkeley. "Most companies divide stores into regions, and then you have a home office of senior management. At Wal-Mart, the regional managers are based in Bentonville; they're on the road Sunday to Wednesday, and then back meeting with management Thursday to Saturday. They're the ones who make the fundamental employee decisions—and the home office knows exactly what they are doing."

The company insists it adequately trains and promotes female managers. But in 2001, a Wal-Mart executive conducted an internal study that showed the company pays female store managers less than men in the same position. "Their focus at Wal-Mart has always relentlessly been on the bottom line and on cost cutting," says Seligman. "Virtually every other consideration is secondary—or third or fourth or fifth."

To protect the bottom line Wal-Mart is as aggressive at fighting off unions as it is at cutting costs. Employees approached by co-workers about joining a union are "scared to even talk," says Ricky Braswell, a "greeter" at the store in Paris. "They're afraid they'll lose their jobs."

In Paris, it was Jennifer McLaughlin's boyfriend, 21-year-old 20 Eric Jackson, who first started talking about a union. Raised by a mother who works in a factory, Jackson always assumed he would find a job after high school rather than go on to college. But the few factory jobs in Paris are highly sought after, so Jackson wound up at Wal-Mart, which employs 350 people out of a local workforce of only 22,000. "People ain't got no other place to go," he says. "There's no other jobs to be had."

Jackson started as an evening cashier earning $5.75 an hour, and it wasn't long before he was regularly asked to perform the duties of a customer service manager, supervising the other cashiers and scheduling their breaks. He asked for a promotion, but three months later he was still doing the extra work for no extra pay. "I took it because I wanted more money, but I never got the raise," Jackson says. "They knew they could do it to me." He fought for the promotion and eventually won, but by then he had already contacted a local union office about organizing the store.

"When Eric first suggested it, I looked at him like he was on crack," says McLaughlin. "I said, 'You can't take down a company like Wal-Mart with a union.'" Nevertheless, Jackson arranged for a UFCW organizer to come to Paris and meet with a small group of workers one June afternoon at the Pizza Inn. But the company soon caught wind of the organizing effort. As one worker left an early meeting of union supporters, he spotted a Wal-Mart manager in the parking lot. From then on, workers seen as pro-union were watched closely by management.

"By the time we had our first meeting, they were holding their first anti-union meeting," says McLaughlin. The response came straight from the company's union-avoidance playbook: Troops from the Bentonville "People Division" were flown in, and employees were required to attend hour-long meetings, where they were shown anti-labor videos and warned about unions. "They tend to treat you like you're simple, and they use real bad scare tactics," says McLaughlin. Those who supported the union, she says, were told, "Some people just don't belong at Wal-Mart."

McLaughlin isn't shy about speaking her mind, and in the meeting she confronted one of the men from the People Division. "Let me tell you, I used to have epilepsy," she told him. "My dad was in a union, and we had health insurance, and I got better. I don't have health insurance. If my child got epilepsy, what would I do? Doesn't a union help you to get company-paid insurance?" The man, she recalls, became flustered. "Jennifer, I don't have an answer about that," he said. "I'll have to get back with you."

The meetings were just beginning. "The videos and group 25 meetings are the surface cosmetics," says Levitt, the former consultant. "Where Wal-Mart beats the union is through a one-on-one process implemented from Bentonville. They carefully instruct management to individually work over each employee who might be a union sympathizer." In Paris, Eric Jackson was called into a back room by five managers and made to watch an anti-union video and participate in a role-playing exercise. "I was supposed to be a manager, and one of them was the associate who came to me with a question about a union," says

Jackson. "So I quoted the video. I said, 'We do not believe we need a union at Wal-Mart,' and they were like, 'Good, good!' and then I said, 'We're not anti-union—we're pro-associate,' just like I'm supposed to say."

Before the onslaught by the company, says McLaughlin, she talked to more than 70 workers at the Paris store who were prepared to sign cards calling for a vote on union representation, but that number quickly dwindled. Those who'd signed cards felt they were being watched. "All of a sudden the cameras start going up," says Chris Bills, who works in the receiving area. "Now there's three in receiving. This one manager took up smoking so he could sit with us on our breaks." Other hourly employees learned for the first time that they were actually counted as managers. "They said we were considered management, so we shouldn't get involved with the union stuff," says Dianne Smallwood, a former customer service manager who worked at the store seven years. Employees opposed to the union were given "pro-associate" buttons to wear, while managers amended the dress code to exclude T-shirts with any kind of writing on them, apparently to prevent workers from wearing union shirts.

Wal-Mart declined to let *Mother Jones* interview store managers or representatives from the People Division in Bentonville, but says it sends out people from corporate headquarters "to answer questions associates may have and to make sure that all store personnel are aware of their legal requirements and meet those requirements exactly." But the company has also made clear that keeping its stores union-free is as much a part of Wal-Mart culture as door greeters and blue aprons. "Union representation may work well for others," says Cynthia Illick, a company spokeswoman. "However, it is not a fit for Wal-Mart."

With the company so determined to ward off unions, the prospects of employees in towns like Paris, Texas, winning significant improvements in wages and working conditions seem awfully slim. "It's a long process," Jennifer McLaughlin concedes. "I wish it could be done in the next year, but people come and go, and for every one union card you get signed, two others ones who signed cards have gotten fired or left. It's real frustrating, and a lot of times I don't want to do it no more. But I'm not going to give up until I end up leaving the store."

In the end, the success of the organizing drives may depend on labor's ability to mobilize more than just store employees. "We'll never bring Wal-Mart to the table store by store," says Bernie Hesse, an organizer for UFCW Local 789 in Minneapolis. "I can get all the cards signed I want, and they'll still crush us. They'll close the frigging store, I'm convinced. We've got to do it in conjunction with the community." That means going to small businesses and religious leaders and local officials, he says, and convincing them that it's in their interest to stand up to Wal-Mart. "As a community we've got to say, 'All right, if you want to come here and do business, here's what you've got to do—you've got to pay a living wage, you've got to provide affordable health insurance.'"

See pp. 44–49 on framing quotations to support your argument.

Putting together such a broad initiative can be "like pulling teeth," Hesse says, but the stakes are high. If employees succeed in improving wages and working conditions at the country's largest employer, they could effectively set a new benchmark for service-sector jobs throughout the economy. Some 27 million Americans currently make $8.70 an hour or less—and by the end of the decade, Hesse notes, nearly 2 million people worldwide will work at Wal-Mart.

"These are the jobs our kids are going to have," he says.

Joining the Conversation

1. This article opens with two paragraphs describing the life of one Wal-Mart employee. How does the opening pave the way for the discussion that follows?

2. This selection comes from *Mother Jones,* a magazine that tends to be pro-union. Go through the article and find examples of pro-union and anti-union discussion. How can you tell which examples represent the author's point of view and which represent opposing viewpoints?

3. Karen Olsson provides many facts and much personal testimony to support her argument against Wal-Mart. How well does she consider positions other than her own? What naysayers does she include?

4. Notice how many quotations this article includes. What do the quotations add to the argument? Try rewriting one or two paragraphs that include direct quotations, replacing the quotations with summaries. How does this change affect the argument? What if anything can you conclude about quoting and summarizing?

5. It's clear that the author assumes her audience is sympathetic to her pro-union viewpoint. What if she were arguing on behalf of Wal-Mart employees to an audience of Wal-Mart executives—how would her argument be different? Try revising several paragraphs to reach those executives.

Progressive Wal-Mart. Really.

SEBASTIAN MALLABY

—▢—

THERE'S A COMIC SIDE to the anti-Wal-Mart campaign brewing in Maryland and across the country. Only by summoning up the most naive view of corporate behavior can the critics be shocked—shocked!—by the giant retailer's machinations. Wal-Mart is plotting to contain health costs! But isn't that what every company does in the face of medical inflation? Wal-Mart has a war room to defend its image! Well, yeah, it's up against a hostile campaign featuring billboards, newspaper ads, and a critical documentary movie. Wal-Mart aims to enrich shareholders and put rivals out of business! Hello? What business doesn't do that?

Wal-Mart's critics allege that the retailer is bad for poor Americans. This claim is backward: As Jason Furman of New York University puts it, Wal-Mart is "a progressive success

SEBASTIAN MALLABY is a columnist for the *Washington Post* and the former Washington bureau chief for the *Economist*. He is also a fellow at the Council on Foreign Relations. Mallaby has written *The World's Banker: A Story of Failed States, Financial Crises, and the Wealth and Poverty of Nations* (2004) and is currently writing a book on hedge funds. "Progressive Wal-Mart. Really." appeared in the *Washington Post* on November 28, 2005.

story." Furman advised John "Benedict Arnold" Kerry in the 2004 campaign and has never received any payment from Wal-Mart; he is no corporate apologist. But he points out that Wal-Mart's discounting on food alone boosts the welfare of American shoppers by at least $50 billion a year. The savings are possibly five times that much if you count all of Wal-Mart's products.

These gains are especially important to poor and moderate-income families. The average Wal-Mart customer earns $35,000 a year, compared with $50,000 at Target and $74,000 at Costco. Moreover, Wal-Mart's "everyday low prices" make the biggest difference to the poor, since they spend a higher proportion of income on food and other basics. As a force for poverty relief, Wal-Mart's $200 billion-plus assistance to consumers may rival many federal programs. Those programs are better targeted at the needy, but they are dramatically smaller. Food stamps were worth $33 billion in 2005, and the earned-income tax credit was worth $40 billion.

Set against these savings for consumers, Wal-Mart's alleged suppression of wages appears trivial. Arindrajit Dube of the University of California at Berkeley, a leading Wal-Mart critic, has calculated that the firm has caused a $4.7 billion annual loss of wages for workers in the retail sector. This number is disputed: Wal-Mart's pay and benefits can be made to look good or bad depending on which other firms you compare them to. When Wal-Mart opened a store in Glendale, Arizona, last year, it received 8,000 applications for 525 jobs, suggesting that not everyone believes the pay and benefits are unattractive.

But let's say we accept Dube's calculation that retail work- 5 ers take home $4.7 billion less per year because Wal-Mart has busted unions and generally been ruthless. That loss to workers would still be dwarfed by the $50 billion-plus that Wal-Mart consumers save on food, never mind the much larger sums that they save altogether. Indeed, Furman points out that the wage suppression is so small that even its "victims" may be better off. Retail workers may take home less pay, but their purchasing power probably still grows thanks to Wal-Mart's low prices.

To be fair, the $4.7 billion of wage suppression in the retail sector excludes Wal-Mart's efforts to drive down wages at its suppliers. *Wal-Mart: The High Cost of Low Price*, the new anti-Wal-Mart movie that's circulating among activist groups, has the requisite passage about Chinese workers getting pennies per day, sweating to keep Wal-Mart's shelves stocked with cheap clothing. But no study has shown whether Wal-Mart's tactics actually do suppress wages in China or elsewhere, and suppression seems unlikely in poor countries. The Chinese garment workers are mainly migrants from farms, where earnings are even worse than at Wal-Mart's subcontractors and where the labor is still more grueling.

Wal-Mart's critics also paint the company as a parasite on taxpayers, because 5 percent of its workers are on Medicaid.

For tips on acknowledging and answering objections, see Chapter 6. Actually that's a typical level for large retail firms, and the national average for all firms is 4 percent. Moreover, it's ironic that Wal-Mart's enemies, who are mainly progressives, should even raise this issue. In the 1990s progressives argued loudly for the reform that allowed poor Americans to keep Medicaid benefits even if they had a job. Now that this policy is helping workers at Wal-Mart, progressives shouldn't blame the company. Besides, many progressives favor a national health system. In other words, they attack Wal-Mart for having 5 percent of its workers receive health care courtesy of taxpayers when the policy that they support would increase that share to 100 percent.

Companies like Wal-Mart are not run by saints. They can treat workers and competitors roughly. They may be poor stewards of the environment. When they break the law they must be punished. Wal-Mart is at the center of the globalized, technology-driven economy that's radically increased American inequality, so it's not surprising that it has critics. But globalization and business innovation are nonetheless the engines of progress; and if that sounds too abstract, think of the $200 billion-plus that Wal-Mart consumers gain annually. If critics prevent the firm from opening new branches, they will prevent ordinary families from sharing in those gains. Poor Americans will be chief among the casualties.

Joining the Conversation

1. This article defends the retail giant Wal-Mart against a variety of criticisms. What arguments in particular is Sebastian Mallaby responding to here?
2. How exactly does the author respond to what critics of Wal-Mart say? Does he agree? Disagree? Agree and disagree? Give specific examples from the text.
3. Does Mallaby anticipate any possible objections to his position? How does he do so, and how effective is he in this regard? Can you come up with other objections? How fair would you say he is in representing the objections?
4. Read the article by Karen Olsson on pp. 606–18. How do you think Olsson would respond to Mallaby's argument? How might Mallaby respond to Olsson?
5. Mallaby concludes by saying that "If critics prevent [Wal-Mart] from opening new branches, they will prevent ordinary families from sharing in those gains. Poor Americans will be chief among the casualties." Respond with an essay of your own, using this quotation as your "they say."

Predatory Lending
and the Devouring of
the American Dream

CONSTANCE M. RUZICH AND A. J. GRANT

—◻—

WHAT IS THE VALUE of the American Dream? How will the worth of that dream be altered after absorbing hundreds of billions of dollars in losses incurred from the subprime mortgage crisis, along with the accompanying rising unemployment, global stock market declines, and forecast recession? And in what ways has the term *predatory lending* shaped perceptions and attitudes of the subprime mortgage crisis, giving rise to images of large, avaricious institutions gobbling up not only American homeowners, but the American Dream itself?

Subprime mortgages are home loans made at higher rates of interest to borrowers who represent higher credit risks and have lower credit scores (Retsinas and Belsky, *Building Assets* 138).

CONSTANCE M. RUZICH teaches at Robert Morris University in Pittsburgh and is the author of a textbook, *The Challenge of Effective Speaking*. **A. J. GRANT** also teaches at Robert Morris. His research focuses on writing in academic disciplines and the history of communications. This article first appeared in the *Journal of American Culture* in 2009.

Ten years ago, few Americans had heard of subprime mortgages or predatory lending, but by 2008, a survey of economists had identified the effects of the mortgage crisis as the number one threat to the U.S. economy, greater than that of terrorism or conflict in the Middle East (Crutsinger A10). The roots of the subprime mortgage crisis are tangled with the housing boom of the 1990s. As Edward Gramlich, economics professor and former member of the Board of Governors of the Federal Reserve, explains in *Subprime Mortgages: America's Latest Boom and Bust*, a number of factors combined to increase the number of loans made to borrowers who had previously been considered poor credit risks: changing federal government laws and policies changed mortgage practices and actively sought to increase homeownership opportunities for minorities and immigrants (including legislation such as the Depository Institutions Deregulatory and Monetary Control Act of 1980 and the Community Reinvestment Act); technological changes in the loan application and approval process expedited the awarding of mortgages; the number of institutions offering securitization of mortgages increased dramatically; and the American economy had been relatively free of recession and inflation since the early 1980s, causing housing values to rise with the economy (4–5). Gramlich's analysis indicates the rapid rise of the subprime loan industry:

> . . . in 1994, subprime mortgage originations were $35 billion, less than 5 percent of total mortgage originations. By 2005, subprime mortgage originations had risen to $625 billion, 20 percent of total originations . . . . a whopping 26 percent annual rate of increase over the whole decade. From being essentially nonexistent in 1994, subprime mortgages are now 7 percent of the total mortgage stock. (6)

As a result of the increase in subprime loans, total home-ownership rates in the United States also rose, and the increase in homeownership was particularly sharp among minorities and those from lower-income levels. As Gramlich notes,

> From 1994 to 2005, the overall ownership rate rose from 64 to 69 percent. The rate for blacks rose from 42 to 49 percent. . . . The rate for Hispanics went from 42 to 50 percent. . . . The rate for households indicating more than one race rose from 52 to 60 percent. . . . The rate for homeowners in the lowest tenth of the income distribution rose from 39 to 43 percent, in the second tenth from 45 to 49 percent. (3–4)

With the dramatic increase in homeownership and in subprime lending, a tipping point was reached. The rate of defaults on subprime home loans was greater than that of prime mortgages, a fact that perhaps should not have been unexpected in loans made to those with less favorable credit histories, but by 2006, the defaults on subprime loans occurred in numbers that created a cascading effect of foreclosures and bankruptcies, not only affecting individual home loans, but the financial stability of the lending organizations themselves (Bajaj and Creswell C1). Initially estimated at over $150 billion in 2006 (House-Layton 1), the global costs of the subprime mortgage crisis have continually been revised upward. In March of 2008, USB Securities estimated that the global costs would reach $600 billion (Hamilton C1), but by October 2008, the International Monetary Fund was predicting that the global costs would double that figure before the crisis had ended (Banyard 18). And ubiquitous in stories covering the crisis has been the use of the term *predatory lending*, a label

used to describe the practices of institutions who wrote subprime home mortgages.

Examining Predatory Lending

The term *predatory lending* contains an implicit metaphor, one
which we will argue has shaped Americans' understandings of
and responses to the subprime mortgage crisis. One of the reasons that the metaphor is worth closer examination is that
predatory lending has no standard legal definition in the United
States (Callaway; Sichelman; United States). While politicians, bankers, and consumer advocates have used the term
as a catch-all phrase to describe illegal activities in the mortgage industry, it is widely acknowledged that some practices
labeled as "predatory lending" are actually legal (although
they may not be in the best interests of homeowners). *Mortgage News Daily* suggests that the definition of *predatory lending* "involves who really benefits in the mortgage transaction.
The fact that the *homeowner does NOT benefit* is what turns
a legal mortgage into a predatory lending practice which can
and should be reported" ("What Is Predatory Lending?"). And
yet, even those who are not legal analysts can discern that
determining "what does not benefit the homeowner" is a problematic definition. When California attempted to devise a
legal definition for the term ("placing consumers in loan products with significantly worse terms and/or higher costs than
loans offered to similarly qualified consumers in the region for
the primary purpose of enriching the originator and with little or no regard for the costs to the consumer"), consumer
groups argued both that the definition was too vague and that
it needed to be broadened (Sichelman). Without a legal def-

inition, the metaphorical implications of the term become even more significant.

Metaphors and Why They Matter

Julian Jaynes notes in *The Origin of Consciousness in the Breakdown of the Bicameral Mind*:

> The most fascinating property of language is its capacity to make metaphors. But what an understatement! For metaphor is not a mere extra trick of language, as it is so often slighted in the old schoolbooks on composition; it is the very constitutive ground of language . . . . Understanding a thing is to arrive at a metaphor for that thing by substituting something more familiar to us. And the feeling of familiarity is the feeling of understanding. (48, 52)

Metaphors matter because they provide us with assurances of familiarity and understanding as we encounter new and strange realities. As Lakoff and Johnson in *Metaphors We Live By* have argued, "Since much of our social reality is understood in metaphorical terms, and since our conception of the physical world is partly metaphorical, metaphor plays a very significant role in determining what is real for us" (146). As our social and economic realities become increasingly complex, metaphor plays an increasingly important role in facilitating and shaping not only understandings of complex and intertwined realities, but in actions and responses that then affect those realities. As Lakoff and Johnson observe,

> Our concepts structure what we perceive, how we get around in the world, and how we relate to other people. Our conceptual system thus plays a central role in defining our everyday realities. . . .

> Metaphors may create realities for us, especially social realities. A metaphor may thus be a guide for future action. (3, 156)

Lakoff and Johnson have noted that just as significant as the ways in which metaphors steer or direct our thinking are the ways in which they limit or restrict other kinds of conceptionalizations, making them less readily apparent or available: "In allowing us to focus on one aspect of a concept . . . a metaphorical concept can keep us from focusing on other aspects of the concept that are inconsistent with that metaphor" (10).

The term *predatory lending* both focuses attention on certain aspects of the mortgage crisis, while diverting attention from other areas. The metaphor implicit in the term provides a window into current American attitudes toward credit and debit, toward the relationships between lending institutions and borrowers, and toward the values of a capitalist economy.

A Historical Examination of Predatory Lending

The *Oxford English Dictionary* (OED) reveals that the first 10 recorded use in English of the word *predatory* appears in 1589 when Puttenham in *The Arte of English Poesie* wrote, "So saith Aristotle that pasturage was before tillage, or fishing or fowling, or any other predatory art or cheuisance." The original sense of the word is defined by the OED as "Of, relating to, of the nature of, or involving plunder, pillage, or ruthless exploitation." The application of the word to predacious or carnivorous animals appears in the second half of the seventeenth century, and the application of the term to "unfairly competitive or exploitative" business practices is noted as appearing first in 1912 in the Trenton, New Jersey *Evening Times* ("Predatory").

The combining of the terms *predatory* and *lending*, however, did not occur until nearly ninety years later. Using LexisNexis (searching "News, All—English, Full-Text") and the
ProQuest Direct (PQD) databases, we found that one of the
earliest recorded uses of the term was on June 12, 1991, when
two articles in the *Boston Globe* each quoted Bruce Marks,
the executive director of the Union Neighborhood Assistance Corporation of America (UNAC), in stories on New
England banks' alleged discriminatory and illegal mortgage
practices:

> "The Bank of New England has done in Massachusetts what Fleet
> has done nationally," Marks said. "UNAC can't allow these two
> companies to merge, to continue their predatory lending practices.
> The Fed has to have a public hearing to analyze these issues we've
> identified." (Canellos, "Probe" 1)

> This is very consistent with what tends to be their [Baybank's]
> predatory lending practices and maximization of profits with no
> consideration of implications, Marks said. (Marantz 1)

The *Globe* used the term three more times that month in
articles related to the same story; in the June 25 article, *predatory lending* was used with quotation marks, suggesting that the
author (Canellos, "Groups") was aware of the term as a new
coinage in the context of banking. The *Boston Herald* and the
Worcester, Massachusetts, *Telegram & Gazette* picked up the
term and used it in articles later that year: the *Herald* ran one
article in September and two in October using the term; the
Telegram & Gazette ran two articles in September. And in a
more geographically remote usage, the term appeared one more

time in 1991: in October, the Queensland, Australia, *Courier Mail's* included the following in its report on the collapse of the Outback wool trade: "The mounting pressure of debt and farm foreclosures have focused anger on rural lenders. Banks and pastoral houses came under fire with accusations of predatory lending practices and heartless action to force people off the land" (Collie).

For the period between the years of 1992 and 1994, PQD contained only two sources that used the term: an article in *Business Atlanta* in January of 1994 and an article in *Forbes* magazine in March of 1994. During the same time span, LexisNexis identified 157 uses of the term, most of them in local newspapers dealing with local bank stories (especially in Boston and Atlanta). However, in 1993, the Associated Press and United Press International both used the term for the first time (Wells; "NYC Consumer"), and *predatory lending* was referenced in a CBS news broadcast on March 3 of 1993 ("A Look at Unscrupulous Contractors"), as well as in an article in *National Mortgage News* (Collins 2).

In the next three years, from 1995 through 1997, the term appeared twelve or fewer times per year in the PQD database and fewer than forty-five times per year in the LexisNexis database, but in 1998, the use of the term *predatory lending* increased to ninety-seven articles indexed by PQD (fifteen in *American Banker*, twenty-two in *National Mortgage News*, and twenty in *Origination News*), and 213 articles indexed by LexisNexis. Both databases revealed an additional slight rise in the frequency of use of the term in 1999, but the year 2000, however, proved to be the tipping point for *predatory lending*, with the term appearing in 920 articles indexed by PQD, (forty-two articles in the *Washington Post*, twenty-nine in the *LA Times*, and twenty-six

TABLE 1. OCCURRENCE OF THE TERM *PREDATORY LENDING*
IN PERIODICALS, 2000–2008

YEAR OF PUBLICATION	NUMBER OF SOURCES INDEXED BY PROQUEST DIRECT USING TERM *PREDATORY LENDING*	NUMBER OF SOURCES INDEXED BY LEXISNEXIS USING TERM *PREDATORY LENDING*
2000	920	1889
2001	1097	2268
2002	1306	3047
2003	1340	3091
2004	1449	2935
2005	1310	2672
2006	1656	3436
2007	2810	7542
2008 (January 1 TO June 30)	1086 (half year)	3344 (half year)

in the *Wall Street Journal*) and 1889 articles indexed by Lexis-Nexis. The metaphor had crossed from the local to the national, from the jargon of mortgage and banking into the popular press, and it has appeared with increasing frequency in the past eight years, as evidenced by Table 1.

Predatory Lending and the American Dream

The phrase *predatory lending* occurs frequently in articles also 15 containing the word victim (PQD searches yielded 379 articles using both terms concurrently in 2007 and 170 articles using both terms in the first six months of 2008; LexisNexis identified 832 instances of the terms used concurrently in 2007 and 467 occurrences during the first six months of 2008). What is perhaps more surprising is the concurrent use of the terms *preda-*

tory lending and *dream* (PQD identified 465 articles using both terms in 2007 and 194 articles in the first six months of 2008; LexisNexis identified 897 articles using both terms in 2007 and 375 articles using both in the first six months of 2008). Presidential candidates repeatedly linked the two ideas, as evidenced by the following speech excerpt from Hillary Clinton.

> Now, homeownership is at the heart of the American dream, and I share your concern about what's happening in the subprime housing market. We have seen for several years now people buying mortgages with rates that suddenly skyrocket, leaving them scrambling to refinance or being forced to default altogether. And frankly, lax standards in this industry have led to our recent market turmoil. Let's work together to curb predatory lending and abusive practices and to educate home buyers.
>
> ("Remarks by Senator Hillary Rodham Clinton")

Barack Obama also linked the ideas in his campaign speeches:

> We haven't come this far because we practice survival of the fittest. America is America because we strive for survival of the nation— a nation where no one is left behind and everyone has a chance to achieve their dreams. That's who we are. And that's who we can be again at this defining moment. This isn't an issue I found along the campaign trail. I introduced legislation to stop mortgage fraud and predatory lending almost two years ago.
>
> ("Remarks of Senator Barack Obama")

The frequent concurrence of the terms *predatory lending* and *dream* implies that it is not only borrowers and American homeowners who are at risk from predatory lenders; frequently, *predatory lending* is charged with killing the American Dream itself. What the metaphor does not as easily allow for is a closer examination of the dream of American homeownership. The Cuyahoga County Treasurer's comments on Cleveland's mortgage crisis suggest such an examination:

> Rokakis [Cuyahoga County Treasurer] said that many homeowners in financial turmoil probably shouldn't have bought homes to begin with. People shouldn't continue to "peddle the notion" that everyone has the right to buy a house. "It's wrong for us to continue talking about the American Dream," he said.
>
> (Murray C1)

According to Alphonso Jackson, "The phrase 'American Dream' was coined in 1931 by historian James Adams, who defined it as a dream 'in which each man and each woman shall be able to attain to the fullest stature of which they are innately capable, and be recognized by others for what they are, regardless of the circumstances of birth or position'" (54). The idea of owning anything, particularly a home, is a cultural construct, but the concept of homeownership in America, has, from the beginning, been closely identified with the nation's identity and promise. Retsinas and Belsky, in *Low-Income Homeownership: Examining the Unexamined Goal*, suggest that American aspirations to land are derived from "agrarian roots in medieval England" and evolved into "the concept of landholding as a precondition of liberty" (1). Jackson notes that early Americans' dreams of land evolved into dreams of homeownership, and the two were connected and supported by governmental actions such as the Homestead Act of 1862, "which promised free land to anybody who agreed to plant it and build a home . . . [so that] By the 1890s, nearly half of all Americans owned a home" (55).

Following World War II, the GI Bill of Rights further helped to support homeownership by offering mortgages that would not have been previously available to returning servicemen: "The overall homeownership rate rose from forty-five to sixty-five percent in little more than a decade," and from the 1950s, overall homeownership rate in America stayed stable until mid-1990s (Gramlich 1). Ira Katznelson, in *When Affirmative Action Was White*, describes the GI Bill as "the most wide-ranging set of social benefits ever offered by the federal government in a single, comprehensive initiative" (113). While acknowledging that the GI Bill "by advancing the momentum toward suburban living, mass consumption, and the creation of wealth and economic security . . . created middle-class America" (113), Katznelson asserts that the middle-class society that was fostered was

> almost exclusively for whites. Written under southern auspices, the law was deliberately designed to accommodate Jim Crow. Its administration widened the country's racial gap. The prevailing experience for blacks was starkly differential treatment. (114)

Retsinas and Belsky offer the following summary perspec- 20 tive: in the 1920s, the typical home mortgage borrowers were wealthy, because

> [b]anks required a 50-percent downpayment and offered a loan of three to five years. . . . By the 1950s, the typical borrower put 20 percent down and got a fixed-rate mortgage for twenty years. That buyer had a moderate income. . . . Today a buyer can put as little as nothing down, get a variable-rate mortgage, and amortize a loan for as long as thirty years. (Low-Income 4)

In his 2008 book, *House Lust: America's Obsession with Our Homes*, Daniel McGinn examines the psychology and behaviors that have driven the recent U.S. real-estate boom and the evolving American Dream of homeownership. McGinn's book provides thought-provoking statistics about the evolving American Dream that is being preyed upon: in 1940, only forty-four percent of Americans owned their homes, a number that had grown to sixty-nine percent of Americans by 2006 (9); between the years 2000 and 2006, the average U.S. home soared in value by fifty-six percent (9); in 1950, the average American home size totaled 938 square feet, but by 2005, the average home measured 2,434 square feet (16–17). In 1984, the ideal "New American Home" featured at a convention of the nation's home builders encompassed 1,500 square feet; by 1988, the show home had grown to 2,400 square feet, and in 2006, the ideal "New American Home" was 10,023 square feet and valued at over $4 million (McGinn 20–22).

As McGinn's analysis demonstrates, the American Dream of land and homeownership is not stable: it continues to grow. As the percentage of Americans owning their own homes has increased, so, too, has the size and cost of those homes expanded. As in so much of American culture, bigger is assumed to be better, both for the homeowner and for society at large. Not surprisingly, then, the mortgage crisis and the predatory lenders who have threatened to prey upon and devour the American Dream have assumed almost mythic proportions themselves.

Examining the Ways in Which the Metaphor of *Predatory Lending* Has Shaped Attitudes and Behaviors

Considering the term *predatory lending*, we can recognize the way in which the metaphor invites thoughts of powerful and muscular meateaters (timber wolves, Bengal tigers, Mako sharks) lying in wait or stalking their helpless and vulnerable victims (young fawns, wide-eyed bunnies, hapless surfers). The very term *predatory* suggests a doomed fight for survival against a vastly superior adversary. And because of these associations, the term has successfully helped to communicate the desperate economic situations of individuals and communities who have been "gutted" by the alarming rate at which mortgage foreclosures have risen. The metaphoric associations of the term have not only implied an unfair and insurmountable advantage possessed by the lenders, but have implicitly assigned blame to financial institutions and to governments who have looked the other way as the slaughter has continued. In these ways, the metaphor itself has helped to galvanize support for quick and decisive action against lenders as well as motivating protection and support of their victims. By substituting the familiar and easily grasped concept of predation for the complex economic policies and laws surrounding mortgage practices, the general public has gained a feeling of familiarity, and "the feeling of familiarity is the feeling of understanding" (Jaynes 52). Yet the metaphor may have other, unintended associations: Cliff Oswick's 2001 examination of the term *corporate predatorship* notes that

> At a surface level, the depiction of the corporation as a predator is a decidedly negative one. . . . At a deeper level, there is perhaps a far more subtle and sophisticated connection at work. The behavioural of predatory animals is perceived as both "natural" and "necessary." . . . Furthermore, devouring other animals is an instinctive rather than cognitive process. In short, being a predatory animal is not primarily a lifestyle choice. Through their public discourse, corporations seek to re-present themselves in a similar light—the

corporatist domination of other small more vulnerable organizations is cleverly framed as "natural" and "unavoidable." Underpinning this perspective is the imperative of competition—"the right of the strongest" and "the survival of the fittest." (22)

Similarly, at a deeper level, the term *predatory lending* also subtly communicates that this predation is part of a natural process that is unavoidable in a capitalist economy.

Not only has the metaphor of *predatory lending* shaped our thinking in one direction, but just as other metaphors operate, so, too, has the term *predatory lending* kept us "from focusing on other "aspects of the concept that are inconsistent with that metaphor" (Lakoff and Johnson, "Metaphors," 462). The metaphor does not easily allow for examining the ways in which some financial institutions have also been harmed by these lending practices, for we do not readily think of the danger to predators in their hunting. And yet, national banks such as Merrill Lynch and Citibank have reported losses or write-offs of over two billion dollars—in one quarter—while many smaller regional banks and lenders have been described as struggling for survival (Ring et al. 38A). Additionally, the metaphor does not easily invite us to think of predators as "small" or mom-and-pop in nature. But whether big or small, national or local, financial institutions have also been gutted. In one particularly convoluted scheme in Ohio, a mortgage fraud ring was laundering money through strip clubs, money that had been gained by buying and reselling houses at artificially inflated prices (with the help of fraudulent appraisals), with the intent of never making payments on the loan and leaving the banks holding mortgages that could never be satisfied ("Home Renovator Accused"). NPR coined the term "predatory borrowing" to describe the scheme ("Home Renovator Accused").

The metaphor implicit in the term *predatory lending* also does not easily allow for a recognition of the ways in which recent changes in lending practices have benefited some borrowers, as we are not accustomed to thinking of any positives accruing to prey who are being hunted. And yet former Federal Reserve Chairman Edward Gramlich has stated that "the subprime mortgage market was a valid innovation," noting that many of the new homeowners "would have been denied mortgage credit in the early 1990s," and estimating that "about eighty-eight percent of these new homeowners are making their payments and retaining their houses" (Schneider 127). While Williams, Nasiba, and McConnell have questioned this "progress" as merely trading one kind of inequality (access to homeownership) for another (predatory loan terms), the point remains that the newly coined metaphor of *predatory loan practices* does not readily allow for a discussion of substitutionary discrimination or of historic problems within U.S. society that although recently manifested in the housing market have long-standing historical antecedents.

Finally, the metaphor does not readily invite us to examine the decisions or choices of borrowers. We are likely to assume that those who are being preyed upon are helpless and at the mercy of the predator, with no option but to fight for their very survival. And yet, an analysis of subprime mortgage lending practices has revealed complicity between lenders and borrowers that has facilitated the crisis. A research study published by BasePoint Analytics examined over three million loans from 1997 to 2006 and found that an estimated seventy percent of "recent early payment defaults had fraudulent misrepresentations on their original loan applications" (Cowen BU6). Economics professor Tyler Cowen points out that "applications with misrepresentations were also five times as likely to go into default," while Malkin identifies fraudulent borrowing practices that included lying about income and falsifying documents with computers, as "mortgage originators and middlemen looked the other way rather than slowing down the process or insisting on adequate documentation of income and assets. As long as housing prices kept rising, it did not seem to matter" (1). A recent blog posting on "Naked Capitalism" sums up the situation in this way:

> [T]hese two world views, the one that blames the borrower versus the one that blames the lender for the housing market woes, aren't necessarily mutually exclusive. . . . But in many cases, *the borrower and lenders were enmeshed*, both aware that they were taking advantage of the liberties that the Brave New World of finance offered them. (Smith)

In addition to forestalling the conceptualization of enmeshed borrowers and lenders, the metaphorical sense of predatory lending carries a subtle infantilization of borrowers who fall victim to unfavorable loan practices. Frequently, discussions of predatory lending practices identify racial minorities and the elderly as being disproportionately victimized and describe these populations in ways that negate their agency and rationality:

> "Predatory lenders have two distinct targets," says James Ballentine, director of community and economic development at the American Bankers Association in Washington, D.C. "They go after minorities, because they consider them to be less financially sophisticated than other ethnic groups." (Billingsley C1)

It is important to reaffirm that the metaphor of the level playing field in America is more myth than reality; real barriers exist that deny individuals and groups access to equal opportunities. However, it may also be important to consider the ways in which metaphors subtly reinforce stereotypes of lower intelligence and rationality.

Conclusion

Massachusetts Representative Barney Frank, currently Chairman of the House Financial Services Committee and cosponsor of the House of Representatives Mortgage Reform & Anti-Predatory Lending Act of 2007, in remarks made in July of 2007 addressing the Federal Housing Finance Reform Act of 2007, stated, "I'm not big on metaphors, but when Samson pulled down the walls of the temple, he got hit in the head." A little later in the same speech, he reiterated, "I'm not a big one for metaphors, but I always learned that the rising tithe lifts all boats" ("Rep. Barney Frank"). This essay suggests that metaphors are more influential on thought and action than many of us, Barney Frank included, might suppose. The use of the metaphor *predatory lending* has allowed the complex story of the subprime mortgage crisis to be reduced to a simple and dramatic narrative. While some aspects of the metaphor have highlighted aspects of American lending practices in ways that have motivated political action, other nuances of the metaphor have blocked discussions of critical factors in the mortgage industry and in American society: discussions of race, gender, agency, psychological motivations, the enmeshed interests of borrowers and lenders, and the very nature of American capitalism. Edward Gramlich has described the housing boom of the mid-1990s as "a great national experiment," and seen in the best possible light, it was an opportunity to harness the inventiveness of the capitalist system,

30

giving low-income families, minorities, and immigrants a chance to own their homes (Klein and Goldfarb A1). Jim Carr, chief operating officer of the National Community Reinvestment Coalition counters, "The mortgage crisis has driven home to many who formerly were not believers in regulation that efficient markets require appropriate regulation" (Reynolds and Hamilton A1). At the heart of the discussions regarding predatory lending are debates regarding the future direction of American capitalism: is the country willing to conduct a great national experiment with its concomitant costs and benefits measured in dollars and dreams, or does the image of blood-thirsty predation signal a shift in American attitudes toward a system of free enterprise that must be tamed by government intervention? That is, do Americans view predators as dangerous marauders to be caged and fettered for the protection of their vulnerable prey, or as a natural part of the economic system and of capitalism, good for the culling of the herd and good for society? As the sharks continue to circle and clouds of recession obscure the horizon, America waits to see the ways in which this storm is shaping the vision of the American economy and of the American Dream.

WORKS CITED

"A Look at Unscrupulous Contractors Disguising Expensive Second Mortgages as Loans for Home Improvements." CBS This Morning 3 Mar. 1993.

Bajaj, Vikas, and Julie Creswell. "Home Lenders Hit by Higher Default Rates." New York Times 22 Feb. 2007: C.1.

Banyard, Peter. "Between a Rock and a Hard Place." Credit Management Dec. 2008: 18–19.

Billingsley, R. "Blacks Hit Hard by Subprime Loans." New Pittsburgh Courier 19 Sept. 2007: C1–2.

Callaway, Brian. "Groups Target Predatory Lending: High Interest and Fees can Push Borrowers to the Financial Breaking Point." *Knight Ridder Tribune Business News* 8 Feb. 2007: 1.

Canellos, Peter S. "Groups Offer 10-Point Plan to Aid Loan Victims." *Boston Globe* 25 June 1991: 17.

———. "Probe Asked of Fleet Finance's Practices." *Boston Globe* 12 June 1991: 1.

Collie, G. "Wool Collapse Brings Outback Economy to Its Knees." *Courier Mail* 4 Oct. 1991.

Collins, Brian. "Fed Will Consider Chrysler First Acquisition." *National Mortgage News* 11 Jan. 1993: 2.

Cowen, Tyler. "So We Thought, But Then Again . . . ." *New York Times* 13 Jan. 2008: BU6.

Crutsinger, Martin. "Unfolding Subprime Loan Crisis Seen as Gravest Economic Threat." *Pittsburgh Post-Gazette* 3 Mar. 2008: A.10.

Gramlich, Edward. *Subprime Mortgages: America's Latest Boom and Bust.* Washington, DC: The Urban Institute Press, 2007.

Hamilton, Walter. "Markets; Stocks Sink on Finance Worries; AIG's Huge Loss and a UBS Report Suggesting More Sub-Prime Woes Send the Major Indexes Down Sharply." *Los Angeles Times* 1 Mar. 2008: C.1.

"Home Renovator Accused of Scamming $18 Million." Narr. Melissa Block. *All Things Considered.* National Public Radio. Washington, DC. 11 Feb. 2008.

House-Layton, Kate. "National Study Finds Mortgage Crisis." *Knight Ridder Tribune Business News* 20 Dec. 2006: 1.

Jackson, Alphonso. "The Dream of Home Ownership is Still Possible." *Is the American Dream a Myth?* Ed. Kate Burns. Detroit: Thomson Gale, 2006. 54–62.

Jaynes, Julian. *The Origin of Consciousness in the Breakdown of the Bicameral Mind.* Boston: Houghton Mifflin, 1990.

Katznelson, Ira. *When Affirmative Action Was White: An Untold History of Racial Inequality in Twentieth-Century America.* New York: Norton, 2005.

Klein, Alec, and Zachary A. Goldfarb. "The Bubble; How Homeowners, Speculators and Wall Street Dealmakers Rode a Wave of Easy Money with Crippling Consequences." *The Washington Post* 15 June 2008: A1.

Lakoff, George, and Mark Johnson. "Metaphors We Live By." *Language: Introductory Readings.* 6th ed. Ed. Virginia Clark, Paul Eschholz, Alfred Rosa, and Beth Lee Simon. Boston: Bedford/St. Martin's, 2008. 458–65.

_____, and _____. *Metaphors We Live By*. Chicago: U of Chicago P, 1980.

Malkin, Michelle. "Let's Hear From Small-Government Conservatives." *Human Events* 64.3 (12 January 2008): 1, 8.

Marantz, Steve. "Link Probed between Bank, Mortgage Lender." *Boston Globe* 12 June 1991: 23.

McGinn, Daniel. *House Lust: America's Obsession with Our Homes*. New York: Doubleday, 2008.

Murray, Teresa Dixon. "U.S. Treasurer Tours Cleveland's Foreclosure Devastation; She Says Borrowers Need to Press Lenders." *Cleveland Plain Dealer* 26 Oct. 2007: C1.

"NYC Consumer Chief Says Big Banks Profiting from Home-Repair Ripoffs." *United Press International* 16 Feb. 1993.

Oswick, Cliff. "The Etymology of 'Corporate Predatorship': A Critical Commentary." TAMARA: *Journal of Critical Postmodern Organization* 1.2 (2001): 21–24.

"Predatory." Def. Oxford English Dictionary. On-line ed. 2008.

"Remarks by Senator Hillary Rodham Clinton, Congressional City Conference of the League of Cities." *Federal News Service* Washington, DC: 13 Mar. 2007.

"Remarks of Senator Barack Obama: Economic Speech." *States News Service* Chicago, IL: 22 Jan. 2008.

"Rep. Barney Frank Holds a Markup of H.R. 1257, the Shareholder Vote on Executive Compensation Act; H.R. 1515, to Amend the Housing and Community Develoment Act of 1974; H.R. 1427, the Federal Housing Finance Reform Act of 2007; the Preservation Approval Process Improvement." *Political Transcript Wire* 30 Mar. 2007.

Retsinas, Nicolas P., and Eric S. Belsky. *Building Assets, Building Credit: Creating Wealth in Low-Income Communities*. Washington, DC: Brookings Institute, 2005.

_____ and _____. Low-Income Homeownership: Examining the Unexamined Goal. Washington, DC: Brookings Institute, 2002.

Reynolds, Maura, and Walter Hamilton. "The Mortgage Meltdown; Fed Imposes New Rules on Lenders." *Los Angeles Times* 15 July 2008: A.1.

Ring, Niamh, Marc Hochstein, Harry Terris, Alan Kline, Rob Blackwell, Will Wade, and Matt Ackermann. "Take One Credit Crunch. Add Deals, Bills, and Exec Shuffles. Shake Well." *American Banker* 30 Nov. 2007: 38A.

Schneider, Howard. "Subprime Bust has its Positives." *Mortgage Banking* 68.4
    (January 2008): 127.
Sichelman, Lew. "Defining Predatory Lending." *Realty Times*. 18 Aug. 2004.
    24 July 2008 http://realtytimes.com/rtpages/20040818_predatory
    lending.htm
Smith, Yves. "Up to 70 Percent of Mortgage Defaults Linked to
    Misrepresentation." [weblog entry] *Naked Capitalism*. 13 Oct. 2007. 26
    July 2008 http://www.nakedcapitalism.com/2007/10/ up-to-70-of-
    mortgage-defaults-linked-to.html
United States. Department of the Treasury. "Remarks by the Honorable
    Sheila C. Bair Assistant Secretary of the Treasury for Financial
    Institutions National Association of Affordable Housing Lenders
    Predatory Lending: Can Best Practices Be Part of the Solution?" 21 Feb.
    2002. 24 July 2008 http://www.ustreas.gov/ press/releases/po1034.htm
Wells, Rob. "Fed Approves NationsBank's Purchase of Chrysler First."
    Associated Press 13 Jan. 1993.
"What Is Predatory Lending?" *Mortgage News Daily* 30 Sept. 2004. 24 July
    2008. http://www.mortgagenewsdaily.com/Mortgage_Fraud/
    Predatory_Lending.asp.
Williams, Richard, Reynold Nasiba, and Eileen Diaz McConnell. "The
    Changing Face of Inequality in Home Mortgage Lending." *Social
    Problems* 52.2 (2005): 181–208.

Joining the Conversation

1. How do Constance Ruzich and A. J. Grant relate the notion
   of predatory lending to the nation's financial crisis and to
   the idea of the American Dream? How were these lending
   practices allowed to take place, according to the authors?

2. According to Ruzich and Grant, why is metaphor important, and how has the metaphor *predatory lending* helped
   shape public attitudes toward certain business practices and
   regulatory actions?

3. Think about this essay in light of Bob Herbert's or Cal Thomas's discussions of the American Dream. Given their positions, how might each of these authors respond to Ruzich and Grant's argument? What might either of them find to agree and/or disagree with?

4. Ruzich and Grant discuss predatory lending from a number of perspectives, including those of lenders, recipients, and government regulators. How would you characterize Ruzich and Grant's own view of this practice? How do they explain and support this view? What other perspectives do they bring up, and how do they respond to these positions?

5. Write an essay responding to Ruzich and Grant's critique of predatory lending. Start by summarizing their views, and then agree, disagree, or both agree and disagree with their views, but you need to explain why.

A More Perfect Union

BARACK OBAMA

—🔲—

"**W**E THE PEOPLE, in order to form a more perfect union."

Two hundred and twenty-one years ago, in a hall that still stands across the street, a group of men gathered and, with these simple words, launched America's improbable experiment in democracy. Farmers and scholars; statesmen and patriots who had traveled across an ocean to escape tyranny and persecution finally made real their declaration of independence at a Philadelphia convention that lasted through the spring of 1787.

The document they produced was eventually signed but ultimately unfinished. It was stained by this nation's original sin of slavery, a question that divided the colonies and brought the convention to a stalemate until the founders chose to allow the

BARACK OBAMA is the President of the United States. Before entering politics, Obama worked as a community organizer and civil rights attorney and taught law at the University of Chicago. Obama has written several books, including a memoir of his youth titled *Dreams from My Father* (1995) and a personal commentary on U.S. politics titled *The Audacity of Hope* (2006). "A More Perfect Union" is a speech Obama delivered in March 2008 responding to controversial statements made by his former pastor. The speech's title comes from the Preamble to the U.S. Constitution.

slave trade to continue for at least twenty more years, and to leave any final resolution to future generations.

Of course, the answer to the slavery question was already embedded within our Constitution—a Constitution that had at its very core the ideal of equal citizenship under the law; a Constitution that promised its people liberty, and justice, and a union that could be and should be perfected over time.

And yet words on a parchment would not be enough to 5 deliver slaves from bondage, or provide men and women of every color and creed their full rights and obligations as citizens of the United States. What would be needed were Americans in successive generations who were willing to do their part—through protests and struggle, on the streets and in the courts, through a civil war and civil disobedience and always at great risk—to narrow that gap between the promise of our ideals and the reality of their time.

This was one of the tasks we set forth at the beginning of this campaign—to continue the long march of those who came before us, a march for a more just, more equal, more free, more caring, and more prosperous America. I chose to run for the presidency at this moment in history because I believe deeply that we cannot solve the challenges of our time unless we solve them together—unless we perfect our union by understanding that we may have different stories, but we hold common hopes; that we may not look the same and we may not have come from the same place, but we all want to move in the same direction—toward a better future for our children and our grandchildren.

This belief comes from my unyielding faith in the decency and generosity of the American people. But it also comes from my own American story.

I am the son of a black man from Kenya and a white woman from Kansas. I was raised with the help of a white grandfather who survived a Depression to serve in Patton's Army during World War II and a white grandmother who worked on a bomber assembly line at Fort Leavenworth while he was overseas. I've gone to some of the best schools in America and lived in one of the world's poorest nations. I am married to a black American who carries within her the blood of slaves and slave-owners—an inheritance we pass on to our two precious daughters. I have brothers, sisters, nieces, nephews, uncles, and cousins, of every race and every hue, scattered across three continents, and for as long as I live, I will never forget that in no other country on Earth is my story even possible.

It's a story that hasn't made me the most conventional candidate. But it is a story that has seared into my genetic makeup the idea that this nation is more than the sum of its parts—that out of many, we are truly one.

Throughout the first year of this campaign, against all predictions to the contrary, we saw how hungry the American people were for this message of unity. Despite the temptation to view my candidacy through a purely racial lens, we won commanding victories in states with some of the whitest populations in the country. In South Carolina, where the Confederate Flag still flies, we built a powerful coalition of African Americans and white Americans.

This is not to say that race has not been an issue in the campaign. At various stages in the campaign, some commentators have deemed me either "too black" or "not black enough." We saw racial tensions bubble to the surface during the week before the South Carolina primary. The press has scoured every exit poll for the latest evidence of racial polarization, not just in terms of white and black, but black and brown as well.

10

And yet, it has only been in the last couple of weeks that the discussion of race in this campaign has taken a particularly divisive turn.

On one end of the spectrum, we've heard the implication that my candidacy is somehow an exercise in affirmative action; that it's based solely on the desire of wide-eyed liberals to purchase racial reconciliation on the cheap. On the other end, we've heard my former pastor, Reverend Jeremiah Wright, use incendiary language to express views that have the potential not only to widen the racial divide, but views that denigrate both the greatness and the goodness of our nation; that rightly offend white and black alike.

I have already condemned, in unequivocal terms, the statements of Reverend Wright that have caused such controversy. For some, nagging questions remain. Did I know him to be an occasionally fierce critic of American domestic and foreign policy? Of course. Did I ever hear him make remarks that could be considered controversial while I sat in church? Yes. Did I strongly disagree with many of his political views? Absolutely—just as I'm sure many of you have heard remarks from your pastors, priests, or rabbis with which you strongly disagreed.

But the remarks that have caused this recent firestorm weren't 15 simply controversial. They weren't simply a religious leader's efforts to speak out against perceived injustice. Instead, they expressed a profoundly distorted view of this country—a view that sees white racism as endemic, and that elevates what is wrong with America above all that we know is right with America; a view that sees the conflicts in the Middle East as rooted primarily in the actions of stalwart allies like Israel, instead of emanating from the perverse and hateful ideologies of radical Islam.

As such, Reverend Wright's comments were not only wrong but divisive, divisive at a time when we need unity; racially charged at a time when we need to come together to solve a set of monumental problems—two wars, a terrorist threat, a falling economy, a chronic health care crisis, and potentially devastating climate change; problems that are neither black or white or Latino or Asian, but rather problems that confront us all.

Given my background, my politics, and my professed values and ideals, there will no doubt be those for whom my statements of condemnation are not enough. Why associate myself with Reverend Wright in the first place, they may ask? Why not join another church? And I confess that if all that I knew of Reverend Wright were the snippets of those sermons that have run in an endless loop on the television and YouTube, or if Trinity United Church of Christ conformed to the caricatures being peddled by some commentators, there is no doubt that I would react in much the same way.

But the truth is, that isn't all that I know of the man. The man I met more than twenty years ago is a man who helped introduce me to my Christian faith, a man who spoke to me about our obligations to love one another; to care for the sick and lift up the poor. He is a man who served his country as a U.S. Marine; who has studied and lectured at some of the finest universities and seminaries in the country; and who for over thirty years led a church that serves the community by doing God's work here on Earth—by housing the homeless, ministering to the needy, providing day care services and scholarships and prison ministries, and reaching out to those suffering from HIV/AIDs.

In my first book, *Dreams from My Father,* I described the experience of my first service at Trinity:

People began to shout, to rise from their seats and clap and cry out, a forceful wind carrying the reverend's voice up into the rafters.

. . . And in that single note—hope!—I heard something else; at the foot of that cross, inside the thousands of churches across the city, I imagined the stories of ordinary black people merging with the stories of David and Goliath, Moses and Pharaoh, the Christians in the lion's den, Ezekiel's field of dry bones. Those stories—of survival, and freedom, and hope—became our story, my story; the blood that had spilled was our blood, the tears our tears; until this black church, on this bright day, seemed once more a vessel carrying the story of a people into future generations and into a larger world. Our trials and triumphs became at once unique and universal, black and more than black; in chronicling our journey, the stories and songs gave us a means to reclaim memories that we didn't need to feel shame about . . . memories that all people might study and cherish—and with which we could start to rebuild.

That has been my experience at Trinity. Like other predominantly black churches across the country, Trinity embodies the black community in its entirety—the doctor and the welfare mom, the model student and the former gang-banger. Like other black churches, Trinity's services are full of raucous laughter and sometimes bawdy humor. They are full of dancing, clapping, screaming, and shouting that may seem jarring to the untrained ear. The church contains in full the kindness and cruelty, the fierce intelligence and the shocking ignorance, the struggles and successes, the love and, yes, the bitterness and bias that make up the black experience in America.

And this helps explain, perhaps, my relationship with Reverend Wright. As imperfect as he may be, he has been like family to me. He strengthened my faith, officiated at my wedding, and baptized my children. Not once in my conversations with him have I heard him talk about any ethnic group in derogatory terms, or treat whites with whom he interacted with anything but courtesy and respect. He contains within him the contradictions—the good and the bad—of the community that he has served diligently for so many years.

I can no more disown him than I can disown the black community. I can no more disown him than I can my white grandmother—a woman who helped raise me, a woman who sacrificed again and again for me, a woman who loves me as much as she loves anything in this world, but a woman who once confessed her fear of black men who passed by her on the street, and who on more than one occasion has uttered racial or ethnic stereotypes that made me cringe.

These people are a part of me. And they are a part of America, this country that I love.

Some will see this as an attempt to justify or excuse comments that are simply inexcusable. I can assure you it is not. I suppose the politically safe thing would be to move on from this episode and just hope that it fades into the woodwork. We can dismiss Reverend Wright as a crank or a demagogue, just as some have dismissed Geraldine Ferraro, in the aftermath of her recent statements,* as harboring some deep-seated racial bias.

But race is an issue that I believe this nation cannot afford to ignore right now. We would be making the same mistake that Reverend Wright made in his offending sermons about America— to simplify and stereotype and amplify the negative to the point that it distorts reality.

****Ferraro's statements** Geraldine Ferraro, the first woman vice-presidential candidate for a major political party, in 1984, and later a supporter of Hillary Clinton's campaign, commented that, given current prejudices, Barack Obama had an easier time running for president as an African American man than Hillary Clinton had as a woman. Ferraro was asked to resign from Clinton's campaign following these remarks.

The fact is that the comments that have been made and the [25] issues that have surfaced over the last few weeks reflect the complexities of race in this country that we've never really worked through—a part of our union that we have yet to perfect. And if we walk away now, if we simply retreat into our respective corners, we will never be able to come together and solve challenges like health care, or education, or the need to find good jobs for every American.

See Chapter 7 for ways of saying why it matters, as Obama does here.

Understanding this reality requires a reminder of how we arrived at this point. As William Faulkner* once wrote, "The past isn't dead and buried. In fact, it isn't even past." We do not need to recite here the history of racial injustice in this country. But we do need to remind ourselves that so many of the disparities that exist in the African American community today can be directly traced to inequalities passed on from an earlier generation that suffered under the brutal legacy of slavery and Jim Crow.[†]

Segregated schools were, and are, inferior schools; we still haven't fixed them, fifty years after *Brown v. Board of Education*,[‡] and the inferior education they provided, then and now, helps explain the pervasive achievement gap between today's black and white students.

Legalized discrimination—where blacks were prevented, often through violence, from owning property, or loans were

---

William Faulkner (1897–1962)   Nobel Prize–winning American novelist most of whose work was set in his native Mississippi.

[†]*Jim Crow*   Refers to laws enforcing segregation between black and white people, primarily in the South, between 1876 and 1965, when the landmark Civil Rights Act was passed by Congress.

[‡]*Brown v. Board of Education*   1954 Supreme Court decision that made separate schools for black and white students unconstitutional.

not granted to African American business owners, or black homeowners could not access FHA mortgages,* or blacks were excluded from unions, or the police force, or fire departments—meant that black families could not amass any meaningful wealth to bequeath to future generations. That history helps explain the wealth and income gap between black and white, and the concentrated pockets of poverty that persist in so many of today's urban and rural communities.

A lack of economic opportunity among black men, and the shame and frustration that came from not being able to provide for one's family, contributed to the erosion of black families—a problem that welfare policies for many years may have worsened. And the lack of basic services in so many urban black neighborhoods—parks for kids to play in, police walking the beat, regular garbage pick-up, and building code enforcement—all helped create a cycle of violence, blight, and neglect that continue to haunt us.

This is the reality in which Reverend Wright and other African Americans of his generation grew up. They came of age in the late fifties and early sixties, a time when segregation was still the law of the land and opportunity was systematically constricted. What's remarkable is not how many failed in the face of discrimination, but rather how many men and women overcame the odds; how many were able to make a way out of no way for those like me who would come after them.

But for all those who scratched and clawed their way to get a piece of the American Dream, there were many who didn't make it—those who were ultimately defeated, in one way or

---

*FHA mortgages Loans backed by the Federal Housing Administration that historically have allowed lower-income Americans to buy homes when they otherwise might not be able to.

another, by discrimination. That legacy of defeat was passed on to future generations—those young men and increasingly young women who we see standing on street corners or languishing in our prisons, without hope or prospects for the future. Even for those blacks who did make it, questions of race, and racism, continue to define their worldview in fundamental ways. For the men and women of Reverend Wright's generation, the memories of humiliation and doubt and fear have not gone away; nor has the anger and the bitterness of those years. That anger may not get expressed in public, in front of white co-workers or white friends. But it does find voice in the barber-shop or around the kitchen table. At times, that anger is exploited by politicians, to gin up votes along racial lines, or to make up for a politician's own failings.

And occasionally it finds a voice in the church on Sunday morning, in the pulpit and in the pews. The fact that so many people are surprised to hear that anger in some of Reverend Wright's sermons simply reminds us of the old truism that the most segregated hour in American life occurs on Sunday morning. That anger is not always productive; indeed, all too often it distracts attention from solving real problems; it keeps us from squarely facing our own complicity in our condition, and prevents the African American community from forging the alliances it needs to bring about real change. But the anger is real; it is powerful; and to simply wish it away, to condemn it without understanding its roots, only serves to widen the chasm of misunderstanding that exists between the races.

In fact, a similar anger exists within segments of the white community. Most working- and middle-class white Americans don't feel that they have been particularly privileged by their race. Their experience is the immigrant experience—as far as they're concerned, no one's handed them anything, they've built it from scratch. They've worked hard all their lives, many times only to see their jobs shipped overseas or their pension dumped after a lifetime of labor. They are anxious about their futures, and feel their dreams slipping away; in an era of stagnant wages and global competition, opportunity comes to be seen as a zero sum game, in which your dreams come at my expense. So when they are told to bus their children to a school across town; when they hear that an African American is getting an advantage in landing a good job or a spot in a good college because of an injustice that they themselves never committed; when they're told that their fears about crime in urban neighborhoods are somehow prejudiced, resentment builds over time.

Like the anger within the black community, these resentments aren't always expressed in polite company. But they have helped shape the political landscape for at least a generation. Anger over welfare and affirmative action helped forge the Reagan Coalition. Politicians routinely exploited fears of crime for their own electoral ends. Talk show hosts and conservative commentators built entire careers unmasking bogus claims of racism while dismissing legitimate discussions of racial injustice and inequality as mere political correctness or reverse racism.

Just as black anger often proved counterproductive, so have these white resentments distracted attention from the real culprits of the middle-class squeeze—a corporate culture rife with inside dealing, questionable accounting practices, and short-term greed; a Washington dominated by lobbyists and special interests; economic policies that favor the few over the many. And yet, to wish away the resentments of white Americans, to label them as misguided or even racist, without recognizing they are grounded in legitimate concerns—this too widens the racial divide, and blocks the path to understanding.

This is where we are right now. It's a racial stalemate we've been stuck in for years. Contrary to the claims of some of my critics, black and white, I have never been so naïve as to believe that we can get beyond our racial divisions in a single election cycle, or with a single candidacy—particularly a candidacy as imperfect as my own.

See Chapter 6 for tips on answering naysayers.

But I have asserted a firm conviction—a conviction rooted in my faith in God and my faith in the American people—that working together we can move beyond some of our old racial wounds, and that in fact we have no choice if we are to continue on the path of a more perfect union.

For the African American community, that path means embracing the burdens of our past without becoming victims of our past. It means continuing to insist on a full measure of justice in every aspect of American life. But it also means binding our particular grievances—for better health care, and better schools, and better jobs—to the larger aspirations of all Americans—the white woman struggling to break the glass ceiling, the white man who's been laid off, the immigrant trying to feed his family. And it means taking full responsibility for our own lives—by demanding more from our fathers, and spending more time with our children, and reading to them, and teaching them that while they may face challenges and discrimination in their own lives, they must never succumb to despair or cynicism; they must always believe that they can write their own destiny.

Ironically, this quintessentially American—and yes, conservative—notion of self-help found frequent expression in Reverend Wright's sermons. But what my former pastor too often failed to understand is that embarking on a program of self-help also requires a belief that society can change.

The profound mistake of Reverend Wright's sermons is not 40 that he spoke about racism in our society. It's that he spoke as if our society was static; as if no progress has been made; as if this country—a country that has made it possible for one of his own members to run for the highest office in the land and build a coalition of white and black, Latino and Asian, rich and poor, young and old—is still irrevocably bound to a tragic past. But what we know—what we have seen—is that America can change. That is the true genius of this nation. What we have already achieved gives us hope—the audacity to hope—for what we can and must achieve tomorrow.

In the white community, the path to a more perfect union means acknowledging that what ails the African American community does not just exist in the minds of black people; that the legacy of discrimination—and current incidents of discrimination, while less overt than in the past—are real and must be addressed. Not just with words, but with deeds—by investing in our schools and our communities; by enforcing our civil rights laws and ensuring fairness in our criminal justice system; by providing this generation with ladders of opportunity that were unavailable for previous generations. It requires all Americans to realize that your dreams do not have to come at the expense of my dreams; that investing in the health, welfare, and education of black and brown and white children will ultimately help all of America prosper.

In the end, then, what is called for is nothing more, and nothing less, than what all the world's great religions demand—that we do unto others as we would have them do unto us. Let us be our brother's keeper, Scripture tells us. Let us be our sister's keeper. Let us find that common stake we all have in one another, and let our politics reflect that spirit as well.

For we have a choice in this country. We can accept a politics that breeds division, and conflict, and cynicism. We can tackle race only as spectacle—as we did in the O.J. trial*—or in the wake of tragedy, as we did in the aftermath of Katrina†—or as fodder for the nightly news. We can play Reverend Wright's sermons on every channel, every day and talk about them from now until the election, and make the only question in this campaign whether or not the American people think that I somehow believe or sympathize with his most offensive words. We can pounce on some gaffe by a Hillary supporter as evidence that she's playing the race card, or we can speculate on whether white men will all flock to John McCain in the general election regardless of his policies.

We can do that.

But if we do, I can tell you that in the next election, we'll 45 be talking about some other distraction. And then another one. And then another one. And nothing will change.

That is one option. Or, at this moment, in this election, we can come together and say, "Not this time." This time we want to talk about the crumbling schools that are stealing the future of black children and white children and Asian children and Hispanic children and Native American children. This time we want to reject the cynicism that tells us that these kids can't

---

*O.J. trial In the mid-1990s, former football star O.J. Simpson was tried and acquitted for the murder of his ex-wife, Nicole Simpson, and her friend Ron Goldman.

†Katrina Hurricane that devastated New Orleans and much of the north-central Gulf Coast in 2005.

learn; that those kids who don't look like us are somebody else's problem. The children of America are not those kids, they are our kids, and we will not let them fall behind in a twenty-first century economy. Not this time.

This time we want to talk about how the lines in the Emergency Room are filled with whites and blacks and Hispanics who do not have health care; who don't have the power on their own to overcome the special interests in Washington, but who can take them on if we do it together.

This time we want to talk about the shuttered mills that once provided a decent life for men and women of every race, and the homes for sale that once belonged to Americans from every religion, every region, every walk of life. This time we want to talk about the fact that the real problem is not that someone who doesn't look like you might take your job; it's that the corporation you work for will ship it overseas for nothing more than a profit.

This time we want to talk about the men and women of every color and creed who serve together, and fight together, and bleed together under the same proud flag. We want to talk about how to bring them home from a war that never should've been authorized and never should've been waged, and we want to talk about how we'll show our patriotism by caring for them, and their families, and giving them the benefits they have earned.

I would not be running for President if I didn't believe with 50 all my heart that this is what the vast majority of Americans want for this country. This union may never be perfect, but generation after generation has shown that it can always be perfected. And today, whenever I find myself feeling doubtful or cynical about this possibility, what gives me the most hope is the next generation—the young people whose attitudes and beliefs and openness to change have already made history in this election.

There is one story in particular that I'd like to leave you with today—a story I told when I had the great honor of speaking on Dr. King's birthday at his home church, Ebenezer Baptist, in Atlanta.

There is a young, twenty-three-year-old white woman named Ashley Baia who organized for our campaign in Florence, South Carolina. She had been working to organize a mostly African American community since the beginning of this campaign, and one day she was at a roundtable discussion where everyone went around telling their story and why they were there.

And Ashley said that when she was nine years old, her mother got cancer. And because she had to miss days of work, she was let go and lost her health care. They had to file for bankruptcy, and that's when Ashley decided that she had to do something to help her mom.

She knew that food was one of their most expensive costs, and so Ashley convinced her mother that what she really liked and really wanted to eat more than anything else was mustard and relish sandwiches. Because that was the cheapest way to eat.

She did this for a year until her mom got better, and she told everyone at the roundtable that the reason she joined our campaign was so that she could help the millions of other children in the country who want and need to help their parents too.

Now Ashley might have made a different choice. Perhaps somebody told her along the way that the source of her mother's problems were blacks who were on welfare and too lazy to work, or Hispanics who were coming into the country illegally. But she didn't. She sought out allies in her fight against injustice.

Anyway, Ashley finishes her story and then goes around the room and asks everyone else why they're supporting the campaign. They all have different stories and reasons. Many bring up a specific issue. And finally they come to this elderly black man who's been sitting there quietly the entire time. And Ashley asks him why he's there. And he does not bring up a specific issue. He does not say health care or the economy. He does not say education or the war. He does not say that he was there because of Barack Obama. He simply says to everyone in the room, "I am here because of Ashley."

"I'm here because of Ashley." By itself, that single moment of recognition between that young white girl and that old black man is not enough. It is not enough to give health care to the sick, or jobs to the jobless, or education to our children.

But it is where we start. It is where our union grows stronger. And as so many generations have come to realize over the course of the 221 years since a band of patriots signed that document in Philadelphia, that is where the perfection begins.

Joining the Conversation

1. Barack Obama gave this speech about the role of race in U.S. life in response to criticism and massive media coverage of inflammatory remarks made by his former pastor, Rev. Jeremiah Wright. He begins by quoting from the Preamble of the U.S. Constitution. How does this quotation set the stage for the speech that follows?

2. After discussing the Constitution and his optimistic belief in "a more just, more equal, more free, more caring, and more prosperous America" (paragraph 6), Obama briefly

tells his own life story. What does he gain by explaining his unusual background? What is his purpose for doing so?

3. Obama discusses at length Reverend Wright, his church, and what he, Obama, gained from entering the world of that church. Reread this discussion (in paragraphs 12 to 21), paying attention to how he begins with what others say about Reverend Wright to frame what he, Obama, says—about Wright, race in America, and more. Summarize Obama's "they say" and "I say."

4. This is a speech about race, and yet we include it in a chapter about economic opportunity. In fact, Obama says in paragraph 25 that the media reactions to Reverend Wright's comments "reflect the complexities of race in this country that we've never really worked through" and that Americans must work through these complexities in order to "solve challenges like health care, or education, or the need to find good jobs for every American." Why, in Obama's view, is it so important that we as Americans engage in a full and frank conversation about all these issues?

5. Some say that this is one of the best campaign speeches ever given in the United States. What do you think? Write an essay or a speech responding to what Obama says here. Start by summarizing or quoting from his speech.

PERMISSIONS
ACKNOWLEDGMENTS

—◻—

Barack Obama: "A More Perfect Union."

Michelle Obama: "Remarks by the First Lady to the NAACP National Convention in Kansas City."

Karen Olsson: "Up Against Wal-Mart." *Mother Jones*, March/April 2003. © 2003, Foundation for National Progress. Reprinted by permission of Mother Jones.

Susie Orbach: Introduction, pp. 3–9. From *Fat Is a Feminist Issue*. Reprinted by permission of the author.

Carrie Packwood Freeman and Debra Merskin: "Having It His Way: The Construction of Masculinity in Fast-Food TV Advertising." From *Food for Thought: Essays on Eating and Culture*. Reprinted with permission of the authors.

Michael Pollan: "Escape from the Western Diet," from *In Defense of Food* by Michael Pollan. Copyright © 2008 by Michael Pollan. Used by permission of The Penguin Press, a division of Penguin Group (USA) Inc.

Joe Posnanski: "Cheating and CHEATING," by Joe Posnanski. *Sports Illustrated* March 1, 2010. Used by permission of Time Inc.

Felisa Rogers: "How I Learned to Stop Worrying and Love Football" by Felisa Rogers. We have made diligent efforts to contact the copyright holder to obtain permission to reprint this selection. If you have information that would help us, please write to Permissions Department, W. W. Norton & Company, Inc., 500 Fifth Avenue, New York, NY 10110.

Mike Rose: "Blue-Collar Brilliance: Questions Assumptions about Intelligence, Work and Social Class." Reprinted from *The American Scholar*, Volume 78, No. 3, Summer 2009. Copyright © 2009 by Mike Rose.

Constance M. Ruzich and A.J. Grant: "Predatory Lending and the Devouring of the American Dream." From *The Journal of American Culture*, Vol. 32. Copyright © 2009 Wiley Periodicals. Reproduced with permission of Blackwell Publishing Ltd.

Wilfrid Sheed: "Why Sports Matter." *The Wilson Quarterly*, Vol. 19, No. 1. We have made diligent efforts to contact the copyright holder to obtain permission to reprint this selection. If you have information that would help us, please write to Permissions Department, W. W. Norton & Company, Inc., 500 Fifth Avenue, New York, NY 10110.

Dana Stevens: "Thinking Outside the Idiot Box" by Dana Stevens, movie critic (and former TV critic) for *Slate*. *Slate Magazine*, April 25, 2005. Reprinted with permission of the author.

Cal Thomas: "Is the American Dream Over?" From *Townhall Daily*, December 20, 2010. Used with permission by TMS Reprints.

Sanford J. Ungar: Originally published as "7 Major Misconceptions about the Liberal Arts," *The Chronicle of Higher Education*, March 5, 2010. Reprinted with the permission of the author.

David Foster Wallace: "Kenyon Commencement Speech," From *This Is Water* by David Foster Wallace. Copyright © 2009 by David Foster Wallace Literary Trust by Permission of Little, Brown and Company.

Judith Warner: "Junking Junk Food." *The New York Times*, November 28, 2010. Copyright © 2010 The New York Times Company. All rights reserved. Reprinted with permission.

Robin Wilson: "A Lifetime of Student Debt? Not Likely." Copyright © 2009 *The Chronicle of Higher Education*. Reprinted with permission.

Jennie Yabroff: "In Defense of Cheering." From *Newsweek*, March 15, 2008. Copyright © 2008 Harmon Newsweek LLC, Inc. All rights reserved. Used by permission and protected by the Copyright Laws of the United States. The printing, copying, redistribution, or retransmission of the Material without express written permission is prohibited.

David Zinczenko: "Don't Blame the Eater." *The New York Times*, November 23, 2002. Reprinted by permission of the author.

Jason Zinser: "The Good, The Bad, and *The Daily Show*." From *The Daily Show and Philosophy: Moments of Zen in the Art of Fake News* by Jason Holt. Copyright © 2008 John Wiley & Sons. Reproduced with permission of Blackwell Publishing Ltd.

Photographs
Chapter 14

p. 176: Walt Handelsman cartoon, "At the rate I'm going, my student loans should be paid off in 3 years": © Tribune Media Services, Inc. All rights reserved. Reprinted with permission.

p. 216: For-profit college billboard: AP Photo

p. 244: Mike Rose's Mother, Rosie: Photo courtesy of Mike Rose

p. 249: Mike Rose's Father, Joe: Photo courtesy of Mike Rose

Chapter 15

p. 274: Brooke Gladstone cartoon: From *The Influencing Machine* 2011, W. W. Norton, pages 142–43

Chapter 16

Chapter 17

Chapter 18

ACKNOWLEDGMENTS

—◻—

We have our superb editor, Marilyn Moller, to thank for this book. It was Marilyn who first encouraged us to write it, and she has devoted herself tirelessly to helping us at every stage of the process. We never failed to benefit from her incisive suggestions, her unfailing patience, and her cheerful good humor.

Our thanks go as well to John Darger, who offered early encouragement to write *"They Say / I Say"*—and to Debra Morton Hoyt for her excellent work on the cover.

For this second edition, we offer our sincere appreciation to the following Norton staff members, whose talents and strong work ethics made the project move smoothly every step of the way: Beth Ammerman helped us develop and refine the study questions that follow each reading; Jane Searle served as production manager extraordinaire, and Christine D'Antonio was an excellent project editor; together, they managed the publication process and kept us on an efficient schedule. Betsye Mullaney, associate editor, offered a wealth of smart and helpful suggestions throughout.

Thanks to Lisa Ampleman, doctoral student in English at the University of Cincinnati, for her invaluable aid in finding effective readings for the book and for writing the instructor's notes that now accompany the book. And a thank you as well to Michal Brody for her work on the superb blog that accompanies this book.

We owe special thanks to our colleagues in the English department at the University of Illinois at Chicago: Mark Canuel, our current department head, for supporting our efforts overseeing the university's Writing in the Disciplines requirement, work that led us to solicit the two new chapters on writing in the sciences and social sciences for the second edition. Walter Benn Michaels, our former department head, and Ann Feldman, Director of University Writing Programs, for encouraging us to teach first-year composition courses at UIC in which we could try out ideas and drafts of our manuscript. Lon Kaufman, Tom Moss, Diane Chin, Vainis Aleksa, and Matt Pavesich have also been very supportive of our efforts. We are especially grateful to Ann and Diane for bringing us into their graduate course on the teaching of writing, and to Ann, Tom, Diane, and Matt for inviting us to present our ideas in UIC's Mile 8 workshops for writing instructors. The encouragement, suggestions, and criticisms we received at these sessions have proved invaluable. Our deep gratitude also goes to our research assistant for the past two years, Matt Oakes.

We are also especially grateful to Steve Benton and Nadya Pittendrigh, who taught a section of composition with us using an early draft of this book. Steve made many helpful suggestions, particularly regarding the exercises. We are grateful to Andy Young, a lecturer at UIC who has tested our book in his courses and who gave us extremely helpful feedback. And we thank Vershawn A. Young, whose work on code-meshing influenced our argument in Chapter 9, and Hillel Crandus, whose classroom handout inspired Chapter 11, "Entering Classroom Discussions."

We are grateful to the many colleagues and friends who've let us talk our ideas out with them and given extremely helpful responses. UIC's former dean, Stanley Fish, has been central in this respect, both in personal conversations and in his incisive articles calling for greater focus on form in the teaching of writing. Our conversations with Jane Tompkins have also been integral to this book, as was the composition course that Jane co-taught with Gerald entitled "Can We Talk?" Lenny Davis, too, offered both intellectual insight and emotional support, as did Heather Arnet, Jennifer Ashton, Janet Atwill, Kyra Auslander, Noel Barker, Jim Benton, Jack Brereton, Tim Cantrick, Marsha Cassidy, David Chinitz, Lisa Chinitz, Pat Chu, Duane Davis, Bridget O'Rourke Flisk, Steve Flisk, Judy Gardiner, Howard Gardner, Rich Gelb, Gwynne Gertz, Jeff Gore, Bill Haddad, Ben Hale, Scott Hammerl, Patricia Harkin, Andy Hoberek, John Huntington, Joe Janangelo, Paul Jay, David Jolliffe, Nancy Kohn, Don Lazere, Jo Liebermann, Steven Mailloux, Deirdre McCloskey, Maurice J. Meilleur, Allan Meyers, Greg Meyerson, Alan Meyers, Anna Minkov, Chris Newfield, Jim Phelan, Paul Psilos, Bruce Robbins, Charles Ross, Evan Seymour, Eileen Seifert, David Shumway, Herb Simons, Jim Sosnoski, David Steiner, Harold Veeser, Chuck Venegoni, Marla Weeg, Jerry Wexler, Joyce Wexler, Virginia Wexman, Jeffrey Williams, Lynn Woodbury, and the late Wayne Booth, whose friendship we dearly miss.

We are grateful for having had the opportunity to present our ideas to a number of schools: Augustana College, Brandeis University, Brigham Young University, Bryn Mawr College, Case Western University, Columbia University, Community College of Philadelphia, California State University at Bakersfield, California State University at Northridge, University of California at Riverside, University of Delaware, DePauw University, Drew University, Duke University, Duquesne University, Elmhurst College, Fontbonne University, Furman University, Gettysburg College, Harper College, Harvard University, Haverford

College, Hunter College, Illinois State University, John Carroll University, Lawrence University, the Lawrenceville School, MacEwan University, University of Maryland at College Park, University of Memphis, University of Missouri at Columbia, New Trier High School, Northern Michigan University, North Carolina A&T University, State University of New York at Stony Brook, University of North Florida, Northwestern University Division of Continuing Studies, University of Notre Dame, Oregon State University, University of Portland, University of Rochester, St. Ambrose University, St. Andrew's School, St. Charles High School, Seattle University, Southern Connec ticut State University, University of South Florida, Swarthmore College, Teachers College, University of Tennessee at Knoxville, University of Texas at Arlington, Tulane University, Union College, Wabash College, Washington College, University of Washington, Western Michigan University, University of West Virginia at Morgantown, Whitney Young High School, and the University of Wisconsin at Whitewater.

We particularly thank those who helped arrange these visits and discussed writing issues with us: Jeff Abernathy, Herman Asarnow, John Austin, Greg Barnheisel, John Bean, Crystal Benedicks, Joe Bizup, Sheridan Blau, Dagne Bloland, Chris Breu, Joan Johnson Bube, John Caldwell, Gregory Clark, Irene Clark, Dean Philip Cohen, Cathy D'Agostino, Tom Deans, Gaurav Desai, Kathleen Dudden-Rowlands, Lisa Ede, Emory Elliott, Anthony Ellis, Kim Flachmann, Ronald Fortune, George Haggerty, Donald Hall, Gary Hatch, Elizabeth Hatmaker, Harry Hellenbrand, Nicole Henderson, Doug Hesse, Joe Harris, Van Hillard, Andrew Hoberek, Michael Hustedde, Sara Jameson, T. R. Johnson, David Jones, Ann Kaplan, Don Kartiganer, Linda Kinnahan, Dean Georg Kleine, Albert Labriola,

Tom Liam Lynch, Thomas McFadden, Sean Meehan, Connie Mick, Margaret Oakes, John O'Connor, Gary Olson, Tom Pace, Emily Poe, Dominick Randolph, Monica Rico, Kelly Ritter, Jack Robinson, Warren Rosenberg, Dean Howard Ross, Deborah Rossen-Knill, Rose Shapiro, Mike Shea, Evan Seymour, Erec Smith, Nancy Sommers, Stephen Spector, Timothy Spurgin, Ron Strickland, Trig Thoreson, Josh Toth, Judy Trost, Charles Tung, John Webster, Sandi Weisenberg, Robert Weisbuch, Martha Woodmansee, and Lynn Worsham.

For inviting us to present our ideas at their conferences, we are grateful to John Brereton and Richard Wendorf at the Boston Athenaeum; Wendy Katkin of the Reinvention Center of SUNY Stony Brook; Luchen Li of the Michigan English Association; Lisa Lee and Barbara Ransby of the Public Square in Chicago; Don Lazere of the University of Tennessee at Knoxville, chair of a panel at the MLA; Dennis Baron of the University of Illinois at Urbana-Champaign, Alfie Guy of Yale University, Gregory Colomb of the University of Virginia, and Irene Clark of the California State University of Northridge, chairs of panels at CCCC; George Crandell and Steve Hubbard, co-directors of the ACETA conference at Auburn University; Mary Beth Rose of the Humanities Institute at the University of Illinois at Chicago; Diana Smith of St. Anne's Belfield School and the University of Virginia; Jim Maddox and Victor Luftig of the Bread Loaf School of English; Jan Fitzsimmons and Jerry Berberet of the Associated Colleges of Illinois; and Rosemary Feal, Executive Director of the Modern Language Association, initiator of a workshop for community college teachers at the 2008 MLA convention.

A very special thanks goes to those who reviewed materials for this new edition: Kathy Albertson (Georgia Southern University); Joseph Aldinger (State University of New York, Buffalo);

Nicolette Amann (Humboldt State University); Sonja Andrus (Collin College); Gail Arnoff (John Carroll University); Lisa Siefker Bailey (Indiana University-Purdue University Indianapolis); John Berteaux (California State University, Monterey Bay); Sonya Blades (University of North Carolina, Greensboro); Elyse Blankley (California State University, Long Beach); Andrew Bodenrader (Manhattanville College); Rachel Bowman (University of North Carolina, Greensboro); Eric Branscomb (Salem State College); Harryette Brown (Eastfield College); Elena Brunn (Borough of Manhattan Community College/City University of New York); Rita Carey (Clark College); Julie Cassidy (Borough of Manhattan Community College); Catherine Chaterdon (The University of Arizona); Amy Lea Clemons (Francis Marion University); Tracey Clough (University of Texas, Arlington); Julie Colish (University of Michigan, Flint); Matt Copeland (San Diego State University); Christopher Cowley (State University of New York, Buffalo); Angela Crow (Georgia Southern University); Susie Crowson (Del Mar College); Sean Curran (California State University, Northridge); Kate Dailey (Bowling Green State University, Firelands); Jill Darley-Vanis (Clark College); Virginia Davidson (Mount Saint Mary College); Page Delano (Borough of Manhattan Community College); Elisabeth Divis (University of Michigan); Will Dodson (University of North Carolina, Greensboro); Patricia Dowcett (Quinnipiac University); Laura Dubek (Middle Tennessee State University); William Duffy (University of North Carolina, Greensboro); Gary Eberle (Aquinas College); Alycia Ehlert (Darton College); Sarah Farrell (University of Texas, Arlington); Joseph Fasano (Manhattanville College); Benjamin Fischer (Northwest Nazarene University); Joan Forbes (Kean University); Courtney Fowler (California State University, Long Beach); Caimeen Garrett

(American University); William Griswold (California State University, Long Beach); Deborah Greenhut (New Jersey City University); Charles Guy-McAlpin (University of North Carolina, Greensboro); Katalin Gyurian (Kean University); Jami Hemmenway (Eureka College); Jane Hikel (University of Hartford); Erin Houlihan (University of North Carolina, Greensboro); Erik Hudak (University of Texas, Arlington); Chris Hurst (State University of New York, Buffalo); Kristopher Jansma (Manhattanville College); Michael Jauchen (Colby-Sawyer College); Jeanine Jewell (Southeast Community College); Antonnet Johnson (University of Arizona); Donald Johnson (Santa Monica College); Lou Ann Karabel (Indiana University Northwest); Rod Kessler (Salem State College); Kristi Key (Newberry College); Kelly Kinney (Binghamton University); Francia Kissel (Indiana University-Purdue University Indianapolis); Geoff Klock, Debra S. Knutson (Shawnee State University); Morani Kornberg-Weiss (State University of New York, Buffalo); David LaPierre (Central Connecticut State University); Ann-Gee Lee (St. Cloud State University); Jerry Lee (University of Arizona); Jessica Lee (University of Arizona); Eric Leuschner (Fort Hays State University); Brian Lewis (Century College); Damon Kraft (Missouri Southern State University); Amy Losi (Hamburg Central School District); Aimee Lukas (Central Connecticut State University); Jaclyn Lutzke (Indiana University-Purdue University Indianapolis); John McBratney (John Carroll University); Heather McPherson (University of Minnesota); Cruz Medina (University of Arizona); Dawn Mendoza (Dean College); Rae Ann Meriwether (University of North Carolina, Greensboro); Catherine Merritt (University of Alabama); Gina Miller (Alaska Pacific University); Tomas Q. Morin (Texas State University); Jenny Mueller (McKendree University); Matt Mullins (University of North

Carolina, Greensboro); Roxanne F. Munch (Joliet Junior College); Charles Nelson (Kean University); Pauline Newton (Southern Methodist University); Pat Norton (University of Alabama); Marsha Nourse (Dean College); Anne-Marie Obilade (Alcorn State University); Adair Olson (Black Hills State University); Nancy Pederson (University of Minnesota, Morris); Christine Pipitone-Herron (Raritan Valley Community College); D. Pothen (Multnomah University); Sarah A. Quirk (Waubonsee Community College); Clancy Ratliff (University of Louisiana, Lafayette); Kelly Ritter (University of North Carolina, Greensboro); Stephanie Roach (University of Michigan, Flint); Jeffrey Roessner (Mercyhurst College); Scott Rogers (Weber State University); Suzanne Ross (St. Cloud State University); Keidrick Roy; Myra Salcedo (University of Texas, Arlington); Ronit Sarig (California State University, Northridge); Samantha Seamans (Central Connecticut State University); Rae Schipke (Central Connecticut State University); Michael Schoenfeldt (University of Michigan); Pat Sherbert (National Math and Science Initiative); Joyce Shrimplin (Miami University of Ohio); Leticia Slabaugh (Texas A&M, Galveston); Lars Soderlund (Purdue University); Summar Sparks (University of North Carolina, Greensboro); David Squires (State University of New York, Buffalo); Alice Stephens (Oldenburg Academy of the Immaculate Conception); Mary Stroud (The University of Arizona); Kimberly Sullivan (Clark College); Doug Swartz (Indiana University Northwest); William Tate (Covenant College); James Tolan (Borough of Manhattan Community College); Dawn Trettin-Moyer (University of Washington, Oshkosh); Clementina Verge (Central Connecticut State University); Norma Vogel (Dean College); Nhu Vu (Seattle Central Community College); Christie Ward (Central Connecticut State University); Stephanie Wardrop (Western New

England College); Rachael Wendler (University of Arizona); Cara Williams (University of North Carolina, Greensboro); Todd Williams (Kutztown University); Robert Wilson (Cedar Crest College); Courtney Wooten (University of North Carolina, Greensboro); Chuck Venegoni (John Hersey High School); William Younglove (California State University, Long Beach).

We also thank those who reviewed materials for the first edition: Marie Elizabeth Brockman (Central Michigan University); Ronald Clark Brooks (Oklahoma State University); Beth Buyserie (Washington State University); Michael Donnelly (University of Tampa); Karen Gardiner (University of Alabama); Greg Glau (Northern Arizona University); Anita Helle (Oregon State University); Michael Hennessy (Texas State University); Asao Inoue (California State University at Fresno); Sara Jameson (Oregon State University); Joseph Jones (University of Memphis); Amy S. Lerman (Mesa Community College); Marc Lawrence MacDonald (Central Michigan University); Andrew Manno (Raritan Valley Community College); Sylvia Newman (Weber State University); Carole Clark Papper (Hofstra University); Eileen Seifert (DePaul University); Evan Seymour (Community College of Philadelphia); Renee Shea (Bowie State University); Marcy Taylor (Central Michigan University); Rita Treutel (University of Alabama at Birmingham); Margaret Weaver (Missouri State University); Leah Williams (University of New Hampshire); and Tina Žigon (State University of New York at Buffalo).

Index of Templates

———⊡———

Introducing What "They Say" *(p. 23)*

▸ A number of _____ have recently suggested that _____

▸ It has become common today to dismiss _____.

▸ In their recent work, Y and Z have offered harsh critiques of _____ for _____.

Introducing "Standard Views"
(pp. 23–24)

▸ Americans today tend to believe that _____.

▸ Conventional wisdom has it that _____.

▸ Common sense seems to dictate that _____.

▸ The standard way of thinking about topic X has it that _____.

▸ It is often said that _____.

▸ My whole life I have heard it said that _____.

▸ You would think that _____.

▸ Many people assume that _____.

MAKING WHAT "THEY SAY" SOMETHING *YOU* SAY *(pp. 24–25)*

▶ I've always believed that _____ .

▶ When I was a child, I used to think that _____ .

▶ Although I should know better by now, I cannot help thinking that _____ .

▶ At the same time that I believe _____ , I also believe _____ .

INTRODUCING SOMETHING IMPLIED OR ASSUMED *(p. 25)*

▶ Although none of them have ever said so directly, my teachers have often given me the impression that _____ .

▶ One implication of X's treatment of _____ is that _____ .

▶ Although X does not say so directly, she apparently assumes that _____ .

▶ While they rarely admit as much, _____ often take for granted that _____ .

INTRODUCING AN ONGOING DEBATE *(pp. 25–27)*

▶ In discussions of X, one controversial issue has been _____ . On the one hand, _____ argues _____ . On the other hand, _____ contends _____ . Others even maintain _____ . My own view is _____ .

▶ When it comes to the topic of _____, most of us will readily agree that _____. Where this agreement usually ends, however, is on the question of _____. Whereas some are convinced that _____, others maintain that _____.

▶ In conclusion, then, as I suggested earlier, defenders of _____ can't have it both ways. Their assertion that _____ is contradicted by their claim that _____.

CAPTURING AUTHORIAL ACTION *(pp. 38–40)*

▶ X acknowledges that _____.

▶ X agrees that _____.

▶ X argues that _____.

▶ X believes that _____.

▶ X denies/does not deny that _____.

▶ X claims that _____.

▶ X complains that _____.

▶ X concedes that _____.

▶ X demonstrates that _____.

▶ X deplores the tendency to _____.

▶ X celebrates the fact that _____.

▶ X emphasizes that _____.

- X insists that _____.

- X observes that _____.

- X questions whether _____.

- X refutes the claim that _____.

- X reminds us that _____.

- X reports that _____.

- X suggests that _____.

- X urges us to _____.

INTRODUCING QUOTATIONS *(p. 46)*

- X states, "_____."

- As the prominent philosopher X puts it, "_____."

- According to X, "_____."

- X himself writes, "_____."

- In her book, _____, X maintains that "_____"

- Writing in the journal *Commentary*, X complains that "_____"

- In X's view, "_____."

- X agrees when she writes, "_____."

- X disagrees when he writes, "_____."

- X complicates matters further when he writes, "_____."

Index of Templates

EXPLAINING QUOTATIONS *(pp. 46–47)*

▶ Basically, X is saying _____.

▶ In other words, X believes _____.

▶ In making this comment, X urges us to _____.

▶ X is corroborating the age-old adage that _____.

▶ X's point is that _____.

▶ The essence of X's argument is that _____.

DISAGREEING, WITH REASONS *(p. 60)*

▶ I think X is mistaken because she overlooks _____.

▶ X's claim that _____ rests upon the questionable assumption that _____.

▶ I disagree with X's view that _____ because, as recent research has shown, _____.

▶ X contradicts herself/can't have it both ways. On the one hand, she argues _____. On the other hand, she also says _____.

▶ By focusing on _____, X overlooks the deeper problem of _____.

AGREEING—WITH A DIFFERENCE *(pp. 62–64)*

▸ I agree that _____ because my experience _____ confirms it.

▸ X surely is right about _____ because, as she may not be aware, recent studies have shown that _____.

▸ X's theory of _____ is extremely useful because it sheds insight on the difficult problem of _____.

▸ Those unfamiliar with this school of thought may be interested to know that it basically boils down to _____.

▸ I agree that _____, a point that needs emphasizing since so many people believe _____.

▸ If group X is right that _____, as I think they are, then we need to reassess the popular assumption that _____.

AGREEING AND DISAGREEING SIMULTANEOUSLY *(pp. 64–66)*

▸ Although I agree with X up to a point, I cannot accept his overall conclusion that _____.

▸ Although I disagree with much that X says, I fully endorse his final conclusion that _____.

▸ Though I concede that _____, I still insist that _____.

▸ Whereas X provides ample evidence that _____, Y and Z's research on _____ and _____ convinces me that _____ instead.

▶ X is right that _____, but she seems on more dubious ground when she claims that _____.

▶ While X is probably wrong when she claims that _____, she is right that _____.

▶ I'm of two minds about X's claim that _____. On the one hand, I agree that _____. On the other hand, I'm not sure if _____.

▶ My feelings on the issue are mixed. I do support X's position that _____, but I find Y's argument about _____ and Z's research on _____ to be equally persuasive.

SIGNALING WHO IS SAYING WHAT *(pp. 71–73)*

▶ X argues _____.

▶ According to both X and Y, _____.

▶ Politicians _____, X argues, should _____.

▶ Most athletes will tell you that _____.

▶ My own view, however, is that _____.

▶ I agree, as X may not realize, that _____.

▶ But _____ are real and, arguably, the most significant factor in _____.

▶ But X is wrong that _____.

▶ However, it is simply not true that _____.

▶ Indeed, it is highly likely that _____.

▸ X's assertion that _____ does not fit the facts.

▸ X is right that _____.

▸ X is wrong that _____.

▸ X is both right and wrong that _____.

▸ Yet a sober analysis of the matter reveals _____.

▸ Nevertheless, new research shows _____.

▸ Anyone familiar with _____ should agree that _____.

EMBEDDING VOICE MARKERS *(pp. 74–75)*

▸ X overlooks what I consider an important point about _____.

▸ My own view is that what X insists is a _____ is in fact a _____.

▸ I wholeheartedly endorse what X calls _____.

▸ These conclusions, which X discusses in _____, add weight to the argument that _____.

ENTERTAINING OBJECTIONS *(p. 82)*

▸ At this point I would like to raise some objections that have been inspired by the skeptic in me. She feels that I have been ignoring _____. "_____," she says to me, "_____."

▸ Yet some readers may challenge the view that _____.

▸ Of course, many will probably disagree with this assertion that _____.

NAMING YOUR NAYSAYERS *(pp. 83–84)*

- Here many *feminists* would probably object that _____ .

- But *social Darwinists* would certainly take issue with the argument that _____ .

- *Biologists,* of course, may want to question whether _____ .

- Nevertheless, both *followers and critics of Malcom X* will probably argue that _____ .

- Although not all *Christians* think alike, some of them will probably dispute my claim that _____ .

- *Non-native English speakers* are so diverse in their views that it's hard to generalize about them, but some are likely to object on the grounds that _____ .

INTRODUCING OBJECTIONS INFORMALLY *(pp. 84–85)*

- But is my proposal realistic? What are the chances of its actually being adopted?

- Yet is it always true that _____ ? Is it always the case, as I have been suggesting, that _____ ?

- However, does the evidence I've cited prove conclusively that _____ ?

- "Impossible," some will say. "You must be reading the research selectively."

MAKING CONCESSIONS WHILE STILL STANDING YOUR GROUND *(p. 89)*

▸ Although I grant that _____, I still maintain that _____.

▸ Proponents of X are right to argue that _____. But they exaggerate when they claim that _____.

▸ While it is true that _____, it does not necessarily follow that _____.

▸ On the one hand, I agree with X that _____. But on the other hand, I still insist that _____.

INDICATING WHO CARES *(pp. 95–96)*

▸ _____ used to think _____. But recently [or within the past few decades] _____ suggests that _____.

▸ These findings challenge the work of earlier researchers, who tended to assume that _____.

▸ Recent studies like these shed new light on _____, which previous studies had not addressed.

▸ Researchers have long assumed that _____. For instance, one eminent scholar of cell biology, _____, assumed in _____, her seminal work on cell structures and functions, that fat cells _____. As _____ herself put it, "_____" (2007). Another leading scientist, _____, argued that fat cells "_____" (2006). Ultimately, when it came to the nature of fat, the basic assumption was that _____.

But a new body of research shows that fat cells are far more complex and that _____.

▸ If sports enthusiasts stopped to think about it, many of them might simply assume that the most successful athletes _____. However, new research shows _____.

▸ These findings challenge neoliberals' common assumptions that _____.

▸ At first glance, teenagers appear to _____. But on closer inspection _____.

ESTABLISHING WHY YOUR CLAIMS MATTER
(pp. 98–99)

▸ X matters/is important because _____.

▸ Although X may seem trivial, it is in fact crucial in terms of today's concern over _____.

▸ Ultimately, what is at stake here is _____.

▸ These findings have important consequences for the broader domain of _____.

▸ My discussion of X is in fact addressing the larger matter of _____.

▸ These conclusions/This discovery will have significant applications in _____ as well as in _____.

▸ Although X may seem of concern to only a small group of _____, it should in fact concern anyone who cares about _____.

COMMONLY USED TRANSITIONS

CAUSE AND EFFECT

accordingly	since
as a result	so
consequently	then
hence	therefore
it follows, then	thus

CONCLUSION

as a result	so
consequently	the upshot of all this is that
hence	therefore
in conclusion, then	thus
in short	to sum up
in sum, then	to summarize
it follows, then	

COMPARISON

along the same lines	likewise
in the same way	similarly

CONTRAST

although	nevertheless
but	nonetheless
by contrast	on the contrary
conversely	on the other hand
despite	regardless
even though	whereas

however	while
in contrast	yet

ADDITION

also	in fact
and	indeed
besides	moreover
furthermore	so too
in addition	

CONCESSION

admittedly	of course
although it is true that	naturally
granted	to be sure
I concede that	

EXAMPLE

after all	for instance
as an illustration	specifically
consider	to take a case in point
for example	

ELABORATION

actually	to put it another way
by extension	to put it bluntly
in short	to put it succinctly
that is	ultimately
in other words	

ADDING METACOMMENTARY *(pp. 135–37)*

▸ In other words, _____.

▸ What _____ really means by this is _____.

▸ Ultimately, my goal is to demonstrate that _____.

▸ My point is not _____, but _____.

▸ To put it another way, _____.

▸ In sum, then, _____.

▸ My conclusion, then, is that, _____.

▸ In short, _____.

▸ What is more important, _____.

▸ Incidentally, _____.

▸ By the way, _____.

▸ Chapter 2 explores _____, while Chapter 3 examines _____.

▸ Having just argued that _____, let us now turn our attention to _____.

▸ Although some readers may object that _____, I would answer that _____.

INTRODUCING GAPS IN THE EXISTING RESEARCH
(p. 163)

▸ Studies of X have indicated _____. It is not clear, however, that this conclusion applies to _____.

▸ _____ often take for granted that _____. Few have investigated this assumption, however.

▸ X's work tells us a great deal about _____. Can this work be
generalized to _____?

INDEX OF AUTHORS AND TITLES

———※———

697

About the Authors

GERALD GRAFF, a professor of English and Education at the University of Illinois at Chicago and 2008 President of the Modern Language Association of America, has had a major impact on teachers through such books as *Professing Literature: An Institutional History*, *Beyond the Culture Wars: How Teaching the*  *Conflicts Can Revitalize American Education*, and, most recently, *Clueless in Academe: How Schools Obscures the Life of the Mind*.

CATHY BIRKENSTEIN is a lecturer in English at the University of Illinois at Chicago and co-director of the Writing in the Disciplines program. She has published essays on writing, most recently in *College English*, and, with Gerald Graff, in *The Chronicle of Higher Education*, *Academe*, and *College Composition and Communication*.  She has also given talks and workshops with Gerald at numerous colleges and is currently working on a study of common misunderstandings surrounding academic discourse.

RUSSEL DURST, who edited the readings in this book, is Head of the English Department at the University of Cincinnati, where he teaches courses in composition, writing pedagogy and research, English linguistics, and the Hebrew Bible as literature. A past President of the National Conference on Research in Lan-  guage and Literacy, he is the author of several books, including *Collision Course: Conflict, Negotiation, and Learning in College Composition*.